AF352420

Politeness Phenomena across Chinese Genres

Pragmatic Interfaces

Series Editors:
Németh T. Enikő, University of Szeged
Dániel Z. Kádár, Hungarian Academy of Sciences
Károly Bibok, University of Szeged

In the last two decades it has become increasingly clear that language and language use cannot be studied separately and independently of each other. This new approach assumes an interaction between grammar (phonology, morphology, lexicon, syntax and semantics) and pragmatics. An analysis of the interfaces between each component of grammar and pragmatics (the 'interface view') can also be applied to hard-pragmatics and soft-pragmatics research. Hard-pragmatics studies the field of language use from philosophical, linguistic and logical points of view, while soft-pragmatics explores phenomena of language use from a social and socio-cultural perspective.

The definitions hard- and soft-pragmatics, adopted around the 1980s, have become somewhat dated since pragmatics has become a field of its own, and so these two trends have merged to some extent. Also, various pragmaticians made important attempts to blend these approaches. Nevertheless, a border between these areas continues to exist: hard-pragmaticians rarely venture into socio-pragmatic issues, and, vice versa, soft-pragmatic studies rarely make use of the formal tools of hard-pragmatics.

Pragmatic Interfaces fills an important knowledge gap in the field of pragmatics as the first major publication project devoted to studying grammar–pragmatics interfaces and the merging of soft-pragmatics with hard-pragmatics. Through this merging many pragmatic phenomena could be essentially revisited. *Pragmatic Interfaces* follows an interdisciplinary approach, allowing scholars from different areas of grammar and pragmatics to collaborate.

Published:
Face and Face Practices in Chinese Talk-in-Interaction: A Study in Interactional Pragmatics
Wei-Lin Melody Chang
Impoliteness in Corpora: A Comparative Analysis of British English and Spoken Turkish
Hatice Celebi

Politeness Phenomena across Chinese Genres

Edited by Xinren Chen

SHEFFIELD UK   BRISTOL CT

Published by Equinox Publishing Ltd

UK: Office 415, The Workstation, 15 Paternoster Row, Sheffield, South Yorkshire S1 2BX

USA: ISD, 70 Enterprise Drive, Bristol, CT 06010

www.equinoxpub.com

First published 2017

British Library Cataloguing-in-Publication Data

A catalogue record for this book is available from the British Library.

ISBN-13 978 1 78179 176 9 (hardback)

Library of Congress Cataloging-in-Publication Data

Names: Chen, Xinren, 1967- editor.

Title: Politeness phenomena across Chinese genres / edited by Xinren Chen.

Description: Sheffield, UK ; Bristol, CT : Equinox Publishing Ltd, [2017] |
    Series: Pragmatic Interfaces | Includes bibliographical references and index. |

Identifiers: LCCN 2016055126 (print) | LCCN 2017021278 (ebook) | ISBN 9781781795866 (ePDF) |
    ISBN 9781781791769 (hb)

Subjects: LCSH: Politeness (Linguistics)--China. | Grammar, Comparative and general--Honorific. |
    Chinese language. | Etiquette--China. | Sociolinguistics--China. | China--Social life and customs.

Classification: LCC P299.H66 (ebook) | LCC P299.H66 P74 2017 (print) | DDC 306.442/951--dc23

LC record available at https://lccn.loc.gov/2016055126

Typeset by Steve Barganski

Printed and bound in the UK by Lightning Source UK Ltd, Milton Keynes and Lightning Source Inc., La Vergne, TN

Contents

Part III

Politeness in various conflictive Chinese situations

Part IV

Backchannelling and politeness in various Chinese interactions

Contributors

Qian Chen is Associate Professor in the College of Foreign Languages and Literature at Northwest Normal University and a doctoral student at the National Key Research Centre for Linguistics and Applied Linguistics in Guangdong University of Foreign Studies, P. R. China. She has published papers in pragmatics in journals such as *Linguistics and Applied Linguistics, Foreign Languages and their Teaching* and *Journal of Gansu Lianhe University*. She has also published papers about language teaching in journals such as *e-Education Research* and *Journal of Northwest Adult Education*.

Rong Chen is Professor of Linguistics at California State University at San Bernardino, USA and Guest Professor at Xi'an International Studies University, P. R. China. His research interests are pragmatics and cognitive linguistics. He has published several books and more than 50 articles in these and other areas of linguistics and serves on the governing and editorial boards of associations and journals.

Xinren Chen is Professor of English and linguistics in the School of Foreign Studies at Nanjing University, P. R. China and is co-editor of *East Asian Pragmatics*. He has published papers in pragmatics and foreign language teaching in journals such as *Journal of Pragmatics, Foreign Language Teaching and Research, Modern Foreign Languages* and *Contemporary Linguistics*. Major monographs he has authored or co-authored include *Contemporary Pragmatics, English Grammar in Use, The Pragmatics of Overinformativeness in Conversation, A Critical Pragmatic Perspective on Public Discourse, Politeness Theories and Foreign Language Learning, Pragmatics and Foreign Language Teaching*.

Tzu-Wei Hsiang is a doctoral student in the Institute of Linguistics at National Chung Cheng University, Taiwan. She has contributed a book chapter on 'Top secret: Hacking and fraud detection in business emails of a Taiwanese company' in Yuan-shan Chen et al. (eds.), *Email Discourse among Chinese Using English as a Lingua Franca* (2016).

Chunmei Hu is Lecturer in the School of English Studies at Xi'an International Studies University, Xi'an, P. R. China. She has published papers in pragmatics and cognitive linguistics in journals such as *Journal of Pragmatics, Intercultural Pragmatics* and *Foreign Language Education.*

Cynthia Lee is Associate Professor in the Centre for Applied English Studies (CAES) at the University of Hong Kong, P. R. China. She has published papers in interlanguage and intercultural pragmatics in journals such as *Journal of Pragmatics, Pragmatics, Multilingua* and *Intercultural Pragmatics.* She is also interested in second language (L2) learning in the academic context, and her work has appeared in journals such as *Language and Education, System, Computer-Assisted Language Learning* and *Teaching in Higher Education.*

Minfen Lin is a PhD candidate in the Department of Chinese and Bilingual Studies of the Hong Kong Polytechnic University. She is an active practitioner in the field of communication and media, and her research interests focus on the sociolinguistic study of new media communication.

Yansheng Mao is Associate Professor in the Foreign Languages Department at Harbin Engineering University, P. R. China, as well as a postdoctoral research fellow in the English Department of East China Normal University. He has published papers in sociopragmatics in journals such as *Language Teaching and Linguistics Studies* and *Applied Linguistics.* He has also co-authored *Linguistic Variation in the Framework of Linguistic Adaptation Theory*, published by Xiamen University Press.

Yonghong Qian is Associate Professor in the School of Foreign Languages at Nanjing University of Auditing, Nanjing, China. She has published several papers on pragmatic teaching, critical pragmatics and interpersonal pragmatics in journals such as *Modern Foreign Languages, Foreign Language Teaching Theory and Practice, Foreign Languages in China, Foreign Languages and their Teaching, Foreign Languages and Literature.* She has contributed book chapters in Xinren Chen (ed.), *Politeness Theory and Foreign Language Learning* (2013) and in Xinren Chen (ed.), *Pragmatics and Foreign Language Teaching* (2013).

Yongping Ran is Professor at the National Key Research Centre for Linguistics and Applied Linguistics in Guangdong University of Foreign Studies, Guangzhou, P. R. China. He is Editor-in-Chief of the journal *Modern Foreign Languages.* He has published papers in *Intercultural Pragmatics, Journal of Pragmatics, Pragmatics and Society* and in some top journals of linguistics in Chinese. He has also published books such as *Pragmatics: Phenomena and their Analyses* (2006), *New Explorations in Lexical Pragmatics* (2013) and some co-authored books of pragmatics, including *Cognitive Pragmatics: Cognition in Verbal Communication* (2006) and *A New Survey of Pragmatics* (2009).

Victoria Rau is Professor in the Institute of Linguistics at National Chung Cheng University, Taiwan. She has published papers in sociolinguistic variation in journals such as *Language Learning, Language and Linguistics* and *Oceanic Linguistics*. She has also co-authored *Yami: Texts, Reference Grammar, and Dictionary*, published by Academia Sinica, and co-edited *Documenting and Revitalizing Austronesian Languages*, published by the *Journal of Language Documentation and Conservation*, University of Hawaii.

Wei Ren is Professor of Applied Linguistics at the National Key Research Centre for Linguistics and Applied Linguistics at Guangdong University of Foreign Studies, P. R. China. His research interests include L2 pragmatics, cross-cultural pragmatics, pragmatics in online communication and in English as a lingua franca. His recent publications include a monograph *L2 Pragmatic Development in Study Abroad Contexts* and articles in *Applied Linguistics, Discourse, Context and Media, ELT Journal, International Journal of Bilingual Education and Bilingualism, Pragmatics* and *System*.

Winnie Shum is Senior Research Assistant in the Centre for Applied English Studies (CAES) at the University of Hong Kong. She has a Master's degree in language studies. She is interested in intercultural/interpersonal communication, pragmatics, discourse analysis and (im)politeness. Winnie has worked for several large-scale research projects which are related to English language diagnostic assessment and e-learning for vocational English communication in Hong Kong.

Xiaoyan Wang is Lecturer in the School of Foreign Languages at Nanjing University of Posts and Telecommunications, Nanjing, P. R. China, and also a PhD candidate of Applied Linguistics in Nanjing University, Nanjing, P. R. China. She has published several papers on pragmatic teaching in journals such as *Foreign Languages and their Teaching*.

Xueyu Wang is Associate Professor in the School of Foreign Studies at Nantong University, P. R. China. She has published papers in pragmatics and discourse analysis in journals such as *Communication and Discourse, Communication and Society, Modern Foreign Languages* and *Contemporary Linguistics*.

Doreen Wu is Associate Professor in the Department of Chinese and Bilingual Studies, The Hong Kong Polytechnic University. Her major research interests and publications have been in the areas of Chinese sociolinguistics and comparative discourse studies of media. Among her works are: *The Discourses of Cultural China in the Globalizing Age* (2008); co-editor of *Media Discourse in Greater China*, a special issue of *Journal of Asian-Pacific Communication* (19(2), 2009); co-editor of *Media Discourses and Cultural Globalisation: A Chinese Perspective*, a special issue of *Critical Arts* (25(1), 2011). Her recent projects and publications include: *Language Use of the Youth on the Internet* and *Researching Human Interactivity and Relational Communication on Chinese New Media*.

Kun Yang is Lecturer in the Foreign Languages Department at Civil Aviation University of China. He has published papers on pragmatics in journals such as *Modern Foreign Languages, Foreign Language Education in China, Journal of Guangdong University of Foreign Studies* and *Journal of Tianjin Foreign Studies University*.

Liyin Zhang is Lecturer in the School of Foreign Languages at Northwest University, Xi'an, P. R. China, and also a PhD candidate of Applied Linguistics at Nanjing University, Nanjing, P. R. China. She has published several research papers on pragmatics and textual analysis of academic discourse in journals such as *Foreign Languages and their Teaching* and presented at several international conferences such as the 6th International Conference on Intercultural Pragmatics and Communication.

Xiyun Zhong is Assistant Professor in the School of Foreign Studies at Hohai University, Nanjing, P. R. China. Her PhD dissertation traces the pragmaticalisation of politeness markers in English. She has published both book chapters and journal articles on English and Chinese pragmatics in general and politeness in particular.

Foreword

Chinese politeness has fascinated researchers for decades because of its vast differences from Western culture and its rich tradition of politeness rituals. More interesting is the fact that drastic societal changes taking place in modern China have given rise to the addition or omission of many politeness expressions and practices. This has created a complex and often misperceived system of Chinese politeness. However, it is this complexity that has inspired many researchers to conduct empirical studies of Chinese politeness behaviour from various aspects, including from historical, comparative, linguistic or cultural perspectives, with an effort to capture the characteristics of politeness practice in China. And yet, with the rapid growth of China's economy and its ever-increasing role on the world stage, Chinese politeness research seems to have entered a new era due to the multitude of changes in communication modes and increased contact with many other cultures.

This volume thus gives a timely, refreshing look into this intriguing issue by investigating a new dimension of the phenomenon of Chinese politeness: the genre effect on politeness practice. It takes the approach of variational pragmatics by examining intracultural differences in politeness behaviour across a variety of genres: daily interactions versus institutional ones, face-to-face communication versus TV- or computer-mediated communication. It is a true delight to read the scholarly works contained in this volume undertaken by so many researchers, all employing a scientific and systematic approach to studying Chinese politeness.

Upon reading the chapters in this book, I can see several unique contributions that these studies make to the area of Chinese politeness research. First, the broad range of social settings covered in the volume is impressive. From a sociolinguistic perspective, language use, or politeness practice in this case, depends greatly on the social setting in which an interaction takes place. The politeness phenomenon cannot be adequately studied without looking into the components of its social setting, such as the scene, participant role and interaction goal. The authors in this volume have endeavoured to undertake studies that cover a variety of social settings: from casual to formal occasions (e.g., dinner table conversation vs dissertation defence), and from private sphere to public domain (e.g., private gatherings vs TV interviews). Their findings not only extend, but also expand previous scholarly works on Chinese politeness.

Another unique contribution is the array of existent and emerging genres of communication in modern Chinese that are represented in this volume. Traditional studies on Chinese politeness have normally focused on either face-to-face or written communication. With the rapid development of technology and the Internet, communication is no longer limited to the two modes of face-to-face versus written. Computer- or electronic device-mediated communication has become more prevalent, and it has presented new grounds for research. The studies in this volume explore emergent genres in the new areas of the Internet and social media, and provide insightful findings as to how interactants employ various linguistic and semiotic devices to signal politeness.

It is also intriguing to see the kinds of linguistic features and genre-related factors under investigation in this volume. In addition to studying the usual linguistic features of lexicons or syntactic structures that express politeness, this volume looks into new dimensions of discursive strategies that show politeness. These new dimensions include types and frequency of responses to a speech act, the presence or absence of self-denigration/other-elevation expressions, the typology of identity construction for politeness sake, the typology of rapport orientations, the manner of disagreement and its degree of explicitness, the manner and politeness function of listener responses (e.g., backchannelling). By studying these new dimensions of discursive strategies, the authors have demonstrated that politeness practice is a more complex issue than the mere use of some politeness words or expressions. Its full picture can only be revealed through a thorough examination of relevant interactional elements and genre-related factors.

Through investigation of all these dimensions in various genres, the studies in this volume not only capture how the traditional Chinese characteristics of modesty, hierarchy, collectivism and implicitness affect politeness behaviour, but also demonstrate how genre brings to light these cultural characteristics. The authors show that in the five genres under study, politeness behaviour varies because of the attention given to a certain culture value in the specific genre. For example, power structure, social status and personal relations among participants play out differently in different genres, and have an effect on the use of politeness expressions and language choice. It is these variations that make politeness behaviour subtle, sensitive and crucial to successful communication in a given communicative event.

After reading this book, the reader will have a much broader view of the intricacies of Chinese politeness practice and a better understanding of how politeness is manifested in the changing modes of communication. However, it is interesting to note that, in spite of the new modes of communication and the rise of dependence on technology in human interaction, the basic core of human interactional needs is unchanging: the need to be connected and the need to be respected. It is this basic core that drives politeness behaviour in human society. The studies in this volume undoubtedly demonstrate this point. Hence this volume is a much welcome addition to the ongoing exploration of Chinese politeness, as well as politeness research in general. It also has significant implications for cross-cultural pragmatics and intercultural communication.

Yuling Pan
Former Principal Researcher and Senior Sociolinguist
at the US Census Bureau

Acknowledgment

This volume is part of a research project entitled 'Empirical Linguistic Perspectives on Politeness in Contemporary Chinese Society' (2017ZDAXM002)

CHAPTER 1

Introduction

Xinren Chen

This volume targets politeness phenomena in China, a country/culture/society that is attracting more and more attention worldwide. The topic has been much dealt with in separate journal articles by scholars like Yueguo Gu, Carl G. Hinze, LuMing Mao, Minchung Yu and Rong Chen, and some monographs, such as *Cross-Cultural Communication: Politeness and Face in Chinese Culture* by Song Mei Lee-Wong, *Terms of (Im)politeness: On the Communicational Properties of Historical Chinese Terms of Address* by Daniel Kádár, *Politeness in Chinese Face-to-Face Interaction* by Yuling Pan, *Politeness in Historical and Contemporary China* by Yuling Pan and Daniel Kádár, *Chinese Discourse and Interaction* by Daniel Kádár and Yuling Pan, to name the most well-known ones. Then, why is this volume still necessary?

Need for this volume

The reason is that there has been no book-length monograph or volume devoted to the study of the effect of genre on politeness in China, i.e., variations in polite behaviour across different genres in Chinese. In this volume, genre is defined, essentially following Norman Fairclough, as referring to 'different ways of (inter) acting discoursally' (2003: 26). The definition emphasises the impact of the communicative situation on the formal and organisational features of the discourse (Charaudeau, Maingueneau and Adam 2002: 278–280). The definition also draws on Bakhtin (1983), who regards genres as socially specified 'modes of speaking or writing', such as 'a TV show', 'dinner talk', 'a university lecture' and 'a job interview'. It is also consistent with Miller's (1984) view of genre as social action. More often than not, different genres correspond to different social contexts of activity or social action and are recognised by a particular culture or community.

As a matter of fact, there has been no similar investigation of such size elsewhere in the world into how polite behaviour may manifest itself differently across genres within the same 'national' culture. Thus, this volume may fill a gap in politeness research in general and Chinese politeness research in particular, against the backdrop of 'a tendency to over-generalise the influence of culture and downplay the individualistic and intracultural differences' (Kong 2013: 310). For a no less important reason, this volume responds to the current situation where '[i]nterest in Chinese discourse and interaction is a relatively new endeavor that needs exploration in different directions' (Kong 2013: 312), wherein the study of 'genres and genre repertoires available to Chinese' and that of 'sociocultural assumptions in different situations and contexts involving Chinese speakers' are among the listed future directions (Kong 2013: 316–317).

Theoretically, this study will provide fairly systematic evidence for how polite linguistic behaviour may vary across genres in China, complementing and even renewing the popular understanding of polite behaviour among Chinese people by those in the West. Existing studies generally treat the phenomenon of Chinese politeness as a monolithic condition, which is far from true. Indeed, all sorts of variation in linguistic politeness behaviour within the Chinese are under studied. This volume will investigate intracultural politeness-related variations in social acts such as introductions and responses, refusals, disagreements, advice-giving, compliments and responses, and some relational acts that are subject to the influence of genre differences, as opposed to such well-studied social factors as gender and age. More crucially, for that purpose, this study will introduce some new factors leading to pragmatic variation and examine some new dimensions of such variation to enrich the existing framework for research on politeness. It is hoped that, by comparing the same category of linguistic politeness behaviour across different genres within a renewed configuration of factors and dimensions, it will turn up some important findings that would otherwise be impossible from the examination of the same act in a single genre.

Practically, this study can help handle Chinese face-to-face conversation and web-mediated interaction by enriching the knowledge of how politeness as probably the single most important type of interpersonal meaning is enacted, constructed and negotiated in different genres.

Categorisation of this volume

The present probe into the effect of genre on the variation of linguistic politeness behaviour falls into the broad scope of variational pragmatics, a subdiscipline of intercultural pragmatics that can be 'conceptualised as the intersection of pragmatics with sociolinguistics or, more specifically, with dialectology as the study of language variation' (see Barron and Schneider 2009 for a detailed account of the field and its methodology).

Variational pragmatics has a couple of 'cousins' clustered under intercultural pragmatics, of which cross-cultural/contrastive pragmatics is best known. Basically, cross-cultural/contrastive pragmatics is concerned with interlingual/intercultural differences as well as similarities in language use, i.e., pragmatic differences as well as universals across different languages and cultures (e.g., Ambady, Koo, Lee and Rosenthal 1996; Bargiela-Chiappini and Kádár 2011; Blum-Kulka, House and Kasper 1989; Fujii 2008; House 1986; Joy 1995; Lee 2011; Pinto 2008; Ruiz de Zarobe and Ruiz de Zarobe 2012; Trosborg 2010; Wierzbicka 2003). One relevant area of comparison and contrast is politeness. For example, Chen (1993) takes responding to compliments as the focus of attention and compares the politeness strategies used by American English and Chinese speakers; Sifianou (1999) compares politeness phenomena in England and Greece; Fukushima (2003) compares politeness in British English and Japanese; Haugh and Hinze (2003) compare 'face' and 'politeness' in Chinese, English and Japanese. These studies reveal some interesting types of variation or relativity in politeness practice in terms of (in)directness, avoidance/approach distinction, weight of negative politeness, value of politeness concepts like modesty and generosity, and so on. The findings from these studies pose challenges to the fundamental claim of universality explicit or implicit in classic models or theories of politeness such as Fraser (1990), Brown and Levinson (1978, 1987) and Leech (1983, 2005, 2007, 2014).

Unlike cross-cultural/contrastive pragmatics, variational pragmatics investigates intralingual differences, i.e., pragmatic variations in language use between and across native varieties of the same language. Such studies on variation across countries or regions speaking the same native language have begun to flourish in recent years (see Barron 2005a, 2005b; Farr and Murphy 2009; García 2008, 2009; Macaulay 2009; Placencia 1994, 2008; Schneider 2005, 2008; Schneider and Barron 2008a, 2008b; Schölmberger 2008, among others). It has been found that 'speakers who share the same native language do not necessarily share the same culture' (Barron and Schneider 2009), including linguistic politeness behaviour. For instance, native speakers of English in Ireland and the United States use language in different ways (Schneider 1999, 2008).

More relevant for the present study, variational pragmatics may also address intracultural differences, i.e., pragmatic variation among people not only speaking the same language, but also having the same citizenship and national culture (which, however, consists of distinct sub-cultures). For example, it has been found that Americans in the US do not use English in the same way (e.g., Barron 2009; Wolfram and Schilling-Estes 2006). Barron (2009) shows how apologies are performed in somewhat different ways across the USA. Tannen (1990, 1996) explores how American males and females behave differently in conversation, including how they attend to politeness. Mills (2003) deals with the relation between gender and politeness in a critical way, challenging some traditional conceptions. Rüegg (2014) investigates the thanks responses in three socioeconomic settings concerning restaurant service encounters in Los Angeles, California, USA in terms of form and frequency of thanks responses from the variational pragmatic approach.

While existing pragmatic variation studies focus almost exclusively on variations triggered by user-related factors like gender and age (e.g. Farr and Murphy 2009; Macaulay 2009; Tannen 1990, 1996), locality (e.g. Barron 2009; Pichler 2009) and economic status (e.g. Rüegg 2014), few studies are oriented to pragmatic variations, including those related to politeness, triggered by genre/register-related factors. According to Halliday and Hasan (1989), language varies according to both its user and genre/register. It thus could be reasonably hypothesised that linguistic politeness behaviour, as an essential part of language use, also varies according to genre. This hypothesis is exactly what this volume aims to verify on an empirical basis, with specific reference to the pragmatic variations of linguistic politeness behaviour across different genres of communication in the context of contemporary China.

Theoretical considerations of this volume

Notion of politeness

This volume embraces a hybrid view of politeness rather than sticking to a single model or paradigm, including at least the following:

A. Geoffrey Leech's (1983, 2005, 2007, 2014) view of politeness, recently embodied in the model of Grand Strategies of Politeness (GSP). His latest view, drawing on the earliest maxim-based conception of politeness (Leech 1983), incorporates ten main orientations of polite behaviour in relation to self and other. It represents a strategy approach to politeness as a kind of interpersonal rhetoric for the purpose of maintaining social equilibrium. For a more detailed introduction to the view in this volume, refer to the studies conducted by Xueyu Wang, Xinren Chen, Yonghong Qian, Yansheng Mao and Kun Yang, and Xiyun Zhong.

B. Brown and Levinson's (1978, 1987) view of politeness, embodied in their Face Theory (FT). According to the theory, face is a public self-image, falling into two types, namely positive face and negative face. While the former has to do with the desire for being admired, liked, appreciated etc., the latter has to do with the desire for freedom of action and autonomous territory. For a detailed introduction to the theory in this volume, refer to the study by Chunmei Hu and Rong

Chen. Reference to the theory is also made in the studies conducted by Doreen Wu and Minfen Lin, and Cynthia Lee and Winnie Shum.

C. Helen Spencer-Oatey's (2000, 2002, 2005, 2008) view of politeness, embodied in her Rapport Management Model (RMM). This view, developed out of Brown and Levinson's (1978, 1987) face-oriented framework, regards politeness as a means of managing interpersonal rapport. It reformulates Brown and Levinson's notions of positive face and negative face, which are individualistic by nature, by incorporating face (including quality face and social identity face, the latter being collectivist by nature) with social rights (including equity rights and association rights), thus avoiding the assumed Western bias concerning negative face. In addition, Spencer-Oatey broadens the scope of rapport management to include that of interactional goal. For a detailed presentation of the model in this volume, refer to the studies conducted by Yongping Ran and Qian Chen, Tzu-Wei Hsiang and Victoria Rau, and Liyin Zhang and Xiaoyan Wang. Reference to the theory is also made in the study by Wei Ren.

D. Constructivists' view of politeness, represented by such scholars as Arundale (1999, 2006, 2010), Eelen (2001), Haugh (2003, 2004, 2007, 2010), Haugh and Bargiela-Chiappini (2010), Kádár and Haugh (2013), Kádár and Mills (2011), Kádár and Pan (2011, 2013), Locher (2004), Locher and Watts (2005), Mills (2003), Watts (2003), and so on. This view takes politeness as a form of relational behaviour, a kind of dynamic social practice, and an emergent property in the form of joint discursive constitution. The approach generally concerns itself with how interlocutors perceive and evaluate each other's behaviour in dynamic discourse in terms of (im)politeness. Although this view is not explicitly reviewed or formally presented in any of the studies in this volume, the discussions of the examples used in the ones conducted by Xueyu Wang, Xinren Chen, Yonghong Qian, Wei Ren, and Xiyun Zhong do embody the spirit of social constructionism.

This volume adopts the hybrid view of politeness for the reason that the models of politeness are not incompatible but complementary to each other. Indeed, politeness as a property of utterances, discourse or social behaviour in a situated context can be viewed from the perspective of the speaker, the hearer or both. The former perspective, as represented by the first three basically 'etic' views above, enables convenient discussion of politeness orientations and pragmalinguistic choices, whereas the latter, basically an 'emic' perspective, helps to reveal how politeness takes place across individuals and how it impacts the development and outcome of the interaction. Though cases where the speaker's politeness intentions do not match the interlocutor's evaluation do exist now and then, the bulk of cases, which this volume looks into, support default interpretations conveyed by the pragmalinguistic choices in question. Ignorance of either the etic or emic approach would prove costly.

Factors bearing on the variation of politeness

This volume will look into how polite linguistic behaviour varies in interactional exchanges that are particularly politeness-sensitive across a variety of Chinese genres, broadly divided into ordinary ones (Chapters 2, 6, 10 and 13) vs institutional ones (medical, educational, academic, recreational, and journalistic; Chapters 3, 4, 5, 7, 8, 9, 11 and 12) or face-to-face ones (Chapters 2, 3, 4, 7, 8, 9 and 11) vs non-face-to-face ones (Chapters 5, 6, 10, 12 and 13), which involve different media and channels of communication, degrees of formality, situated role-configurations etc.

This book will investigate the impact of genre on the production and interpretation of Chinese politeness, demonstrating genre-specific preferences and features in the use of politeness resources. Specifically, the effect of such genre-related factors as formality of occasion (e.g. Chapter 2 vs Chapter 4; Chapter 5 vs Chapter 6), institution-specific power and distance (e.g. Chapter 7 vs Chapter 8; Chapter 12 vs Chapter 13) and channel of communication (Chapter 5 vs Chapter 6) will be explored. Other factors leading to pragmatic variation under study mainly include: i) presence or absence of the interlocutor (e.g. Chapter 8 vs Chapter 10; Chapter 11 vs Chapter 12) and ii) direct participation or non-direct-participation of the third party (e.g. Chapter 2 vs Chapter 3).

Dimensions of pragmatic variation analysis

Existing cross-cultural pragmatics in general or variational pragmatics in particular have generally adopted a few dimensions of politeness strategies for comparison or contrast, such as (in)directness of speech and redressive effort at face-work, like internal and external modification on account of vertical power (P), horizontal distance (D) and rank of imposition (R). Or, in the case of research on compliment and thanks responses, researchers focus on how people from different cultural backgrounds may vary in the types and frequency of responses (like accepting, denying or declining etc.) to complimenting and thanking respectively.

In the present volume, some new dimensions, which are characteristically related to linguistic politeness behaviour in contemporary China, are introduced for the purpose of cross-genre comparison and contrast. These dimensions of pragmatic variation mainly include: i) presence/absence and degree of self-denigration/other-elevation, as in Chapters 1, 2 and 3; ii) typology of identity construction for politeness's sake, as in Chapters 4, 5 and 6; iii) typology of rapport orientations, as in Chapters 2, 6, 7 and 8; iv) manner of disagreement and its degree of explicitness, as in Chapters 8 and 9; and v) manner and politeness function of listener responses, as in Chapters 10, 11, 12 and 13. These dimensions are characteristic of the Chinese context and are worthy of exploration so as to empirically confirm, complement, modify or refute the following long-standing generalisations about Chinese politeness-related practices. First, Chinese people have long been conceived of as placing a high value on modesty, as captured in Gu's (1990) Self-Denigration Maxim. Second, China has long been a hierarchical society, where the choice, presentation and even ad hoc construction of appropriate identities are crucially linked with politeness evaluations. Thirdly, Chinese culture is generally believed to be of a collectivist kind that encourages attention to the management of not only public self-image and equity rights, but also social identities and association rights, as documented in Spencer-Oatey (2002) and Spencer-Oatey and Xing (1998). Fourthly, Chinese culture is also one that favours implicitness and avoidance when people are in disagreement, as evidenced by the richness of related idioms and proverbs in the Chinese language such as 和而不同 (literally 'stay harmonious while holding different views'), 仁者见仁，智者见智 (literally 'The benevolent see benevolence and the wise see wisdom', as a way of reconciliation between each other). Lastly, Chinese people are said to use only a moderate amount of listener responses like backchannelling, taking the behaviour as a sign of impolite interruption, as documented in Clancy, Thompson, Suzuki and Tao (1996). The modification and even dismissal of these long-established views of Chinese people will prove most beneficial to international people in direct or indirect contact with them.

Hopefully, these dimensions of variational pragmatic analysis proposed in this volume can serve as a reference for the study of pragmatic variation in other languages and cultures while enriching the existing literature about Chinese linguistic politeness in the research field.

Methodological considerations of this volume

By nature, the present research on pragmatic variation in politeness phenomena in China is empirical. Instead of basing the analysis on impressionistic episodic evidence or so-called introspective (i.e., intuitive and fabricated) data, each and every researcher in this volume has gathered sizable naturally occurring data for discussion.

Regarding the question of what types of data or data collection method can or should be used in the analysis, Schneider and Barron (2008a) point out that variational pragmatics, unlike approaches permitting no other type than naturally occurring conversation, acknowledges that each and every data type including naturally occurring discourse and each data collection method has its advantages as well as its shortcomings, and that the choice of method depends entirely on the aims and research questions of a project, and that a method suitable for one purpose may not be suitable for other purposes (cf. Bardovi-Harlig 1999; Kasper 1990; also Jucker 2009). While it seems easier to use elicitation methods that allow a high degree of variable control, this volume will depend almost exclusively on the use of naturally occurring data, spoken or written, a practice generally encouraged in recent literature on politeness (the cost of this practice is obvious, too, such that solid generalisation will be unavailable from this volume).

The data have been gathered by the following means: i) for the daily genre, recordings were made of guest-welcoming dinner talks to study other-introductions and responses, radio conversations were recorded to study how complaints about public service affairs were handled with a view to demonstrating rapport management, and public discussions in Internet forums were collected to study the performance of disagreement and relational acts respectively; ii) for the academic genre, recordings of lectures and panel discussions were made to study other-introduction and identity construction; iii) for the journalistic genre, episodes of TV interviews were recorded to study other-introduction and backchannelling; iv) for the medical genre, recordings were made of medical consultants' promotional discourse on radio; v) for the recreational genre, data were collected from popular Chinese TV dating shows in mainland China and Taiwan to study rapport management in making refusals, and from social media to study how celebrities managed their impressions on others.

Instead of focusing solely or primarily on individual utterances, the researchers would sometimes delve into extended scenarios to observe how particular speech acts were performed across turns or lines to reveal the interactional dynamics and mechanisms.

Summary of the chapters

The volume is composed of, apart from the Introduction, four parts, each dealing with three genres across which politeness behaviour in Chinese may vary.

Part I

Part 1 examines how politeness behaviour unfolds in harmonious situations, specifically when Chinese people introduce each other. It will demonstrate how Chinese speakers elevate others when introducing them and how Chinese people denigrate themselves when responding to others' elevating introductions in three representative genres: private gatherings, lectures and TV interviews. These dimensions of politeness are brought under study because, in the Chinese culture, approbation and, more importantly, modesty, are often assumed to be important forms of politeness, as documented in a number of studies (e.g. Gu 1990; Leech 1983, 2005, 2014).

In Chapter 2, Xueyu Wang explores, within the framework of Leech's (2014) GSP, how speakers 'do' politeness in guest-introducing and responding acts at the

Chinese dinner table. The results show that Chinese dinner-table talk is a very complex social interaction involving different participant roles. In most guest-introducing and responding acts, both the Approbation Maxim and the Modesty Maxim are used and realised linguistically with the use of typical address terms, adjectives, verbs and nouns carrying a positive semantic load and some syntactic structures such as rhetorical questions and exclamatory sentences. In addition, in both guest introductions and responses at dinner tables, powers, social status and interpersonal relations among participants are found to influence the use of politeness strategies and language choice.

In Chapter 3, also following Leech (2014), Xinren Chen directs attention to the introductory part of lecture activity in Chinese universities and demonstrates how the hosts' and visiting professors' interaction at this phase serves as a site of interpersonal work such that they attach an additional interpersonal meaning to the basically academic activity. His study shows that the hosts are profuse in the use of approbation strategy, directed to different aspects of the visiting professors, including their popularity and fame, prolificacy and achievement, expertise and authority, contribution, conduct, lecture value, and sometimes a combination of several of the aforesaid aspects; in reaction to the hosts' complimentary introductions, the visiting professors demonstrate a variety of responses, including acknowledgment, approbation downgrading, approbation denial, phatic communion, and compliment return, sometimes in singular ways and sometimes in combined ways.

In Chapter 4, still within Leech's (2014) framework, Yonghong Qian examines how hosts and guests interact at the opening stages of three Chinese TV celebrity interview programmes, with a special focus on the compliments hosts pay to the guests and the responses the guests make, in order to reveal their respective efforts directed at politeness. Her study indicates that both the hosts and the guests resort to politeness strategies. The primary strategy adopted by the hosts is to observe the Approbation Maxim, exalting the positive qualities of the guests. By comparison, the guests resort to a variety of strategies of politeness, abiding by such maxims as modesty, agreement, obligation and approbation. The use of these strategies on both sides helps to maintain or establish a harmonious relationship between them, as well as with the audience present. For the guests, it also contributes to the building and maintaining of their nice public image.

Comparing the three studies in this part, we can detect some variations in the extent and way Chinese people use other-elevation and self-denigration across the three genres in question. For example, in lecture openings, the introducers apparently use a lot more elevation than in the other two genres. It is presumed that the preponderance of the hosts' elevation in the invited and co-ordinated academic lectures in China is due to the fact that these lectures are sometimes more complimentary than academic, and are more crucially intended to strengthen the ties between the visiting professors and the host affiliations, particularly the inviters (usually the hosts on this occasion). Besides, the introducees in the TV interview openings use much less self-denigration than those at table dinners and especially in lecture openings. This might be due to the fact that the introducees interviewed are not given adequate time to respond to the approbation before they are asked serious questions in the activity, whereas in the lecture context, academic people are generally expected to behave modestly, a quality assumably inherent in scholarship. In addition, it is found that oftentimes in private gatherings, but not so often in lecture openings or TV interview openings, Chinese people also observe the Intimacy Maxim, so to speak, a maxim that is not included in previous scholars' classification. This finding may result from the fact that the interlocutors in this genre are generally friends engaging in more private activities, where a third party is often actively involved.

Part II

This part addresses the issue of identity construction in relation to politeness considerations across three genres of Chinese interactions, namely call-in programmes, computer-mediated communication (CMC) via social media, and PhD oral defences. Understanding that face is 'a particularly important facet of identity' (Tracy and Robles 2013: 24), the three studies in this part each seek to reveal how the participants in these contexts of communication construct appropriate identities for the sake of politeness and together highlight possible variations in the typology of identities across the different genres.

In Chapter 5, Wei Ren investigates the linguistic strategies employed by the host in a radio-mediated call-in programme in China as a means of identity construction. His study reveals five partly overlapping local identity categories: caring helper, responsible helper, authoritative host, media propagandist and public authority, which influence the host's choices of linguistic strategies, including (im)politeness based on the argument that the use of (im)politeness is a linguistic index for the host's identity construction.

In Chapter 6, Doreen Wu and Minfen Lin examine the types of facework made possible by Chinese celebrities in the performance of various kinds of relational acts on Sina Weibo, the leading Social Network Service Site (SNS) in the Cultural China region. They argue that reputable individuals used these relational acts as well as related features to build relational connectedness with their followers. They discover that such SNSs have formed a new literary practice that reflects both traditional and new ways of constructing facework (see Davies 2012; Wu and Feng 2015; Zhao, Grasmuck and Marin 2008).

In Chapter 7, Yongping Ran and Qian Chen focus on advice-giving in PhD oral defences in Chinese universities and explore how supervisors construct identities in relation to the management of interpersonal rapport between the participants. It is found that, while supervisors provide students with some help for the improvement of their dissertations, they also take into account interactional goals which are about the management of personal or interpersonal relationships with the students. As a consequence, supervisors are found to adopt some strategies for constructing collective identities as well for managing rapport relations with students.

This part indicates that, while a range of identities are constructed by Chinese consultants and experts, some variation in the typology of identity construction for the sake of politeness is still visible. For one thing, the various identities constructed by the two kinds of professionals are closely related to the type of context and activity these people are engaged in at the moment. For another, while both hosts and supervisors construct authoritative identities and manage interpersonal relations at the same time, celebrities only pay attention to the construction of close identities, so to speak, that may serve to enhance their connection with their followers and friends. The first variation might be due to the fact that hosts and supervisors enact different roles in their respective activity. As for the second variation, the cause might be that both hosts and supervisors assume some institutional power over their addressees in their contexts whereas the celebrities, who crave the favour and support of their followers, choose to maintain a low yet intimate profile in the eyes of the latter. In addition, the fact that the celebrities are being engaged in less formal interaction than the former two groups of people is also likely to makes a difference to the type of politeness conveyed.

Part III

The chapters in this part investigates how linguistic politeness behaviour unfolds in face-sensitive interactions, specifically when Chinese people do face-threatening acts (FTAs, Brown and Levinson 1978, 1987) such as making refusals and expressing disagreements. Chapters 7 and 8, plus Chapter 6 in Part II, will demonstrate, by adopting Spencer-Oatey's (2000, 2002, 2008) rapport management model of politeness, how rapport orientations may vary across three genres, namely TV dating shows, conference discussions and PhD oral defences. Chapter 9 serves as an additional comparison with Chapter 8 on the issue of disagreement.

In Chapter 8, Tzu-Wei Hsiang and Victoria Rau explore the strategies of refusals used by Chinese women on TV dating shows in Taiwan and Mainland China. Using an interactive sociolinguistic approach to discourse analysis, the authors analyse the females' refusal strategies with a focus on two Chinese versions of the dating show 'Take Me Out', showing that in the context of TV dating shows, women in Taiwan and those in Mainland China employ drastically different strategies, revealing different interpersonal attentiveness and face systems.

In Chapter 9, Liyin Zhang and Xiaoyan Wang focus on how panellists do rapport management when expressing disagreement at conference discussions. Based on an in-depth analysis of the utterances collected from academic conference discussions in the field of linguistics, they show the strategies the panellists adopt to manage face and sociality rights and interactional goals in the activity, and investigate the influencing factors concerned. The study demonstrates that disagreement, though a risky communicative act, is not necessarily meant to be face-threatening, but rather it can be a site for the management of rapport between or among interlocutors. Panellists craftily combine the components of disagreement with other strategies to fulfil the purpose of rapport management.

In Chapter 10, Cynthia Lee and Winnie Shum manifest how in Internet discussion forums, the Cantonese interlocutors present opposite views when they disagree. Their study indicates that the interlocutors adhere to their traditional values to do justice and make moral judgments, and shows that the interlocutors employ these as tactics for implicit disagreement and empowerment, leaving the implied meaning to others. They argue that such implicit disagreement is particularly enacted with the aim of preserving others' face and avoids hurting the positive face directly (Brown and Levinson 1987), a speaking practice that is largely in line with Chinese interpersonal communication practice, politeness and face work (Gao 1998; Gao and Ting-Toomey 1998; Kádár and Pan 2011; Pan 2000).

This part also testifies to the hypothesis that genre makes a lot of differences to how Chinese people behave politely. Specifically, the rapport management in dating shows, though variable between females from Mainland Chinese and those from Taiwan, is essentially oriented towards separation face or connection face, while that in conference discussions is primarily targeted at the value of the interlocutor's research, and that in PhD oral defences is multiply targeted, including not only the interpersonal aspect, but also the interactional goal. This type of variation can be explained by the difference in the institution-specific power and distance, the medium of communication, as well as the type of acts involved. Specifically, since the dating programmes are televised, the females' direct refusals will incur huge face threat to the male guests; in the conference discussion setting, the panellists, who are often on equal footing, are expected to respect others' research; in the case of the PhD oral defence, supervisors have the mixed role of quality control and emotional support. Another variation concerns the manner and nature of disagreement: while panellists use hedges or downtoners to soften their disagreement, which is not necessarily meant or interpreted to be face-threatening in such settings, interlocutors in Internet discussion forums use verbatim quotes, words and phrases from Chinese classical works as a form of softened disagreement, which is nevertheless face-threatening. The variation in the nature of disagreement, which is more noteworthy, is reasonable for the reason that the panel discussion setting encourages (constructive) disagreement, whereas the Internet discussion forum, which involves a lot of hostility, seldom does.

Part IV

This part addresses how Chinese people's linguistic politeness behaviour with specific reference to the use of backchannels may vary across three genres: TV interviews, call-in programmes and Internet interactions.

In Chapter 11, Chunmei Hu and Rong Chen explore the interconnection between backchannelling and politeness in TV interviews aired in Mainland China, Hong Kong and Taiwan. They demonstrate that while the function of backchannelling varies a great deal in this particular genre, it is motivated by the speakers' consideration for the dominant speakers' positive face. Simply put, positive politeness undergirds almost all instances of backchannelling in Chinese TV interviews.

In Chapter 12, Yansheng Mao and Kun Yang explore the use of backchannels in Chinese consultant–caller communication as a form of politeness. They find that consultants use backchannels for the primary purpose of following, followed by those performing the functions of agreeing, responding, rephrasing, adding, interrupting, repeating and commenting. These functions, discussed within Leech's GSP (2014), are found to have implications of politeness.

In Chapter 13, Xiyun Zhong, by combining quantitative and qualitative analyses, and integrating interviews with observations, examines the backchannel practice on Chinese Internet forums. She discovers that backchannels, represented in an Internet style, occur more frequently on Internet forums than in daily conversations and perform a variety of politeness functions, each function corresponding to a certain sub-maxim of Leech's General Strategy of Politeness.

This part reveals that while the use of backchannels has the overtone of politeness in all the three genres in question, it also exhibits considerable variations in terms of the relative weight of specific politeness considerations resulting from the distribution of corresponding interaction functions. For example, while Chunmei Hu and Rong Chen's study points to the prominence of agreement as a way of politeness, Yansheng Mao and Kun Yang's study brings to the fore conformity to the Tact Maxim as a salient way of politeness. This difference is explicable in that the genre under the former study involves a lot more idea exchanges than that under the latter, whereas the genre under the latter study involves a lot more attention acknowledgments than that under the former. Also, Xiyun Zhong's study seems to show that the use of backchannels in Chinese Internet forums is more frequent than that in face-to-face conversation (like the TV interviews under study), a finding that can be accounted for by the lack of synchronicity and low level of formality in the former.

Limitations of this volume and future directions

Like many other volumes of the present kind, this volume suffers from some 'holes' that are more or less difficult to mend, notably the lack of theoretical unity, topical coherence and methodological comparability. First, although the present volume deliberately adopts a hybrid view of politeness, the disadvantage of this choice is also obvious in that no general discussion of the four modules or parts is available from a common theoretical perspective. Secondly, although all the chapters centre on the general topic of linguistic politeness behaviour in various Chinese genres, the topics for the modules are diverse and discrete. They do touch upon some key areas characteristic of Chinese politeness, yet they fail to present a panoramic picture of how Chinese people behave politely in verbal communication. Thirdly, while all the chapters are qualitative studies using naturally occurring data from the Chinese context, some involve quantitative analysis whereas others do not. Although we can acquire a general impression about some quantitative differences in politeness across observed genres, no solid or valid conclusion can be drawn on a statistical basis. Consequently, our findings with regard to some cross-genre variations in politeness must be interpreted with reservation and caution.

In view of the above serious inherent defects in the design of this volume, we call on future researchers to work better and further in the following directions. First, it would be more beneficial to adopt a unified theoretical framework throughout all the component studies so that consistent interpretation and discussion could be achieved. Second, future work needs to focus exclusively on one aspect of certain linguistic politeness behaviour across a variety of genres in Chinese to enable appropriate comparison and contrast. Third, to better bring out the genre-specific characteristics of Chinese politeness, inferential statistics need to be included if we aim at valid generalisations about cross-genre differences. All things considered, what the present volume has done is make an initial step towards these future endeavours and improvements, at least or at most.

References

Ambady, N., Koo, J., Lee, F. and Rosenthal, R. (1996) More than words: Linguistic and nonlinguistic politeness in two cultures. *Journal of Personality and Social Psychology* 70(5): 996–1011. https://doi.org/10.1037/0022-3514.70.5.996

Arundale, R. (1999) An alternative model and ideology of communication for an alternative politeness theory. *Pragmatics* 9: 119–153. https://doi.org/10.1075/prag.9.1.07aru

Arundale, R. (2006) Face as relational and interactional: A communication framework for research on face, facework, and politeness. *Journal of Politeness Research* 2(2): 193–216. https://doi.org/10.1515/PR.2006.011

Arundale, R. (2010) Constituting face in conversation: Face, facework and interactional achievement. *Journal of Pragmatics* 42(8): 2078–2105. https://doi.org/10.1016/j.pragma.2009.12.021

Bakhtin, M. M. (1983) Epic and novel. In M. Holquist (ed.) *The Dialogic Imagination: Four Essays*. Austin: University of Texas Press.

Bardovi-Harlig, K. (1999) Exploring the interlanguage of interlanguage pragmatics: A research agenda for acquisitional pragmatics. *Language Learning* 49: 677–713. https://doi.org/10.1111/0023-8333.00105

Bargiela-Chiappini, F. and Kádár, D. Z. (2011) *Politeness across Cultures*. Palgrave Macmillan. https://doi.org/10.1057/9780230305939

Barron, A. (2005a) Variational pragmatics in the foreign language classroom. *System* 33(3): 519–536. https://doi.org/10.1016/j.system.2005.06.009

Barron, A. (2005b) Offering in Ireland and England. In A. Barron and K. P. Schneider (eds) *The Pragmatics of Irish English* 141–176. Berlin and New York: Walter de Gruyter. https://doi.org/10.1515/9783110898934.141

Barron, A. (2009) Apologies across the USA. In K. Turner and B. Fraser (eds) *Language in Life, and a Life in Language* 9–17. Chennai: Emerald.

Barron, A. and Schneider, K. P. (2009) Variational pragmatics: Studying the impact of social factors on language use in interaction. *Intercultural Pragmatics* 6(4): 425–442. https://doi.org/10.1515/IPRG.2009.023

Blum-Kulka, S., House, J. and Kasper, G. (1989) Investigating crosscultural pragmatics: An introductory overview. In S. Blum-Kulka, J. House and G. Kasper (eds) *Cross-cultural Pragmatics: Requests and Apologies* 1–34. Norwood, NJ: Ablex.

Brown, P. and Levinson, S. (1978) Universals in language usage: Politeness phenomena. In E. Goody (ed.) *Questions and Politeness* 56–310. Cambridge: Cambridge University Press.

Brown, P. and Levinson, S. (1987) *Politeness: Some Universals in Linguistic Usage*. Cambridge: Cambridge University Press.

Charaudeau, P., Maingueneau, D. and Adam, J. (2002) *Dictionnaire d'analyse du discours*. Paris: Seuil.

Chen, R. (1993) Responding to compliments: A contrastive study of politeness strategies between American English and Chinese speakers. *Journal of Pragmatics* 20(1): 49–75. https://doi.org/10.1016/0378-2166(93)90106-Y

Clancy, P., Thompson, S. A., Suzuki, R. and Tao, H. (1996) The conversational use of reactive tokens in English, Japanese and Mandarin. *Journal of Pragmatics* 26(1): 355–387. https://doi.org/10.1016/0378-2166(95)00036-4

Davies, J. (2012) Facework on Facebook as a new literacy practice. *Computers and Education* 59: 19–29. https://doi.org/10.1016/j.compedu.2011.11.007

Eelen, G. (2001) *Critique of Politeness Theories*. Manchester: St Jerome Press.

Fairclough, N. (2003) *Analysing Discourse: Textual Analysis for Social Research*. London: Routledge.

Farr, F. and Murphy, B. (2009) Religious references in contemporary Irish-English: 'For the love of God almighty…I'm a holy terror for turf'. *Intercultural Pragmatics* 6(4): 535–559. https://doi.org/10.1515/IPRG.2009.027

Fraser, B. (1990) Perspectives on politeness. *Journal of Pragmatics* 14: 219–236. https://doi.org/10.1016/0378-2166(90)90081-N

Fujii, Y. (2008) 'You must have a wealth of stories': Cross-linguistic differences between addressee support behaviour in Australian and Japanese. *Multilingua* 27(4): 325–370. https://doi.org/10.1515/MULTI.2008.016

Fukushima, S. (2003) *Requests and Culture: Politeness in British English and Japanese.* Bern: Peter Lang.

Gao, G. (1998) 'Don't take my word for it.' – Understanding Chinese speaking practices. *International Journal of Intercultural Relations* 22: 163–186. https://doi.org/10.1016/S0147-1767(98)00003-0

Gao, G. and Ting-Toomey, S. (1998) *Communicating Effectively with the Chinese.* Thousand Oaks, CA: Sage.

García, C. (2008) Different realisations of solidarity politeness: Comparing Venezuelan and Argentinean invitations. In K. P. Schneider and A. Barron (eds) *Variational Pragmatics: A Focus on Regional Varieties in Pluricentric Languages* 269–305. Amsterdam and Philadelphia: John Benjamins.

García, C. (2009) Intra-lingual pragmatic variation in the performance of reprimanding. *Intercultural Pragmatics* 6(4): 443–472. https://doi.org/10.1515/IPRG.2009.024

Gu, Y. (1990) Politeness phenomena in modern Chinese. *Journal of Pragmatics* 14(2): 37–257. https://doi.org/10.1016/0378-2166(90)90082-O

Halliday, M. A. K. and Hasan, R. (1989) *Language, Context, and Text: Aspects of Language in a Socialsemiotic Perspective.* Oxford: Oxford University Press.

Haugh, M. (2003) Anticipated versus inferred politeness. *Multilingua* 22(4): 397–413. https://doi.org/10.1515/mult.2003.020

Haugh, M. (2004) Revisiting the conceptualisation of politeness in English and Japanese. *Multilingua* 23(1/2): 85–109. https://doi.org/10.1515/mult.2004.009

Haugh, M. (2007) The discursive challenge to politeness theory: An interactional alternative. *Journal of Politeness Research* 3(2): 295–317. https://doi.org/10.1016/j.pragma.2009.12.018

Haugh, M. (2010) Jocular mockery, (dis)affiliation and face. *Journal of Pragmatics* 42(8): 2106–2119. https://doi.org/10.1016/j.pragma.2009.12.018

Haugh, M. and Bargiela-Chiappini, F. (2010) Face in interaction. Special issue of *Journal of Pragmatics* 42(8): 2073–2171. https://doi.org/10.1016/j.pragma.2009.12.013

Haugh, M. and Hinze, C. (2003) A metalinguistic approach to deconstructing the concepts of 'face' and 'politeness' in Chinese, English and Japanese. *Journal of Pragmatics* 35(10/11): 1581–1611. https://doi.org/10.1016/S0378-2166(03)00049-3

House, J. (1986) Cross-cultural pragmatics and foreign language teaching. In K. Bausch, Fr. G. Königs and R. Kogelheide (eds) *Probleme und Perspektiven der Sprachlehrforschung* 281–295. Frankfurt a. M.: Scriptor.

Joy, H. (1995) *Wrapping Culture: Politeness, Presentation, and Power in Japan and Other Societies.* Oxford: Oxford University Press.

Jucker, A. H. (2009) Speech act research between armchair, field and laboratory. The case of compliments. *Journal of Pragmatics* 41: 1611–1635. https://doi.org/10.1016/j.pragma.2009.02.004

Kádár, D. Z. and Haugh, M. (2013) *Understanding Politeness.* Cambridge: Cambridge University Press. https://doi.org/10.1017/CBO9781139382717

Kádár, D. Z. and Mills, S. (2011) *Politeness in East Asia.* Cambridge: Cambridge University Press. https://doi.org/10.1017/CBO9780511977886

Kádár, D. Z. and Pan, Y. L. (2011) Politeness in China. In D. Z. Kádár and S. Mills (eds) *Politeness in East Asia* 125–146. Cambridge: Cambridge University Press. https://doi.org/10.1017/CBO9780511977886.008

Kádár, D. Z. and Pan, Y. L. (eds) (2013) *Chinese Discourse and Interaction.* London: Equinox.

Kasper, G. (1990) Linguistic politeness: Current research issues. *Journal of Pragmatics* 14: 193–218. https://doi.org/10.1016/0378-2166(90)90080-W

Kong, K. (2013) Epilogue: What makes Chinese unique in discourse and interaction? In D. Z. Kádár and Y. L. Pan (eds) *Chinese Discourse and Interaction* 310–320. London: Equinox.

Lee, Y. C. (2011) Comparison of politeness and acceptability perceptions of request strategies between Chinese learners of English and native English speakers. *Asian Social Science* 7(8): 21–34. https://doi.org/10.5539/ass.v7n8p21

Leech, G. (1983) *Principles of Pragmatics.* London: Longman.

Leech, G. (2005) Politeness: Is there an East–West divide? *Journal of Foreign Languages* (6): 3–31.

Leech, G. (2007) Politeness: Is there an East–West divide? *Journal of Politeness Research* (3): 167–206. https://doi.org/10.1515/PR.2007.009

Leech, G. (2014) *The Pragmatics of Politeness.* Oxford: Oxford University Press. https://doi.org/10.1093/acprof:oso/9780195341386.001.0001

Locher, M. (2004) *Power and Politeness in Action: Disagreements in Oral Communication.* Berlin: Mouton. https://doi.org/10.1515/9783110926552

Locher, M and Watts, R. (2005) Politeness theory and relational work. *Journal of Politeness Research* 1: 9–33. https://doi.org/10.1515/jplr.2005.1.1.9

Macaulay, R. K. S. (2009) Adolescents and identity. *Intercultural Pragmatics* 6(4): 597–612. https://doi.org/10.1515/IPRG.2009.029

Miller, C. (1984) Genre as social action. *Quarterly Journal of Speech* 70: 151–167. https://doi.org/10.1080/00335638409383686

Mills, S. (2003) *Gender and Politeness.* Cambridge: Cambridge University Press. https://doi.org/10.1017/CBO9780511615238

Pan, Y. L. (2000) *Politeness in Chinese Face-to-Face Interactions.* Stamford, CT: Ablex Publishing Corporation.

Pichler, H. (2009) The functional and social reality of discourse variants in a northern English dialect: I DON'T KNOW and I DON'T THINK compared. *Intercultural Pragmatics* 6(4): 561–596. https://doi.org/10.1515/IPRG.2009.028

Pinto, D. (2008) Passing greetings and interactional style: A cross-cultural study of American English and Peninsular Spanish. *Journal of Cross-Cultural and Interlanguage Communication* 27(4): 371–388. https://doi.org/10.1515/MULTI.2008.017

Placencia, M. E. (1994) Pragmatics across varieties of Spanish. *Donaire* 2: 65–77.

Placencia, M. E. (2008) Requests in corner shop transactions in Ecuadorian Andean and Coastal Spanish. In K. P. Schneider and A. Barron (eds) *Variational Pragmatics: A Focus on Regional Varieties in Pluricentric Languages* 307–332. Amsterdam and Philadelphia: John Benjamins.

Rüegg, L. (2014) Thanks responses in three socio-economic settings. A variational pragmatics approach. *Journal of Pragmatics* 71: 17–30. https://doi.org/10.1016/j.pragma.2014.07.005

Ruiz de Zarobe, Y. and Ruiz de Zarobe, L. (2012) *Speech Acts and Politeness across Languages and Cultures*. Bern: Peter Lang International Academic Publishers. https://doi.org/10.3726/978-3-0351-0438-7

Schneider, K. P. (1999) Compliment responses across cultures. In M. Wysocka (ed.) *On Language in Theory and Practice: In Honour of Janusz Arabski on the Occasion of his 60th Birthday* 162–172. Katowice: Wydawnictwo Uniwersytetu Śląskiego.

Schneider, K. P. (2005) 'No problem, you're welcome, anytime': Responding to thanks in Ireland, England, and the USA. In A. Barron and K. P. Schneider (eds) *The Pragmatics of Irish English* 101–139. Berlin and New York: Mouton de Gruyter.

Schneider, K. P. (2008) Small talk in England, Ireland, and the USA. In K. P. Schneider and A. Barron (eds) *Variational Pragmatics: A Focus on Regional Varieties in Pluricentric Languages* 99–139. Amsterdam and Philadelphia: John Benjamins.

Schneider, K. P. and Barron, A. (eds) (2008a) *Variational Pragmatics: A Focus on Regional Varieties in Pluricentric Languages*. Amsterdam and Philadelphia: John Benjamins. https://doi.org/10.1075/pbns.178

Schneider, K. P. and Barron, A. (2008b) Where pragmatics and dialectology meet: Introducing variational pragmatics. In Klaus P. Schneider and A. Barron (eds.), *Variational Pragmatics: A Focus on Regional Varieties in Pluricentric Languages* 1–32. Amsterdam and Philadelphia: John Benjamins.

Schölmberger, U. (2008) Apologizing in French French and Canadian French. In K. P. Schneider and A. Barron (eds) *Variational Pragmatics: A Focus on Regional Varieties in Pluricentric Languages* 329–350. Amsterdam and Philadelphia: John Benjamins. https://doi.org/10.1075/pbns.178.15sch

Sifianou, M. (1999) *Politeness Phenomena in England and Greece: A Cross-Cultural Perspective*. Oxford: Oxford University Press.

Spencer-Oatey, H. (2000) Rapport management: A framework for analysis. In H. Spencer-Oatey (ed.) *Culturally Speaking: Managing Rapport through Talk across Cultures* 11–46. London: Continuum.

Spencer-Oatey, H. (2002) Managing rapport in talk: Using rapport sensitive incidents to explore the motivational concerns underlying the management of relations. *Journal of Pragmatics* 34: 529–545. https://doi.org/10.1016/S0378-2166(01)00039-X

Spencer-Oatey, H. (2005) (Im)politeness, face and perceptions of rapport: Unpacking their bases and interrelationships. *Journal of Politeness Research* 1: 95–119. https://doi.org/10.1515/jplr.2005.1.1.95

Spencer-Oatey, H. (2008) Face, (im)politeness and rapport. In H. Spencer-Oatey (ed.) *Culturally Speaking: Culture, Communication and Politeness Theory* 11–47. London: Continuum.

Spencer-Oatey, H. and Xing, J. (1998) Relational management in Chinese–British business meetings. In S. Hunston (ed.) *Language at Work* 31–46. Clevedon: British Association for Applied Linguistics in association with Multilingual Matters.

Tannen, D. (1990) *You Just Don't Understand: Women and Men in Conversation.* New York: William Morrow & Co.

Tannen, D. (1996) *Gender and Discourse.* Oxford: Oxford University Press.

Tracy, K. and Robles, J. (2013) *Everyday Talk: Building and Reflecting Identities* (2nd edn). New York: Guilford Press.

Trosborg, A. (ed.) (2010) *Pragmatics across Languages and Cultures.* Berlin: Mouton De Gruyter. https://doi.org/10.1515/9783110214444

Watts, R. (2003) *Politeness.* Cambridge: Cambridge University Press. https://doi.org/10.1017/CBO9780511615184

Wierzbicka, A. (2003) *Cross-Cultural Pragmatics: The Semantics of Human Interaction.* Berlin and New York: Mouton De Gruyter. https://doi.org/10.1515/9783110220964

Wolfram, W. and Schilling-Estes, N. (2006). *American English: Dialects and Variation* (2nd edn) London: Blackwell.

Wu, D. and Feng, W. (2015) Pragmatist, evangelist, or sensualist?: Emotional branding on Sina Weibo. In P. P. K. Ngand C. S. B. Ngai (eds) *Role of Language and Corporate Communication in Greater China* 225–239. Heidelberg: Springer.

Zhao, S., Grasmuck, S. and Marin, J. (2008) Identity construction on Facebook: Digital empowerment in anchored relationships. *Computers in Human Behaviour* 24: 1816–1836. https://doi.org/10.1016/j.chb.2008.02.012

PART I

Politeness in various Chinese introduction/ response settings

Guest introductions and responses at Chinese dinner tables

Xueyu Wang

Introduction

Natural conversation has long been regarded as the orthodox data in the field of discourse analysis and pragmatics. Accordingly, dinner talk, one of the typical forms of natural conversation, which is 'neither public, nor entirely private and informal' (Aronsson 1999), deserves attention. It is, however, a relatively unexplored source for research in these two fields (but see Blum-Kulka 1997; Brumark 2003a, 2003b, 2006; De Geer, Tulviste, Mizera and Tryggvason 2002; Leung 2009; Tryggvason 2006).

There are exceptions, though. Blum-Kulka's research monograph *Dinner Talk: Cultural Patterns of Sociability and Socialisation in Family Discourse* (1997) might be considered pioneering in the investigation of dinner talk, in which the author offers a rich introduction to this particular genre, exploring such multifaceted topics as participation framework and topic management, narratives and narrative roles, dimensions of directives and other speech acts. Throughout the book, Blum-Kulka focuses on the relation between language practices and age and gender in family dinner talk. For example, she finds that it is usually mothers who like to use more syntactically indirect directives traditionally connected with politeness (Blum-Kulka 1997). Brumark (2003a, 2003b, 2006) also has interesting findings related to gender influence on language use at the family dinner table. In Brumark (2003a), she shows that 50% of mothers' directives addressed to children aged from 6 to 11 were conventionally indirect, whereas fathers were either proportionately more direct or non-conventionally indirect. In another article,

Brumark (2003b) focuses on metapragmatic comments during family dinner talk, showing that mothers and children are considerably more sensitive to flouts and violations made by other interlocutors. In a recent article, Brumark (2006) addresses the issue of indirect speech and implication in family dinner talk from a Gricean perspective, illustrating the gender influence on speakers observing and violating the Cooperative Principle (Grice 1975). De Geer et al. (2002) investigate the socialisation function of family dinner talk, focusing on the use of comment, one of the linguistic tools of socialisation in Estonian, Finnish and Swedish family dinner talk, showing that families from different cultural backgrounds use different comments to socialise their children. Tryggvason (2006) compares the amount of talk at dinner tables in three Nordic groups – Finnish, Swedish-Finnish and Swedish families – proving that cultural background does influence communicative practice at dinner tables.

Though scholars have probed the linguistic features, constraining contextual factors and socialisation function of dinner talk, most of these studies focus on a particular kind of dinner talk, i.e. family dinner talk, with little attention directed to dinner talk in other social settings, like that between friends, with strangers and so on (but see Leung 2009). Also, no study has concerned itself with polite behaviour at the opening part of dinner talk such as self- and other-introduction. In addition, all the previous studies on dinner talk are limited to English or other Western languages, with Chinese dinner talk unexplored.

In China, dinner engagements with friends, colleagues, business partners or rivals, or so-called *fanju* (饭局) in Chinese, constitute an interesting social phenomenon. They can be important social encounters, either for exchanges between friends and colleagues or for negotiations between business partners or rivals. More often than not, *fanju* in China have both transactional and interpersonal functions, offering very important opportunities for doing business, establishing and maintaining human relations, and constructing social identities. Thus, in such social interaction at dinner tables, politeness is a relevant and salient factor. To maintain good relationships and construct desirable self images, the dinner participants are often found to go to great lengths to 'do' politeness, by either giving a high value to others' aspects or by giving a low value to their own. We can often observe that people behave politely in the process of guest introductions and responses at Chinese dinner tables. It is based on these observations that the present study aims to explore how the participants 'do' politeness in guest introductions and responses in Chinese dinner talk within the theoretical framework of Leech's (2014) newly revised model of politeness. In addition, drawing on research findings, I also aim to discover some possible social parameters that underlie the participants' language practice.

Theoretical framework of the study

This study is targeted at exploring different types of politeness maxims employed to maintain and enhance interpersonal relations in the process of guest introductions and responses at Chinese dinner tables. For this purpose, Leech's new model of politeness provides a useful theoretical framework.

In the field of pragmatics, scholars like Lakoff (1973), Brown and Levinson (1978/1987) and Leech (1983, 2005, 2014) have proposed inspiring models and principles to deal with the matter of 'politeness' in an interaction.

Leech (1983) proposes the Politeness Principle as complementary to Grice's Cooperative Principle. The general assumption of the principle is that interactants, on the whole, prefer to express or imply polite beliefs rather than impolite beliefs. In this principle, there are two pairs of core concepts, Self and Others, and Costs and Benefits. Based on these concepts, Leech further postulates six maxims to account for linguistic politeness behaviour, namely, the Tact Maxim, the Generosity Maxim, the Approbation Maxim, the Modesty Maxim, the Agreement Maxim and the Sympathy Maxim.

The Politeness Principle has been criticised on many grounds. One of the common criticisms is that it displays a Western bias and ignores the differences of language use in Eastern and Western cultures (e.g., Gu 1990; Xu 1992; Ide 1989; Spencer-Oatey 2008). Therefore, Leech (2005) restates the original Politeness Principle from the perspective of cross-cultural communication, attempting to construct a universal theory applicable to all languages and cultures, i.e. the Grand Strategy of Politeness. In 2014, in his academic monograph *Pragmatics of Politeness*, Leech further improves the new model of politeness. Based on the original politeness maxims, borrowing Brown and Levinson's consideration for social parameters, and combining the cultural analysis of the politeness phenomenon by scholars such as Gu (1990), Ide (1989) and Spencer-Oatey (2008), this new politeness model seems to be more applicable to the analysis of the politeness phenomenon in different cultures.

Specifically, according to Leech (2005, 2014), to understand communicative politeness, it is necessary to distinguish some pairs of politeness concepts, including bivalent and trivalent politeness and pos-politeness and neg-politeness. Leech's distinction between bivalent and trivalent politeness is based on the social parameters involved. According to Leech (2014: 10), 'bivalent politeness' is realised through forms such as honorifics which 'are normally selected on the basis of two sociopragmatic dimensions, vertical and horizontal distance (also referred to as "power" and "distance", or "power" and "solidarity")'. In contrast, 'trivalent politeness' involves a third dimension, the weightiness of the transaction. For

Leech, bivalent politeness is more central in Eastern cultures and trivalent politeness in the English-speaking world.

In his new model, Leech includes all the original six politeness maxims under one large umbrella, a superconstraint, which he calls the General Strategy of Politeness (or GSP):

> In order to be polite, S expresses or implies meanings that associate a favorable value with what pertains to O (O = other, hearer) or associates an unfavorable value with what pertains to S (S = self, speaker).

(Adapted from Leech 2014: 90)

According to the values assigned to S and O, Leech further postulates ten concrete GSP maxims. Here they are illustrated within Chinese contexts.

(M1) Give a high value to O's wants (Generosity Maxim)

In many languages and cultures, making offers, invitations and promises is considered 'generous'. The more direct these speech acts are, the more sincere and polite the speaker appears to be. For example, in Chinese, invitations can be direct or even sound imposing to Westerners. For example:

(1)

你一定饿了吧，快坐下吃！

You must be very hungry! Sit down and eat something!

In this example, the speaker gives a high value to the hearer's want of food since she assumes the hearer 'must be very hungry'. She is behaving politely, although her offer is direct and even sounds like a command.

(M2) Give a low value to S's wants (Tact Maxim)

This is a speaker-oriented maxim. Usually, to show politeness, the speaker needs to give a low value to her own wants. For example:

(2)

你先吃，我刚吃过一点，不怎么饿的。

Enjoy your meal. I've just had some food, and am not very hungry now.

In this example, the speaker gives a low value to her want of food, telling the hearer that she is 'not very hungry now'. She is polite in so doing.

(M3) Give a high value to O's qualities (Approbation Maxim)

This maxim finds ample expression in the use of compliments in communication, in which the speaker gives a high value to O's qualities. For example:

(3)

您的园艺技术果然一流，看看您花园的花多漂亮啊！

You are really good at gardening. How attractive the flowers are!

In Example (3), the speaker behaves politely by giving a high value to the hearer's skills in gardening.

(M4) Give a low value to S's qualities (Modesty Maxim)

This happens when one responds to another person's compliments. The speaker gives a low value to her own qualities through the use of self-deprecating expressions, or the refusal of the compliment, or the attribution of a particular achievement to others. For example:

(4)

Teacher:	你的字写得很好啊！
Student:	您过奖了，写得还不好。
Teacher:	Your handwriting is beautiful.
Student:	Well, thanks for your compliment. It's not good enough.

In this example, the student behaves politely by giving a low value to his own handwriting in the comment that 'It's not good enough'.

(M5) Give a high value to S's obligation to O (Obligation of S to O Maxim)

The speaker acts politely by stating that she has an obligation to do something for the hearer, thus making the hearer feel at ease in making a request. For example:

(5)

别客气啊，有事您说话，应该的。

Do not hesitate to let me know should you want any help from me. It's my duty.

In this example, the speaker is polite because she emphasises that it is her duty to help the hearer, thus giving a high value to her obligation to the hearer.

(M6) Give a low value to H's obligation to S (Obligation of O to S Maxim)

Here, the speaker is polite because she downplays the hearer's obligation to her. For example:

(6)

您是客人啊，哪能让您来倒水呢？我来给您倒!

You are the guest. How could I let you pour water for me? Let me do it for you.

In this example, the speaker behaves politely in that she emphasises that the hearer as a guest has no obligation to pour water for her, thus giving a low value to H's obligation.

(M7) Give a high value to O's opinions (Agreement Maxim)

When responding to others' opinions or judgments, the speakers sound polite when they employ the Agreement Maxim. The use of intensifiers like '完全' ('completely') '绝对' ('absolutely') and '毫无疑问' ('doubtlessly') further enhances the degree of politeness to the hearers. For example:

(7)

Boss:	你怎么看，小陈？
Employee:	我完全同意您的决定。
Boss:	What's your opinion, Chen?
Employee:	I totally agree with you.

In this example, when being asked to express his opinion, the employee adopts the Agreement Maxim to show his politeness. With the use of the verb phrase 'totally agree', he is giving a high value to his boss's opinion.

(M8) Give a low value to S's opinions (Opinion-reticence Maxim)

When expressing her own opinion, the speaker needs to use some hedges like 'I think', 'I guess' and 'I suppose' to indicate uncertainty so as to show politeness. This maxim is especially applicable to communication in Eastern cultures. For example, in China, expressing opinions (especially to a superior) might be seen as potentially offensive. As a result, speakers employ various linguistic devices to restrain their own opinion to show politeness to others. For example:

(8)

就这个问题呢，我觉得大家已经说得很多了，我也没有可添加的了。

To this question, I think you all have contributed a lot, and I have nothing to add.

In this example, the speaker, when asked to express her own opinion on the question mentioned, emphasises that all the others have contributed a lot to this question, and holds back her own opinion by saying that 'I have nothing to add', thus giving a low value to her own opinion. By doing so, she actually aims to show her politeness to others.

(M9) Give a high value to O's feelings (Sympathy Maxim)

This maxim is best illustrated in such speech events as congratulations, good wishes and condolences. In these events, speakers express their politeness by sharing the hearers' feelings: feeling sad when the hearers have suffered misfortune, and feeling happy when they have good luck. For example:

(9)

真的很难过听到这样的事，但不管怎样你要振作。

I'm really sad to hear it, but anyway you should not be discouraged.

In Example (9), when hearing the misfortune of the hearer, the speaker shows her sympathy, which is a polite act according to the GPS.

(M10) Give a low value to S's feelings (Feeling-reticence Maxim)

In daily communication, it is considered polite not to tells others one's bad experiences or feelings, thus preventing them from worrying. For example, when responding to the question '最近怎么样啊' ('How have you been?'), the answer is always preferably '挺好' ('fine') or '还行' ('not bad'). For example:

(10)

A:	怎么样？伤得厉害吗？
B:	没关系，一点刮伤而已。
A:	How are you feeling? Does it hurt seriously?
B:	It doesn't matter. Just a few scratches.

In this example, when responding to A's question about the injury, B answers that 'it doesn't matter', and refers to the injury as 'a few scratches', downplaying the seriousness of her injury, thus preventing A from worrying about her injury. B is behaving politely to A by so doing.

All the above ten maxims of the GSP are summarised in Table 2.1.

Table 2.1 The component maxims of GSP

Maxims	Label for this maxim	Typical speech event type(s)
(M1) give a high value to O's wants	Generosity	Commissives
(M2) give a low value to S's wants	Tact	Directives
(M3) give a high value to O's qualities	Approbation	Compliments
(M4) give a low value to S's qualities	Modesty	Self-devaluation
(M5) give a high value to S's Obligation to O	Obligation (of S to O)	Apologising, thanking
(M6) give a low value to O's obligation to S	Obligation (of O to S)	Responses to thanks and apologies
(M7) give a high value to O's opinions	Agreement	Agreeing, disagreeing
(M8) give a low value to S's opinions	Opinion-reticence	Giving opinions
(M9) give a high value to O's feelings	Sympathy	Congratulating, commiserating
(M10) give a low value to S's feelings	Feeling-reticence	Suppressing feelings

As it is more likely for the speech acts of compliments and self-devaluation to occur at dinner-table introductions and responses, my analysis mainly focuses on the Approbation Maxim and the Modesty Maxim. Besides, it should be noted that, though Leech provides these ten politeness maxims in his new model, as he himself mentions, 'the list of constraints of M1–M10 may be incomplete' and 'other instances … could be elaborated'. I shall demonstrate the addition of a new maxim or maxims, if at all, on the basis of my data.

In addition to the politeness maxims, Leech, based on Brown and Levinson's analysis on D (distance), P (Power) and R (Rank of imposition), proposes some social factors which might influence the use of politeness, among which the most important three are:

(1) Vertical distance between S and O (in terms of status, power, role, age, etc.)
(2) Horizontal distance between S and O (intimate, familiar, acquaintance, stranger)
(3) Cost/benefit: how large is the benefit, the cost, the favor, the obligation, etc., that is, the real socially defined value of what is being transacted.

(Leech 2014: 103)

As for the analysis of dinner-table introductions and responses, the consideration of power and relationship between S and O is much more important than cost/benefit, as the latter does not seem relevant. Thus, I limit the contextual factors to the first two, the vertical distance between S and O and the horizontal distance between S and O. Figure 2.1 provides the theoretical framework for this analysis:

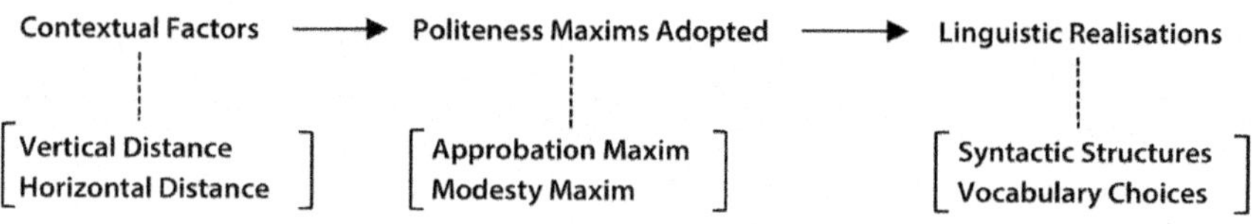

Figure 2.1 Theoretical framework of the present research

Methodology

Research questions

In this study, I shall focus on how speakers adopt the GSP to 'do' politeness at Chinese dinner tables and how the vertical and horizontal distances between participants influence their choice of politeness maxims as finally realised linguistically. Specifically, my aim is to answer the following three research questions:

1. What politeness maxims are enacted in guest introductions and responses at Chinese dinner tables?
2. How are these maxims realised linguistically?
3. How do vertical distance and horizontal distance between S and O influence the choice of politeness maxims?

Data collection and analysis

Despite the advantage of data from spontaneous conversations, it is not convenient to collect a large number of naturally occurring conversations at Chinese dinner tables. For this reason, the present study mainly adopts the dinner talks from two Chinese novels as the research data for the description of politeness maxims observed and their linguistics realisations.

The two Chinese novels *History of Officer Hou* (《侯卫东官海沉浮》) and *Years in Officialdom* (《官场风月》) are both officialdom novels. These two novels are mainly about the career advancement of two young Chinese officials, Hou Weidong in the former one and Liu Mingqiang in the latter one. It is assumed that these Chinese novels provide adequate chances for us to get a full picture of what China's dinner talks are like. Although an element of simulation is involved in novel writing, these simulated interactions in novels can still reflect the mutual exchange and interactive communication between speakers and thus are applicable to pragmatic analysis (Biber and Finegan 1992; Lakoff and Tannen 1984). In addition, in officialdom novels there are more considerations of power and relationships among the different participants. Thus, data in Chinese officialdom novels could be helpful enough in the analysis of contextual factors influencing the enactment of politeness maxims during dinner-table introductions and responses.

The present study mainly adopts a qualitative method, and is descriptive and explanatory in nature. Data analysis has been carried out by describing the roles of dinner-table introductions and responses, identifying the politeness maxims adopted in these speech acts and explaining the influence of the contextual factors on language use. To describe the participant roles of dinner-table introductions and responses, I first of all provide a simple description of the process of a typical dinner-table introduction and response activity, and then analyse the different roles and role shifts involved in this process. To identify the politeness maxims adopted in dinner-table introductions and responses, I mainly adopt Leech's analysis of the Approbation and Modesty Maxims. In order to explain the contextual influence, I mainly focus on the influence of vertical distance and horizontal distance among the participants of language use.

'Doing' politeness in introductions and responses at dinner tables

Roles in dinner-table introductions and responses

A typical dinner-table introduction and response goes like this: the introducer sends the introducing message related to one participant (the participant being introduced, or simply the introduced) to the other participant(s) or addressee(s) to get them acquainted with each other, and then the addressee gives back a responding message, usually directly to the participant being introduced. The whole process is depicted in Figure 2.2:

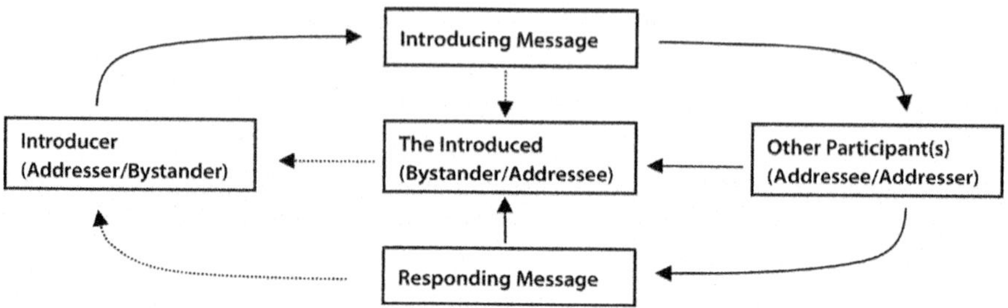

Figure 2.2 Process of dinner-table introduction and response

From Figure 2.2 we can detect different roles in a typical dinner-table introducing and responding interaction. When sending the introducing message, the targeted addressee of the introducer is the other participant(s), so the solid arrow is used to connect the introducer, the introducing message and the other participants. In this process, the introducer acts as the addresser, the other participant(s) as the addressee(s) and the participant being introduced as a bystander. When responding to the introduction, the other participant(s) now acts as the addresser, the participant being introduced as the addressee and the introducer as the bystander. Though the targeted audience in the responding process is the person being introduced, the addresser indirectly conveys the message to the introducer while responding to the introduction. Hence, the dotted arrow is used to connect the responding message and the introducer.

As is seen in Figure 2.2, the dinner-table introduction and response can be considered as a very complex three-party interaction. However, once two of the participants overlap – the introducer and the participant being introduced – this three-party interaction may be reduced to a simple two-party interaction, with one participant introducing himself to other participant(s) and the other participant(s) responding to his introduction.

To understand the whole process of dinner-table interaction better, look at (11) selected from the Internet novel *History of Officer Hou*, in which a three-party conversation takes place on the occasion of guest introduction and response.

(11)

Hou:　　这是益扬报社的段英，才从上青林下来，她是我的大学同学。

Zeng:　　段记者采访工作细致……段记者是什么时候到的报社，报社的美女记者我都熟悉，以前怎么没有见过你？"

Hou:　　This is Duan Yin from Yiyang News Agency, my college classmate. She has just returned from Shangqinglin County.

Zeng:　　Ms. Duan is really meticulous in interviewing … When did Ms. Duan start to work in Yiyang News Agency? I know all the pretty ladies there. How could it be possible that I've never seen you before?

In (11), Hou acts as an introducer to send the introducing message related to his former classmate Duan to Zeng. At this stage, Zeng is his targeted addressee and Duan a bystander. Hou's introduction mainly focuses on Duan's identity as being a journalist from 'Yiyang News Agency' and their relation as being 'college classmates'. The addressee, Zeng, after hearing the introduction, responds directly to Duan, shifting Duan from a bystander to a direct addressee, and Hou from the addresser to a bystander.

Politeness maxims adopted in dinner-table introductions

At Chinese dinner tables, other-introduction often unfolds in a three-party conversation. The present study focuses on the analysis of the politeness maxims adopted in this process, as exemplified by the data.

A. The Approbation Maxim in dinner-table introductions

Most frequently, when making an introduction of one participant to others, the speaker is generally found to adopt the Approbation Maxim, i.e., to give a high value to those being introduced, focusing either on the latter's positive personal qualities, skills and competence, or on their high social status and identities. For example:

(12)

 Tang: 这是新来的大学生侯卫东，以后就在工作组工作。

 Tang: This is Hou Weidong, a newly coming college graduate. He will work in our group.

In this example, as the introducer, Tang introduces Hou Weidong to all the participants by referring to him as a '大学生' ('college graduate'). College students are usually regarded as a cultivated group with relatively high qualities and competence. Thus, by referring to Hou as a 'college graduate', the addresser aims to imply that Hou is a person with good education and competence. Through giving such a high value to Hou, Tang shows politeness to Hou by enacting the Approbation Maxim. Here is another example:

(13)

 Su Mingjun: 这是杨柳，办公室主任，笔头功夫很不错，综合协调能力很强。

 Su Mingjun: This is Yang Liu, office chief. She is excellent in writing and coordinating.

In this episode, the addresser, Su Mingjun, introduces Yang Liu to the other guests. In his introduction, he gives very positive comments on Yang, complimenting her as being 'excellent in writing and coordinating', thus giving a high value to the personal qualities of Yang, expressing his politeness through the use of the Approbation Maxim.

In addition to personal qualities, the addresser may also give a high value to the person's social identities. This happens especially when the person being introduced enjoys a relatively high social status. We can refer to Examples (14) and (15). In both instances, the social roles and identities are mentioned in the introduction discourse.

(14)

Liang Bifa: 这是沙洲道路工程公司的李晶，李总。

Liang Bifa: This is Lijingin Shaozhou Road Construction Company, General Manager Li.

(15)

Zhou: 这是我们科委侯主任，一把手。

Zhou: This is Hou, Head in Science and Technology Commission, our chief leader.

In (14), Liang Bifa, the addresser introduces one of his guests, Li Jing, to the other guest, Hou Weidong. He praises Li Jing by referring to her social identity, notably general manager of the company. This is a display of the Approbation Maxim, realised by giving a high value to the social identity of the one being introduced. In (15), when introducing Hou to the other guests, the addresser, Zhou, attempts to show politeness to Hou by telling other guests of Hou's high social identity, '科委主任' ('Head in Science and Technology Commission') and '一把手' ('our chief leader').

B. The Modesty Maxim in dinner-table introductions

In the introduction phase of Chinese dinner tables, if the one being introduced happens to be an 'in-grouper' of the introducer, the Modesty Maxim in the GSP is sometimes used. For example:

(16)

Hou: 这是我兄弟媳妇小佳，才工作没几年，没什么经验，还望各位领导多多关照。

Hou: This is my sister-in-law Xiaojia. She has just started to work and has no working experience. Hope you can help in her work.

In this instance, when Hou Weiguo is introducing his sister-in-law to the other guests, he complies with the Modesty Maxim. Considering Xiaojia is his family member, who can be regarded as an 'in-grouper', Hou, gives a low value to Xiaojia, his 'in-grouper', to show his politeness to all the other guests.

C. The Intimacy Maxim in dinner-table introductions

Based on the data, I would venture a further maxim to be added to Leech's ten maxims, i.e. the Intimacy Maxim: specifically, give a high value to self's attachment to the other. This makes perfect sense because, in Chinese culture, showing intimacy to others is seen as polite in interpersonal interaction (Jia 1997). By showing his or her intimate relationship with the other, the addresser satisfies the addressee's wants of being cared and loved. Linguistically, this maxim is usually realised through the use of endearment names, nicknames or expressions indicating a close relationship. As a matter of fact, this kind of politeness maxim is frequently found in dinner-table talks. For example:

(17)

Guo Lan: 这是李俊，我的好朋友。

Guo Lan: This is Lijun, my good friend.

In (17), when the addresser Guo Lan makes an introduction of Li Jun to other guests, she refers to Li as '我的好朋友' ('my good friend'), which sounds polite to Li Jun in this context.

(18)

Jin: 他啊，我的秘书，刘明强，同时也是我的干儿子，哈哈。

Jin: He? My secretary, Liu Mingqiang. He is also my adopted son.

In this instance, the addresser Jin invites some of his old friends to dinner. He brings Liu with him. When introducing Liu, he first refers to him as 'my secretary' in an official way. However, being a secretary suggests a relatively lower social status, inferior to the addresser himself and his other guests. To show politeness, Jin adopts the Intimacy Maxim by calling Liu 'my newly adopted son'. In China, people occasionally establish such non-blood-type parent–child relationships as a means of endearment to each other. Jin's words testify to this cultural practice.

Politeness maxims adopted in responses to dinner-table introductions

In response to the addressers' introductions, the addressee now makes a shift to take on the role of the addresser, usually with the participant being introduced as his direct addressee, and the former addresser of the introduction as a bystander. The addresser has to be very sensitive in 'doing' politeness, as he has to show politeness to both his direct addressee (the one being introduced) and the bystander (the introducer). Hence, when this speech act is performed, various politeness maxims are adopted, including the Approbation Maxim, the Modesty Maxim as proposed by Leech (2014) and the Intimacy Maxim as illustrated above.

A. The Approbation Maxim in responses to guest introductions

A typical politeness maxim used to respond to guest introductions at Chinese dinner tables is the Approbation Maxim, in which a high value is given, in most cases, to qualities of the one being introduced in an explicit way. This kind of responding act is to some degree similar to a complimenting act, 'characteristically both in terms of semantics and syntax' (Wolfson 1989: 21). In terms of semantics, most of the complimenting acts make use of adjectives, adverbs and noun phrases to carry the positive semantic load. The following is an example from the data:

(19)

Zhou:	这是我们科委侯主任，一把手。
Guest:	侯主任恐怕是科委系统最年轻的主任了。
Zhou:	This is Hou, Head in Science and Technology Commission, our chief leader.
Guest:	Mr Hou might be the youngest leader in Science and Technology Commission.

In this interaction, after Zhou Yongtai introduces Hou to another guest at the dinner table, the guest responds to his introduction by complimenting his addressee, Hou, as the 'youngest leader', giving a high value to Hou's qualities, since in this context being young is considered quite desirable. Hence, in the above example, the responding speech act is conducted with observance of the Approbation Maxim, realised by the positive adjective on the semantic layer.

In terms of syntax, when responding to guest introductions at Chinese dinner tables, the Approbation Maxim is realised by such typical sentence structures as exclamatory sentences and rhetorical questions as shown in (20) and (21).

(20)

Zhu Yan:	这是益扬新管会主任侯卫东。
Liang:	好年轻的新管会主任呀！
Zhu Yan:	This is Hou Weidong, chief leader in Yiyang Management Committee for New Urban Construction.
Liang:	What a young leader!

(21)

Hou:	这是我老婆张小佳。
Guo:	张小佳肯定不是在益杨工作的吧？
Xiaojia:	你怎么知道？
Guo Lan:	（指了指小佳漂亮的小卷发以及身上的衣服）益杨女孩子可穿不出这样的味道。
Hou:	This is my wife Zhang Xiaojia.
Guo:	Couldn't Zhang be working in Yiyang?
Xiaojia:	How could you know that?
Guo Lan:	(pointing to Xiajia's delicate hair and dress) Girls in Yiyang can't have your taste in dress.

In (20), an exclamatory sentence is used to realise the Approbation Maxim. When responding to Zhu's introduction about Hou, Liang utilises an exclamatory sentence 'What a young leader!' to strongly express his emotion, complimenting Hou on his quality of being young. In (21), the Approbation Maxim is realised in two conversational turns. In the first turn, after Hou's introduction to his girlfriend Zhang, Guo responds with a rhetorical question 'Couldn't Zhang be working in Yiyang?', which elicits Zhang's question 'How could you know that?', and the second turn starts. Guo's compliment act becomes more obvious after she finally gives her answer 'Girls in Yiyang cannot have your taste in dress', implicitly conveying that Zhang is a girl with fine taste in dress, giving a high value to Zhang, Hou's girlfriend, showing politeness to both Zhang and Hou.

B. The Modesty Maxim in responses to guest introductions

In some cases, the response is made by the person being introduced at the dinner table. In such cases, the Modesty Maxim is often adopted to give a low value to the speaker's own qualities. For example, in (22), when being introduced to others, the speaker adopts the Modesty Maxim to show his politeness.

(22)

Liang Bifa:	这是沙州道路工程公司的李晶，李总。
Li Jing:	侯卫东，好几次听到梁大哥说起你，我是沙州道路工程公司的李晶，我哪里是老总，只是为了好听，挂了一个副总的名字。
Liang Bifa:	This is Li Jing in Shaozhou Road Construction Company, General Manager Li.
Li Jing:	Hou Weidong, I've long heard about you from Brother Liang. I'm Li Jing in Shaozhou Road Construction Company. I'm not a real general manager at all, but a vice manager in name only.

In (22), it is Liang who first acts as the addresser to introduce Li Jing to Hou Weidong. He shows his politeness by referring to Li's social identity, Manager of Shazhou Road Construction Company, calling her '李总' ('General Manager Li'). Following this introduction, Li takes the floor to respond to this complimentary introduction with a rejection strategy, declining to be called '李总' ('General Manager Li'). Instead, she tells Hou that she is 'just a vice manager in name only', implying that she is not entitled to be a general manager or even a vice manager, giving a low value to herself. This is a clear instance of observing the Modesty Maxim.

C. The Intimacy Maxim in responses to guest introductions

In responding to guest introductions at Chinese dinner tables, we find the Intimacy Maxim is also frequently used to give a high value to the addressees' wants to be on close terms with the addressers. For example:

(23)

Jin:	今天我们改下规矩，这是我的秘书小刘，今天给大家介绍介绍，方便你们以后汇报工作，所以今天小刘就坐在我边上吧。
Liu:	在座的各位领导，我叫刘明强，以后就麻烦大家多多照顾照顾。
Qin:	刘秘书你好，欢迎到我们这开发区来，今天老弟可要多喝几杯啊。
Jin:	Today let's change the seat arrangement. I will introduce my secretary, Little Liu, to you so that you can report your work to him later. So let him sit next to me today.
Liu:	Dear leaders, I'm Liu Mingqiang. Hope you can help me in my future job.
Qin:	Welcome, Secretary Liu. My good brother, you must enjoy your drink here.

In (23), Jin first introduces Liu to all other guests present, followed by Liu's self-introduction. After the introduction sequence, one of the guests, Qin, acts as the addresser to respond to the introduction act. To show his politeness to Liu, he first expresses his welcome to Liu formally, and then uses an informal kinship term '老弟' ('my good brother') to indicate that he has already considered Liu to be in his group, showing his intimacy with Liu. Hence, the informal kinship term is actually one of the linguistic realisations of the Intimacy Maxim. In our data, we can find other such kinship terms in Chinese as '嫂子' ('sister-in-law') and '小子' ('guy').

It is worthwhile to point out that in our data, the addresser might adopt different kinds of politeness maxims to give either a high value to the addressees or a low value to herself. As a matter of fact, in some cases, two or three maxims are combined in the same responding act. For example, in (24), the addresser observes both the Approbation Maxim and the Intimacy Maxim to show his politeness to the addressee.

(24)

Li:	咦，老金，这位是？
Jin:	他啊，我的秘书，刘明强，同时也是我的干儿子，哈哈。
Li:	小伙子不错，人精神，不错，小子，你好福气啊，跟着老金好好干，早晚会飞黄腾达的。
Li:	Jin, who is this?
Jin:	He? My secretary, Liu Mingqiang. He is also my newly adopted son.
Li:	This young guy is not bad, very energetic. Good, guy, you are really lucky. Work hard with Jin, and you will succeed sooner or later.

In this instance, after hearing Jin's introduction to Liu Mingqiang, Li first gives a very positive comment on Liu with the use of some evaluative expressions like '不错' ('not bad') and '人精神' ('very energetic'), giving a high value to Liu, which is a display of the Approbation Maxim. Then he continues his response with the enactment of the Intimacy Maxim, as realised by the use of the term of endearment '小子' ('guy'), showing his affection towards Liu, the young man being introduced.

It is very interesting that, when responding to guest introductions at Chinese dinner tables, though the one being introduced is always the targeted addressee, the addresser would take into consideration not only the value of the one being introduced, but the value of the original introducer. Thus, the use of politeness maxims is not only oriented to the introduced, but also to the introducer. For example, in (22), when Li Jing responds to Liang's introduction to Hou, Li's utterance not only shows politeness to Hou, the one being introduced, but also to Liang, the introducer. She adopts the Modesty Maxim to show politeness to the direct addressee Hou, and at the same time she also shows politeness to the original addresser Liang by referring to him as '梁大哥' ('Brother Liang'), a kinship term in Chinese culture to indicate a close relationship. Also, in (23), when Li responds to Jin's introduction of Liu, his speech act is oriented to both Liu and Jin. Overtly, he is making comments on Liu's being 'not bad' and 'energetic', but when congratulating Liu on his being 'lucky' and encouraging him to 'work hard' so as to be 'successful in the future', he implicitly gives a high value to Jin's potential of being an influential and competent leader. Hence, in such a speech event with complex participant roles, when responding to guest introductions, the addressers generally go to great lengths to 'do' politeness to smooth the interaction.

Contextual factors influencing China's dinner talks

According to Leech (2014), three very important contextual factors might influence the use of politeness: 1) vertical distance between speaker and others, 2) horizontal distance between speaker and others (intimate, familiar, acquaintance, stranger etc.) and 3) cost/benefit of the transaction. The vertical distance between speaker and others concerns their relative power, social status, roles and ages, and the horizontal distance concerns whether the participants of the interaction are intimate, familiar, acquainted or strangers.

In guest introductions and responses at Chinese dinner tables, the two types of distance might play important roles, since these speech events involve complex participant roles as mentioned above. Thus, the following sections will focus on the influence of vertical and horizontal distance in two speech events respectively: the guest introduction event and the responding event.

A. Influence of vertical and horizontal distance on introductions

In the phase of guest introduction, when the one being introduced has a lower social status, is less powerful or is younger than the other participants including the introducer, either the Intimacy Maxim or no politeness maxim has been observed in my data. On the linguistic layer, the former is realised in the use of informal or endearment address terms. For example, in (18) and (24), when Jin introduces Liu, he directly refers to his full name 'Liu Mingqiang' without the use of any politeness term. Then, to show his intimacy, he adds to his introduction by calling him 'my newly adopted son' to give a high value to Liu.

The addresser also prefers to refer to the one being introduced with a 'little + family name' structure, which in Chinese is used to refer to younger ones or ones with relatively lower social status. For instance, in (23), Jin, who is obviously more powerful than all the other participants including Liu, the one being introduced, tells the addressee that 'This is my secretary, little Liu'. Here is another example:

(25)

Department Head Ma:	这是小池。
Department Head Ma:	This is little Chi.

In this instance, Ma is the head of the department, and Chi is only a member of staff in this department. Thus, the addresser Ma has a relatively higher social status and is more powerful than Chi, the one being introduced. As a result, in the introduction, Ma simply refers to Chi as '小池' ('little Chi').

However, if the one being introduced has a higher social status and is more powerful than the introducer or the direct addressee, the Approbation Maxim is frequently used, realised in the use of very formal or respectful address terms indicating the social identity of the one being introduced. For example:

(26)

Liang Yunshan:	我是茂云组织部的，梁云山。
Someone nearby:	这是组织部梁部长。
Liang Yunshan:	I'm Liang Yunshan from MaoYun Organisation Department.
Someone nearby:	This is Director Liang of Organisation Department.

In (26), after Liang Yunshan's self-introduction, someone nearby introduces him to Hou Weidong, 'This is Director Liang …' In this interaction, Liang is the one with higher social status and is more powerful than both the introducer and the one being introduced, so in the introduction act, Liang's official title '组织部长' ('Director of Organisation Department') is stressed.

Thus, we can draw the following conclusion: in dinner-table introductions, the relative power, social status and age of the participants might influence the choice of politeness maxims. When the introduced has a lower social status, is less powerful or is younger than the other participants, the politeness consideration is not so clear, and various linguistic devices are used to refer to him, including the full name of the person, informal address terms and the 'little + family name' structure; when the introduced has a higher social status, is more powerful or is older than the other participants, respectful titles or official titles are usually used to refer to him, giving a high value to his social position.

In addition to the influence of vertical distance among the participants, horizontal distance is also an important contextual factor at work in Chinese dinner-table introductions, as our data reveal. To be specific, when introducing one guest to others, if the introducer is familiar with both the one being introduced and the addressee, the language used might be more casual. For example:

(27)

Jin:	你女朋友？
Liu:	（开玩笑道）别瞎说，我们是同事，我给你们介绍一下，这位是金倩同志，是我的一个朋友，这位呢，是张云佳同志，我和她是革命战友。
Jin:	Your girlfriend?
Liu:	(joking) Stop that nonsense. She's my comrade. Let me introduce her to you. This is Jin Qian, my friend, and this is Comrade Zhang Yunjia. We're 'comrades-in-arms'.

In (27), the introducer Liu Mingqiang is familiar with both Jin Qian and Zhang Yunjia. Thus, the horizontal distance among these three participants is relatively small. Hence, when introducing both girls, Liu avoids using very formal address terms. Instead, he refers to both Jin and Zhang as 'comrade', an obviously inappropriate term to be used among friends today. However, this 'comrade' is not used seriously, which can be detected from the expression '开玩笑道' ('joking'). Thus, both 'comrade Jin Qian' and 'comrade Zhang Yunjia' are used in an informal and humorous way. In addition, when introducing Zhang Yunjia, Liu adds that they are 'comrades-in-arms', which is another illustration of the informality in this introduction act.

In contrast, if there is certain horizontal distance between the introducer and the one being introduced, then the introduction speech act might be relatively formal, avoiding jokes, informal address terms or nicknames. For instancee, in (11) discussed above, Hou Weidong introduces Duan Ying to the other guests. Though Hou and Duan were once college classmates, Hou purposefully keeps a certain distance from Duan, since Duan is the girlfriend of his friend. Thus, when introducing Duan to others, Hou formally refers to Duan by telling others her identity as a journalist 'from Yi Yang News Agency', giving a high value to her social position.

B. Influence of vertical and horizontal distance on responses

When responding to a guest introduction at Chinese dinner tables, the addresser is found to take into consideration the power, social status and age of both the introducer and the one being introduced. If the addresser has a relatively higher social status, then his language tends to be casual and informal.

(28)

Xiaojia:	局长，这是我的爱人侯卫东。
Hou:	张局长你好。
Zhang:	小侯在哪里工作？
Hou:	我在益杨科委工作。
Xiaojia:	Director, this is my husband Hou Weidong.
Hou:	Hello, Director Zhang.
Zhang:	Where do you work, Little Hou?
Hou:	I work in Yiyang Science and Technology Commission.

In this instance, Xiaojia is the subordinate to Director Zhang, and Hou is her husband. She is introducing her husband to her leader. In this interaction, Director Zhang has a higher social status and is more powerful than both Xiaojia and Hou. As a result, in responding to Xiaojia's introduction of Hou, Director Zhang simply calls the one being introduced '小侯' ('little Hou'), an address term usually adopted by the superior to the inferior, or the senior to the junior.

However, if the addresser has a relatively lower social status or is less powerful than the one being introduced or the introducer, his language might display a high degree of politeness. For instance, in (19), when Zhou Yongtai introduces Hou Weidong to all the participants, one of them, an office head, who obviously has a lower social status compared to Hou, responds to the introduction by giving a high value to Hou's qualities, addressing him as '侯主任' ('Director Hou'), complimenting him on being the 'youngest leader in Science and Technology Commission'.

We now turn to the effect of horizontal distance on the use of politeness and linguistic realisations in dinner-table responding speech events. When responding to guest introductions, if the introducer and the other two parties (the one being introduced and the one the introduction oriented to) are very close in horizontal distance, then in the responding act the new addresser tends to adopt the Intimacy Maxim to show politeness, linguistically realised in the use of kinship terms. For example,

(29)

Hou Weidong:	这是我老婆，小佳。
He Hongfu:	大嫂，欢迎到上青林。
Hou Weidong:	This is my wife, Xiaojia.
He Hongfu:	My sister-in-law, welcome to Shangqinlin.

Example (29) is an interaction between Hou Weidong, He Hongfu and Hou's wife Xiaojia. In this instance, the introducer, Hou, is familiar with both Xiaojia, the one being introduced and He Hongfu, his targeted addressee. Thus, the horizontal distance among them is very small. He Hongfu realises the intimate relationship between Hou and Xiaojia. As a result, he adopts the Intimacy Maxim to show his closeness not only to his targeted addressee, Xiaojia, but also to the introducer, Hou. Linguistically, he uses the Chinese kinship term '大嫂' ('sister-in-law') to convey politeness.

Conclusion

The aim of the present study was to explore how speakers 'do' politeness at China's dinner tables. Specifically, it has sought to illustrate how Leech's politeness maxims are realised in dinner-table interactions and responses and how such contextual factors as vertical distance and horizontal distance among the participants influence the language use.

Chinese dinner-table talks have been analysed as a kind of very complex social interaction with different participant roles. Both guest introductions and responses place stress on either giving a high value to others or giving a low value to the speakers themselves. Thus, both speech acts are examples of politeness as proposed by Leech. From the data analysis, in most guest introducing and responding acts, such GSP maxims as the Approbation Maxim and the Modesty Maxim are used to give different values to others and to the speaker herself, which are realised with the use of typical address terms, adjectives, verbs and nouns carrying positive semantic load and some syntactic structures like rhetorical questions and exclamatory sentences. In addition, I have added a new maxim of GPS, the Intimacy Maxim, as supported by my data. Finally, in both guest introductions and responses, power, social status and personal relations among participants are found to influence the use of politeness use and language choice.

This study has suggested that Leech's GSP is applicable not only to Western interactions, but also to Eastern interactions such as Chinese dinner-table talks. In addition, it has also proved that culture plays an important role in the use of polite language at Chinese dinner tables. First of all, Chinese culture makes clear hierarchical differences among people, emphasising that there are differences between the superior and the inferior, the noble and the humble, as well as the old and the young (Jia 1997). As a result, in Chinese culture, to 'do' politeness requires understanding the differences between self and others. Quite often, though not always, a polite speaker may denigrate himself and elevate others, lending partial but not whole support to Gu's (1990) Self-denigration Maxim. The choice of polite language at Chinese dinner tables has been deeply influenced by Chinese culture. When making guest introductions or responses, speakers also make clear the differences between self and others, denigrating self by giving a low value to their own qualities, and elevating others by giving a high value to their qualities. Therefore, the Modesty Maxim and the Approbation Maxim are the two maxims most frequently adopted by speakers at Chinese dinner tables. Furthermore, Chinese culture emphasises the blood relations among people, which are usually realised in the kinship-based address terms in the Chinese language (Jia 1997). For a Chinese person, regarding others as one of their family is actually polite behaviour. 'Doing' politeness requires being intimate. Therefore, it is not hard to understand the frequent resort to the Intimacy Maxim at Chinese dinner talks when making guest introductions and responses.

It should be noted that, though the present study has some interesting findings about how people 'do' politeness at Chinese dinner tables, there are still some limitations. To start with, the data of the study are mainly from Internet novels. Though these data are relevant, they are, unquestionably, less 'authentic' for pragmatic analysis compared with those from real-life face-to-face conversational data. In addition, as has been mentioned, this study provides qualitative analysis for Chinese dinner-table talks. A quantitative method can render the analysis more convincing.

References

Aronsson, K. (1999) Review on *Dinner Talk. Journal of Pragmatics* 31: 287–292. https://doi.org/10.1016/S0378-2166(98)00048-4

Biber, D. and Finegan, E. (1992) The linguistic evolution of the five written and speech-based genres from the 17th to the 20th century. In M. Rissanen, O.Ihalainen and T. Nevalainen (eds) *History of Englishes: New Methods and Interpretations in Historical Linguistics* 699. Berlin: Mouton de Gruyter. https://doi.org/10.1515/9783110877007.688

Blum-Kulka, S. (1997) *Dinner Talk: Cultural Patterns of Sociability and Socialisation in Family Discourse.* Mahwah, NJ: Lawrence Erlbaum.

Brown, P. and Levinson, S. C. (1978/1987) *Politeness: Some Universals in Language Usage.* Cambridge: Cambridge University Press.

Brumark, A. (2003a) Regulatory talk and politeness at the dinner table in 20 Swedish families. *Sodertorn University College Working Papers* 2.

Brumark, A. (2003b) Reconsidering meta-pragmatic comments in family dinner table conversation. *Sodertorn University College Working Papers* 4.

Brumark, A. (2006) Non-observance of Gricean maxims in family dinner table conversation. *Journal of Pragmatics* 38: 1206–1238. https://doi.org/10.1016/j.pragma.2005.03.014

De Geer, B., Tulviste, T., Mizera, L. and Tryggvason, M. (2002) Socialisation in communication: Pragmatic socialisation during dinnertime in Estonian Finnish and Swedish families. *Journal of Pragmatics* 34: 1757–1786. https://doi.org/10.1016/S0378-2166(01)00059-5

Grice, P. (1975) Logic and conversation. In P. Cole and J. Morgan (eds) *Syntax and Semantics 3: Speech Acts* 41–58. New York: Academic Press.

Gu, Y. (1990) Politeness phenomena in modern Chinese. *Journal of Pragmatics* 3: 237–257. https://doi.org/10.1016/0378-2166(90)90082-O

Ide, S. (1989) Formal forms and discernment: Two neglected aspects of universals of linguistic politeness. *Multilingua* 8: 223–248. https://doi.org/10.1515/mult.1989.8.2-3.223

Jia, Y. (1997) *Intercultural Communication.* Shanghai: Shanghai Foreign Language Education Press.

Lakoff, R. (1973) The logic of politeness; or, minding your p's and q's. *Papers from the Ninth Regional Meeting of the Chicago Linguistic Society*: 295–305.

Lakoff, R. T. and Tannen, D. (1984). Conversational strategy and metastrategy in pragmatic theory: The example of scenes from a marriage. *Semiotica* 49: 323–346.

Leech, G. (1983) *Principles of Pragmatics.* London: Longman.

Leech, G. (2005) Politeness: Is there an East–West divide? *Wai Guo Yu: Journal of Foreign Languages* 6: 3–31.

Leech, G. (2014) *The Pragmatics of Politeness.* Oxford: Oxford University Press.

Leung, C. B. (2009) Collaborative narration in preadolescent girl talk: A Saturday luncheon conversation among three friends. *Journal of Pragmatics* 41: 1341–1357. https://doi.org/10.1016/j.pragma.2009.02.011

Spencer-Oatey, H. (2008) *Culturally Speaking: Culture, Communication and Politeness Theory.* London and New York: Continuum.

Tryggvason, M. (2006) Communicative behaviour in family conversation: Comparison of amount of talk in Finnish, Swedish Finnish and Swedish families. *Journal of Pragmatics* 38: 1795–1810. https://doi.org/10.1016/j.pragma.2006.02.001

Wolfson, N. (1983) An empirically based analysis of complimenting in English. In N. Wolfson and J. Elliot (eds) *Sociolinguistics and Language Acquisition* 82–95. Rowley, MA: Newbury House.

Xu, S. (1992) On a new model of politeness. *Foreign Language Research* 2: 1–7.

CHAPTER 3

Hosts' introductions and visiting professors' responses in lecture openings

Xinren Chen

Introduction

Giving lectures or talks at universities other than one's own is part of scholars' academic life. Such activity provides the speakers, generally successful and reputed researchers, with an opportunity to publicise their research work as well as to help the audience develop their research ability. So far, academic talk has attracted plenty of scholastic attention from linguists of diverse backgrounds, with focus on the interactive discourse structuring (e.g., Camiciottoli 2004) including the use of metadiscourse (e.g., Deroey and Taverniers 2012; Grant 2011; Lee and Subtirelu 2015; Thompson 2003) and the use of questions (e.g., Camiciottoli 2008; Chang 2012), the interaction between the lecturer (or visiting professor) and the audience such as the use of modifiers in seminars and interactive lectures (e.g., Lin 2015), the occurrence of laughter (e.g., Carey 2014; Nesi 2012) and the use of body language (e.g., Khuwaileh 1999), the function of personal pronouns (e.g., Fortanet 2004; Yeo and Ting 2014) for interpersonal purposes, the use of repetition (Giménez-Moreno 2012), the use and perception of humour (Wang 2014), and so on.

However, while some attention has been given to the discussion sessions following visiting professors' talks (e.g., Wulff, Swales and Keller 2009) and closings of lectures (e.g., Cheng 2012), scant attention has been directed to an auxiliary part, so to speak, of the lecture activity, i.e. the introductory part undertaken by the host on each occasion. An exception is the analysis of the moves of engineering lecture introductions (Shamsudin and Ebrahimi 2013). More effort is called for, given the length and complexity of openings observed on many occasions. In particular, the introductory part is not entirely an informative process, but rather involves a flow of interpersonal meaning as well, as shall be demonstrated later.

Thus, this study examines this specific part and demonstrates how the host's and visiting professor's interaction at this phase serves as a site of interpersonal work such that they attach an additional interpersonal meaning to the basically academic activity. Specifically, we shall focus on the approbation and modesty issues involved in the situated discourse. Despite enormous research done on compliments (e.g., Chen 1993; Spencer-Oatey and Ng 2001; Yuan 2002), no attention has been paid to compliments in the academic setting. Also, while existing literature claims that modesty plays a central role in interpersonal communication in Chinese societies, the claim is based primarily on ancient Chinese philosophy, analysts' intuitions and the like (e.g., Chen 1993; Gu 1990). Except for Spencer-Oatey and Ng (2001) and Wu (2011), very few empirical studies, let alone on the basis of naturally occurring data, have been conducted to testify to the role (Wu 2011). To fill in these gaps, first-hand data will be collected from co-ordinated lecture events in some Chinese universities. In the analysis part, Leech's (2014) new model of politeness (omitted here to reduce repetition; for a detailed introduction, refer to Chapter 2), M3 (Approbation Maxim) and M4 (Modesty Maxim) in particular will be adopted and specified when characterising the host's and the visiting professor's conversational behaviour in the introductory part. Meanwhile, reference will be made to Gu Yueguo's (1990) proposal regarding Chinese politeness.

Maxims of politeness: approbation and modesty

In general, people involved in interpersonal communication have a positive face goal and/or a negative face goal, definable as:

> **Positive face goal:** the goal of gaining or enhancing face (i.e., the heightening or maintaining of a person's self-esteem as a result of the heightening or maintaining of that person's estimation in the eyes of others.)

> **Negative face goal:** the goal of avoiding loss of face. (Loss of face is a lowering of that self-esteem as a result of the lowering of that person's estimation in the eyes of others.)

> (Leech 2014: 25)

To fulfil the positive or negative face goal, people can avail themselves of some maxims under 'a single superconstraint' that Leech calls the 'General Strategy of Politeness' (GSP), where the term 'maxim' is a descriptive rather than normative concept meaning a 'constraint influencing speakers' communicative behaviour' (Leech 2014: 90):

General Strategy of Politeness: In order to be polite, *S* expresses or implies meanings that associate a favourable value with what pertains to *O* or associates an unfavourable value with what pertains to *S* (*S* = self, speaker; *O* = the other person(s), who is probably *H*, hearer).

(adapted from Leech 2014: 90)

The maxims pertaining to the achievement of positive face goal include:

(M1) Generosity Maxim: give a high value to O's wants (as realised by commissive speech acts).

(M3) Approbation Maxim: give a high value to O's qualities (as realised by the speech act of complimenting).

(M5) Obligation (of S to O) Maxim: give a high value to S's obligation to O (as realised by such speech acts as apologising and thanking).

(M7) Agreement Maxim: give a high value to O's opinions (as realised by the speech act of agreeing).

(M9) Sympathy Maxim: give a high value to O's feelings (as realised by the speech acts of congratulating and commiserating).

(adapted from Leech 2014: 90)

The maxims pertaining to the achievement of negative face goal include:

(M2) Tact Maxim: give a low value to S's wants (as realised by directive speech acts).

(M4) Modesty Maxim: give a low value to S's qualities (as realised by the speech act of self-devaluation).

(M6) Obligation (of S to O) Maxim: give a low value to O's obligation to S (as realised by such speech acts as responses to thanks and apologies).

(M8) Opinion Reticence Maxim: give a low value to S's opinions (as realised by the speech act of giving opinions).

(M10) Feeling Reticence Maxim: give a low value to S's feelings (as realised by the speech acts of suppressing feelings).

(adapted from Leech 2014: 90)

Considering the theme of this chapter, we shall focus on two of the maxims:

Approbation and Modesty. Earlier, Leech (1983: 135) defined the two maxims respectively as follows:

> Approbation Maxim: MINIMIZE DISPRAISE OF OTHER; MAXIMIZE PRAISE OF OTHER

> Modesty Maxim: MINIMIZE PRAISE OF SELF; MAXIMIZE DISPRAISE OF SELF

While the new definitions are clearer in wording and less demanding in force (because placing a high/low value to S/O is enough to be polite, minimising or maximising is too strong to hold true in real-life interaction), they allow for elaborations with respect to the notion of 'O's/S's qualities', just like 'OTHER'/ 'SELF' in the old formulation.

Therefore, to operationalise, 'O's/S's qualities' or 'OTHER/SELF' are understood, in this study, to encompass SELF's or OTHER's ability, intelligence, knowledge, appearance, influence, resourcefulness, social position, possessions or belongings, children etc. They also cover SELF's or OTHER's achievement, accomplishment, participation, devotion, contribution, gains, sacrifice, gift etc. Thus, to observe the Approbation Maxim (M3), the speaker is expected to elevate OTHER by giving a high value on a particular aspect or more than one aspect of OTHER mentioned above. Correspondingly, to observe the Modesty Maxim (M4), the responder is supposed to denigrate SELF by giving a low value on the particular aspect(s) commented on by the initiator of the approbation. For example:

(1)

    a.   How clever of you!

   ?b.   How clever of me! (Leech 1983: 136)

In (1a), the speaker is abiding by the Approbation Maxim because he or she is giving a high value to the addressee's intelligence; however, in (1b), the speaker is violating the Modesty Maxim because he or she is giving a high value to his or her own intelligence. Consider (2):

(2)

    a.   Please accept this small gift as a token of our esteem.

   ?b.   Please accept this large gift as a token of our esteem. (Leech 1983: 136)

In (2a), the speaker is observing the Modesty Maxim because he or she is giving a low value to his or her gift to the addressee. In (2b), by contrast, the speaker is violating the maxim as a result of speaking highly of his or her gift.

According to Leech, face is 'the positive self-image or self-esteem that a person enjoys as a reflection of that person's estimation by others' (Leech 2014: 25). In this light, the Approbation Maxim, as executed in compliments, is aimed at face enhancement (Kerbrat-Orecchioni 1997) and is thus consistent with pos-politeness (Leech 2014). By contrast, the Modesty Maxim, as executed in self-denigration, is aimed at face-mitigation (since the acceptance of OTHER's elevation would risk impressing OTHER as pompous and committing 'the social transgression of boasting' (Leech 1983: 136) and is thus consistent with neg-politeness (Leech 2014).

Among the five constraint pairs, there is an issue of asymmetry. According to Leech, 'the Tact Maxim (M2) is generally felt, at least in Anglophone societies, to be more powerful than the Generosity Maxim (M1)' (Leech 2014: 91) , in the sense that people are more expected to consider the former than the latter, which means the hearer-oriented maxims are generally more 'powerful' than the speaker-oriented ones. He points out that '[in] some activity types complimentary language is a virtual necessity, as when guests praise a host(ess)'s meal, or an academic introduces the lecture of a visiting senior professor' (Leech 2014: 93). To use his own example:

(3)
很荣幸邀请到在XX领域做出杰出贡献的XX教授来给我们做报告。

It's a great honour for us to have invited Professor XX to give us a lecture. Professor XX has made great contribution to the XX field.

We find that, in (3), the host is doing pos-politeness, or face enhancement, by executing the Approbation Maxim through giving a high value to Professor XX's contribution in the XX field.

It is interesting, therefore, to examine whether it is also the case in China that Chinese academics pay compliments when they introduce visiting professors. On the other hand, now that 'self-dispraise is regarded as quite benign, even when it is exaggerated for comic effect' (Leech 1983: 136), it is also worthwhile to investigate whether the Chinese visiting professors behave modestly in the face of the hosts' compliments. In China, as well as in Japan, where 'the Modesty Maxim is more powerful than it is as a rule in English-speaking societies' (Leech 1983: 137), it would be a high expectation that they do so.

Methodology

This section states the research questions to be addressed, describes the data collected for the study, and specifies the method of data analysis.

Research questions

In order to demonstrate how the interaction between hosts and visiting professors at the introductory phase of lecture events pertains to the issue of politeness,

I set out to examine the following three research questions, with particular attention paid to the content orientations of the approbation used by the hosts:

A. How do the hosts introduce the visiting professors to the audience? What is the former's approbation, if at all, directed at?

B. How do the visiting professors respond to the hosts' complimentary introductions in the face of the audience?

C. How can the hosts' introductions and the guests' responses be interpreted in terms of politeness?

Data collection

To answer the research questions above, I collected, with the assistance of my post-graduate and doctoral students, 16 lecture sessions that took place in several universities located in Nanjing, as summarised in Table 3.1.

Table 3.1. Summary of the lectures

No.	Visiting professor	Topic Area	Venue	Host
1	JX	Linguistics	NJU	CH
2	ZD	Linguistics	NJUST	ZX
3	QG	Linguistics	GDUFS	MA
4	WS	Literature	GDUFS	ZF
5	MZ	Linguistics	NJU	SY
6	LJ	Linguistics	NJU	SY
7	CJ	Linguistics	NAU	PY
8	QF	Linguistics	NJNU	ZH
9	SJ	Linguistics	SISU	ZR
10	GY	Ethnography	ECNU	TZ
11	ZJ	Literature	NKU	SW
12	SW	Literature	SJTU	ZY
13	CC	Linguistics	ECNU	LX
14	SL	Literature	TJI	GY
15	ZQ	Literature	NJU	CT
16	CX	Linguistics	SZU	SX

Of the 16 pieces of data, 6 were audio-recorded by my MA students with their mobile phone while the other 10 were video-recorded with the assistance of Beijing Centennial Superstar Corporation, which, devoted to the production of an academic video website, had collected over 80,000 academic lectures covering such disciplines as philosophy, religion, sociology, politics, cultural studies, literature, linguistics, art and history. A noticeable feature of variation was observed in terms of the length of the introductory part. Some lasted quite long, up to 5–6 minutes, whereas a limited few others were very brief, involving only a few words of exchange. To ensure authenticity of the data, none of the hosts or visiting professors was informed of the recording. Also, to secure anonymity, only the initials of the hosts' or visiting professors' names would be used in the following text development, as indicated in Table 3.1.

All the hosts had a relatively high position in their university departments or schools, acting as dean or vice-dean of the school, or chair of the department. All the visiting professors were aged between 45 and 60, were usually on familiar or even close terms with the hosts, and were well known in their own field. The audience for the lectures, the size of which ranged from 25 to 60, was mostly composed of postgraduate students or doctoral students and, in some cases, a small number of faculty members.

Data analysis

This study is basically qualitative and exploratory. Thus, in accordance with the research questions, I analysed the data in two steps.

Step 1: I dug into the hosts' introductions. First, the 'factual' content orientations of the introductions were categorised on the basis of a variety of information pertaining to what defined a researcher, such as professional title, research interests and academic achievements. Then, I looked for subjective content that represented the hosts' complimentary evaluation of the visiting professors. Little mention was made of the pragmalinguistic resources used by the hosts, though, which was consistent with the analytic orientations of Leech's Grand Strategy of Politeness. Finally, discussion of the two types of information followed in terms of politeness.

Step 2: I focused on the visiting professors' responses. The responses were carefully differentiated into two big categories: responses to the host's invitation and responses to the host's approbation (the visiting professors often combined the two categories in their response). I then focused on the visiting professors' second category of responses, classified them into several types in accordance with the tripartite system: Acceptance, Deflection/Evasion and Rejection (Chen 1993; Holmes 1988; Tang and Zhang 2009) and discussed the different types of response in terms of politeness, as Chen (1993) does.

Hosts' complimentary introductions

Overall, the hosts' introductions can be differentiated into two categories: presentation of factual information about the visiting professors and subjective evaluation of them. Despite the distinction, I argue that both involve approbation and thus are politeness oriented. In addition, the hosts may make other attempts at politeness, as I shall demonstrate in passing.

'Factual' content of the hosts' introductions

Despite some variation, the hosts' introductions generally include the following 'factual' aspects: professional title + family name (e.g., Prof. Shi), affiliation (e.g., XX University), lecture title or topic, academic background, academic achievement, and perhaps some other information. Among others, the content under the category of academic background covers such information as universities from which one obtained one's degree(s), research interests or directions, visiting scholarship, etc.; the content under the category of academic achievement includes information related to publications, academic titles, awards, adjunct or guest professorship, etc.

Apart from the commonly expected strands of information, some other types of apparently objective information were found in use by some hosts. For example:

(4)

SX:　　也许大家不知道，CX教授是我们学校的校友，差不多20年前他曾在这里读研究生。

SX:　　You may not know, Prof. CX is our alumnus. He did his MA here some 20 years ago.

(5)

TZ:　　GY教授与我们有长期的合作关系。

TZ:　　Prof. GY has a long term of collaboration with us.

In (4), the host makes mention of the fact that Prof. CX had once studied in this university. Welcoming back alumni who have achieved some success is often a proud thing in China and perhaps elsewhere. In (5), the host's emphasis on the long-term collaboration also makes the visiting professor more welcome than otherwise.

The reason I label the content above as 'factual' is that it is not as totally factual as it stands. I will return to this point later.

Use of explicit approbation by the hosts

Apart from the 'factual' content, there is invariably an element of subjective evaluation, mostly describable as approbation in Leech's terms, i.e. giving a high value to O's qualities. Examination of the data, however, reveals that there is significant variation in the use of approbation among the hosts, as summarised below.

To start with, variation manifests itself along the dimension of the content of approbation. Throughout the data, I found that the hosts' approbation points to the following major categories in the order of frequency of occurrence:

A. Popularity and fame (14 occurrences)

Hosts may speak highly of the visiting professors by asserting that the latter are well known and that the audience is familiar with them. In the academic circle, those who are well known are likely to be those who are very successful. Thus, asserting somebody's fame is approbatory. For example:

(6)

    PY: 其实很多老师应该对我们CJ教授比较熟悉。

    PY: As a matter of fact, I believe many teachers here should be familiar with Prof. CJ.

In (6), PY states assumed familiarity of the audience with the visiting professor, implying Prof. CJ's fame.

(7)

    CT: 今天我们请到了ZQ教授。ZQ老师是主攻中国古代文学。他是中国古代文学界非常著名的教授…

    CT: Today we have Prof. ZQ with us. Prof. ZQ specialises in ancient Chinese literature. He is a very famous professor in the circle of ancient Chinese literature …

In (7), CT the host points out that Prof. ZQ is a very famous professor in the field of Chinese classic literature. It is a subjective evaluation to describe some as famous, as there is no solid proof to verify somebody's fame.

B. Prolificacy and achievement (12 occurrences)

Most of the hosts in question make reference to the guests' productive career in their introductions, as the data suggest. For example:

(8)

    ZF: WS教授主要从事英语语言文学的教学和研究工作，他的研究方向是英美文学和英语教育，并取得了丰硕的成果。

    ZF: Prof. WS engages himself primarily with the teaching and research of English literature. His research interests include British and American literature and English education, where he has obtained abundant achievements.

In (8), the host ZF, following the statement of Prof. WS's research interests, comments that the latter has accomplished a lot in his areas of study. The term '丰硕的' ('abundant') used is a fuzzy one, whose interpretation varies from person to person and from situation to situation. Nevertheless, it conveys the meaning of 'a huge amount'. Here is another example:

(9)

    LX: 他（CC教授）在语言学、认知语言学、语料库语言学、汉语语言的教学和习得等方面都有许多的建树。

    LX: He (Prof. CC) has made plentiful achievements in general linguistics, cognitive linguistics, corpus linguistics, teaching Chinese as CFL, and CFL acquisition.

In (9), the host LX commends the visiting professor by listing a few areas in which the latter has gleaned a plentiful harvest. Like the term '丰硕的' ('abundant'), the adjective '许多的' ('plentiful') may also involve a degree of amplification from the host's perspective, as it is not an easy thing for a researcher to accomplish a lot in a variety of fields.

C. The value of the lecture (8 occurrences)

In the data, we find that a few hosts would comment appreciatively on the lecture to be given by the visiting professors, which may arouse the audience's interest and raise their expectation. For example:

(10)

ZF: 他(WS教授)今天的《外国文学与中国》的报告定会使我们有 "听君一席话，胜读十年书" 的收获。

ZF: He (Prof. WS) will give us a talk on the topic 'Foreign Literature and China'. I'm sure this talk will benefit us a lot; just as a saying has it, 'listening to you for a while counts more than reading alone for ten years'.

In (10), the host ZF cites a well-known saying in China to express his as well as the audience's expectation about Prof. WS's lecture. Since the saying involves a high degree of commendation, ZF is being complimentary by conveying a high appraisal of the upcoming lecture. Here is another example:

(11)

ZH: QF教授是心理学出身的，她在心理语言学方面发表了很多文章，许多发表在国外很有影响的期刊上，我觉得这是我们很好的学习机会，下面我们请QF教授为我们做报告

ZH: Prof. QF is essentially a psychologist. She has published a lot of articles in psycholinguistics, many of them in influential journals abroad. I believe her lecture today gives us as a good learning opportunity. Now let's have Prof. QF to talk to us.

In (11), instead of directly assessing the guest's lecture, the host ZH exalts Prof. QF's lecture as 'a good learning opportunity', thus implying the value of it to the audience present. A similar practice is found in (12), where the host speaks highly of the value of time available for the lecture:

(12)

MA: 下面我们就把这宝贵的时间交给QG教授，大家欢迎！

MA: Now let's leave the following precious time to Prof. QG. Applause, please!

In (12), clearly, the adjective '宝贵的' ('precious') used by MA is a transferred epithet. It is not that time is precious; rather, it is Prof. QG's lecture to occupy the time that is precious.

D. Expertise and authority (6 occurrences)

Hosts are found to claim that the invited guests are experts or authorities in some field. For example:

(13)

MA: QG教授是我国最早在国外语用学刊物上发表文章的学者之一，可以说是当前在语言哲学研究方面、语用学方面集资历与权威于一身的专家

MA: Prof. QG is one of the earliest Chinese scholars who published in international pragmatics journals. I can say that he is both a senior and an authority in the philosophy of language and pragmatics.

In (13), the host MA depicts Prof. QG as both a senior and an authority in the fields the latter engages himself. Such depiction is often based on personal judgment and evaluation, though. Here is another example:

(14)

FX: WJ教授一直在做这方面的研究，是这方面的专家，大家可以看到，在她演讲的时候会发现她有很深的造诣…

FX: Prof. WJ has been doing this research for long and thus is an expert in this area. As you all will find during her lecture, she has a lot of experience and insights …

In (14), the host FX presents Prof. WJ as an experienced and insightful expert. Again, the presentation is not grounded on supplied evidence but on personal appraisal.

E. Contribution (5 occurrences)

Hosts are also frequently found to use profuse words of praise for their guests in regard to the latters' academic contribution in a particular area of inquiry or in a discipline. For example:

(15)

ZF: WS教授在英美文学、英语教育领域进行的开拓性工作，对我们在全球化语境下研究中西文学、文化的相互融合、吸收、碰撞和影响具有深刻的启迪意义。

ZF: Prof. WS has conducted a lot of pioneering work in British and American literature and English education, which has profound implications for the integration, absorption, interaction and impact of Sino-Western literature and culture in the context of globalisation.

In (15), the host ZF calls Prof. WS a pioneer whose work has contributed to the development of Sino-Western literature and culture. This line of comment is highly complimentary in the academic field, because pioneers are generally those who have done ground-breaking work and thus can enjoy incomparable repute and respect. Here is another example:

(16)

> TZ:　GY教授是中国著名的民族学家，原来是XX大学民族学的负责人，在古文化研究，民族文化研究等多方面作出很多贡献⋯。
>
> TZ:　Prof. GY is a famous ethnographer in China. He used to be in charge of the ethnography research in XX University. He has contributed immensely to the research on ancient Chinese culture and ethnographical studies …

In (16), TZ alludes to Prof. GY's huge contribution in the field of ancient Chinese culture and ethnographical studies. As no specific details are used to evidence this evaluation, the host can be understood to be complimentary in this case.

F. Conduct (2 occurrences)

Hosts are occasionally found to speak highly of the visiting professor's personality and personhood. For instance:

(17)

> MA:　QG教授治学严谨、宽以待人，无论是做人还是做学问，钱教授都不愧为教师、学者的典范、广大学者的楷模⋯
>
> MA:　Prof. QG is serious about scholarship and forgiving to others. When it comes to conducting oneself or doing research, Prof. QG is an exemplar and role model for teachers and researchers …

In (17), the host MA portrays the guest as 'an exemplar and role model for teachers and researchers'. This is quite a personal evaluation, although it may be appropriate to the latter.

In addition to content variation, the hosts vary in terms of the quantity of approbation used. While most hosts compliment the visiting professors on one or two aspects, a few give 'multiple compliments'. For instance:

(18)

> PY:　其实很多老师应该对我们CJ教授比较熟悉。名气很大，呵，这个，名气很大，哎，是XX大学著名教授，博士生导师，然后最重要的是在专门用途英语教学方面，非常的，⋯有见解，有思想，有造诣。⋯成果非常多，⋯所以不仅仅是学术研究，也在英语教学方面是我们外语界的领军人物⋯
>
> PY:　As a matter of fact, I believe many teachers here should be familiar with Prof. CJ. He is very famous, yeah, very famous. He is a famous professor and PhD supervisor from XX University. Most importantly, he has a lot of insights and great ideas and achievements in teaching English for Specific Purposes … Prof. CJ has published a lot … So he is a leading person of the foreign language circle not only in the field of academic research but also in English teaching …

In (18), the host PY directs his approbation towards his guest in the following directions: 1) his fame, 2) his expertise and authority and 3) his achievement.

Naturally, the multitude of approbation has a more complimentary effect than simple and singular commendation. As a consequence, in the face of such flattery, visiting professors often may feel a bit uneasy or fidgety, which I have both experienced and witnessed myself.

Visiting professors' response strategies

Overall, the visiting professors' responses to the hosts' introductions are quite limited in type and size, as our data suggest. Generally, despite one or two exceptions, the professors make a quick transition into their lectures after a brief reaction to the introductions. But almost all visiting professors start by thanking the hosts, or their affiliations, for the lecture invitation, as in (19):

(19)

ZQ:　谢谢ZH老师的邀请。今天我与大家交流的是…

ZQ:　Thanks a lot for Professor ZH's invitation. What I want to exchange with you all today is …

In (19), the invited professor ZQ expresses her gratitude to the host Prof. ZH for his invitation.

After thanking the hosts, visiting professors are frequently found in the data to move on to greet the audience by saying that they are pleased to have a chance to meet the audience, including students in most cases and/or sometimes faculty members. For example:

(20)

WJ:　很高兴与各位同学一起见面。我今天要谈的话题是…

WJ:　I'm very happy to meet all of you students here. What I want to talk about today is …

In (20), WJ expresses his pleasure of meeting the students on the spot.

What most concerns us here is how visiting professors respond to the hosts' approbation. It is found that visiting professors' responses all fall within the framework proposed by Holmes (1988) and used elsewhere (e.g., Chen 1993; Tang and Zhang 2009).

A. Deflecting or evading the approbation (13 occurrences)

Three of the visiting professors made no direct or explicit response to the hosts' approbation but rather jumped to their talk after acknowledging their invitation or greeting the audience, as exemplified in (19) and (20)

Furthermore, three visiting professors were found to lower the degree of the hosts' approbation. For example:

(21)

> ZY: 商教授是才子，确实是才子。那我们下面欢迎商教授给我们做学术报告。
>
> SW: 谢谢。非常感谢赵院长的介绍，呵呵，过奖了，还有建平兄的邀请。今天第一次到XX大学来，看到五千亩的校园，非常大，也非常高兴和大家见面。我今天报告的题目是⋯
>
> ZY: Prof. Shang is a talent, surely a talent. Now let's welcome Prof. Shang to give us an academic report.
>
> SW: Thank you. Thank you for your introduction, Dean Zhao. You've flattered me too much. Thanks also for Jianping's invitation. Today it's the first time that I've been here in XX University. The university has an area of five thousand *mu*. It's so huge. Also, I feel pleased to meet all of you. The topic of my talk is …

In (21), after the host ZY finishes his introduction piling up a lot of praise, Prof. SW expresses his thanks for it. Yet he immediately uses '过奖了' ('You've flattered me too much') to downgrade ZY's approbation.

Four visiting professors were found to downgrade the approbation by devaluing their lectures. In (19), for instance, Prof. ZQ says he is pleased to have an opportunity to '交流' ('exchange ideas') with the audience instead of '做报告' ('give a talk'). In Chinese, whereas people in superior positions give talks, people on an equal footing exchange ideas. More effort for modesty sake is found in (22):

(22)

> SL: 非常荣幸能够来到XX，与大家进行一个交流，其实刚才XX老师呢，多有溢美，其实呢我称不上是大师，也是一个正在学习的人。⋯⋯我们中国古代的这个文化经典啊，确实是博大精深，永无止境的。⋯⋯所以呢，每次当我接触到这个话题的时候，都是有点儿这个如履薄冰啊，有这个感觉。尤其是今天来到这里的都是这方面的专家和爱好者，所以呢，我也觉得心里特别虚。今天呢，我充其量就是在这方面做一个汇报和交流，不当之处呢，请大家多批评。
>
> SL: I feel very much honoured to be here in XX University and have an exchange of ideas. Just now, Mr XX spoke too highly of me. Actually I can't be called a master but rather I'm someone on the way of learning … The classics of the Chinese culture are really profound and seem endless … So each time I touch upon this topic, I feel as if I were walking on the thin ice. Really I have this feeling. Especially today, you are all experts and lovers in this area, so I feel pretty uncertain. For this reason, I can do no better than give a report and have an exchange of ideas. Please criticise whatever I say improperly.

In (22), Prof. SL shows tremendous modesty in several ways: 1) regarding his being invited as an honour to him, 2) stating that the host was speaking too highly of him, 3) rejecting the host's address form for him, 4) considering himself as 'someone on the way of learning', 5) expressing his uncertainty about what he is going to talk about, 6) defining his lecture as an exchange of ideas or even a report (in Chinese, an inferior '汇报' ('report') to a superior) and 7) admitting possible inadequacies in his upcoming lecture.

Three visiting professors were found to evade the approbation by returning a compliment. For instance, in (21), Prof. SW commends the size of the host's university. Here are more examples:

(23)

    CJ: 你们潘老师很会说话啊。我们上次碰到以后，她就抓住我，她说一定要到我们学校给我们讲讲。我感到XX学院还是很有特色的学校，所以我觉得还是很有必要跟大家一起交流一下。我今天要讲的这个题目⋯

    CJ: Your Mr Pan is a nice speaker. Last time she met me, she insisted that I come and talk here. I feel XX University is one with a lot of characteristics. So I think it quite necessary to exchange my mind with you all. The topic of my talk today is …

In (23), CJ the guest pays two compliments, one to the host, Mr Pan, and the other to the university. The latter is rarely found in purely interpersonal encounters, though, but is explicable because the host and the audience come from the university that finances the guest's visit. Take another example:

(24)

    SJ: 那么，也是非常感谢赵院长给我这样一个这么宝贵的机会，向XX大学老师和同学请教的机会。我这个，客气话我就不多说了，然后就进入正题。

    SJ: Then, I'd like to thank Dean Zhao for giving me this precious opportunity, an opportunity to learn from the faculty members and students from XX University. Now I don't want to say any more on the courtesy side, but revert to business right away.

In (24), SJ, apart from acknowledging Dean Zhao's arrangement of this visit, takes the opportunity as one to learn from the faculty members and students from XX University.

It should be pointed out that the different strategies of deflecting or evading approbation may co-occur in the same visiting professor's response. For example, in (23), CJ devalues his talk by using '交流' ('exchange ideas') in addition to returning a compliment.

B. Accepting the approbation (3 occurrences)

Occasionally, visiting professors would express their thanks not for their invitation but for their complimentary introductions, as in (25):

(25)

    SD: 谢谢主持人的介绍。很高兴今天有这个机会与XX大学的同学一起交流⋯

    SD: Thank you for your introduction, host. I'm very pleased to have this opportunity to exchange ideas with students from XX University …

In (25), SD says that he is happy to have this opportunity to exchange ideas with the students from XX University. His thanking act might be interpreted as an implicit way of accepting the host's approbation apart from acknowledging the latter's introduction.

C. Rejecting the approbation (2 occurrences)

Visiting professors may even reject an explicitly or implicitly overdone praise cast on them by their hosts. For example:

(26)

ZY: 今天我们非常荣幸地请到XX外国语大学的著名教授SW给我们做学术报告。SW教授是北京大学的高才生。…在北大毕业也是提前毕业是吧？

SW: 呵呵，其实也没有。

ZY: 哦，是留校的是吧。嗯，后来到哈佛大学，又继续攻读学位。现在是XX大学中国文学教授，获得XX大学杰出教授奖。可以说是国际知名学者，商教授的研究领域主要是元、明、清文学，尤其是喜剧小说为主，涉及明清时代的书籍印刷文化以及思想史和文化史，可以说知识面很广，尤其以思考深刻见长。…哟，商教授还是硬笔书法的专家。

SW: 哟，这是从哪里造来的。呵呵。

ZY: Today we're honoured to have a famous professor, Prof. SW, from XX University to talk to us. Prof. SW used to be a big talent in Peking University … You graduated there ahead of time, am I right?

SW: As a matter of fact, no.

ZY: Oh. You stayed on and became a teacher there after you graduated, right? Then, you went to Harvard University for further degree education. And now you are a professor of Chinese literature in XX University. You once won the title of 'Distinguished Professors' of XX University. We can say Prof. SW is a scholar with international reputation. His major research interests cover Chinese literature in the Yuan, Ming and Qing dynasties. He particularly excels in comic fiction studies. His research also involves book printing culture, historical development of thinking and culture in the Ming and Qing dynasties. I can say he has a wide scope of knowledge and especially profound depth of thinking … Yes, he is also an expert at hard pen calligraphy.

SW: Haha, how have you invented all this?

In (26), Prof. SW makes two denials: one denial when the host ZY ventures to say he graduated ahead of time, the other denial when ZY mentions the title of 'Distinguished Professors', his research interests, his knowledgeability and thinking ability, and his expertise at hard pen calligraphy. In the former case, it is complimentary in China to say somebody graduates ahead of time because graduation in advance presupposes greater talent and better academic performance than usual. In the latter case, it is complimentary in China and perhaps elsewhere to say somebody is distinguished, knowledgeable, penetrating and versatile, especially on the basis of details that might not be totally true. In both cases, there is a need to tone down the approbation.

The discussion above on the one side lends support to Holmes's (1988) classification of compliment responses and Chen's (1993) modification, and on the other lends further evidence for Spencer-Oatey and Ng's (2001) finding that compliment responses may vary in complex ways.

Discussion

The hosts' politeness orientation

As our data indicate, the hosts utilise a variety of politeness strategies when introducing visiting professors. For instance, the hosts may resort to the Self-denigration Maxim in Gu's (1990) terms or, in Leech's (2014) terms, the Modesty Maxim (Gu's self-denigration, in his terms, 'absorbs the notions of respectfulness and modesty'). Indeed, we can find it a consistent practice among almost all the guest introductions, probably because the general Chinese culture of modesty plays an important role in this academic context. Thus, the hosts often use the honorific term '荣幸地' ('We feel honoured that …') almost invariably at the beginning of the introductions, as in (27):

(27)

WY: 今天我们非常荣幸地请到XXX外国语大学的著名教授SW给我们做学术报告。

WY: Today we're honoured to have a famous professor, Prof. SW, from XX University to talk to us.

Sometimes, the host may attempt at politeness by means of, in Gu's (1990)'s terms, 'attitudinal warmth'. For example, the host generally calls on the audience to applaud for the start of the guest's lecture, as in (28) below. This is not unique to the Chinese academic context in question, though. It might be found elsewhere. For instance:

(28)

ZR: 让我们用热烈的掌声，欢迎SJ教授的讲座。

ZR: let's welcome with warm applause Prof. SJ to give us a talk.

Still, the host may occasionally express thanks to the visiting professor, as illustrated in (29).

(29)

FXG: 我想借此机会感谢WJW教授特意为这个讲演做了很长时间的准备，另外也是给了我们的学习机会。

FXG: I like to take this opportunity to express my thanks to Prof. WJW, for preparing long for this lecture and giving us this learning opportunity.

In (29), FXG is being polite by expressing his gratitude to the guest on two counts:

spending a long time preparing for this lecture and giving a learning opportunity to the audience. Thus, he is observing the Obligation (of S to O) Maxim: namely, he is giving a high value to his obligation to Prof. WJ.

Despite these and some other non-discussed means of politeness, the hosts' observance of the Approbation Maxim is most salient, lending support to Leech's observation that 'in some activity types complimentary language is a virtual necessity, as when guests praise a host(ess)'s meal, or an academic introduces the lecture of a visiting senior professor' (Leech 2014: 93). The salience is manifested in two ways: the presentation of the 'factual' content and the varied use of explicit compliment strategies. The former way merits a little further discussion. Specifically, some strands of the 'factual' content, such as academic titles, awards, adjunct or guest professorship, are not objective in effect but rather complimentary as well. The reason is that these titles, awards and adjunct or guest professorship all presuppose the winners' or owners' respectable great achievements in their field and help to build images of importance and influence, thus enhancing their face. Sometimes, when talks are given at mediocre universities, even the names of the guests' affiliations are not wholly objective if they point to the best universities in China. Similarly, it sounds complimentary to mention the guests' supervisors, if the latter are big names in the field, to mention the names of the universities where the guests received their degree education and even visiting scholarship, and to list the guests' research interests, etc.

Examination of the data indicates that the hosts opt to abide by the Approbation Maxim even at the risk or expense of the Quality Maxim (Grice 1989). In other words, they may sometimes elevate their guests beyond the point of factuality. For example:

(30)

LX: CC教授呢这次安排了一系列的活动，那么我们呢是第一站。那么CC教授呢，我做一个简单的介绍。其实大家都非常熟悉了。…

LX: Prof. CC is on a series of visits this time. His visit to us is the first one. Now let me say a few words about him. As a matter of fact, all here are familiar with him …

In (30), LX seems to assert that the audience all know the visiting professor. Given our background knowledge, this assertion cannot hold true, in all probability. Similar practices may concern the provision of the guests' titles, such as introducing a vice chair as the chair, a vice-president of an association as the president. To my mind, this observation testifies to what Leech discusses with regard to the role of hyperbole and litotes in enhancing politeness:

[T]he justification for hyperbole and litotes is politeness. There will naturally be a preference for overstating polite beliefs, and for understating impolite ones: While an exaggeration such as *that was a delicious meal!* is favoured in praising others, an uninformative denial – a typical device of understatement—is frequently used in criticism: *I wasn't overimpressed by her speech.* The understating of praise will normally be directed towards *s* rather than *h*.

(Leech 1983: 146)

Indeed, there is counterpart practice in other domains of life. For instance, as mentioned by Leech himself, the Japanese may claim 'this is a gift which will be of no use to you, but …' and may even go to the extreme of denying the existence of the food he is offering: 'there is nothing (to eat), but please …' (Leech 1983: 138). Again, a maxim of politeness, that of Modesty in this case, may overrule the Maxim of Quality.

How, then, do we explain this salience or pervasiveness of the approbation strategy in this activity type? One reason is that the invited professors come from prestigious universities or enjoy high prestige in the academic circle. But we also presume that, in the current Chinese sociocultural context, invited and coordinated academic lectures in China are sometimes more complimentary than academic. Despite their role in popularising disciplinary knowledge and activating the host affiliations' academic atmosphere, the lectures are more crucially intended to strengthen the ties between the visiting professors and the host affiliations, particularly the inviters (usually the hosts on this occasion). Such being the case, the hosts are expected to enhance the visiting professors' face, to the extent that 'where the Approbation Maxim is in force, a failure to commit oneself to a favourable opinion implied that one cannot (truthfully) do so. In other words, the lack of praise implicates dispraise' (Leech 1983: 136). Last but not least, speaking highly of the visiting professors may help attract the audience's attention and raise their interest, a concern on the part of the host not to be ignored in this type of academic context.

It is worth mentioning in passing that some expressions used in the hosts' introductions at this setting have gradually become conventionalised as a result of politeness-driven frequent usage. They include '今天很荣幸…' ('Today we feel honoured to …'), '著书等身' (which literally means 'publications pile up as tall as one stands'), '用热烈的掌声欢迎…' ('Let's welcome sb. with warm applause') and '请…给我们做报告/指导' (which literally means 'Let's have sb. give us a talk/instructions').

The visiting professors' politeness orientation

As summarised earlier, the visiting professors demonstrated three major types of response to the hosts' approbation in the activity type in question, apart from acknowledging the invitation and greeting the audience: 1) accepting the approbation, 2) deflecting or evading the approbation by downgrading or returning a compliment, and 3) denying the approbation. All these responses are politeness oriented. Specifically, when they acknowledge the hosts' invitation, the visiting professors indicate their gratefulness and thus abide by the Obligation (of S to O) Maxim; when they greet the audience by saying that they feel pleased to meet them, they are conducting phatic communion, a general token of politeness; when they accept the hosts' approbation by thanking them for their complimentary introduction, they are abiding by the Agreement Maxim; when they downgrade the hosts' approbation, they are sticking to the Modesty Maxim; when they deny the hosts' approbation, they are still giving priority to the Modesty Maxim over the Agreement Maxim; when they return a compliment to the hosts, they are following the Approbation Maxim. Thus, the findings indicate, as Wu (2011) does, that Gao and Ting-Toomey's claim that 'to blatantly accept a compliment is considered impolite' (1998: 47) is a 'misleading over-simplification' (Spencer-Oatey and Ng 2001: 193).

Despite the variety of responses, each of which is consistent with a particular maxim of politeness, we find from our data, though not conclusively, that the visiting professors opt to deflect or evade the hosts' approbation in the majority of cases. This finding points to their priority of observing the Modesty Maxim in the face of approbation. This is particularly to be expected in academic encounters in Chinese culture, because scholars are supposed to be well educated and subject to the influence of traditional Chinese values such as modesty. In other words, the claim that one would behave modestly in the face of approbation, a claim relying completely on ancient philosophy or the analysts' intuitions in explicating Chinese modesty, is largely true in the academic context, if not in all kinds of context.

Another observation needs to be mentioned. Specifically, the visiting professors acknowledge the invitation more often than they respond to the hosts' approbatory introduction. How, then, do we explain the priority of this response type? It might be said that they give priority to the Obligation Maxim. In China, such an invitation is often made on a personal and relational basis. Quite often, it is a mode of building, maintaining and strengthening the friendship and partnership between researchers from different affiliations. This explains why the visiting professors' expression of gratitude at the beginning is most often directed to the hosts, who they are familiar with and who are usually their inviters. Also, when the hosts make approbatory remarks about the visiting professors, they are doing publicity for them. This also makes it necessary that the visiting professors express their gratitude to the hosts. Basically, negotiation with the hosts on the issue of approbation is not a central concern to them on this occasion. Last but not least, the visiting professors' thanking the hosts for their invitation as well as their complimentary introduction in the face of the audience does pos-politeness to the hosts, too, in that, apart from indicating their 'debt', it implies the hosts' ability that makes the current lecture possible. This explains why, in (26), Prof. CJ mentions the host's special effort that '(last) time she met me, she insisted that I come and talk here'.

Likewise, some expressions in the visiting professors' responses at this setting have also become conventionalised. They include '很高兴有机会…' ('I'm very pleased to have an opportunity …'), '客气话我就不多说了' ('I don't want to say any more on the courtesy side'), and so on.

Conclusion

This study concerns itself with a much-neglected aspect of academic communication that has increasing importance in Chinese universities, notably introductions and responses at the opening part of invited lectures. In response to the lack of empirical research on this particular phase of the activity type and, more crucially, politeness behaviour such as approbation and modesty thereof, I have examined a sizable amount of naturally occurring data, yielding a couple of implicative findings.

First, the hosts of the invited lectures unanimously adopt approbation in their introductions to the visiting professors, apart from resorting to other strategies of politeness in Leech's (1983, 2014) or Gu's (1990) terms. Their approbation, however, varies because it is directed to different aspects of the professors, sometimes to their multiple aspects, covering their popularity and fame, prolificacy and achievement, expertise and authority, contribution, conduct, and lecture value. It is realised by the use of both explicit appraisal expressions and of implicitly favourable identity-building or image-building content. In either form, the ubiquitous use of approbation in Chinese invited lectures is considered to have stemmed from the often-complimentary nature of the activity type in the current Chinese sociocultural context, apart from other factors like the prestige of the visiting professors and the situational need to attract and sustain the audience's interest.

Second, in reaction to the hosts' complimentary introductions, the visiting professors demonstrate a variety of responses, including acknowledgment, approbation downgrading, approbation denial, phatic communion, and compliment return, sometimes in singular ways and sometimes in combined ways. Each type of the responses is representative of the visiting professors' choice of communicative strategy consistent with a maxim of politeness. Despite the variety of the response types, acknowledgement of the hosts' invitation and introduction in the observance of the Obligation Maxim occurs more often than deflecting or rejecting the hosts' approbation for modesty sake. The priority and preponderance of the former result from the fact that invited lectures in Chinese universities are more of an interpersonal activity than a purely academic event. Yet, when the visiting professors do respond to the hosts' approbation, they give priority to deflecting or evading approbation over accepting, a behaviour best characterised in terms of modesty and appropriate to their identity as academic people.

Despite some regularities detected in both the hosts' and visiting professors' politeness behaviour, variations of different forms have also been discovered across hosts and visiting professors alike. Such variations include the content, quantity and degree of approbation on the hosts' side, and manner and degree of modesty on the professors' side. Yet, no systematic investigation has been attempted to reveal what factors underlay the variations owing to the limited size of our data. Presumably, these factors might include the distance between the host and the visiting professor, the personality of the two, the fame of the visiting professor, the level of the host university, the preparedness of the host's introduction, and the like. Future research may operate on the basis of larger-scale data to verify the assumption. In addition, by focusing on the explicit content or direction of approbation used, this study has given little attention to the pragmalinguistic resources the hosts exploit in their approbation. It might be worthwhile to look into possible variations in pragmalinguistic ways among the hosts. Also, this study has failed to provide a systematic account of hosts' implicit approbation, although some mention has been made in passing. More work might be expected in this direction. Last by not least, this study is basically a qualitative one, providing no exact frequency information about the distribution of each introduction strategy or response strategy. This leaves room for a quantitative discussion of the issue in the future.

References

Camiciottoli, B. C. (2004) Interactive discourse structuring in L2 guest lectures: Some insights from a comparative corpus-based study. *Journal of English for Academic Purposes* 3(1): 39–54. https://doi.org/10.1016/S1475-1585(03)00044-4

Camiciottoli, B. C. (2008) Interaction in academic lectures vs. written text materials: The case of questions. *Journal of Pragmatics* 40(7): 1216–1223. https://doi.org/10.1016/j.pragma.2007.08.007

Carey, R. (2014) A closer look at laughter in academic talk: A reader response. *Journal of English for Academic Purposes* 14: 118–123. https://doi.org/10.1016/j.jeap.2014.03.001

Chang, Y. Y. (2012) The use of questions by professors in lectures given in English: Influences of disciplinary cultures. *English for Specific Purposes* 31(2): 103–116. https://doi.org/10.1016/j.esp.2011.08.002

Chen, R. (1993) Responding to compliments: A contrastive study of politeness strategies between American English and Chinese speakers. *Journal of Pragmatics* 20: 49–75. https://doi.org/10.1016/0378-2166(93)90106-Y

Cheng, S. W. (2012) 'That's it for today': Academic lecture closings and the impact of class size. *English for Specific Purposes* 31: 234–248. https://doi.org/10.1016/j.esp.2012.05.004

Deroey, K. L. B., and Taverniers, M. (2012) *Just remember this*: Lexicogrammatical relevance markers in lectures. *English for Specific Purposes* 31: 221–233. https://doi.org/10.1016/j.esp.2012.05.001

Fortanet, I. (2004) The use of 'we' in university lectures: Reference and function. *English for Specific Purposes* 23: 45–66. https://doi.org/10.1016/S0889-4906(03)00018-8

Gao, G. and Ting-Toomey, S. (1998) *Communicating Effectively with the Chinese*. Thousand Oaks, CA: Sage Publications.

Giménez-Moreno, R. (2012) The interdependence of repetition and relevance in university lectures. *Journal of Pragmatics* 44: 744–755. https://doi.org/10.1016/j.pragma.2012.02.013

Grant, L. E. (2011) The frequency and functions of *just* in British academic spoken English. *Journal of English for Academic Purposes* 10: 183–197. https://doi.org/10.1016/j.jeap.2011.05.006

Grice, P. (1989) *Studies in the Way of Words*. Cambridge, MA: Harvard University Press.

Gu, Y. (1990) Politeness phenomena in modern Chinese. *Journal of Pragmatics* 3: 237–257. https://doi.org/10.1016/0378-2166(90)90082-O

Holmes, J. (1988) Compliments and compliment responses in New Zealand English. *Anthropological Linguistics* 28: 485–508.

Kerbrat-Orecchioni, C. (1997) A multilevel approach in the study of talk-in-interaction. *Pragmatics* 7(1): 1–20. https://doi.org/10.1075/prag.7.1.01ker

Khuwaileh, A. A. (1999) The role of chunks, phrases and body language in understanding co-ordinated academic lectures. *System* 27(2): 249–260. https://doi.org/10.1016/S0346-251X(99)00019-6

Lee, J. J. and Subtirelu, N. C. (2015) Metadiscourse in the classroom: A comparative analysis of EAP lessons and university lectures. *English for Specific Purposes* 37: 52–62. https://doi.org/10.1016/j.esp.2014.06.005

Leech, G. (1983) *Principles of Pragmatics*. London: Longman.

Leech, G. (2014) *The Pragmatics of Politeness*. Oxford: Oxford University Press. https://doi.org/10.1093/acprof:oso/9780195341386.001.0001

Lin, C. Y. (2015) Seminars and interactive lectures as a community of knowledge co-construction: The use of modifiers. *English for Specific Purposes* 38: 99–108. https://doi.org/10.1016/j.esp.2015.02.002

Nesi, H. (2012) Laughter in university lectures. *Journal of English for Academic Purposes* 11(2): 79–89. https://doi.org/10.1016/j.jeap.2011.12.003

Shamsudin, S. and Ebrahimi, S. J. (2013) Analysis of the moves of engineering lecture introductions. *Procedia – Social and Behavioural Sciences* 70: 1303–1311. https://doi.org/10.1016/j.sbspro.2013.01.191

Spencer-Oatey, H. and Ng, P. (2001) Reconsidering Chinese modesty: Hong Kong and

Mainland Chinese evaluative judgements of compliment responses. *Journal of Asian Pacific Communication* 11(2): 181–201. https://doi.org/10.1075/japc.11.2.05spe

Tang, C. H. and Zhang, G. Q. (2009) A contrastive study of compliment responses among Australian English and Mandarin Chinese speakers. *Journal of Pragmatics* 41(2): 325–345. https://doi.org/10.1016/j.pragma.2008.05.019

Thompson, S. E. (2003) Text-structuring metadiscourse, intonation and the signalling of organisation in academic lectures. *Journal of English for Academic Purposes* 2(1): 5–20. https://doi.org/10.1016/S1475-1585(02)00036-X

Wang, Y. (2014) Humor in British academic lectures and Chinese students' perceptions of it. *Journal of Pragmatics* 68: 80–93. https://doi.org/10.1016/j.pragma.2014.05.003

Wu, R. J. R. (2011) A conversation analysis of self-praising in everyday Mandarin interaction. *Journal of Pragmatics* 43: 3152–3176. https://doi.org/10.1016/j.pragma.2011.05.016

Wulff, S., Swales, J. M. and Keller, K. (2009) 'We have about seven minutes for questions': The discussion sessions from a specialised conference. *English for Specific Purposes* 28(2): 79–92. https://doi.org/10.1016/j.esp.2008.11.002

Yeo, J. Y. and Ting, S. H. (2014) Personal pronouns for student engagement in arts and science lecture introductions. *English for Specific Purposes* 34: 26–37. https://doi.org/10.1016/j.esp.2013.11.001

Yuan, Y. (2002) Compliments and compliment responses in Kunming Chinese. *Pragmatics* 12(2): 183–226. https://doi.org/10.1075/prag.12.2.04yua

Celebrity introductions and responses in the openings of Chinese TV celebrity interview programmes

Yonghong Qian

Introduction

There has been enormous research on TV interviews as mediated public discourse, involving political and celebrity people (e.g., Bell and van Leeuwen 1994; Chilton and Schäffner 2002; Clayman 1992; Clayman and Heritage 2002; Fetzer and Weizman 2006; Jucker 1986; Martínez 2003). Among others, a major line of studies focuses on how the two sides of the event behave during the interview. A few scholars (e.g., Bell and van Leeuwen 1994; Fairclough 1995; Lauerbach 2006) investigate the role of the interviewers primarily on the basis of the questions they ask and the evaluative comments they make. Clayman and Heritage consider response tokens in news interviews, noting that the interviewer generally avoids such tokens, because they could 'be treated as offering support for an interviewee, or as exerting an inappropriate influence on the shape and trajectory of interviewee responses' (2002: 128). Norrick (2010) describes the listening practices of interviewers in American television celebrity interviews within the framework of a more general account of listener activities and reveals how interviewers signal listenership, emotional involvement and the uptake of information, how they prompt, aid and act as a foil to interviewees, and how these practices may affect the audience and the trajectory of the interview in progress. Weizman (2006) addresses the division of roles between the interviewer and interviewee, and their asymmetrical rights and obligations to ask questions, offer judgments, interrupt and so on. Gnisci, Zollo, Perugini and Conza (2013), in a cross-national comparative research on interview styles, take English and Italian journalistic styles as good representatives of the 'Atlantic' and the 'Mediterranean' models of media systems and compare them in terms of the face-threatening acts and coercion involved.

So far, however, no special attention has been directed to how the interviewer pays compliments to celebrities, if at all, and how the interviewee responds to them in the opening part of TV celebrity interview programmes, where the host as the interviewer introduces a celebrity guest to the audience. Assuming that conversational openings are generally an important site of cultural practice and interpersonal work, the present study will investigate the compliments and compliment-responses in the introductory part of Chinese TV celebrity interview programmes, with special regard to the politeness strategies employed. Collecting data from Chinese celebrity interview programmes and drawing on Leech's GSP theory (2014), this study will reveal what strategies are used in compliments by the programme hosts and what responses are made by the celebrity interviewees.

Existing studies on compliments and responses

Compliments are regarded as an important speech act in a sociocultural context, which has attracted a wealth of research interest from scholars of diverse backgrounds. According to Hobbs, a compliment is 'a speech act which explicitly or implicitly bestows credit upon the addressee for some possession, skill, characteristic, or the like, that is positively evaluated by the speaker and addressee' (2003: 249). Pragmatically, compliments serve to satisfy the addressee's positive face wants and thus to increase or consolidate solidarity between each other (2003: 262). In general, a compliment must point to something considered positive by both sides (2003: 254).

The earliest pragmatic research on compliments and compliment responses (CRs) dates back to those scholars who examined the phenomena in different varieties of English: American English by Herbert (1986, 1990), Manes (1983), Pomerantz (1978, 1984) and Wolfson (1983), South African English by Herbert (1989) and New Zealand English by Holmes (1988). These pioneering studies serve to bring out the various aspects of both compliments and CRs: the things that are most likely to be complimented on, the kinds of interlocutors that one is likely to pay a compliment to, and the syntactic structures that are most often used in English for compliments and CRs, and the strategies adopted in performing CRs in each of these English-speaking communities. The majority of later research beginning from the 1990s is devoted to the strategies of CRs in different cultures: Nigerian English by Mustapha (2004), Polish by Herbert (1991) and Jaworski (1995), German by Golato (2002), Spanish by Lorenzo-Dus (2001),

Turkish by Ruhi (2006), Persian by Sharifian (2005), Jordanian Arabic by Farghal and Al-Khatib (2001) and Migdadi (2003), Kuwaiti Arabic by Farghal and Haggan (2006), Japanese by Daikuhara (1986), Baba (1997), Fukushima (1990), and Saito and Beecken(1997), Korean by Han (1992), Thai by Gajaseni (1995). Although quite a number of studies have touched upon compliment behaviour among the Chinese (e.g., Chen 1993; Chen and Yang 2010; Spencer-Oatey and Ng 2001; Tang and Zhang 2009; Yu 1999, 2004; Yuan 2002), no study has been found that concerns itself with the observation of the use of compliments by TV interviewers as a special group of complimenters in the Chinese context.

On a related track, pragmatic research on CRs also has a long story, starting from Pomerantz (1978). Existing studies have discovered many subtleties about the similarities and differences among diverse languages. Speakers of German, for instance, are not found to use appreciation tokens (e.g., 'Thank you') in CRs, although they accept compliments as much as do Americans (Golato 2002). In Thai, social status is found to be a factor influencing speakers' CR behaviour (Gajaseni 1995). Instances of 'impoliteness' are found in the Turkish data, whereby the complimenter explicitly challenges the assumption of the compliment (Ruhi 2006:70). Arabic speakers, on the other hand, are found to routinely 'pay lip-service' (Farghal and Haggan 2006:102) to the complimenter, using a set of formulaic utterances to offer the object of the compliment to the complimenter without meaning it. In addition, gender-based differences in CRs have been attested in a number of languages. Herbert (1990), for example, finds that compliments delivered by American males are twice as likely to be accepted than those delivered by females, and females are twice as likely to accept compliments than are males. However, no study has been conducted to show how celebrities as a special group of complimentees respond to compliments.

In addition, there have been explorations into how compliments and CRs convey politeness. However, previous studies have depended on Brown and Levinson's (1987) politeness theory (e.g., Holmes 1988) or Leech's (1983) Modesty Maxim (e.g., Chen 1993), or Chen's (2001) notion of self-politeness (e.g., Ruhi 2006). None of them is adequate enough to capture the richness of the internal connections between compliments and CRs on the one side and politeness on the other.

Finally, previous research concerning compliments and CRs has been mainly based on data collected in Discourse Completion Tests (DCTs) or daily life situations, with social factors such as gender, power and relationships considered. Comparative studies between different cultures and languages have also been made. However, compliments made in public discourses such as TV interview programmes have not been studied so far. As the TV interview programme is a form of public discourse, it deserves investigation in its own right. Therefore, the present study, using data from Chinese TV celebrity interview programmes, will investigate the content orientations of compliments and CRs as well as the politeness issues relating to them in the opening part of interview programmes, especially how the host makes introductions about the guest invited and how the latter responds.

Methodology

In this section, I shall outline the research questions, data collection and methods of analysis.

Research questions

In view of the above issues, the present study aims to address the following questions:

A. What are the hosts' compliments to the celebrities targeted at, if at all, when the former introduce the latter to the audience in the openings of Chinese TV celebrity interview programmes? In what sense are the compliments conceivable as polite?

B. How do the celebrity interviewees respond to the compliments, if at all, in the openings of Chinese TV celebrity interview programmes? Is there any element of self-denigration involved in these responses? In what sense are their responses conceivable as polite?

Data collection

This study is conducted on the basis of naturally occurring data collected from three Chinese TV celebrity interview programmes. They include *Art Life* (《艺术人生》), *Very Quiet Distance* (《非常静距离》), and *Yang Lan One on One* (《杨澜访谈录》). In these programmes, celebrities such as highly accomplished singers, actors and actresses, movie directors and painting artists are invited to talk about their life stories. There are some other similar programmes, such as *A Date with Lu Yu* (《鲁豫有约》), *Kefan Listening* (《可凡倾听》), and *Music and Life* (《音乐人生》), but no data were collected from them because most of the guest introductions were not made by the host, but via a prepared digital video. Table 4.1 summarises the general information of the three programmes from which our data were collected:

A total of ten episodes of each programme in 2014–2015 were randomly selected and downloaded from the Internet. The data met three requirements: first, each of the interviews involved one interviewee only; second, the interviewee came from the mainland of China; third, there was explicit introduction about the interviewee and it was made by the host instead of via a digital video. Table 4.2

Table 4.1. A sketch of the TV interview programmes

Programmes	Broadcaster	Starting year	Host	Guests	Duration
Art Life	CCTV-3	2000	Zhu Jun	Singers, directors, dancers, artists, performers	50 min
Very Quiet Distance	Anhui Satellite TV	2009	Li Jing	Actors, actresses, singers	40 min
Yang Lan One on One	Dragon TV	2001	Yang Lan	Political figures, scientists, artists, athletes, cultural elites, etc.	45 min

Table 4.2. A description of the data collected

Programmes	Guests/episodes
Art Life	岳红 Yue Hong/20140804; 王二妮 Wang Erni/20140811; 王杰 Wang Jie/20141016; 宋佳 Song Jia/20141021; 陈国星 Chen Guoxing/20141120; 李雪健 Li Xuejian/20141213; 尤小刚 You Xiaogang/20141218; 马少骅 Ma Shaoye/20141225; 库尔班江·赛买提 Kuerbanjiang Saimaiti/20150122; 吴子牛 Wu Ziniu/20150129
Very Quiet Distance	钟汉良 Zhong Hanliang/20140104; 俞飞鸿 Yu Feihong/20140222; 刘恺威 Liu Kaiwei/20140323; 宁静 Ning Jing/20150613; 李小鹏 Li Xiaopeng/20140615; 王丽坤 Wang Likun/20140706; 朱丹 Zhu Dan/20141130; 陈赫 Chen He/20141220; 胡歌 Hu Ge/20141228; 娄艺潇 Lou Yixiao/20150704
Yang Lan One on One	李彦宏 Li Yanhong/20141012; 敬一丹 Jing Yidan/20150429; 杨振宁 Yang Zhenning/20150606; 丁俊晖 Ding Junhui/20150613; 陈凯歌 Chen Kaige/20150704; 佟大为 Tong Dawei/20150627; 徐克 Xu Ke/20150314; 崔永元 Cui Yongyuan/20150210; 马未都 Ma Weidu/20150203

presents the general information about the guests and issues. After the data were collected, I transcribed only the opening part, including the hosts' introductions and the guests' responses, into text forms for analysis.

Data Analysis

The data analysis was targeted at the two research questions raised above. First, the discourse structure of the opening part of the collected TV talk show programmes was examined. Special attention went to the targets of the compliments, if at all, that the TV hosts employed in their introductions. It was hypothesised that the hosts would comment on the guests' appearance/possessions, performance/abilities and personalities, especially the first two categories, on the basis of the findings from some previous studies that the topics of compliments seem to be commonly shared across different cultures (e.g., Daikuhara 1986; Holmes 1986, 1988, 1995; Knapp, Robert and Robert 1984; Wang and Tsai 2003; Wolfson

1983, 1989; Yu 2004). It was also expected that some variations would occur under the assumption that each culture has its preference for, or acceptance of, certain topic categories and specific attributes within the categories[1] (e.g., Holmes and Brown 1987; Wolfson 1983). In this study, I will include the aspects or topics of compliments involved based on the data collected.

Next, the analysis of the strategies of CRs the guests employed in the Chinese TV interview programmes was undertaken. While numerous taxonomies of CRs have been proposed (e.g., Chen 1993; Han 1992; Herbert 1986; Holmes 1988; Pomerantz 1978; Yu 2004; Yuan 2002), the present study adopted the most popular one, notably Holmes's (1988) tripartite system: Acceptance, Deflection/Evasion and Rejection (see Ruhi 2006; Tang and Zhang 2009). Meanwhile, the celebrities' responses were addressed in response to Chen and Yang's (2010) study to highlight their peculiar features.

Finally, the compliments and CRs in terms of politeness on the basis of Leech (2014) were discussed. It was assumed that Leech's GSP Model, which combines many of the features of other models, while disagreeing with others on some of the points of view, could serve as a more viable framework. According to the model, there are altogether ten maxims, of which the following five are particularly relevant:

(M3) Approbation Maxim: give a high value to O's qualities (as realised by the speech act of complimenting).

(M4) Modesty Maxim: give a low value to S's qualities (as realised by the speech act of self-devaluation).

(M5) Obligation (of S to O) Maxim: give a high value to S's obligation to O (as realised by such speech acts as apologising and thanking).

(M7) Agreement Maxim: give a high value to O's opinions (as realised by the speech act of agreeing).

(M8) Opinion Reticence Maxim: give a low value to S's opinions (as realised by the speech act of giving opinions).

Clearly, the use of compliments follows the Approbation Maxim, whereas accepting a compliment observes the Agreement Maxim, accepting a compliment with an expression of gratitude observes the Obligation Maxim as well as the Agreement Maxim, rejecting a compliment follows the Modesty Maxim, and deflecting or evading a compliment complies with the Opinion Reticence Maxim. Thus, we can examine how the hosts and interviewees behaved politely in accordance with these maxims.

Hosts' compliments to the celebrities

Based on the data collected, we find that, usually, the opening part of the programmes includes several stages: 1) greeting the audience, 2) introduction of the guest before the guest comes to the stage and 3) greeting exchanges after the guest comes to the stage. In this study, however, we shall only investigate the second and the third stages, because compliments and compliment-responses occur in these two stages.

Working on the data, we find the hosts phrased their compliments to the guests in the following directions.

A. Stating attention and interest

In daily life, attention and interest means care, friendship and even love. Showing attention to or interest in someone is to convey the message that he or she is valued and respected. This at least partly explains why Leech (1983) proposed the Interest Principle as one of the politeness principles. The principle, in my opinion, is basically compatible with, or sometimes can be subsumed under, the Approbation Maxim, in that if speaker A pleases speaker B by saying B has caught A's attention or interest, A is complimenting B for the sake of politeness.

No doubt, winning and maintaining public attention and interest is crucial to celebrities. Thus, we can almost predict that they care, sometimes even too much, about whether the public, especially their fans, still remember them and expect news of them. This prediction is confirmed by finding that the hosts sometimes compliment the interviewees by expressing attention to and interest in the latter. For example:

(1)

Zhu Jun:　亲爱的观众朋友们大家好，欢迎大家来到艺术人生的演播现场。今年，因为一部电视连续剧的热播，让我们对一位演员产生了浓厚的兴趣，高度的关注。这就是电视连续剧《历史转折中的邓小平》这部剧中，邓小平的扮演者马少骅…

Zhu Jun:　Dear audience, welcome to our Art Life studio. This year, a hot TV series has successfully attracted our keen attention to an actor, Ma Shaohua, who starred as Deng Xiaoping, the great leader in Chinese history in *Deng Xiaoping at the Historical Turning Point…*

In (1), Zhu Jun, the host, draws the audience's attention to the guest's role in a popular TV series, stating that the guest has attracted intense interest and aroused immense attention. To the guest, such a statement is complimentary, as it implies the success of his role.

It is worth mentioning that, in the introduction, Zhu Jun does not give the name of the guest straightforwardly, but delays it until the end. This is a very common pattern when introducing the guest, adopted by the hosts in all three programmes.

B. Emphasising popularity

For celebrities, especially actors/actresses and singers, popularity is their lifeline. Their career largely depends on how many fans they have. To say they are popular is equal to saying they are successful. Thus, mentioning the popularity of a celebrity in the face of the audience can be highly complimentary to him or her. For example:

(2)

Li Jing: 钟汉良，<u>这两年你的知名度也好，个人魅力也好，都是急剧上升</u>。我看了一下，因为我每天都在做采访嘛，我觉得你的粉丝对你的热爱，真的是由衷的，而且力量很大。<u>你去天涯论坛，天涯瘫痪了；你去新浪，新浪瘫痪了。听说你是在做活动，然后那是在哪，世贸天街大屏幕，你把人家搞瘫了</u>，你有没有内疚啊，哈哈哈。

Li Jing: Hello, Zhong Hanliang, <u>your popularity and personal charm have seen a sharp rise in the past two years</u>. As I do interview programmes every day, I do think that your fans' love for you is really true and huge. <u>When you went onto the BBS, Tianya, you paralysed it because too many fans followed you there; when you went to Sina, you paralysed it, too; when you held an activity at Shima Tianjie, you got the big screen there out of operation</u> … so, have you ever felt guilty about that? ha, ha, ha, ha …

In (2), Li Jing makes explicit mention of the guest's popularity in recent years in her direct exchange with him. She even goes a step further by exaggerating how the guest's appearance in some net spaces may cause 'jams' due to the visit by throngs of his fans. Here is another example:

(3)

Zhu Jun: 亲爱的观众朋友们大家好，欢迎来到艺术人生的演播现场。<u>一上台吓我一跳，今天我们演播现场装了我们平常两倍以上的观众。由此可见，今天做客艺术人生的这位嘉宾，他的人气到底有多旺。</u>他是一位歌手，从出道到现在，出了50多张专辑，发行量呢已经达到8700万张。应该说，创下了一个唱片界的奇迹。一直以来，他以他的独特的嗓音，以及他传奇的人生，被歌迷称之为浪子。他为大家演绎了许许多多经典的歌曲。比如说《一场游戏一场梦》《是否我真的一无所有》等等。记得十年前，他曾经做客艺术人生，那一次我们聊得非常的畅快。不知道他是否还记得。十年过去了，他的人生，又有了什么样的变化呢？来，让我们掌声有请王杰！

Zhu Jun: Hello, my dear audience friends, welcome to *Art Life*. <u>Actually, it's such a surprise to see more than twice as big an audience as usual today, which indicates how popular our guest today is</u>. He is a singer, who has released more than 50 albums with a circulation reaching 87 million since his career in this line. It proves to be a miracle of the music industry. For a long time, he, with his unique voice and his legendary life, has been regarded as a prodigy by his devoted fans. He has played out so many classic songs for everyone, such as 'A Game, A Dream', 'Do I Really Have Nothing', and so on. I still remember our carefree talk ten years ago when he joined our programme as a guest. What changes have taken place to his life in the recent ten years? Let us welcome Wang Jie with warm applause!

Unlike the case in (2), in (3), Zhu Jun addresses his comment on the guest's popularity to the audience. Likewise, though, he also exaggerates his complimentary expression by saying he is 'startled' to find an audience twice the usual size.

C. Commending good appearances

Celebrities generally pay a lot of attention to their public image, of which physical appearance is an essential part. This explains, to some extent, why some good-looking celebrities, especially actors or actresses, are paid by advertisers to speak for their products. Even an ordinary person likes to be complimented on their appearance, let alone the celebrities. Our data suggest that the hosts very often resort to the strategy of appearance commendation, sometimes even in exaggerated ways. For example:

(4)

Li Jing: 今年是他出道第十个年头，我们说十年磨一剑。然后不光是事业有成，最重要的是人家事业是跟着十年走，然后长相还停留在十年前。… 掌声有请，胡歌。

Li Jing: This year is his tenth year in his career. A saying goes like this: 'it takes ten years to sharpen a sword'. Now he has achieved a lot. More importantly, despite his big achievement in the ten years, he looks as young as ten years ago. Let's welcome Hu Ge with applause.

In (4), Li Jin comments indirectly and somewhat humorously that the guest looks young and equally handsome despite a successful career over the past ten years. Let us take another example:

(5)

Host: 来。我们看看他年轻时候的照片。哎呀，这位大姐说，比濮存昕还要帅。

Host: Let's take a look at our guest's photos in his younger age. Aha, this lady says that he was even more handsome than Pu Cunxin.

In (5), Zhu Jun commends the guest's handsomeness by cleverly citing the admiring words of a woman in the audience, which involve a comparison with Pu Cunxin, a well-known handsome artist in China.

If it is natural that the hosts comment on the good looks of actors or actresses, it is less expected that they do so to someone who is not in the same field. This, however, does happen. For example:

(6)

Yang Lan:　大家好！随着盛大、百度和分众在美国纳斯达克的上市，人们普遍认为中国网络股的第二个浪潮又出现了，其中百度呢是在2005年8月5日登陆纳斯达克的，它的股份从最初的27美元，曾经一度飚升到154美元，最近呢也回落到80美元左右，市盈率高达1000倍以上，从而成为在纳斯达克上市值最高的中国公司。<u>它的董事长兼CEO李彦宏可以称得上是一位帅哥</u>，不过他没有成为娱乐圈的偶像，反而成为网络界炙手可热的明星，那么，李总，你好！

Yang Lan:　Hello, everybody. Since Shengda, Baidu and FenZhong were listed in Texas of the United States, it has been widely believed that China's Internet stocks are witnessing a second wave. Baidu was listed in NASDAQ on August 5, 2005. Its shares once soared from the initial $27 to $154 before falling to about $80, with PE ratio rising as high as more than 1000 times, becoming China's most valuable company among the listed companies in NASDAQ. <u>Its chairman and CEO Li Yanhong is a handsome guy</u>. He did not become an entertainment icon, but turned out to be a hot star in the cyber-world instead. So, Hello, Mr. Li!

In (6), Mr Li Yanhong is a successful business person who has created economic wonders. Yang Lan, the host, remarks that he is a handsome guy after presenting the background information about his financial achievements. Her compliment on his good looks is a bit surprising, as this might divert the audience's attention to something other than the story of his economic wonders.

D. Focusing on talent

Another important dimension that is pertinent to celebrities is their talent in their profession as an actor, a singer, an athlete, an artist, etc. Thus, they are likely to receive compliments in terms of their talent, as in (7):

(7)

Zhu Jun:　今年，因为一部电视连续剧的热播，让我们对一位演员产生了浓厚的兴趣，高度的关注。这就是电视连续剧《历史转折中的邓小平》这部剧中，邓小平的扮演者马少骅…但是我跟大家说句实话啊，<u>这个片子刚开始，我看第一集和第二集的时候，我也觉得从形象上，不是十分的相像；但我看到最后的时候，我认定，你就是邓小平。正是那种出神入化的表演，完全吸引了我</u>…

Zhu Jun:　This year, a hot TV series has successfully attracted our keen attention to a famous actor, Ma Shaohua, who starred as Deng Xiaoping, the great leader in Chinese history in *Deng Xiaoping at the Historical Turning Point*

> ... To be honest, <u>when I watched the first two episodes at the beginning, I didn't think the actor looked like Deng Xiaoping in appearance. However, as I watched more episodes, especially towards the end of the story, I was fully convinced that he was Deng himself. I was fully overwhelmed by his superb acting</u> ...

In the above example, when introducing the guest, Ma Shaohua, Zhu Jun, the host, speaks highly of his excellent acting skills. Zhu uses '出神入化的表演' ('superb acting') and '完全吸引了我' ('I was fully overwhelmed') to describe his own feeling and judgment. More than that, he even admits that he almost took Ma Shaohua to be Deng Xiaoping himself by the end of the TV series. These complimentary remarks were doubtless very pleasant to Ma's ear.

E. Stressing achievement

Last but not least, as the data suggest, the hosts quite often compliment their guests on their achievements, yet another aspect of celebrities' life that the public want to know about. For example:

(8)

Yang Lan:　在中国啊如果谁谈到台球谈到斯诺克，丁俊晖这个名字几乎是脱口而出的，<u>在这个英国人占据绝对优势的体育项目之中呢，丁俊晖15岁就获得了第一个世界性的冠军，十几年来他几乎囊括了所有斯诺克大赛的冠军，并且曾经问鼎了世界第一的排名</u>，在一方小小的球台之上、在似乎非常沉稳和内敛的表情背后我们看到的是一个少年不寻常的成长之路。

Yang Lan:　In China, when talking about billiards and snooker, Ding Junhui is always a household name. <u>In this British-dominated sport, Ding Junhui won the first world champion at the age of 15. In the following more than a dozen years, he almost won the championship of all the snooker competitions, once ranking No. 1 in the world.</u> On a small snooker table, behind his calm and reserved expressions, we see the unusual growth path of a young boy.

In (8), Yang Lan draws the audience's attention to the remarkable achievements that Ding Junhui, the guest, who has ranked as a world-class snooker player in the past dozen years. As an athlete, Ding is expected to feel proud of himself when hearing the host's account to the audience of his record-breaking career.

In introductions on similar occasions, it seems quite customary in Chinese culture to compliment a person on the prizes he or she has won. Here is another example:

(9)

Zhu Jun:　今天做客我们艺术人生节目的嘉宾，是一位大叔级的帅哥，他毕业于北京电影学院，78级表演系。他们这个班呢，出现了很多大家都非常熟悉和喜欢的著名的演员，比如说张丰毅，谢园等。但是我们这位大叔级的帅哥，毕业之后有点不务正业，去当导演了。<u>这一当导演可不得了，拍出了像《孔繁森》、《黑眼睛》、《横空出世》等等这样经典的影片。他呢，还是一个获奖专业户。</u>用现在的话来讲，<u>他获奖获得手发软。</u>如果你走进他的工作室，<u>一定会被那一排一排金光灿灿的奖杯所震撼。</u>他就是非常帅气的导演，陈国星。

Zhu Jun: Today we are very much honoured to have a senior handsome guy with us in our studio. He graduated from Beijing Film Academy in 1978, majoring in performing art. Many of his classmates have now become famous performing artists, among whom there is Zhang Fengyi, Xie Yuan. Unlike them, however, our guest switched to become a director, which proved to be equally successful, and <u>several classic movies like *A Public Servant Kong Fansen*, *Black Eyes*, *Renounce the World Splendidly* were all directed by him. He is also a professional prize-winner</u>, receiving so many awards that people will be stunned by the piles of golden cups if they make a visit to his studio. He is our handsome director, Chen Guoxing.

As in (8), Zhu Jun the host in (9) also exalts the guest, Chen Guoxing, in the face of the audience by making special mention of the celebrity's splendid achievements apart from his handsomeness. In particular, Zhu vividly describes Chen as 'a professional prize-winner' and imagines how people might be 'stunned by the piles of golden cups if they make a visit to his studio'. There is an element of exaggeration in this description, but it may work as a complimentary effect in the ongoing context.

A striking feature of the hosts' complimenting act is that they more often than not use multiple compliments in introducing the celebrities to the audience, something ordinary people seldom do in daily life. For example, Song Jia was complimented as follows:

(10)

Zhu Jun: 大家一定都记得，上世纪的八十年代，琼瑶剧呢非常的火爆，很多人都追着看。我相信我们现场的很多观众啊，就曾经是琼瑶迷。<u>我们今天来到艺术人生现场的嘉宾，就是第一批的琼瑶剧的演员。人长得漂亮，戏也演得好。而且最近呢，在热播的电视连续剧《历史转折中的邓小平》当中，她又成功地饰演了曹慧这个人物，</u>又深深地吸引了我们。说到这儿，大家一定都知道她是谁了。来，我们掌声有请---宋佳。

Zhu Jun: I guess most of us still remember that in the 80s of last century, Qiongyao TV series were passionately followed and adored by a large number of fans, just like some of our audience present. <u>Today our guest was exactly one of the first few famous actors in Qiongyao series. She is beautiful and has excellent acting skills. Recently, she has again played a successful role of</u>

Cao Hui in a hot Chinese historical TV series, *Deng Xiaoping at the Historical Turning Point*, and once again enchanted us by her superb acting skills. So have you figured out who we've invited to our programme today? Yes, exactly. Let's welcome Song Jia with warm applause.

In (10), Zhu Jun the host employs a variety of complimentary words in his introduction to the guest, covering the latter's appearance ('长得漂亮', 'she is beautiful'), talent ('戏也演得好', 'has excellent acting skills'), achievements ('成功地饰演', 'played a successful role'), etc. A similar practice is also found in (11) below:

(11)

Zhu Jun: 在他几十年的表演生涯里，他塑造了许多风格各异的角色。他力求每一个角色的多样性。用他的话说，他的表演，是一个撕标签的过程。我先列举几个他饰演的角色，让大家来猜一猜，他是谁。他在《渴望》中，饰演宋大成；在《焦裕禄》中，饰演焦书记；在《水浒》中饰演宋江。没错，他就是我们都非常熟悉的，著名表演艺术家，李雪健。来，掌声有请。

Zhu Jun: During the dozens of years of his acting career, he has acted in a wide variety of roles of different styles. He seeks to show the variety of characters. To quote his own words, his performance is a mould-breaking process. Let me name a few of the roles he has staged to enable you to guess who our guest is today. He is the performer of Song Dacheng in the TV drama *Yearning for Happiness*, Secretary Jiao in the movie *A Devoted Public Servant Jiao Yulu*, Song Jiang in *Water Margin*. Yes, exactly. Our guest today is a well-known performing artist, Mr Li Xuejian. Let's give him a warm welcome!

Here, Zhu Jun, in addition to highlighting the guest's familiarity, also gives praise for the latter's experience (that is, he has acted in diverse and distinct roles in the past decades) and talent (that is, he brings out the individuality of each role or, to use his own words, his performance is a process of 'mould-breaking', which means that he stages a brand new style each time he performs a new role). It is worth mentioning that Zhu Jun, in (9) earlier, also makes reference to Chen Guoxing's handsomeness twice apart from focusing on the latter's great achievements.

Our data show that, while Zhu Jun makes consistent use of multiple compliments, he is not the only person to shower more than one compliment on the guests. For instance, in (13), Li Jing also exalts her guest, Zhong Hanliang, on both his popularity and charisma. Yang Lan, the other host, does not do the same thing in her introductions, though, perhaps because of her own preference not to do it.

The guests' responses

Faced with the host's approbatory introduction, how do the guests respond in the opening section of Chinese TV celebrity interview programmes? What strategies do they employ, and how do these politeness strategies embody politeness? In this section, we shall examine our data in this regard.

A careful analysis of the data reveals that most often, or even as rule in Yang Lan One on One, the hosts switch to interview questions immediately after finishing the complimentary introduction, 'depriving' the guests of the opportunities to respond to their compliments. For example,

(12)

Zhu Jun:	亲爱的观众朋友们大家好，欢迎来到艺术人生的演播现场。一上台吓我一跳，今天我们演播现场装了我们平常两倍以上的观众。由此可见，今天做客艺术人生的这位嘉宾，他的人气到底有多旺。他是一位歌手，从出道到现在，出了50多张专辑，发行量呢已经达到8700万张。应该说，创下了一个唱片界的奇迹。一直以来，他以他的独特的嗓音，以及他传奇的人生，被歌迷称之为浪子。他为大家演绎了许许多多经典的歌曲。比如说《一场游戏一场梦》《是否我真的一无所有》等等。记得十年前，他曾经做客艺术人生，那一次我们聊得非常的畅快。不知道他是否还记得。十年过去了，他的人生，又有了什么样的变化呢？来，让我们掌声有请王杰！
Zhu Jun:	<u>好久不见。</u>
Wang Jie:	好久不见。

Zhu Jun: Hello, my dear audience friends, welcome to *Art Life*. Actually, it's such a surprise to see more than twice as big an audience as usual today, which indicates how popular our guest today is. He is a singer, who has released more than 50 albums with a circulation reaching 87 million since his career in this line. It proves to be a miracle of the music industry. For a long time, he, with his unique voice and his legendary life, has been regarded as a prodigy by his devoted fans. He has played out so many classic songs for everyone, such as 'A Game, A Dream', 'Do I Really Have Nothing', and so on. I still remember our carefree talk ten years ago when he joined our programme as a guest. What changes have taken place to his life in the recent ten years? Let us welcome Wang Jie with warm applause!

Zhu Jun: <u>Long time no see.</u>

Wang Jie: Long time no see.

In (12), Zhu the host gives a long introduction to the guest, Wang Jie, and then welcomes the latter onto the stage. Before the guest has a chance to respond to the introduction, Zhu greets him with '好久不见' ('Long time no see'). In return, Wang returns the greeting. Look at another example:

(13)

Li Jing:	钟汉良，这两年你的知名度也好，个人魅力也好，都是急剧上升。我看了一下，因为我每天都在做采访嘛，我觉得你的粉丝对你的热爱，真的是由衷的，而且力量很大。你去天涯论坛，天涯瘫痪了；你去新浪，新浪瘫痪了。听说你是在做活动，然后那是在哪，世贸天街大屏幕，你把人家搞瘫了，<u>你有没有内疚啊</u>，哈哈哈。
Zhong Hanliang:	<u>其实我，都蛮担心的，都担心影响别人</u>。因为，我们欢乐是我们自己的事情，就是，我喜欢看到大家，跟大家喜欢看到我，大家都很开心，我们很欢乐。后来经过那几次呢，我其实觉得，我们都还算是有规矩。
Li Jing:	Hello, Zhong Hanliang, your popularity and personal charm have seen a sharp rise in the past two years. As I do interview programmes every day, I do think that your fans' love for you is really true and huge. When you went onto the BBS, Tianya, you paralysed it because too many fans followed you there; when you went to Sina, you paralysed it, too; when you held an activity at Shima Tianjie, you got the big screen there out of operation … so, <u>have you ever felt guilty about that</u>? ha, ha, ha, ha …
Zhong Hanliang:	<u>Actually, I worried about all those troubles I have caused to others</u>. I sincerely believe that our happiness is our own business. I like to see you, and you like to see me, and everybody is very happy. Then after a few times like that, I really think that we are having fun within our own boundaries.

Unlike (12), where Zhu makes complimentary remarks about Wang in the absence of the latter (although Wang could hear what Zhu was saying behind the curtain), Li Jin addresses her commendation of her guest, Zhong Hanliang, directly to him. Yet, she seals her compliment with a question '你有没有内疚啊' ('Have you ever felt guilty about that?'), to which Zhong has no choice but to respond instead of responding to her complimentary introduction.

In cases where guests do make response to the host's positive introduction, however, they show diverse reactions, as listed below.

A. Acceptance

This type of response occurs only three times, all in Art Life. The guests' acceptance of the compliments is most obviously signalled by their use of 'thanks', a common strategy documented in Chen and Yang's (2010) study. For example:

(14)

Zhu Jun:	马少骅呢，曾经在多部影视剧当中出演过各种各样的角色，比如说警察、民工、生活在底层的小人物，以及国父孙中山等。但用他自己的话来说，他的今天，依然还是北漂一族。年近六旬的他，到底经历过怎样的内心挣扎、彷徨与追求，就让我们一起，来聆听他的心声。掌声有请，马少骅！

Ma Shaohua:	大家好！拍手
Zhu Jun:	大家看到了吗，我完全把您跟荧幕上那个邓小平联系不起来。大家这么看他像吗？有说像的，有说不像的。但是我跟大家说句实话啊，这个片子刚开始，我看第一集和第二集的时候，我也觉得从形象上，不是十分的相像；但我看到最后的时候，我认定，你就是邓小平。
Ma Shaohua:	<u>谢谢，谢谢。</u>（鞠躬）
Zhu Jun:	Ma Shaohua has successfully acted in a number of TV dramas in a wide variety of roles such as police officer, migrant worker, a grassroots man, and Sr. Sun Yet-san, etc. But in his own words, today he is still one of the 'north drift gens'.[a] Now a veteran actor approaching 60 years old, how much inner struggle, hesitation and pursuit has he experienced and suffered? Let us listen to his inner voice today. Ma Shaohua, welcome!
Ma Shaohua:	Hello, everybody! (applause)
Zhu Jun:	You see, I can't associate you with Deng Xiaoping on the screen at all. Do you feel the same? Some said yes, some no. But I'll tell you the truth. While watching this movie at the beginning, especially in the first and second episodes, I didn't think you looked like Deng Xiaoping at all; But towards the end of that TV drama, I was fully convinced that you were Deng Xiaoping himself indeed.
Ma Shaohua:	<u>Thank you, thank you.</u> (bow)

[a] 'North drift gens' relates to those young people who migrate to Beijing to make a living.

In (14), following Zhu Jun's complimentary comment, Ma Shaohua accepts it and acknowledges it with '谢谢，谢谢' ('Thank you. Thank you'). Here is another example:

(15)

Zhu Juan:	在他几十年的表演生涯里，他塑造了许多风格各异的角色。他力求每一个角色的多样性。用他的话说，他的表演，是一个撕标签的过程。我先列举几个他饰演的角色，让大家来猜一猜，他是谁。他在《渴望》中，饰演宋大成；在《焦裕禄》中，饰演焦书记。在《水浒》中饰演宋江。没错，他就是我们都非常熟悉的，著名表演艺术家，李雪健。来，掌声有请。
Li Xuejian:	<u>谢谢，谢谢</u>，很高兴，能有缘分和大家在朱老师的指挥下，来完成今天我们这一期的艺术人生节目。谢谢大家！
Zhu Juan:	During his dozens of years of his acting career, he has in acted a wide variety of roles of different styles. He seeks to show the variety of characters. To quote his own words, his performance is a mould-breaking process. Let me name a few of the roles he has staged to enable you to guess who our guest is today. He is the performer of Song Dacheng in the TV drama *Yearning for Happiness*, Secretary Jiao in the movie *A Devoted Public Servant Jiao Yulu*, Song Jiang in *Water Margin*. Yes, exactly. Our guest today is a well-known performing artist, Mr Li Xuejian. Let's give him a warm welcome!

Li Xuejian: <u>Thanks. Thanks</u>. It's a great pleasure to have the honour to be here, together with all of you and to finish today's programme *Art Life* under the command of Teacher Zhu. Thank you all.

In response to the host's commendations, Li Xuejian the guest, a famous and respected performing artist, also accepts Zhu's compliment with a thanking response.

In addition, it was found that celebrities might accept the compliments by returning a compliment, as we shall see below. However, none of the other strategies found in Chen and Yang's (2010) study, such as agreeing and expressing gladness, were found in the celebrities' responses. Why this happens is yet to be explained.

It is worth mentioning that guests sometimes accept the hosts' compliments tacitly by using non-verbal responses like a bow, a nod or a smile only, or together with a thanking act, as in (14).

B. Deflection/evasion

This type of response occurs only once, in Very Quiet Distance. Here is the exchange:

(16)

Li Jing: 观众朋友们大家好，欢迎收看我们的《非常静距离》。今天我们要请到的这位嘉宾呢，怎么说呢，跟我一样，都是节目主持人。但是呢，我跟她不一样，我是干一行，爱一行，她呢，是见异思迁，干一行，换一行。呵呵。但是人家就是有这个本事。那么她是谁呢？最近，听说她刚从农村回来。我相信现场的每一位朋友，都比她白。我再说下去估计她不出来。准备好你们的掌声了吗？有请朱丹！

Zhu Dan: （出场。笑。）<u>我听着我都不愿意出来了</u>。

Li Jing: Hello, my dear audience friends. Welcome to our *Very Quiet Distance*. Today we are going to have a special guest, how to say, who is like me, an acting show hostess. But she is different from me, as I have stuck to this path since the beginning of my career. She is so fickle, changing from path to path. Ha ha, but she is endowed with this ability to be adaptable to a wide variety of professions. So, who is this versatile lady? Recently, I heard that she just got back from the countryside. I guess she must be suntanned. OK, I'll just save my speech and invite her out. Ready to give her applause? Please welcome our guest today, Zhu Dan!

Zhu Dan: (Onto stage. Smiling) <u>I was just listening to her speech and almost became unwilling to come out</u>.

In (16), after taking the stage, Zhu Dan the guest could not help smiling as a result of hearing Li Jing's humorous and complimentary introduction. Instead of accepting the compliment, Zhu deflects from it by saying that '我听着我都不愿意

出来了' ('I was just listening to her speech and almost became unwilling to come out').

Again, no other strategies like offering, doubting and seeking confirmation, which appear in Chen and Yang's (2010) study were found in our data. This might be due to the fact that the celebrities tended to accept instead of evade or deflect the hosts' compliments.

C. Rejection

This type of response occurs twice, once in Art Life and once in Very Quiet Distance.

(17)

Zhu Jun:	来。我们看看他年轻时候的照片。哎呀，这位大姐说，比濮存昕还要帅。
Chen Guoxing:	哎呀，没有，没有。
Zhu Jun:	Let's take a look at our guest's photos in his younger age. Aha, this lady says that he was even more handsome than Pu Cunxin.
Chen Guoxing:	No, no, no, not at all.

As is shown in (17), in response to the host's positive comments on his looks, Chen Guoxing the guest chooses to deny it by saying '没有，没有' ('no, no, no, not at all'). Here is the other example:

(18)

Li Jing:	今天我们请到的这一位呢，要怎么形容她呢，现在特别喜欢用什么女神呀，这个呀那个，我觉得都不够有特色，所以出场之前呢，我想了一个词，特别适合今天叫"安徽卫视一姐"。特别神，我算了一下，她所有的电视剧都在安徽卫视播，而且都是每一部戏都很红，最近卫视在播一个热播剧叫《你是我的姐妹》你们有看吗？（观众：有）来，我们掌声欢迎娄艺潇，有请。
Lou Yixiao:	静姐，抱抱。
Li Jing:	欢迎（一起对着观众打招呼）"安徽卫视一姐"你好！
Lou Yixiao:	不敢当，不敢当！
Li Jing:	有没有人叫你这个称呼呀？
Li Jing:	Today we get to this Lady, how to describe her … well people might feel urged to use 'goddess', but still I feel this word is not good enough to capture all her charm and brilliant talents. So, before this show, I finally came up with a more suitable address for her, which is 'No. 1 lady of Anhui Satellite TV', as I notice that all her drama has been broadcast in Anhui Satellite TV, and every play is instantly popular with the audience. Have you watched a recent TV series called *You are My Sisters*? (audience: Yes) Let's welcome Lou Yixiao, please!

Lou Yixiao:	My dear sister. Give me a hug.
Li Jing:	Welcome! (Both greet the audience) Hello, 'No. 1 lady of Anhui Satellite TV'!
Lou Yixiao:	<u>No, no, no, I dare not bear it!</u>
Li Jing:	Has anyone addressed you with this title before?

In (18), when greeted by Li Jing with a complimentary address form '安徽卫视一姐' ('No. 1 lady of Anhui Satellite TV'), Lou Yixiao the guest immediately responds with a formulaic denial expression '不敢当，不敢当' (which literally means 'I dare not bear it).

Apart from the three CRs, we detect a further type of CR not captured in Holmes's (1988) taxonomy; that is, the guests may downgrade the compliments paid to them and return a compliment to the host, two types of responses that are included in Chen's classification (1993) and Chen and Yang's classification (2010). For example:

(19)

Zhu Jun:	啊呀你，你离我远点儿(嘉宾站远了一些)。对，一上来你惊着我们大家了。你看你往我们演播室走一圈，我们现场的观众，尤其是年轻漂亮的美眉，全部都是 "哇~好帅啊"，发出这样的惊叹。你觉得你帅吗？
Saimaiti:	<u>一般吧</u>。
Zhu Jun:	不是，你要一般的话，还怎么定义那个帅呢？
Saimaiti:	这个我就不知道了。我觉得帅应该不光只看表面，应该是内在的魅力吧。<u>就像朱军哥，他在这里是绝对是最帅的，大家说对吧？</u>
Zhu Jun:	啊呀，哈哈，谢谢，终于找到自信了，是吧，终于找到自信了。
Zhu Jun:	There, there, please don't stand so close to me (the guest steps away a little from the host). Ok, that's right. Your presence here really gave us a surprise. As soon as you walked into our studio, our audience, especially the young and beautiful girls, couldn't help but letting out a cry: 'wow – how handsome!' Do you think you are handsome?
Saimaiti:	Well, not really.
Zhu Jun:	Ok, if you are not handsome, then how should we define 'handsome'?
Saimaiti:	That I really don't know. But I suppose by 'handsome', it does not only mean one's appearance, but also it should have to do with one's inner charm and qualities. Take our brother Zhu for example. <u>He is the most handsome man in this studio. Don't you think so, everybody?</u>
Zhu Jun:	Aha, thank you so much for your compliment. I have found confidence eventually. Alright, finally I have found my confidence.

In (19), Saimaiti the guest downgrades the host's compliment by saying '一般吧' ('Well, not really').

Another type of response worthy of note in (19) is that Saimaiti also tries to pay a compliment back to the host when he says to the audience '就像朱军哥，他在这里是绝对是最帅的，大家说对吧？' ('He is the most handsome man in this studio. Don't you think so, everybody?').

Similarly, earlier in (15), Li Xuejian the guest also compliments Zhu Jun by addressing him as 'Teacher Zhu' and saying '在朱老师的指挥下' ('under the command of Teacher Zhu'), thus elevating Zhu's status relative to himself.

However, such strategies as disagreeing and expressing embarrassment, documented in Chen and Yang's (2010) study, were not found in the celebrities' responses, perhaps because it was impolite to disagree or perhaps because it was a pleasant thing to hear nice words about themselves.

General discussion

Our data clearly indicate that TV celebrity interview programmes are invariably a site of interpersonal work. For instance, the hosts generally greet the audience first by using some friendly terms like '亲爱的观众朋友们' ('my dear fellow friends') and some appreciating expressions like '欢迎大家来到我们的节目现场' ('welcome to our studio') to show friendliness and hospitality to the audience. Despite all this, our primary attention in this study has been focused on how the hosts behave politely towards the celebrity guests, particularly in the compliment to the latter in the introductions they make at the opening part of the programmes. Also, we have probed into how celebrities act politely in their response to the hosts' compliments.

On the complimenter side, in the introduction part of Chinese TV interview programmes, all of the three hosts invariably pay compliments to their guests in one form or another in almost all of their introductions. In other words, the most frequently used politeness strategy they employ is observance of the Approbation Maxim. According to Leech (2014), the maxim stipulates that one gives a high value to O's qualities. In our data, the celebrities' qualities to which the hosts assign a high value encompass such aspects as attraction, popularity, appearance, talent, achievement etc. The coverage of approbation has to do with the type of interviewees in question, who are all highly successful artists with a high reputation in China. Furthermore, since the purpose of the programme is to invite those highly successful people to share their experiences and stories, the guests are placed at the centre of the programmes. When the hosts introduce them to the audience, it is natural for them to expend a lot of effort to exalt the positive aspects of the guests and set up a high profile for them. In order to make the guests favourably known to the audience in particular and the public in general, the hosts need to make relatively detailed introductions about the guests, highlighting their eye-catching achievements as well as good qualities, which pertains to the Approbation Maxim. Clearly, the hosts' practice of politeness is situation-bound and appropriate to the kind of interactants they face. The hosts' use of approbation-featured politeness at the opening stage of the interviews is expected to heighten the mood of the celebrities and leave a good impression on them. Given that, the approbatory introductions will pave a smooth interview path for the hosts.

On the complimentee side, the CRs in this study also have explicit programme-specific features. Above all, the hosts seldom give the celebrities a chance to respond to their complimentary introductions, which they seem to direct to the audience instead of the guests themselves. They are 'indirect compliments' in the sense that the compliments are within the reach of the guests, and thus are indirectly paid to them. This leaves much less chance for them to respond, especially when interview questions are addressed to them immediately after they are brought to the stage. Thus, we should not be led by the data to think that celebrities are too proud to respond to compliments showered on them by their hosts; indeed, they are apt to respond when they have a chance, as our data indicate. Examination of the limited number of cases lends evidence to this point. From the earlier analysis, we can see that the guests demonstrate different CRs. These CRs can be analysed in terms of strategies of politeness according to Leech (1983, 2014) and Gu (1990), including: 1) observing the Modesty Maxim, i.e. giving a low value to their own qualities, by devaluing their appearance or status, or by deflecting from the hosts' compliment; 2) resorting to the Approbation Maxim, i.e. giving a high value to the hosts' qualities, by returning a compliment to them; 3) complying with the Obligation Maxim, i.e. giving a high value to their obligation to the hosts, as well as the Agreement Maxim, by making appreciative acknowledgment of gratitude when accepting the hosts' compliment. Presumably, all these strategies function to maintain an easy-going and approachable image for the celebrities themselves. This is especially important to them, as their good performance on this interview occasion may bring a lot of fans to them.

To sum up, both the hosts and the guests are sensitive to the situation-bound needs and practice of politeness, which may contribute to the construction of a harmonious relationship between the two sides and a favourable atmosphere for the speech events to develop in a smooth way. In the long run, the hosts' use of politeness strategies makes themselves welcome to the celebrities, whereas the latter's use of polite CRs may add to their own popularity.

Conclusion

The present study examined how hosts and guests interact at the opening stages of three Chinese TV celebrity interview programmes, with a special focus on the compliments hosts pay and the responses the guests make, in order to reveal their respective effort directed at politeness.

Our data have indicated that, while the hosts almost invariably pay compliments to the celebrities in the opening exchanges of the programme, the latter vary from accepting, declining or evading the compliments, whenever they have a chance to respond to the former's compliment. Thus, it can be concluded that both the hosts and the guests resort to politeness strategies. The primary strategy adopted by the hosts is to observe the Approbation Maxim, exalting the positive qualities of the guests. By comparison, the guests resort to a variety of strategies of politeness, abiding by such maxims as modesty, agreement, obligation and approbation. The use of these strategies on both sides helps to maintain or establish a harmonious relationship with each other, as well as the audience present. For the guests, it also contributes to the building and maintaining of their nice public image.

It is worthwhile to point out that there is substantial variation observed among the hosts' compliments and guests' responses. For the hosts, their compliments may be targeted at different aspects of the guests, depending on what field the latter come from. Also, their compliments may vary in terms of quantity across hosts and guests, a finding that calls for further explanation, though. For the guests, their responses vary. For one thing, they sometimes make a response to the compliments and sometimes do not, depending on whether the hosts hold it back or not. For another, they opt for different strategies of politeness, for which a further explanation is also yet to be sought. Nevertheless, the genre of our data is at least partly responsible for the variation.

Due to the limited size of our data, this study suffers from a lack of generalisation. In addition, a lot of factors have been left unconsidered, including the familiarity and distance between the hosts and the guests, the gender and experience of the hosts, the relative fame or status of the guests, and so on. Therefore, more research might be conducted to explore the effects of those factors on the hosts' and the guests' polite behaviour in the activity examined in this study.

Note

1. For example, possession compliments in American English included those relating to children and spouses (Wolfson 1983). Nevertheless, such compliments were regarded as inappropriate in New Zealand English (Holmes and Brown 1987). Holmes and Brown (1987) indicated that, in New Zealand, it was unacceptable to compliment a man on his wife in that this reflected a view of his wife as a possession. If we use this continuum as a basis for comparing CRs across languages, some generalisations can be made. For instance, we can say that Arabic (Farghal and Haggan 2006), German (Golato 2002) and English – including American English, Australian English, British Eng-

lish and South African English – are all at or towards the accepting end of the continuum, with sizable percentages of CR utterances accepting compliments. Thai (Gajaseni 1995) appears to be in the middle. At or towards the rejecting end are Turkish (Ruhi's 2006), Korean (Han 1992), Japanese (Daikuhara 1986, but see below) and Chinese (prior to the findings reported in this study).

References

Baba, J. (1997) A study of interlanguage pragmatics: Compliment responses by learners of Japanese and English as a second language. PhD dissertation, University of Texas at Austin.

Bell, P. and van Leeuwen, T. (1994) *The Media Interview*. Kensington: The University of New South Wales Press.

Brown, P. and Levinson, S. C. (1987) *Politeness: Some Universals in Language Use*. Cambridge: Cambridge University Press.

Chen, R. (1993) Responding to compliments: A contrastive study of politeness strategies between American English and Chinese speakers. *Journal of Pragmatics* 20: 49–75. https://doi.org/10.1016/0378-2166(93)90106-Y

Chen, R. (2001) Self-politeness: A proposal. *Journal of Pragmatics* 33: 87–106. https://doi. org/10.1016/S0378-2166(99)00124-1

Chen, R. and Yang, D. (2010) Responding to compliments in Chinese: Has it changed? *Journal of Pragmatics* 42: 1951–1963. https://doi.org/10.1016/j.pragma.2009.12.006

Chilton, P. and Schäffner, C. (2002) *Politics as Text and Talk*. Amsterdam: John Benjamins. https://doi.org/10.1075/dapsac.4

Clayman, S. and Heritage, J. (2002) *The News Interview: Journalists and Public Figures on the Air*. Cambridge: Cambridge University Press. https://doi.org/10.1017/CBO9780511613623

Clayman, S. (1992) Footing in the achievement of neutrality: The case of news interview discourse. In P. Drew and J. Heritage (eds) *Talk at Work* 163–198. Cambridge: Cambridge University Press.

Daikuhara, M. (1986) A study of compliments from a cross-cultural perspective: Japanese vs American English. *Penn Working Papers in Educational Linguistics* 2: 23–41.

Fairclough, N. (1995) *Media Discourse*. London: Edward Arnold.

Farghal, M. and Al-Khatib, M. A. (2001) Jordanian college students' responses to compliments: A pilot study. *Journal of Pragmatics* 33(9): 1485–1502. https://doi.org/10.1016/S0378-2166(01)00006-6

Farghal, M. and Haggan, M. (2006) Compliment behaviour in bilingual Kuwaiti college students. *International Journal of Bilingual Education and Bilingualism* 9(1): 94–118. https://doi.org/10.1080/13670050608668632

Fetzer, A. and Weizman, E. (2006) Political discourse as mediated and public discourse. *Journal of Pragmatics* 38: 143–153. https://doi.org/10.1016/j.pragma.2005.06.014

Fukushima, N. J. (1990) A study of Japanese communication: Compliment-rejection production and second language instruction. PhD dissertation, Department of Linguistics, University of Southern California.

Gajaseni, C. (1995) A contrastive study of compliment responses in American English and Thai including the effect of gender and social status. PhD dissertation, Department of Linguistics, University of Illinois.

Gnisci, A., Zollo, P., Perugini, M. and Conza, A. D. (2013) A comparative study of toughness and neutrality in Italian and English political interviews. *Journal of Pragmatics* 50: 152-167. https://doi.org/10.1016/j.pragma.2013.01.009

Golato, A. (2002) German compliment responses. *Journal of Pragmatics* 34(5): 547–571. https://doi.org/10.1016/S0378-2166(01)00040-6

Gu, Y. (1990) Politeness phenomena in modern Chinese. *Journal of Pragmatics* 14 (2): 37–257. https://doi.org/10.1016/0378-2166(90)90082-O

Han, C. H. (1992) A comparative study of compliment responses: Korean females in Korean interactions and in English interactions. *Working Papers in Educational Linguistics* 8(2): 17–31.

Herbert, R. K. (1986) Say 'thank you' – or something. *American Speech* 61: 76–88. https://doi.org/10.2307/454710

Herbert, R. K. (1989) The ethnography of English compliment responses: A contrastive sketch. In O. Wieslaw (ed.) *Contrastive Pragmatics* 3–35. Amsterdam: John Benjamins.

Herbert, R. K. (1990) Sex-based differences in compliment behaviour. *Language in Society* 19: 201–224. https://doi.org/10.1017/S0047404500014378

Herbert, R. K. (1991) The sociology of compliment work: An ethnographical study of Polish and English compliments. *Multilingua* 10(4): 381–402. https://doi.org/10.1515/mult.1991.10.4.381

Hobbs, P. (2003) The medium is the message: Politeness strategies in men's and women's voice mail messages. *Journal of Pragmatics* 35(2): 243–262. https://doi.org/10.1016/S0378-2166(02)00100-5

Holmes, J. (1986) Compliments and compliment responses in New Zealand English. *Anthropological Linguistics* 28: 485–508.

Holmes, J. (1988) Paying compliments: A sex-preferential positive politeness strategy. *Journal of Pragmatics* 12(3): 445–465. https://doi.org/10.1016/0378-2166(88)90005-7

Holmes, J. (1995) *Women, Men and Politeness.* Harlow: Longman.

Holmes, J. and Brown, D. F. (1987) Teachers and students learning about compliments. *TESOL Quarterly* 21: 523–545. https://doi.org/10.2307/3586501

Jaworski, A. (1995) 'This is not an empty compliment!': Polish compliments and the expression of solidarity. *International Journal of Applied Linguistics* 5(1): 63–94. https://doi.org/10.1111/j.1473-4192.1995.tb00073.x

Jucker, A. (1986) *News Interviews: A Pragmalinguistic Analysis.* Amsterdam: John Benjamins. https://doi.org/10.1075/pb.vii.4

Knapp, M. L., Robert H. and Robert A. B. (1984) Compliments: A descriptive taxonomy. *Journal of Communication* 19: 12–31. https://doi.org/10.1111/j.1460-2466.1984.tb02185.x

Lauerbach, G. (2006) Discourse representation in political interviews: The construction of identitiies and relations through voicing and ventriloquizing. *Journal of Pragmatics* 38: 196–215. https://doi.org/10.1016/j.pragma.2005.06.015

Leech, G. (1983) *Principles of Pragmatics*. London: Longman.

Leech, G. (2014) *The Pragmatics of Politeness*. Oxford: Oxford University Press. https://doi.org/10.1093/acprof:oso/9780195341386.001.0001

Lorenzo-Dus, N. (2001) Compliment responses among British and Spanish university students: A contrastive study. *Journal of Pragmatics* 33(1): 107–127. https://doi.org/10.1016/S0378-2166(99)00127-7

Manes, J. (1983) Compliments: A mirror of cultural values. In N. Wolfson and J. Elliot (eds) *Sociolinguistics and Language Acquisition* 96–102. Rowley, MA: Newbury House.

Martínez, E. R. (2003) Accomplishing closings in talk show interviews: A comparison with news interviews. *Discourse Studies* 5(3): 283–302. https://doi.org/10.1177/14614456030053001

Migdadi, F. H. (2003) Complimenting in Jordanian Arabic: A socio-pragmatic analysis. PhD dissertation, Ball State University.

Mustapha, A. S. (2004) Gender variation in Nigerian English compliments. PhD dissertation, University of Essex.

Norrick, N. R. (2010) Listening practices in television celebrity interviews. *Journal of Pragmatics* 42: 525–543. https://doi.org/10.1016/j.pragma.2009.07.002

Pomerantz, A. (1978) Compliment responses: Notes on the cooperation of multiple constraints. In J. Schenkein (ed.) *Studies in the Organisation of Conversational Interaction* 79–112. New York: Academic Press.

Pomerantz, A. (1984) Agreeing and disagreeing with assessments: Some features of preferred/dispreferred turn shapes. In M. Atkinson and J. Heritage (eds) *Structures of Social Action* 57–101. Cambridge: Cambridge University Press.

Ruhi, S. (2006) Politeness in compliment responses: A perspective from naturally occurring exchanges in Turkish. *Pragmatics* 16(6): 43–101. https://doi.org/10.1075/prag.16.1.03ruh

Saito, H. and Beecken, M. (1997) An approach to instruction of pragmatic aspects: Implications of pragmatic transfer by American learners of Japanese. *The Modern Language Journal* 81: 363–377. https://doi.org/10.1111/j.1540-4781.1997.tb05497.x

Sharifian, F. (2005) The Persian cultural schema of *shekasteh-nafsi*: A study of compliment responses in Persian and Anglo-Australian speakers. *Pragmatics and Cognition* 13(2): 337–361. https://doi.org/10.1075/pc.13.2.05sha

Spencer-Oatey, H. and Ng, P. (2001) Reconsidering Chinese modesty: Hong Kong and Mainland Chinese evaluative judgements of compliment responses. *Journal of Asian Pacific Communication* 11(2): 181–201. https://doi.org/10.1075/japc.11.2.05spe

Tang, C. H. and Zhang, G. Q. (2009) A contrastive study of compliment responses among Australian English and Mandarin Chinese speakers. *Journal of Pragmatics* 41(2): 325–345. https://doi.org/10.1016/j.pragma.2008.05.019

Wang, Y. F. and Tsai, P. H. (2003) An empirical study on compliments and compliment responses in Taiwan Mandarin conversation. *Concentric: Studies in English Literature and Linguistics* 29(3): 118–156.

Weizman, E. (2006) Roles and identities in news interviews: The Israeli context. *Journal of Pragmatics* 38: 154–179. https://doi.org/10.1016/j.pragma.2005.06.018

Wolfson, N. (1983) An empirically based analysis of complimenting in English. In N. Wolfson and J. Elliot (eds) *Sociolinguistics and Language Acquisition* 82–95. Rowley, MA: Newbury House.

Wolfson, N. (1989) *Perspectives: Sociolinguistics and TESOL*. Boston, MA: Heinle & Heinle Publishers.

Yu, M. C. (1999) Cross-cultural and interlanguage pragmatics: Developing communicative competence in a second language. PhD dissertation, Harvard University.

Yu, M. C. (2004) Interlinguistic variation and similarity in second language speech act behaviour. *The Modern Language Journal* 88(1): 102–119. https://doi.org/10.1111/j.0026-7902.2004.00220.x

Yuan, L. (2002) Compliments and compliments responses in Kunming Chinese. *Pragmatics* 12(2): 183–226. https://doi.org/10.1075/prag.12.2.04yua

PART II

Identity construction and politeness in various Chinese interactions

CHAPTER 5

Identity construction in responses to radio-mediated call-in complaints

Wei Ren

Introduction

The study of identity has constituted one of the main foci in sociolinguistic research (De Fina 2007) and has been considered as an alternative to expand the bases of politeness research (Garcés-Conejos Blitvich 2009). Current research on language and identity relies heavily on perspectives of social constructionism, which view identity as a process, emergent through local interaction, rather than a pre-existing given product (De Fina, Schiffrin and Bamberg 2006). The concept of identity is understood in this study as 'the social positioning of self and other' (Bucholtz and Hall 2005: 586) and will be investigated through an analysis of the variability of its linguistic representation in interactions. One important channel through which we negotiate identity is politeness. Combining research on politeness and that on identity construction has been shown to yield fruitful results (Locher 2008). Building on these concepts, this study presents a linguistic analysis of the manner in which the host in a radio-mediated call-in programme constructs his/her identity in the handling of public service complaints.

The choice of complaint responses in this study stems from a gap in the literature, as a limited number of studies have examined responses to complaints, particularly responses to indirect complaints (Migdadi, Badarneh and Momani 2012; Traverso 2009). Complaints can be categorised as direct complaints or indirect complaints. A direct complaint is typically a face-threatening act (Brown and Levinson 1987) because it is delivered directly to the recipient. An indirect complaint is addressed to 'a (non-present) third-party who is not the recipient of the complaint' (Heinemann and Traverso 2009: 2382). Therefore, depending on the response, an indirect complaint has great potential to be a rapport-inspiring speech act (Boxer 2010). Researchers have analysed the structural features of indirect complaints in conversations between friends in French (Traverso 2009) and between caregivers and care recipients in Danish (Heinemann 2009). However, although some studies have investigated direct complaints in Chinese (e.g., Chen, Chen and Chang 2011; Du 1995), little empirical research has explored indirect complaints and/or responses in Chinese. This study could thus be regarded as a contribution to existing knowledge about the linguistic strategies employed by Chinese speakers in response to indirect complaints, particularly in radio call-in programmes.

The radio call-in programme is 'an increasingly popular site for sociological and discourse analytic attention' (Fitzgerald and Housley 2002: 579), as manifested in numerous studies devoted to analysing radio call-ins (e.g., Bücker 2013; Dori-Hacohen 2014; Hutchby 1996, 1999, 2006; Migdadi et al. 2012; to name just a few). The interaction in radio call-ins should be regarded as an institutional discourse because it is 'a public form of unscripted live talk' (Bücker 2013: 31). The interaction takes place between speakers who align themselves in institutionally prefabricated roles, such as 'host-caller', 'introducer and questioner – introduced and then questioned' (Bücker 2013; Fitzgerald and Housley 2002). To date, only a few studies have examined the interactional behaviour of Chinese speakers in radio call-in programmes. For example, analysing Chinese call-in consultations, Gao (1995) summarises two types of conversation structures in a Chinese call-in programme: counsellor-centred and caller-centred structures. Based on data drawn from naturally occurring medical consultations, Yuan and Chen (2013) reveal that the consultant constructed three types of identities to adapt to the situated communicative acts, that is, as an expert, as a companion and as a sales representative. Thus, by examining radio call-in programmes in Chinese, this study contributes to the body of research that examines aspects of (institutional) telephone conversations in languages other than English (Reiter 2005; Schegloff 1986).

Identity and (im)politeness

Identity and (im)politeness are widely discussed in sociolinguistics and pragmatics literature. It is impossible to give a comprehensive review of the theoretical work on identity and (im)politeness in this study (see Garcés-Conejos Blitvich 2013; Locher 2008; Spencer-Oatey 2007 for detailed introductions). This section instead briefly discusses some of the approaches and concepts that have had the greatest impact on current visions of identity construction and its relation to (im) politeness.

Identity research can be summarised from two perspectives: the essentialist perspective and the constructivist perspective. The former references identity as pre-established attributes prior to interaction (e.g., age, gender, occupation, ethnicity), whereas the latter regards identity as a social construct that is interactively negotiated to fulfil a specific communicative purpose during said interactions (Bucholtz and Hall 2005; Garcés-Conejos Blitvich, Bou-Franch and Lorenzo-Dus 2013). The present study adopts the constructivist perspective, regarding identity as neither a given entity nor a product. Instead, identities are 'performed, enacted and embodied' (De Fina et al. 2006: 3) through the moment-to-moment choices that people make about how to interact. Identity is *how individuals define, create, or think of themselves in terms of their relationships with other individuals and groups*, whether these others are real or imagined' (Kiesling 2013: 450; italics original). In other words, identity is not attributes preceding interaction; instead, it 'emerges within [interaction], as speakers jointly construct temporary identity positions to meet the socially contextualised demands of ongoing talk' (Hall and Bucholtz 2013: 124).

This view of identity emphasises the importance of discourse analysis in researching identity construction, thus coinciding with the discursive approach to politeness (e.g., Locher and Watts 2005; Spencer-Oatey 2008), which notes that discourse, rather than an utterance, is the locus of (im)politeness studies. Unlike second-order approaches to politeness (e.g., Brown and Levinson 1987; Leech 1983), first-order approaches (e.g., Locher and Watts 2005, 2008; Spencer-Oatey 2005, 2008) contest the idea that an utterance is inherently polite or impolite. Instead, they highlight the importance of locally made judgments on language use, which lead interactants to come up with a more diverse way of labelling behaviours beyond them being simply polite and impolite (see Eelen 2001; Kádár and Haugh 2013; Watts 2003 for detailed discussions on first-order and second-order approaches to politeness). In addition, judgments about an utterance may differ from one interaction to the next.

(Im)politeness and identity construction are 'inextricably linked' (Garcés-Conejos Blitvich 2009: 295). On the one hand, negotiating identities influences the employment of (im)politeness. On the other hand, linguistic (im)politeness is arguably one of the indices of people's identities that are interactionally constructed (Garcés-Conejos Blitvich 2009; Locher 2008). Linguistic behaviour is evaluated as polite or impolite when it is assessed as a benefit or a threat to the hearer's identities (Garcés-Conejos Blitvich 2013; Garcés-Conejos Blitvich et al. 2013; Holmes, Marra and Schnurr 2008). The purpose of this study is to investigate the identities that the host constructs and the strategies that the host employs. The extent to which this identity construction involves (im)politeness will also be discussed.

Methodology

The data used for the present study are collected from the *Zhengfeng Hotline*, a radio-mediated call-in programme broadcast in Jiangsu Province, China. This programme is devoted to the handling of public service complaints. Since 27 September 2003, it has aired every day on the state-owned Jiangsu People's Radio. On weekdays, the programme invites people to call in; on Saturdays, it addresses previous complaints, and it repeats the Wednesday programme on Sundays. This programme invites the general public to call in to complain about issues such as lack of public services, infrastructure problems, acts of public negligence, bureaucracy and malfeasance, and policies and issues harming people's interests. The programme has two formats: a male and female host receive and handle calls, and the host invites some special guests (normally leaders in public service departments) to sit on panels that receive and handle calls. The researcher listened to the programme for a month (April 2014), during which callers participated in 21 episodes. The callers complained about various issues, and they regularly complained about housing and finance issues. Thus, the researcher decided to focus on these two issues in this study. The selection resulted in eight episodes (totalling 69,462 words). Four episodes were handled by the hosts alone, and the other four were handled by the panel.

The eight episodes were transcribed and subjected to qualitative, discourse-analytic reading. Because the present study only focuses on the host's linguistic strategies, detailed transcription of pauses, prosody and/or intonation was not attempted. For the sake of readability, the chosen transcription attempted to minimise the use of conventions (refer to the Appendix for an illustration of the symbols used in the examples), following Bremer and colleagues (Bremer, Roberts, Vasseur, Simonot and Broeder 1996). The analytical framework is broadly social-constructivist and discursive, with special attention paid to the identity construction represented in the host's responses to complaints. Identities in this study are viewed as constructed and negotiated during concrete, local and interactional occasions (Bucholtz and Hall 2005; Garcés-Conejos Blitvich et al. 2013), yielding constellations of identities rather than individual, monolithic constructs (De Fina et al. 2006: 2). In the present study, the host's responses to callers' complaints were examined qualitatively to reveal the strategies that the host employed in constructing various desirable personal identities for him/herself. At the clause level, personal pronouns and speech acts were analysed, while at the discourse level, semantic content and interruptions were considered.

Results and discussion

This section analyses the ways in which the host constructed various identities by drawing upon different linguistic choices in the handling of callers' phone-in complaints. The findings are discussed in terms of five local identity categories that have emerged from the complaint-handling discourse and are labelled as follows: caring helper, responsible helper, authoritative host, media propagandist and public authority. As noted by Garcés-Conejos Blitvich et al. (2013), the locally constructed identity categories experienced significant overlap in the data collected. However, these categories are clearly delineated to aid in the clarity of exposition.

A caring helper

When the host answered the call without a panel, he/she first introduced the caller, as illustrated in (1).

(1)

H: 工作人员告诉我们有一位南京的张先生反映问题，我们把他的电话接入直播间。张先生，您好！

H: The working staff told us that Mr Zhang from Nanjing called to report some issues. We now answer his call. Mr Zhang, Hello!

When a panel is handling the complaint, the host will ask the caller for some demographic information, including his/her last name and location, before the caller initiates his/her complaint, as shown in (2).

(2)

H: 好的，丁局长，我们来接听第一位朋友的电话。喂，您好。

C: 您好。

H: 您是哪里的听众啊？

C: 我是南京的。

H: 贵姓？

C: 姓崔。

H: 崔先生有什么问题可以和丁局长交流？

H: Ok, Director Ding, let's answer the first call. Hi, Hello.

C: Hello.

H: Where are you from?

C: I'm from Nanjing.

H: What's your (honourable) family name?

C: (My family name is) Cui.

H: Mr Cui, do you have any question you'd like to ask Director Ding?

As the two examples above indicate, the format of the programme affects the ways in which the host introduces the caller. When the host answers the call alone, a monitor informs him/her about the caller's demographic information (as in (1)). However, when he/she handles the call with the help of special guests, the leader of the guest panel is treated as the primary mediator. Thus, the host has to elicit the caller's demographic information for the guests, as illustrated in (2).

After introducing/receiving the caller's demographic information, the host invites the caller to share his/her problems. When the caller starts discussing his/her complaint, the host shows empathy by expressing his/her interest and concern. As such, the host realises a particular local identity: the caring helper.

Locher and Hoffmann (2005: 94) label comments as empathetic 'when they were displaying awareness of the questioner's particular (emotional) situation'. As found in other studies of complaint responses (Migdadi et al. 2012; Traverso 2009), the host often agrees or supports the caller to encourage him/her to present the complaint clearly and freely. Three types of agreement are identified by Pomerantz (1984): the upgrade, the same evaluation and the downgrade. The first two types are observed in the hosts' responses to callers in the present study, as shown in the following example.

(3)

C:	问了，他说我们要等待人家验收，验收没成功，验收比较慢，等等等等。我们现在就是说什么了，晓东老师，就是我们气愤在什么地方，我们每次去，比如说他讲3月份，好了，我们就3月份去了，他又说5月份。
H:	<男>我明白你的意思，就这样拖着我们。
<女>	好，杨先生，理解你的心情，就是说这个事情感觉你在不断地被忽悠。
C:	I asked. He said they had to wait to be inspected. The inspection didn't go through. The inspection was slow, etc. etc. Now, we, I mean, Teacher Xiaodong, what we're angry about is, every time we went there, for example, he said March, OK, we went there in March, then he said May.
H:	<M>I understand what you mean. Just delaying us in this way.
<F>	Ok, Mr Yang. (I) understand what you're feeling. That is to say, you feel like you're being continuously conned in this matter.

In (3), the male host shows his empathy by summarising the content of the caller's prior statement, indicating that he evaluates the situation in a similar way as the caller. On the other hand, the female host not only shows that she understands how the caller feels, but she also criticises that the real estate company is deceiving the caller. In other words, she uses a stronger evaluative term to describe the caller's situation, a common technique for upgrading evaluations (Pomerantz 1984: 65).

In addition, the hosts often employ one or two words to show their agreement with the caller, like '好' ('OK') in the female host's response in (3). The hosts do not necessarily side with callers, but they generally show their solidarity in the sense that they recognise that the caller's complaint is justified (Migdadi et al. 2012; Traverso 2009).

In addition, the hosts at times explicitly comfort the caller, for example, by telling them not to worry, as in (4):

(4)

    H: 卢先生不要着急，好不好？

    H: Don't worry, Mr Lu, all right?

Usually after comforting the caller, the host will help the caller address the problem by addressing the issue to the parties responsible, thus constructing another identity, 'a responsible helper', to which we now turn.

A responsible helper

In response to the caller's complaint, the host not only shows his/her compassion but also commits him/herself to helping solve the problem, thus constructing 'a responsible helper' identity.

A. Addressing the responsible party on air

After hearing the caller's complaint, the host would directly address the party that was responsible for the caller's problem. When officials were present on the panel, a host would directly engage with them. In both instances, this host would reiterate the caller's complaint and ask the parties responsible for explanations or solutions, as in the following two examples:

(5)

    H: <对房地产开发商>当地有一位业主啊买了你们的房子，叫连云港灌南县华锦园二期，说呢是一个问题啊，说是现在已经过了交房的时间。现在开发商的态度是什么呢，说如果放弃违约金，那么就马上给你交钥匙。我想问一下我们听众反映的情况是这样吗？

    H: <to the real estate developer> A local owner bought a flat from your company in Hua Jin II, Guannan, Lianyungang. There's a problem. It's passed the delivery time, but now your company's attitude is 'If you waive all claims to the penalty, you will receive the key immediately'. I'd like to confirm with you the problem our audience reported.

(6)

    H: <对一位嘉宾>他这个情况，如果可以证明这个车已经购买过，他又重复购买，这个情况一般怎么处理，我们是把他后来购买的车船税费用退还还是怎么样？

    H: <to a special guest> For his (the caller's) situation, if he can prove that the car tax had been paid, but he paid it again, how will this be handled normally? Will we refund the vehicle tax he paid or what?

As indicated in the two examples above, by reiterating the caller's complaint, the host not only acknowledges the caller's sociality right (Spencer-Oatey 2005, 2008) to request a solution or explanation from the parties or authorities responsible, but also strengthens the caller's legitimacy by adopting and reproducing the complaint. The host's acceptance of the caller's complaint serves as a positive politeness strategy (Brown and Levinson 1987), in which both the host and the caller are included in the same activity (Migdadi et al. 2012) of requesting help or a solution from the parties responsible.

B. Promising to help

Another strategy the host employed to show his/her responsibility was committing him/herself to following up on the problem with the appropriate authorities or responsible parties. This follow-up was performed because the issue had not been resolved, either due to the neglect or delay of the responsible party, as shown in (7).

(7)

    H: 好，这个事情这样吧，你告诉你的邻居们，我们节目之后连线一下下关区拆迁办。因为我们的记者一直在打他们的电话，也没有人接听。<u>节目之后我们来联系，好吗？</u>

    H: OK, let's handle the issue in this way. You tell your neighbours. We'll contact the housebreaking office in Xiaguan District. Because our reporter has kept calling them but no one answers, <u>we'll contact them after the programme, all right?</u>

This strategy is also used even if the official present offers a solution or promises to solve the problem, as indicated in the following example.

(8)

    H: 好了，我们这个听众朋友啊，没关系，今天银监局和交通银行的领导都做了明确的表态，<u>节目之后我们会主动联系你的，好不好？</u>

    H: OK. Our friend in the audience, don't worry. The leaders of the Banking Bureau and the Bank of Communications all expressed themselves clearly. <u>We'll contact you after the programme. Is that OK?</u>

In the example above, the special guests have expressed how they will solve the caller's problem. Nonetheless, once again, the host explicitly assures the caller that they will contact him, thus portraying an image of a responsible helper.

It is worth noting that the promise also indicates that the host is going to end the call. Therefore, in the present study, it frequently co-occurred with tag questions, such as '好吗' ('all right?') in (7) and '好不好' ('Is that OK?', literally, 'good or bad?') in (8). The most general function of tag questions is attenuating or softening the illocutionary force of the speech acts in which they occur (Holmes 1984). In addition, tag questions are commonly used as 'appealers' (Blum-Kulka,

House and Kasper 1989), which function to elicit a hearer's signal of understanding. Because the complaint has not been solved, the host, although promising to help, employs such appealers to ask for the caller's understanding of the situation and agreement to end the call. In exploring public service complaint responses on a Jordanian radio call-in programme, Migdadi et al .(2012) find that Jordanian hosts often employ 'alerters' (e.g., 'dear sir', 'dear brother') with their promises to help. Although we cannot generalise the results from Migdadi et al. (2012) and the present study, it might be interesting to conduct future studies that investigate whether cross-cultural differences exist in terms of the strategies employed in the host's promise to help in response to call-in complaints.

An authoritative host

The host presents his/her role as an authoritative helper by employing the following strategies: showing expert knowledge, offering advice, interrupting the speaker and requesting future contact.

A. Showing expert knowledge

In the programme, callers sometimes reveal little background information when discussing their complaints. Thus, to avoid confusion and to clarify things for the audience, the host provides his/her encyclopaedic knowledge (Example (9)) and describes problems and present facts (Example (10)).

(9)

H: 给大家介绍一下啊，拆迁安置房和经济适用房两者到底有什么区别。/…/

H: Let me introduce what on earth is the difference between arrangement housing because of dismantling and economically affordable housing? /…/

(10)

H: 目前我们江苏并没有试点或者出台相关的房地产征收的政策，这里我们要跟大家明确一下。

H: At present, our Jiangsu Province hasn't experimented with or published any policy on relevant housing taxation. We need to clarify this with you all here.

As previous literature (Garcés-Conejos Blitvich et al. 2013; Locher and Hoffmann 2005; Lorenzo-Dus 2005; Simon-Vanderbergen 2007) has shown, experts discursively construct their knowledge in a particular field through the formulation of impersonal views, the presentation of facts, and specialist jargon. By showing his/her expert knowledge, the host constructs a well-informed, trustworthy and reliable identity.

In addition, the host often conveys a determined attitude towards his/her propositions, as shown in (11).

(11)

> H:　这个开发商<u>明显</u>是违规操作，而且是违反我们商品房买卖合同的这个事情。
>
> H:　This developer is <u>obviously</u> against regulations. And it is violating our Commercial Housing Sales Contracts in this matter.

Modality can show the speaker's judgment of a proposition's meaning in relation to probability, obligation and inclination (Halliday 2002) and can be linked to the speaker's relative power and discourse status in the situation at hand (He 1993). The use of the modal adjunct '明显' ('obviously') in the first sentence and the absence of modality in the second sentence show that the host has no reservations about the proposition he/she has made, indicating that he/she believes the developer is undoubtedly wrong regarding the issue identified in the caller's complaint and signalling the host's relative power and authoritative status in this interaction. In the examples above, the host constructs an identity as an authoritative host by displaying him/herself as a competent and knowledgable source of accurate information.

B. Offering advice

After listening to callers' complaints, the host sometimes summarises the issue and offers advice to the callers, as in (12).

(12)

> C:　/…/我曾经办理过中国银行的信用卡，用过一段时间之后因为没有经常消费了，就没有用这个卡。后来银行发信息提醒我说产生了年费，后来我确认核实了一下，确实有此事，是因为我一年没有刷卡就产生了200多块钱的年费，我很快就把年费还上了。我现在去贷款，
>
> H:　刘女士你这个关键是跟银行要合同看一下，我们要确定当时在办这张卡的时候银行或者联名方有没有明确的告诉你如果一年不刷卡就要有200块钱的年费。如果有告知的话，我们消费者也是有一定责任的。最后说我有4个月的利息记录说不可以给我贷款。我认为这个不应该只是给我短信提醒，影响我现在贷款不合理。
>
> C:　当时是有合同的，只要签个名就可以了。
>
> C:　/…/ I had a credit card with the Bank of China. I didn't use the card after a while because I did not consume regularly. The bank texted me alerting that there was an annual fee. I verified that. It was a 200 RMB annual fee because I hadn't used the card for a year. Then, I paid the annual fee. Now I applied for a loan but was rejected due to a balance due of four months accrued interest. I think the bank should not just send me a text alert. It affected my loan application.
>
> 　/…/
>
> H:　Ms Liu, the key to your problem is you need to ask for the contract from the bank. We need to be certain whether the bank or the joint party had told you explicitly that there would be a 200 RMB annual fee if you did not use the card for a year. If they had, we consumers were also responsible to some extent.
>
> C:　There was a contract. I only needed to sign.

In (12), the caller complains that her credit card is charged a 200 RMB annual fee because she has not used it for a year. Later, her loan application is denied due to this debt. The host advises her to confirm whether there is any reference to an annual fee in the contract. Hutchby (1995: 221) maintains that offering advice 'involves a speaker assuming some deficit in the knowledge state of a recipient', which 'assumes or establishes an asymmetry between the participants'. As such, the host's advice could be considered a face-threatening act because it challenges the hearer's identity as a competent and autonomous social actor (Goldsmith and MacGeorge 2000). The host's advice to check the terms in the contract could even be taken as a reproach of the caller's carelessness for not reading the contract carefully. Nevertheless, as indicated by the caller's response in (12), the caller has not interpreted the host's advice as a face-threatening act. On the contrary, the caller likely interprets the host's advice as a sign of solidarity, reflecting Hinkel's (1997) stance that in many cultures, such as Chinese, Japanese, Korean and Indonesian cultures, offering advice could be a rapport-building strategy.

C. Interrupting a speaker

The host often asserts his/her position of authority in the programme by interrupting the special guest or the responsible party when he/she is dissatisfied with an answer. Consider (13):

(13)

G: /…/在办理信用卡的过程中履行的叫三亲见原则，第一叫亲见本人，第二叫亲见原件#

H: #这些刚才丁局长已经给我们讲过了，您不必重复。我们想听的是发生在两地中行这个客户被冒名办卡的事情。

G: 呃。刚才主持人讲的两地，我个人认为核心就是她这个身份证的丢失。/…/一个呢核实是否是本人，第二个呢核实他以往的信用报告，是否具备办卡的条件#

H: #对不起，我打断一下。我个人的理解是这样的，我同意您的一点，确实是大家把身份证遗失了才有后来的。但是似乎今天想跟您说的并不是客户的身份证是怎么遗失的，遗失的对不对，而是我们遗失之后难道就能够在中行被人随随便便办信用卡吗？

G: /…/ In the process of credit card processing, three witness principles have to be fulfilled. The first is called 'witness the person'; the second 'witness the original'#

H: # Director Ding has already told us these. You don't need to repeat. What we want to hear is the issue that happened in the Bank of China in the two cities, where the clients' names were used to establish credit card accounts without permission.

G: Oh. The two cities that the host just talked about, I personally think the key issue is that she lost her identity card. /…/ The first is to verify the person's identity. The second is to check his credit report, to see if he meets the requirement #

H: # Sorry to interrupt. My personal understanding is this: I agree with one of your points. It's true that they lost their identity cards, and then the issue happened. But it seems what we want to discuss with you today is not how the clients lost their identity cards, whether it is right to lose them, but how can our names be used casually to establish credit card accounts in the Bank of China after we lost our identity cards?

In (13), the host interrupts a special guest (a director from the Bank of China) twice. First, the host interrupts and says the guest is talking about something that has already been discussed; thus, there is no point in repeating this information. The interruption is dispreferred, as indicated by 'Oh' in the guest's response. The guest then shifts his talking points by stressing the problem that the host has introduced. However, the host interrupts him again. This time, the host explicitly reproaches the guest, although the direct target is the Bank of China, the institution that the special guest represents.

Interrupting is face threatening for both parties. For the interruptee, his/her positive face (Brown and Levinson 1987) or sociality rights to finish his/her point (Spencer-Oatey 2005, 2008) are harmed. For the interrupter, he/she is altercasted negatively as a rude person (Tracy and Robles 2013: 134). However, the host deploys interruption strategically because the guest's answer does not solve the complaint. Although the host might be assessed as impolite for interrupting the guest, he strategically interrupts and criticises the guest (who represents the institution at which the complaint is targeted) to establish a rapport with the caller. The double role of impoliteness is also noted in Garcés-Conejos Blitvich's (2009, 2010) analysis of the host's identity construction in the American news media. Garcés-Conejos Blitvich (2009: 286) argues that, on the one hand, impoliteness could be a negative identity practice for the host, whereas, on the other hand, impoliteness towards a particular addressee could be used as a strong rapport-building device with a target audience that embodies different values from those of the addressee.

D. Requesting future contact

The host also shows his authoritative role by requesting that the special guest responsible take further action in contacting the caller after the programme, as shown in (14).

(14)

H: 节目以后，我们主动联系一下这位听众。

G: 我回头跟你联系一下，具体协调解决问题。

H: After the programme, we take the initiative to contact the audience.

G: I will contact you afterwards to coordinate specifically to solve the problem.

In the example above, the host makes a very direct request of the special guest by uttering an imperative, 'we take the initiative to contact the audience'. Although the first-person plural pronoun '我们' ('we') used in (14) sounds more polite than the second-person pronoun '你' or '你们' ('you'), it refers only to the special guest or his department. In addition, the host uses an imperative to make his request. According to Blum Kulka et al. (1989), the imperative is 'mood derivable', which is the most direct strategy for realising a request. Therefore, the host's request may be perceived as impolite in this situation. However, as previously discussed, the host could strategically employ being seen as impolite to construct an authoritative host identity, but strengthen the rapport with the caller at the same time.

A media propagandist

Apart from a caring helper, a responsible helper and an authoritative host, the host also constructs an identity as a media propagandist using various strategies, such as commenting on the programme and making earnest warnings.

A. Commenting on the programme's contribution

When the special guests and the host finish solving callers' problems, the host sometimes explicitly comments on the programme's contribution. This strategy only occurs when the host receives and handles calls with special guests. Because episodes with special guests normally focus on particular aspects of public service, it is easy for the host to summarise the episode. In addition, because special guests are present, the host speaks highly of the episode to acknowledge the guests' positive qualities (Spencer-Oatey 2005, 2008) as experts with extensive knowledge of the issue under discussion. Therefore, the strategy is face enhancing to the special guests. For example:

(15)

H: 今天提到的这些问题，收音机前没有打进电话的很多朋友非常关心，因为很多的情况不是个案，涉及到房产交易的问题，很多人都会遇到，我们希望大家认真听节目，这里面会学到很多关于税收的知识。

H: The problems we talked about today are the concern of many friends in front of radio but with no chance to call, as many problems are not individual cases. They involve the housing trade problem, which many people will encounter. We hope that everybody listens to the programme carefully. You can gain a lot of tax knowledge from it.

In (15), the host maintains that the problems discussed in that episode are the concern of many in the audience, and they could gain considerable knowledge by listening to the programme. It is worth noting that the host does not use any hedge to soften his/her claim. Giving such a high appraisal to one's programme appears to be against the Modesty Maxim (Leech 1983) and the Maxim of

Self-denigration (Gu 1990). However, by commenting on the programme, the host does not address himself to the previous caller but to the entire audience. The use of '我们' ('we') in (15) demonstrates the host's categorisation of his institutional role. Therefore, the host's self-promotion, while enhancing the positive face of the special guest, intends to get the entire audience to listen to the programme and to encourage listeners to call, thus fulfilling his identity as a member of a media institution.

B. Making earnest warnings

As a representative of a state-owned radio station, a host must do more than simply speak highly of his/her programme. It appears that the host is aware of this requirement. Because the programme aims to reach a larger audience than those phoning in, the host chooses to highlight relevant policies and to provide earnest warnings against potential missteps when commenting on the issue at hand, as illustrated in the following example.

(16)

> H: 我们借这个多说两句。正好是给大家做一个普及。是不是我们买车之前可能先要了解一下这个车在征收的时候最低计税价格是多少。你知道了之后就不用在开发票的时候再动那些歪脑筋了。

> H: <u>We</u> say a little bit more regarding this. It happens to be disseminated to <u>everybody</u>. <u>We</u> probably need to know the minimum tax rate for the car before we buy it. After <u>you</u> know this, you don't need to use a crooked head when you ask for the invoice.

In (16), the host highlights the necessity of checking about the minimum tax rate before purchasing a car. He warns the audience not to cheat on taxes. The host's use of personal pronouns is worth noting. The pronoun is a form of deixis. Its referent therefore depends heavily on the context and can thus vary widely. De Fina (2003: 52) notes that 'the investigation of the use of pronouns as a window into the analysis of identity has a long-standing tradition in linguistics'. The first '我们' ('we') in '*we* say a little bit more' refers to the host's institutional role, as discussed in the previous section. '大家' ('everybody') is used to explicitly address the audience, not just the caller. The second '我们' ('we') might have referred to anyone buying a car. In contrast, when the host warns against illegal action via tax evasion, he uses the second-person singular '你' ('you'), thus distancing him/herself and other law-biding listeners and singling out those who want to 'use a crooked head'. This distinctive pronoun use indicates the host's institutional role as a media propagandist who preaches to his/her audience.

A public authority

The host also plays the role of a public authority through his/her explicit affiliation with special guests. This strategy is employed only when the special guests are sitting on a panel during the programme. Consider the following examples.

(17)

G:	不同的行业，不同的规模，包括从事不同的领域，有一些不同的政策。
H:	其实我们给他定的一些标准已经非常的详细了。
G:	For different industries, different scales, including different fields, there are different policies.
H:	Actually, some standards <u>we</u> have made for him are already very clear.

(18)

H:	我们张局长就这个问题的表态是非常明确的，在需要必要的情况下<u>我们马上就去做</u>。
H:	<u>Our Director Zhang</u> stated very clearly his position on this issue. <u>We will do it right away</u> under necessary circumstances.

As the examples above show, after the special guests from official public service departments explain the situation, the host sometimes speaks positively of the guests' explanations (as in (17)) or compliments the guests (as in (18)). In these examples, the host employs '我们' ('we') and '我们张局长' ('our Director Zhang') to conflate the special guest and him/herself, thus constructing an identity as part of a public authority. This conflation, which is a token of promoting positive face, is also indicated by the changing footing (Goffman 1979) in (18), when the host repeats the director's words, '我们马上就去做' ('We will do it right away').

Conclusion

The aim of the present study has been to examine the host's identity construction, as well as its politeness implications, in handling public service complaints on a Chinese radio-mediated call-in programme. The study investigates the linguistic strategies employed to contribute to identity construction through a bottom-up analysis of eight episodes of the programme. The analysis has revealed five partly overlapping local identity categories: caring helper, responsible helper, authoritative host, media propagandist and public authority.

These constructed identities are necessary and relevant to the programme. As the host of a radio call-in programme devoted to handling public complaints, he/she should first demonstrate his/her compassion regarding the caller's problem (constructing the caring helper identity); he/she should also have a sense of responsibility (constructing the responsible helper identity) and exercise his/her institutional power (constructing the authoritative host identity). In addition, because the programme is broadcast by a state-owned radio station, the host must consider the wider social context and perform his/her role as part of a propaganda institution (constructing the media propagandist identity). Finally, when special guests from public service departments are present, the host must use strategies, such as the conflation of first-person pronouns, to show his/her proximity to the official leaders and to seek their help and collaboration (constructing the public authority identity).

The present study has shown that, on the one hand, negotiating identities influences the host's choices of linguistic choices, including (im)politeness. On the other hand, the use of (im)politeness is a linguistic index for the host's identity construction. (Im)politeness and identity construction are 'inextricably linked' (Garcés-Conejos Blitvich 2009: 295). In addition, the host's construction of identities is also influenced by factors such as the programme's format (with or without special guests), the programme's institutional role, and the programme's larger audience.

It needs to be admitted that this study only examines eight episodes of a radio call-in programme in a Chinese province. The findings obtained and conclusions drawn are at best tentative. Indeed, the study is not designed to exhaustively analyse the identities constructed and linguistic strategies employed in Chinese radio call-in programmes. Further research involving a sample with more programmes in different areas would be undoubtedly required if any attempt is to be made to achieve more generalisable results.

Appendix: Transcription symbols

H: the speaker is the host
C: the speaker is the caller
G: the speaker is the guest
bbb#
bbb interruption
<> additional comments
/.../ speech not included in the example to save space
<u>underlining</u> to highlight a feature of interest

References

Blum-Kulka, S., House, J. and Kasper, G. (eds) (1989) *Cross-cultural Pragmatics: Requests and Apologies*. Norwood, NJ: Ablex.

Boxer, D. (2010) Complaints: How to gripe and establish rapport. In A. Martínez-Flor and E. Usó-Juan (eds) *Speech Act Performance: Theoretical, Empirical and Methodological Issues* 163–178. Amsterdam and Philadelphia: John Benjamins.

Bremer, K., Roberts, C., Vasseur, M.-T., Simonot, M. and Broeder, P. (1996) *Achieving Understanding: Discourse in Intercultural Encounters*. London: Longman.

Brown, P. and Levinson, S. C. (1987) *Politeness: Some Universals in Language Usage*. Cambridge: Cambridge University Press.

Bucholtz, M. and Hall, K. (2005) Identity and interaction: A sociocutural linguistic approach. *Discourse Studies* 7(4–5): 585–614. https://doi.org/10.1177/1461445605054407

Bücker, J. (2013) Position offerings in German radio phone-in talk shows. *Journal of Pragmatics* 45(1): 29–49. https://doi.org/10.1016/j.pragma.2012.10.007

Chen, Y. S., Chen, C. Y. D. and Chang, M. H. (2011) American and Chinese complaints: Strategy use from a cross-cultural perspective. *Intercultural Pragmatics* 8(2): 252–275. https://doi.org/10.1515/iprg.2011.012

De Fina, A. (2003) *Identity in Narrative: A Study of Immigrant Discourse*. Amsterdam: John Benjamins. https://doi.org/10.1075/sin.3

De Fina, A. (2007) Code-switching and the construction of ethnic identity in a community of practice. *Language in Society* 36: 371–392. https://doi.org/10.1017/S0047404507070182

De Fina, A., Schiffrin, D. and Bamberg, M. (2006) Introduction. In A. De Fina, D. Schiffrin and M. Bamberg (eds) *Discourse and Identity* 1–23. Cambridge: Cambridge University Press.

Dori-Hacohen, G. (2014) Spontaneous or controlled: Overall structural organization of political phone-ins in two countries and their relations to societal norms. *Journal of Pragmatics* 70: 1–15. https://doi.org/10.1016/j.pragma.2014.05.010

Du, J. S. (1995) Performance of face-threatening acts in Chinese: Complaining, giving bad news, and disagreeing. In G. Kasper (ed.) *Pragmatics of Chinese as Native and Target Language* 165–206. Honolulu: University of Hawai'i at Manoa.

Eelen, G. (2001) *A Critique of Politeness Theories*. Manchester: St. Jerome.

Fitzgerald, R. and Housley, W. (2002) Identity, categorization and sequential organization: The sequential and categorical flow of identity in a radio phone-in. *Discourse and Society* 13(5): 579–602. https://doi.org/10.1177/0957926502013005275

Gao, Y. (1995) "咨询员中心" 与 "来话者中心"：两种电话心理咨询模式的会话结构特点 ('Counsellor-centred' and 'Caller-centred': Conversation structures of two types of telephone counselling. 语言文字应用 (*Applied Linguistics*) 3: 100–105.

Garcés-Conejos Blitvich, P. (2009) Impoliteness and identity in the American news media: The 'Culture Wars'. *Journal of Politeness Research* 5: 273–303.

Garcés-Conejos Blitvich, P. (2010) A genre approach to the study of im-politeness. *International Review of Pragmatics* 2: 46–94. https://doi.org/10.1163/187731010X491747

Garcés-Conejos Blitvich, P. (2013) Face, identity and im/politeness. Looking backward, moving forward: From Goffman to practice theory. *Journal of Politeness Research* 9(1): 1–33. https://doi.org/10.1515/pr-2013-0001

Garcés-Conejos Blitvich, P., Bou-Franch, P. and Lorenzo-Dus, N. (2013) Identity and impoliteness: The expert in the talent show *Idol. Journal of Politeness Research* 9(1): 97–121. https://doi.org/10.1515/pr-2013-0005

Goffman, E. (1979) Footing. *Semiotica* 25: 1–29. https://doi.org/10.1515/semi.1979.25.1-2.1

Goldsmith, D. J. and MacGeorge, E. L. (2000) The impact of politeness and relationship on perceived quality of advice about a problem. *Human Communication Research* 26(2): 234–263. https://doi.org/10.1111/j.1468-2958.2000.tb00757.x

Gu, Y. (1990) Politeness phenomena in Modern Chinese. *Journal of Pragmatics* 14: 237–257. https://doi.org/10.1016/0378-2166(90)90082-O

Hall, K. and Bucholtz, M. (2013) Facing identity. *Journal of Politeness Research* 9(1): 123–132. https://doi.org/10.1515/pr-2013-0006

Halliday, M. (2002) *Linguistic Studies of Text and Discourse.* London: Continuum.

He, A. W. (1993) Exploring modality in institutional interactions: Cases from academic counselling encounters. *Text* 13: 503–528.

Heinemann, T. (2009) Participation and exclusion in third party complaints. *Journal of Pragmatics* 41: 2435–2451. https://doi.org/10.1016/j.pragma.2008.09.044

Heinemann, T. and Traverso, V. (2009) Complaining in interaction. *Journal of Pragmatics* 41: 2381–2384. https://doi.org/10.1016/j.pragma.2008.10.006

Hinkel, E. (1997) Appropriateness of advice: DCT and multiple choice data. *Applied Linguistics* 18(1): 1–26. https://doi.org/10.1093/applin/18.1.1

Holmes, J. (1984) Modifying illocutionary force. *Journal of Pragmatics* 8(3): 345–365. https://doi.org/10.1016/0378-2166(84)90028-6

Holmes, J., Marra, M. and Schnurr, S. (2008) Impoliteness and ethnicity: Māori and Pākehā discourse in New Zealand workplaces. *Journal of Politeness Research* 4(2): 193–220. https://doi.org/10.1515/JPLR.2008.010

Hutchby, I. (1995) Aspects of recipient design in expert advice-giving on call-in radio. *Discourse Processes* 19(2): 219–238. https://doi.org/10.1080/01638539509544915

Hutchby, I. (1996) Power in discourse: The case of arguments on a British talk radio show. *Discourse and Society* 7(4): 481–498. https://doi.org/10.1177/0957926596007004003

Hutchby, I. (1999) Frame attunement and footing in the organisation of talk radio openings. *Journal of Sociolinguistics* 3(1): 41–64. https://doi.org/10.1111/1467-9481.00062

Hutchby, I. (2006) *Media Talk: Conversation Analysis and the Study of Broadcasting.* New York: Open University Press.

Kádár, D. Z. and Haugh, M. (2013) *Understanding Politeness.* Cambridge: Cambridge University Press. https://doi.org/10.1017/CBO9781139382717

Kiesling, S. F. (2013) Constructing identity. In J. K. Chambers and N. Schilling (eds) *The Handbook of Language Variation and Change* (2nd edn) 448–467. Oxford: Wiley-Blackwell. https://doi.org/10.1002/9781118335598.ch21

Leech, G. (1983) *Principles of Pragmatics.* London: Longman.

Locher, M. A. (2008) Relational work, politeness and identity construction. In G. Antos, V. Eija and W. Tilo (eds) *Handbooks of Applied Linguistics 2: Interpersonal Communication* 509–540. Berlin and New York: Mouton de Gruyter.

Locher, M. A. and Hoffmann, S. (2005) The emergence of the identity of a fictional expert advice-giver in an American Internet advice column. *Text & Talk* 26(1): 69–106. https://doi.org/10.1515/TEXT.2006.004

Locher, M. A. and Watts, R. J. (2005) Politeness theory and relational work. *Journal of Politeness Research* 1(1): 9–33. https://doi.org/10.1515/jplr.2005.1.1.9

Locher, M. A. and Watts, R. J. (2008) Relation work and impoliteness: Negotiating norms of linguistic behaviour. In D. Bousfield and M. A. Locher (eds) *Impoliteness in Language: Studies on its Interplay with Power in Theory and Practice* 77–99. Berlin: Mouton de Gruyter.

Lorenzo-Dus, N. (2005) A rapport and impression management approach to public figures' performance of talk. *Journal of Pragmatics* 37: 611–631. https://doi.org/10.1016/j.pragma.2004.09.003

Migdadi, F., Badarneh, M. A. and Momani, K. (2012) Public complaints and complaint responses in calls to a Jordanian radio phone-in program. *Applied Linguistics* 33(3): 321–341. https://doi.org/10.1093/applin/ams011

Pomerantz, A. (1984) Agreeing and disagreeing with assessments: Some features of preferred/dispreferred turn shapes. In J. M. Atkinson and J. Heritage (eds) *Structures of Social Action: Studies in Conversation Analysis* 57–101. Cambridge: Cambridge University Press.

Reiter, R. M. (2005) Complaint calls to a caregiver service company: The case of *desahogo*. *Intercultural Pragmatics* 2/4: 481–514. https://doi.org/10.1515/iprg.2005.2.4.481

Schegloff, E. (1986) The routine as achievement. *Human Studies* 9(2–3): 111–151. https://doi.org/10.1007/BF00148124

Simon-Vanderbergen, A. M. (2007) Lay and expert voices in public participation programmes: A case of generic heterogeneity. *Journal of Pragmatics* 39: 1420–1435. https://doi.org/10.1016/j.pragma.2007.04.002

Spencer-Oatey, H. (2005) (Im)Politeness, face and perceptions of rapport: Unpackaging their bases and interrelationships. *Journal of Politeness Research* 1: 95–119. https://doi.org/10.1515/jplr.2005.1.1.95

Spencer-Oatey, H. (2007) Theories of identity and the analysis of face. *Journal of Pragmatics* 39(4): 639–656. https://doi.org/10.1016/j.pragma.2006.12.004

Spencer-Oatey, H. (2008) Face, (im)politeness and rapport. In H. Spencer-Oatey (ed.) *Culturally speaking: Culture, Communication and Politeness Theory* (2nd edn) 11–47. London: Continuum.

Tracy, K. and Robles, J. S. (2013) *Everyday Talk: Building and Reflecting Identities.* (2nd edn). New York and London: The Guilford Press.

Traverso, V. (2009) The dilemmas of third-party complaints in conversation between friends. *Journal of Pragmatics* 41: 2385–2399. https://doi.org/10.1016/j.pragma.2008.09.047

Watts, R. (2003) *Politeness.* Cambridge: Cambridge University Press. https://doi.org/10.1017/CBO9780511615184

Yuan, Z. and Chen, X. (2013) 语言顺应论视角下的语用身份建构研究——以医疗咨询会话为例 (A study of pragmatic identity construction from the perspective of linguistic adaptation theory – A case study of medical consultations). 外语教学与研究 (*Foreign Language Teaching and Research*) 45(4): 518–530.

CHAPTER 6

Relational acts and identity construction by Chinese celebrities on Weibo

Doreen Wu and Minfen Lin

Introduction

As the affordance of new media technologies in supporting interpersonal messaging capacities emerges, attention to the process of interaction and relational management on social media has become critical (Sashi 2012; Chambers 2013). Recent research on social media, also termed as Social Network Service Sites (henceforth, SNSs), has indicated that such SNSs have formed a new literary practice that reflects both traditional and new ways of constructing facework (see Davies 2012; Wu and Feng 2015; Zhao, Grasmuck and Marin 2008).

Weibo, a hybrid of Twitter and Facebook, is a popular microblogging service platform originating from China, and has become one of the leading SNSs in the Cultural China[1] region. It has been expanding since its launch in the first decade of the twenty-first century, and has been well utilised as a social platform by celebrities as well as other individuals to construct self-presentation and interpersonal interactions (Huang 2011; Mo andLeung 2015). As of March 2014, Weibo boasts 143.8 million monthly active users, of whom 66.6 million are daily active users.[2]

Nonetheless, linguistic studies on the interactional and politeness behaviour of Chinese on SNSs (e.g., He and Chen 2015) are few and far between. Therefore, this study attempts to identify the types of relational acts and facework that are used to build connectedness by reputable individuals with their followers on Sina Weibo. In the process, we will revisit the notions of 'face' and 'speech acts' in pragmatics, contributing to interactional linguistics in our study of social media language.

Theoretical background

Face and politeness theories

As Goffman (1967) points out, there is no such thing as faceless communication. It is widely acknowledged that face is a key and invaluable analytical concept for understanding the process of human interaction. It is beyond the aim of this study to review the great amount of work devoted to face and politeness, but we will focus on a number of notions and definitions that have formed the basis for further exploration in this study. Goffman (1967: 5) defines *face* as 'an image of self delineated in terms of approved social attributes' and states that all human interactions engage facework; i.e., people collaboratively protect and support each other's face in interaction. Further to Goffman (1955, 1967), Brown and Levinson (1987) point out that face is something that is emotionally invested, can be lost, maintained or enhanced, and must be constantly attended to in interaction. They define two universal types of face: positive face and negative face, with the former referring to a person's desire for approval and being appreciated by others, while the latter referring to a person's desire for autonomy of action. Positive face is thus aligned with affiliation motives, such as the need for affiliation, communion and positive regards, while negative face is aligned with disaffiliation motives, such as the desire for independence, freedom of action and freedom from imposition. A detailed mechanism for engaging facework with a list of possible linguistic features and strategies appealing to people's need for positive face and negative face is also provided by Brown and Levinson (1987).

Nonetheless, in recent re-examination of face theory, scholars such as Bargiela-Chiappini (2003) and Arundale (2006, 2010) point out that the account provided by Brown and Levinson (1987) is confined to an individual's wants, ignoring face as a relational and interactional phenomenon. They urge a return to Goffman and attention to the 'social self' rather than the 'individual self'. Unlike the 'individual self', the 'social self' is seen as a 'person', an individual inseparably entwined with the other individuals with whom she/he interacts (Arundale 2006: 200). Arundale (2010: 2085) states that face does not belong to a single individual and can only be achieved conjointly, in relation with others and is explained as participants' interpreting of relational connectedness or separateness. Thus, the appropriate unit of analysis in studying interpersonal communication should not be any single isolated utterance of the monadic individual, but we need to take the dyad as the minimum unit of analysis and explain communication as the conjoint outcome of the dyad.

Apart from the theories of face by the Western scholars, Chinese scholars such as Gu (1990) and Tsou and You (2007) have also postulated maxims for Chinese face and politeness behaviour. While Tsou and You (2007) emphasise the importance of modesty and respect in Chinese interactions, Gu (1990: 249) indicates the important variables of power and hierarchy governing the choice of politeness strategies in Chinese and postulates the maxim of self-denigration and other-elevation for Chinese terms of address. Nonetheless, Kádár and Pan (2013) have indicated that, with profound changes in contemporary Cultural China, many of these maxims of Chinese politeness have been transformed and varied; for example, the self-denigration/other-elevation principle for Chinese terms of address has collapsed and been replaced by a single, uniform and unisex term of address *tongzhi* ('comrade').

Recent studies of interaction on social media have started to pay attention to face and politeness behaviour and found that positive face and its related strategies are prevalent on Facebook, Weibo and Twitter (see Lillqvist and Louhiala-Salminen 2013; West and Trester 2013; Wu and Feng 2015; Wu and Li forthcoming). Different from the conceptualisation by Chinese scholars (e.g., Gu 1990; Tsou and You 2007) regarding face and politeness behaviour by Chinese in offline interactions, Wu and Li (forthcoming) point out that solidarity politeness rather than power politeness is largely performed on Chinese SNSs. Nonetheless, their study is only confined to the act of greeting performed by the brand corporations in China. No further elaboration has been provided on other types of relational acts performed by the Chinese on the SNSs.

Speech act theories

The notion of speech act was first proposed by Austin (1962) to refer to an utterance that has performative function in language and communication. Over the years, the term has been utilised to describe and understand the messages and their meanings in human interaction. Nonetheless, linguists differ on the means of analysing speech acts as well as their criteria of classifying the speech acts. Austin (1962) suggests that speech acts can be analysed at three levels: *a locutionary act* (the literal meaning of the utterance), *an illocutionary act* (the intention of the speaker of the utterance) and *a perlocutionary act* (the effect of the utterance on the hearer). Searle (1976) further refines Austin's idea of illocutionary act and classifies illocutionary speech acts in terms of *assertives, directives, commissives, expressives* and *declaratives*.

As new media technologies have emerged in the last decades, scholars have turned increasing attention to how the new tools of communication alter the exchanges of messages and meaning. The frameworks by Austin (1962) and Searle (1976) have thus been utilised in the research on computer-mediated communication. For example, Hassell, Beecham and Christensen (1996) compare speech acts in three media – email, face-to-face and telephone –and conclude that assertives are the most common speech act across all three modes of communication, while imperatives, commissives, expressives and declaratives are more common in email and telephone communication than in face-to-face contexts, and expressive are more common in email than in face-to-face communication. Concerning SNSs, Carr, Schrock and Dauterman (2012) examine the use of speech acts on Facebook status messages and find that the messages are mostly frequently constructed with expressive acts, followed by assertives. Also examining Facebook status updates, Ilyas and Khushi (2012) conclude with the frequency ranking of expressives, assertives, imperatives and commissives.

Nonetheless, as we can observe, while Austin and Searle orient towards the use of language for factual, truthful assertions to the affective and social functions of language, their definition and classification of speech acts is largely dependent on the 'individual self', not the 'social self', with insufficient attention given to the process of relational communication by the speaker with the hearer. This study serves to fill this knowledge gap.

Methodology

Research aims and questions

This study aims to identify the linguistic acts performed by Chinese celebrities on Sina Weibo that represent their 'social self', i.e., contributing to their relational management with their followers. Specifically, the research questions for this study are as follows:

1. What are the prevalent relational speech acts performed by Chinese celebrities on Sina Weibo?
2. How do these relational speech acts contribute to their construction of their social self?

Data collection and unit of analysis

The data were collected in a twelve-month period (June 2012 to June 2013) from six of the most influential verified public figures in Mainland China: three males and three females. The selection of these six public figures was based on the results of the Most Influence Ranking List (最具风云影响力榜) released by the Sina Weibo System in July 2013. The minimum criterion was that the celebrity Weibo users should have used Weibo and published their posts for at least one year, with a minimum of five entries in any single week, i.e., at least twenty entries in a single month. This was to ensure that the account examined was not any fake computer-controlled account (僵尸账户). In accordance with the criterion, the celebrity Weibo users selected for the present study had used Weibo for a mean of 24.4 months (SD = 22.3; ranging from 13 to 64 months). More detailed personal information of the six selected public figures is shown in Table 6.1.

Table 6.1. Profile information of six selected public figures on Sina Weibo

Nickname	Gender	Area of residence	Verified identity statement	Joined Weibo
Ms Yao	Female	Beijing, PRC	Actress	28 August 2009
Ms Zhao	Female	Beijing, PRC	Actress	28 October 2009
Mr Wang	Male	Taipei, Taiwan	Singer	16 August 2010
Mr Chen	Male	Chongqing, PRC	Actor	13 November 2009
Mr He	Male	Beijing, PRC	TV anchor	28 August 2009
Ms Xie	Female	Beijing, PRC	TV anchor	28 August 2009

The most popular posts, i.e., the posts by these six celebrities that received the highest number of likes and responses, were selected for the analysis. Consequently, a total of 4,012 posts were collected, which contain a total number of 11,323 utterances. The unit of analysis is each utterance in each post, with the whole tweet/post as the context for interpreting the relevant speech act(s).

Data analysis

Facework for this study is defined as the cluster of speech acts as well as their discursive features that the reputable individuals use to build relational bonds with their followers on Sina Weibo. It is similar to what Wu and Feng (2015) have indicated as 'solidarity politeness' and to what Arundale (2010) has defined as face strategies contributing to 'relational connectedness'.

While reference to the framework of Speech Act Taxonomy by Searle (1976) will be made, the interpreting of speech acts in this study will not be conducted according to the models by Austin and Searle because they are not relation-oriented. Rather, the speech acts will be classified in terms of how they serve to contribute to the construction of relational identity by the celebrities. In the present study, each utterance in the collected tweets by celebrities will be examined at two levels: 1) the semantic level, in which we look into the meaning of the words in the tweets; 2) the overall intention of the act, i.e., what relational acts the celebrity users of social media are trying to accomplish with the utterance within the context of the post.

As we have observed, sometimes the relational acts are quite manifest and obvious, as the utterances directly present the information or the intent of the Sina Weibo users. But there are other times when the meaning of a certain utterance is not explicitly expressed but is conveyed via implications and connotations; i.e., the relational acts have to be inferred from the context of the utterance. Further discussion and illustration of these relational acts are presented in the following section of analysis.

Analysis of the data

Table 6.2 presents the types of relational acts we have located as used by the celebrity figures from the present sample, with operational criteria and illustrations given for each identified relational act.

Table 6.2. Types of relational acts performed by the celebrities on Sina Weibo

Relational acts	Definitions	Illustrations
Birthday greeting	Celebrities' act of greeting or expressing birthday wishes to others on Sina Weibo.	生日快乐！青春永在！ 'Happy Birthday! Stay young as you are!'
Congratulating	Celebrities' act of telling the other users how happy or proud they are of the others' achievements.	恭喜啊！ 'Congratulations!'
Daily greeting	Celebrities' act of conveying daily greeting or wishes to the other users.	早上好，神经病的一天开始了！ 'Morning, a new day of "psycho" begins!'
Festival greeting	Celebrities' act of conveying good wishes on a festival event	端午节快乐！ 'Happy Dragon Boat Festival!'
Fierce directives; Explicit directives	Celebrities' act of expressing a request directly, explicitly, and/or forcefully to the other users	請安靜，(錄音中) 'Please be quiet, (recording on air)'
Modest directives; Indirect directives	Celebrities' act of expressing a request modestly or indirectly to the other users	敬请期待呀 'Please stay tuned'
Promising	Celebrities' act of expressing to the other users a commitment to do or not to do something	香港见 'See you in Hong Kong'
Promoting assets	Celebrities' act of promoting their own as well as other relevant works and activities	工艺与艺术完美结合！ 'The perfect combination of technology and art'

Self-deprecating	Celebrities' act of critiquing or criticising themselves in front of other users	居然看到有人提问姚明，郭敬明，何炅躺在地上能不能组成个三角形！更气！因为我居然还很忐忑地算了一下！ 'When I saw a question regarding whether the three persons, Yao Ming, Guo Jingming, and He Jiong lying on the floor can form a triangle, I just responded with an estimation! How stupid I am!'
Sharing information	Celebrities' act of presenting facts, beliefs, and/or personal stories to other users	会自嘲但不能自贱，要自信但不要骄傲。 'You can deprecate self verbally, but never depreciate your self-esteem; You can be self-confident, but never be arrogant.'
Showing appreciation	Celebrities' act of conveying gratitude or appreciation to other users	大家都尽力了，谢谢！辛苦了！未来就靠有爱的观众了！感谢！ 'Everybody has made efforts. Thank you very much! And let's see how it is going with our lovely audience! Thank you !'
Showing concern	Celebrities' act of conveying concern or care to other users or for the general public	北京的好心朋友帮忙留意这位老人。 'Friends in Beijing please help when you see this senior citizen.'
Showing stance	Celebrities' act of expressing attitude or emotion towards people or different life issues	我喜欢这样的朋友。 'I like this type of friend.'

Table 6.3 presents a statistical summary of the relational acts we have identified as used by the celebrities on Sina Weibo. We can observe that, as taking place in daily offline interactions, the act of 'daily greeting' is performed regularly by the Chinese celebrities on Sina Weibo, constituting 876 out of a total of 12,285, 7.13% of the collected acts. In addition, relational acts of birthday or festival greetings are also regularly used.

Table 6.3. Distribution of speech acts by celebrities on Sina Weibo

Speech act*	Relational acts	No. of speech acts	% of speech acts
Assertives	Promoting assets (e.g., events, endorsed products, personal movies)	568	4.62
	Sharing information (e.g., life wisdom, personal stories)	2,762	22.48
Directives	Modest directives; Indirect directives	1,838	14.96
	Fierce directives; Explicit directives	348	2.83
Expressives	Birthday greeting	374	3.04
	Congratulating	183	1.48
	Daily greeting	876	7.13
	Festival greeting	407	3.31
	Self-deprecating	393	3.19
	Showing appreciation	964	7.84
	Showing concern	763	6.21
	Showing stance	2,434	19.81
Commissives	Promising	348	2.83
TOTAL		12,285	100

*Speech acts in this column are based on Searle's taxonomy.

The following example contains all such greeting acts.

(1)

早上好！哇？我怎么么睡醒了？ 虽然在北京但还是过美国时间。 祝各位童鞋六月快乐，儿童节快乐！

2013-6-1 02:46來自新浪微博

Morning! Wow? Why did I wake up? Though I am in Beijing, my time is still US time *Happy June to every* schoolmate (童鞋), *Happy Children's Day!*

June 1, 2013 from SinaWeibo.com

From Table 6.3, we can also observe that the most frequent relational act found from the present collection is 'sharing information', constituting 2,762 out of a total of 12,285, 22.48% of the collected acts. The celebrities frequently share their personal stories and life wisdom as well as various sorts of news about themselves and others with their peers or followers on Sina Weibo. An example of sharing information can be seen in (2).

(2)

温暖的声音，致青春 

◆◆

@伍洲彤

今天，我的新书「听话」终于出版了。它是你我20年的青春记念册，也是一本治愈情伤的语典，里面还有一张我特别为你录制的唱片。它适合放在枕边，会给你幻想的空间和内心的温暖。真心期待你打开它，犹如你我第一次见面⋯⋯

2013-6-24 10:51來自iPhone客户

Warm voice, to Youth

@Wu Zhoutong:

Today, my new book Ting Hua finally got published. It is a collection of 20 years of youth for you and me; it could also be used for healing hurt, with an album I have recorded for you. It is suitable to be placed by your pillow, for bedtime reading and imagination. Sincerely hope you can open it, just like the first encounter of you and me …

June 24, 2013, 10:51 from Weibo APP iPhone

Besides 'sharing information', 'showing stance' is another frequent relational act, constituting 2,434 out of a total of 12,285, 19.81% of the collected acts. Illustrations of this act can be seen in (3) and (4).

(3)

我真的，很不喜欢自拍！！！ 一个演员，真的需要这样么？ 早上好，神经病的一天开始了！

2013-6-29 10:06來自iPhone客户端

I really, really do not like selfie!!! As an actor, do you really need to do this? Good morning, a new day of a 'physo' begins!

June 29, 2013, 10:06 from Weibo APP iPhone

(4)

你是那么的合适，放在哪儿都合适，怎么扮都合适，和谁搭都合适！合适到常常让人忘了，你毕竟是个女人！非常地爱你啊！闪电般光彩夺目的女人！@贾玲生日快乐！

2013-4-29 00:09來自iPhone客户端

You can be fitted in any place: you can be fitted for any role in our TV show and perform well with anybody! You can be so fitted that often people forget that you are a woman after all! Love you very much! *Dazzling woman!* @ Jia Ling Happy birthday!

Apr 29, 2013 00:09 from Weibo APP iPhone

We can also observe that there can be more than one relational act expressed within an utterance. For example, the italicised utterances in (4) can be performing not only the act of 'showing stance' but also the act of 'showing appreciation'.

It merits our special attention that another frequent relational act by the celebrities on Sina Weibo is 'directives' and that the act of 'modest directives' is much more frequent than that of 'fierce directives', 14.96% versus 2.83%. This indicates that, while the Chinese celebrities on Weibo like to spread their impact by persuading people to their ideas and action plans, they show special care in managing their relations with their followers by presenting their directives in a modest or implicit manner. An example of this can be seen in the last utterance from (1): '真心期待你打开它，犹如你我第一次见面…' ('Sincerely hope you can open it, just like the first encounter between you and me …'). Further illustrations for a modest directive can be seen in (5):

(5)

以后喝前尽量把手机藏起来 😷😷😷 好咯，好好学习才是硬道理，发张在米国做英语作业的学生照片还可以吧 😨 有没有同学给我推荐很快记单词的方法呀 😐

2013-6-30 08:05來自iPhone客户端

I would try to hide my cell phone before drinking 😷😷😷OK, should study hard, how about posting a picture of doing home assignments in US? 😨 *is there any* <u>classmate</u> *who can recommend shortcut of memorising vocabularies?* 😐

June 30, 2013 from Weibo APP of iPhone

Other relatively frequently used relational acts by the celebrities on Sina Weibo include 'showing appreciation' (7.84%), 'showing concern' (6.21%) and 'promoting assets' (4.62%). Further illustration of 'showing appreciation' can be seen in (6).

(6)

耶！*谢谢难民署对过去三年的认可！以后带小土豆一起去探访难民！*

@华谊姚晨工作室

今天是世界难民日，联合国难民署总部发来消息，感谢@姚晨为提高公众对难民问题的认识所做出的努力，鉴于她在过去三年中持之以恒的工作态度，对难民发自内心的真诚关怀，和她杰出的人道主义精神，以及对推动难民事业做出的努力和贡献，正式升任姚晨为联合国难民署中国亲善大使！！

2013-6-20 10:26來自iPhone客户端

Ye! *Thank the Refugee Agency for recognition of the past three years' work!* Can bring Xiao Tudou to visit the refugees in the future!

@from the office of Yao Chen

Today is the international day for the refugees! The UN Refugee Agency has announced that they are grateful to Yao Chen for her efforts in getting the public in recognising the issues and phenomena of the refugees. In recognition of her persistent attitude, sincere care for humanity, and contribution to the work related to refugees, the United Nations has decided to promote her to be the China Ambassador for the UN Refugee Agency!!

June 20, 2013 10:26 from Weibo APP iPhone

In (6), we can also observe the act of 'promoting assets', as it releases the information about Ms Yao in achieving the recognition of the United Nations with the award of 'China Ambassador for the UN Refugee Agency'. A further example of the act of 'showing appreciation' can also be seen in (7).

(7)

超级有爱的青春团队！你们为了电影充分展示了自己的魅力才华，以及对@致我们终将逝去的青春movie的热爱！大家都尽力了，谢谢！辛苦了！未来就靠有爱的观众了！感谢！

2013-4-29 20:31來自iPhone客户端

Super lovely young team! You demonstrate your talents and your love for our movie. So young! Everybody has made efforts, thank you very much! And let's see how it goes with our audience! Thank you!

Apr 29, 2013 20:31 from Weibo APP iPhone

In (7), Ms Zhao expresses her gratitude to her young team for their contribution to her new movie.

Last but not least, 'showing concern' is also a relatively frequently used relational act performed by the celebrities on Sina Weibo. See (8) for a further illustration.

(8)

考完了吧？觉补过来了吧？撒丫子了吧？都注意安全别疯过头啊！结伴出门的话互相照应点啊！

(23719)|轉發(9585)|收藏|評論(14827)2013-6-10 08:46來自iPhone客户端

So exams finished? Relaxed and made up sleep? Must have been having fun and crazy? Be safe. Do not be over crazy! Take care of each other when you are outside together!

June 10, 2013 08:46 from Weibo APP iPhone

In (8), Mr He reminds his student fans to take care of themselves and their friends and not to exhaust themselves when having fun.

Discussion

Work from social psychology (e.g., Forgas and Williams 2002) has indicated that our positive self-concept is often derived from the social self. One important aspect of the social self is 'including the other in the self' (Crisp and Turner 2014: 208). The greater the inclusion of the other in the self, the greater the satisfaction, commitment and investment in the relationship. We can infer that Chinese celebrities have invested much of their time and space on Sina Weibo in performing relational acts with their followers, and consequently, they can derive stronger and more positive self-concept. Furthermore, being in a collectivism-oriented Chinese culture, the followers as well as the celebrities have demonstrated a higher sense of social self with the 'collective self', i.e., attending more to group memberships and their relationships with one another.

The conclusion above can be supported not only via the amount of relational acts being performed, but also via the large amount of solidarity-oriented linguistic features used on Sina Weibo, e.g., frequent use of personal pronouns, intimate address forms, hedging, affective expressions or emoticons like 🙂😄😆❤ in (6), etc. These discursive features help to define the acts performed by the celebrities as relational by nature.

Terms of address, according to Tracy (2002), can show the relational identity constructed by the speaker in communication, and the choice of appropriate terms of address shows his or her ability to understand and to apply the rule of politeness during communication. In discussing Chinese politeness, Gu (1990) has indicated the important consideration of power and hierarchy in the choice of terms of address. Nonetheless, it is worth noting that the rules of power and hierarchy he discussed do not seem to be quite applicable but are largely overcome by the rules of building solidarity on Weibo: as our data reveal, frequent use of intimate address forms have been used among parties of unequal power status on Sina Weibo, such as '童鞋' ('schoolmate') (as in (1)), '童鞋们' ('schoolmates'), '亲爱的' ('dear'), '亲' ('dear'/'darling'), '亲们' ('my darlings'), '我亲爱的们' ('my darlings'), '各位亲' ('dear all', lit. 'dear every darling'), '小伙伴们' ('my buddies'), and '小盆友们' ('my little friends').

Furthermore, to appear cute, some non-standard orthography is deliberately used by the celebrities in many of these terms of address, e.g., the deviant form '盆友们' ('friends') is used instead of the standard form '朋友们', '小盆友' ('little friends') used instead of the standard form '小朋友', '童鞋' ('schoolmate') instead of '同学', and '筒子' ('pipe') used to replace the unisex term of address '同志' ('comrade'; 筒子 and 同志 are homophones in Chinese). It is also worth noting that, in addressing people in more powerful positions, non-standard orthography is also used to show intimacy or solidarity, e.g., '湿兄' ('wet brother') as an intimate form to address a senior male friend of which the original standard form should be '師兄' ('master brother'). Likewise, '大湿' ('big wet') is used instead of '大師' ('big master').

Arundale (2006) points out that a relational account of the social self and of face implies that the much-used distinction between 'self-face' and 'other face' is problematic. With this relational view, self and other are dialectically linked because both persons link the other to the self, mutually defining one another in their communication. The classification of relational acts by the Chinese celebrities on Sina Weibo has lent further support to the argument that face is achieved conjointly, in relation with others and does not belong to a single individual (see also Arundale 2010: 2085).

Conclusion

Given that Weibo, like any of the other types of SNSs, functions as an interpersonal medium even though the medium is embedded in the mass media of the Internet, the present study has attempted to investigate what relational acts and facework Chinese celebrities have constructed on SinaWeibo towards their multiple audiences, both known and unknown. Different from the existing studies on speech acts on Facebook (e.g., Carr et al. 2012; Ilyas and Khushi 2012) which rely heavily on the criteria and taxonomy of Searle (1976), the present study adopts a relational perspective and re-defines speech acts in terms of how they contribute to the 'social self' in the interaction.

It is found that the cluster of relational acts performed by Chinese celebrities on Sina Weibo include daily and festive greetings, congratulating, directives, promising, promoting assets, sharing information, showing stance, showing appreciation, showing concern, and self-deprecating, etc. Furthermore, the characteristic linguistic features used by the celebrities represent an informal and sometimes non-standard style, a style popular among Chinese netizens (see also Chen 2008). It is worthy of special notice that the celebrities on Weibo no longer adhere to the Chinese traditions of face and politeness or to the principles of power and hierarchy in interaction; instead, they focus primarily on building affiliation and solidarity politeness with their followers on Weibo, adhering to the informal and sometimes non-standard style of Chinese writing.

In emphasising the communication-immanent side of facework as relational and interactional achievement, Arundale (2006) points out that 'all conversational action, topic managing and turn-taking is … conjointly co-constituted' (2006: 196) and that 'in the moment of talk, participants draw opportunistically on the normative resources of their language to interactionally achieve not only conventional, but also non-conventional face interpretings' (2006: 208).

While the present study has attempted a relational perspective in defining and classifying speech acts performed by Chinese celebrities on Sina Weibo, the interpreting of relational acts has been based primarily on our analysis without access to the exchanges between the celebrities and their followers. Such analysis is only preliminary, revealing the conventional but not the unconventional interpretings which can take place between the participants in interaction. Furthermore, any potential impoliteness or other conflict-driven speech acts on Chinese social media have not been examined. Future study in this field can be conducted so as to further reveal the interactional process of facework achievement and the multi-layered characteristics of face on Chinese social media.

Notes

1. The notion 'Cultural China' has been defined in various ways. For this chapter, it refers to the Chinese communities who use the Chinese language regularly for daily communication, including not only those living in mainland China, but also in Hong Kong, Macao, Taiwan, Singapore and other overseas Chinese diasporas.
2. Retrieved from Baidu, introduction to Sina Weibo, http://baike.baidu.com/view/2762127.htm

Acknowledgment

This work was supported by RGC Directly Allocated Research Grant, Hong Kong (#4-ZZFB).

References

Arundale, R. B. (2006) Face as relational and interactional: A communication framework for research on face, facework and politeness. *Journal of Politeness Research* 2: 193–216. https://doi.org/10.1515/PR.2006.011

Arundale, R. B. (2010) Constituting face in conversation: Face, facework, and interactional achievement. *Journal of Pragmatics* 42: 2078–2105. https://doi.org/10.1016/j.pragma.2009.12.021

Austin, J. L. (1962) *How to Do Things with Words* (2nd edn). Oxford: Clarendon Press.

Bargiela-Chiappini, F. (2003) Face and politeness: New (insights) for old (concepts). *Journal of Pragmatics* 35(10/11): 1453–1469. https://doi.org/10.1016/S0378-2166(02)00173-X

Brown, P. and Levinson, S. C. (1987) *Politeness: Some Universals in Language Usage.* Cambridge: Cambridge University Press.

Carr, C. T., Schrock, D. B. and Dauterman, P. (2012) Speech acts within Facebook status messages. *Journal of Language and Social Psychology* 31(2): 176–196. https://doi.org/10.1177/0261927X12438535

Chambers, D. (2013) *Social Media and Personal Relationships: Online Intimacies and Networked Friendship.* Basingstoke: Palgrave Macmillan. https://doi.org/10.1057/9781137314444

Chen, J. (2008) "火星文"："火星文"：网络语言的新发展 ('Language from Mars': The new development of Netspeak). 修辞学习 (*Rhetorical Studies*) 4: 41–46.

Crisp, R. J. and Turner, R. N. (2014) *Essential Social Psychology*. London: Sage.

Davies, J. (2012). Facework on Facebook as a new literacy practice. *Computers and Education* 59: 19–29. https://doi.org/10.1016/j.compedu.2011.11.007

Forgas, J. P. and Williams, K. D. (eds) (2002) *The Social Self: Cognitive, Interpersonal, and Intergroup Perspectives*. New York: Psychology Press.

Goffman, E. (1955) On facework: An analysis of ritual elements in social interaction. *Psychiatry* 18: 213–231. https://doi.org/10.1080/00332747.1955.11023008

Goffman, E. (1967) *Interaction Ritual: Essays on Face-to-Face Behaviour*. New York: Pantheon Books.

Gu, Y. (1990) Politeness Phenomena in Modern Chinese. *Journal of Pragmatics* 14(2): 237–257. https://doi.org/10.1016/0378-2166(90)90082-O

Kádár, D. Z. and Pan, Y. (2013) *Chinese Discourse and Interaction*. London: Equinox.

Hassell, L., Beecham, S. and Christensen, M. (1996) Indirect speech acts and their use in three channels of communication. *Communication Modeling – The Language/Action Perspective* 9: 1–14.

Huang, L. (2011) Presenting ideal self: A study of the impact of narcissism of uses and gratification of microblog in Mainland China. MA thesis, Hong Kong Baptist University.

He, H. and Chen, X. (2015) 网店店主关系身份建构的语用研究 (The pragmatic study of the construction of the identities of the online business owners). 现代外语 (*Modern Foreign Languages*) 38(3): 347–356.

Ilyas, S. and Khushi, Q. (2012) Facebook status updates: A speech act analysis. *Academic Research International* 3(2): 500–507.

Lillqvist, E. and Louhiala-Salminen, L. (2013) Facing Facebook: Impression management strategies in company–consumer interactions. *Journal of Business and Technical Communication* 28(1): 3–30. https://doi.org/10.1177/1050651913502359

Mo, R. and Leung, L. (2015) Exploring the roles of narcissism, uses of, and gratifications from microblogs on affinity-seeking and social capital. *Asian Journal of Social Psychology* 18(2): 152–162. https://doi.org/10.1111/ajsp.12087

Sashi, C. M. (2012) Customer engagement, buyer–seller relationships, and social media. *Management Decision* 50(2): 253–272. https://doi.org/10.1108/00251741211203551

Searle, J. R. (1976) A classification of illocutionary acts. *Language in Society* 5(1): 1–23. https://doi.org/10.1017/S0047404500006837

Searle, J. R. (1979) *Expression and Meaning: Studies in the Theory of Speech Acts*. Cambridge: Cambridge University Press. https://doi.org/10.1017/CBO9780511609213

Tracy, K. (2002) *Everyday Talk: Building and Reflecting Identities*. New York: Guilford Press.

Tsou, B. K. and You, R. J. (2007) *Introduction to Sociolinguistics*. Taipei: Wunan Book Co.

West, L. and Trester, A. M. (2013) Facework on Facebook. In D. Tannen and A. M. Trester (eds) *Discourse 2.0: Language and New Media* 113–153. Washington, DC: Georgetown University Press.

Wu, D. and Feng, W. (2015) Pragmatist, evangelist, or sensualist? Emotional branding on Sina Weibo. In P. P. K. Ngand C. S. B. Ngai (eds) *Role of Language and Corporate Communication in Greater China* 225–239. Heidelberg: Springer. https://doi.org/10.1007/978-3-662-46881-4_12

Wu, D. and Li, C. (forthcoming) Emotional branding on social media: A cross-cultural discourse analysis of global brands on Twitter and Weibo. In A. Curtis and R. Sussex (eds) *Intercultural Communication in Asia: Education, Language and Values.* Heidelberg: Springer.

Zhao, S., Grasmuck, S. and Martin, J. (2008) Identity construction on Facebook: Digital empowerment in anchored relationships. *Computers in Human Behaviour* 24: 1816–1836. https://doi.org/10.1016/j.chb.2008.02.012

Experts' identity construction and rapport management in the Chinese context of PhD oral defences

Yongping Ran and Qian Chen

Introduction

Advice-giving, or suggestion making, abounds in daily and institutional interactions. As a face-threatening act (FTA; Brown and Levinson 1987), it has been extensively studied in different fields along various approaches, yielding rich literature (e.g., DeCapua and Dunham 1993; Heritage and Sefi 1992; Locher 2006; Martinez-Flor 2005; Vehviläinen 2001, 2009). Among others, some attention has been paid to advice-giving in the setting of educational counselling, where advising or supervising students is a core practice (Bresnahan 1992; Vehviläinen 2001, 2009). Yet, despite numerous studies, the issue of how identity construction in the course of advice-giving serves politeness purposes has seldom been explored.

Power, identity and social distance are essential constraining factors in speech acts of advice-giving and advice-seeking, and there is always an underlying asymmetry between the participants in academic contexts since specific institutional roles empower advisers to be professionals and authorities. Vehviläinen (2001: 373) holds that advice itself positions the participants asymmetrically, 'regardless of the ostensible role of advice in a particular situation, there are inescapable messages of authority, expertise and intimacy in advice' (DeCapua and Huber 1995: 128). Basically, there exists an assumption that the advice seeker or receiver is short of some professional knowledge, or is incapable in some respect. Thus, advice-giving is an activity embodying such asymmetrical relationships between the participants. As a result, the use of pragmatic strategies and linguistic forms is most likely to be influenced by such factors, and identity construction is closely interwoven with advice-giving patterns. While much research on institutional advice-giving has paid attention to the relation between language forms and identity construction (DeCapua and Huber 1995), the dynamic process of identity construction and its connection with politeness need further exploring.

This study aims to focus on advice-giving in PhD oral defences in Chinese universities and to explore how the supervisors construct identities in relation to the management of interpersonal rapport between the participants so as to shed light on the cultural and institutional practice of advice-giving in Chinese educational settings. Out of the naturally occurring data collected, typical instances of advice-giving are identified to show the relationship between identity construction and politeness. Firstly, the strategies of advice-giving that are reflected by linguistic structures are presented; secondly, the identities constructed by the supervisors in utilising those strategies are discussed. Finally, why the supervisors construct these identities dynamically is explored in relation to politeness.

Advice-giving in institutional contexts

The nature of advice

Longman Dictionary of Contemporary English (2014) defines advice as 'an opinion that you give someone about what they should do', and according to *Oxford Advanced Learner's English–Chinese Dictionary* (2009) it is an 'opinion given about what to do or how to behave'. Indeed, advice-giving is a type of directive speech act in nature and has often been explored within the speech-act framework (Searle 1969). Searle (1969: 70) contrasts advising with the speech act of request, stressing that 'advising you is not trying to get you to do something in the sense that requesting is, which is more likely telling you what is best for you'. Banerjee and Carrell (1988: 319) hold that suggesting is 'an utterance that the speaker intends the hearer to perceive as a directive to do something that will be to the hearer's benefit'. Although the speech act of suggesting would always benefit the advisee, it is still a kind of face-threatening behaviour. According to Martínez-Flor (2010: 258), 'the interlocutor who makes the suggestion somehow intrudes into the hearer's world through performing an act to get the latter to do something'. In a number of studies, the speech act of suggesting and advising are employed interchangeably, referring to the same speech act (Banerjee and Carrell 1988; Searle 1969). Following this practice, the present study will not differentiate between suggestion and advising, either.

In institutional interaction, advising is more likely to be considered as a problem-solving activity (Ren 2014: 49), in which the advice-giver offers an option about how to solve a particular problem and by doing so implies that the suggested course of action is beneficial to the advice-seeker (Locher 2006: 3).

Vehviläinen (2001: 373) also finds that 'advice contains a normative dimension, a recommendation towards a course of action that the advice giver prefers, and it is given with the expectation that the recipient will treat it as relevant, helpful, or newsworthy and accept it ... Therefore, advice-giving is a potentially problematic activity', and a similar viewpoint is restated in his later study (Vehviläinen 2009).

Goal orientation is a fundamental feature of institutional discourse (Sun 2013), where people construct identities to negotiate and maintain relationships in accomplishing institutional tasks. In the context of academic supervision or instruction, fixing problems during students' work on dissertations is an important stage. Advice-giving provides students with support and instruction so as to solve problems in their research. Naturally, problem fixing has become the focus of attention in some studies, while the 'process orientation', that is, the process of trial and error, is one of the main concerns in recent literature.

Studies on advice-giving in institutional contexts

A. Features of advice

Advice-giving in the institutional contexts of health care, medical service, radio counselling and online communication have been broadly explored. Heritage and Sefi (1992) study those initial visits of health visitors to first-time mothers, focusing on requesting, delivering and receiving advice in these visits. They find that advice can be given in three different ways. First, overt recommendations are employed, e.g., 'I would recommend giving her a bath everyday'; second, modal verbs of obligation are used, e.g., 'And I think you should involve your husband as much as possible'; third, less commonly factual generalisation is made, e.g., 'lots of mums do' (1992: 368–369). In general, health visitors 'deliver their advice explicitly, authoritatively and in so doing decide a fashion as to project their relative expertise on health and baby-management issues' (1992: 369). Basing her research questions and methodology on Heritage and Sefi's (1992) study, Leppänen (1998) explores the advice-rendering in interaction between Swedish district nurses and patients, and explicates the features of advice-giving in the context. She analyses the advice sequences and compares them with those in Heritage and Sefi (1992), finding that advice is delivered through imperative forms and modal verbs of obligation. Pilnick (1999, 2001) investigates the counselling given by pharmacists to patients or caregivers in a hospital in the UK, with the support of data consisting of 45 tape-recorded consultations. The 'approach to advice-giving' could be accomplished by a question, a statement, or dispensed with altogether (Pilnick 2001: 1939), which indicates that advice-giving is different from information-giving.

Some studies have examined the linguistic and discourse features of advice in radio programmes (DeCapua and Dunham 1993; Hudson 1990; Hutchby 1995).

On the basis of three hours of talk broadcast on the *Robbie Vincent Show* from Radio London, Hutchby identifies a two-part format consisting of an answer to the caller's question and 'an auxiliary response in which subsidiary information or advice is conveyed' (1995: 223). The expert is thus 'both exhibiting his knowledgeability and "doing expertise", while at the same time exhibiting his sensitivity to the public context in which he is deploying that expertise' (1995: 228). Hutchby's study is helpful in understanding the authority of the advice-giver in public settings. Similarly, DeCapua and Dunham (1993) emphasise the public context of advice-giving. In their investigation of two American radio advice programmes, they find that the principal goals of the advice-giver are 'to help callers clarify their problems, to help them explore their options, and to offer direction, usually regarding some action to be taken in the future' (DeCapua and Dunham 1993: 519). Hudson (1990) examines the interactions of 23 different callers with an expert and authority figure in one Californian radio broadcast. His linguistic analysis of the advice suggests that it occurs in 'prototypical grammatical form for directive advice' which is 'the non-agent imperative of the form "*Go ahead and do it*" or perhaps just "*Do it*"' (1990: 285), and that it is softened by 'interpersonal markers' (1990: 286). In his study, recommendations and knowledge presentation are also regarded as advice-giving in this context.

Kouper (2010) depicts the features of advice in a computer-mediated context. Focusing on online peer advice, he demonstrates the ways in which participants solicit and give advice in an online community. For giving advice, four strategies are found: direct advice, hedged advice, indirect advice and description of personal experience. According to Kouper (2010: 17), advice takes on various roles in an online community, such as for establishing rapport, showing sympathy, providing information and warning of consequences. He finds that 'through personal examples, advice givers establish their authority and yet avoid responsibility and shift the agency of advice, because they do not explicitly tell advice seekers what to do'. This finding demonstrates that advice-givers construct their identity as an expert without creating a power imbalance.

The above studies about advice-giving are helpful for us to understand the speech act of advising in institutional contexts. However, how participants with authority and power adopt strategies to construct appropriate identities and, in so doing, lessen the possible face-threatening effects in academic practices needs to be examined more closely.

B. Advice in educational contexts

Some scholars have examined academic counselling through which advice is given by professionals with a higher-ranking social status than the advice-seekers (Bresnahan 1992; He 1993, 1994, 1995, 1996a, 1996b; He and Keating 1991; Vehviläinen 2001, 2009), and their work needs to be examined for its scholarly importance.

The contradictory roles that supervisors play in giving advice are fully discussed by Bresnahan (1992). He studies 14 advising interviews with respect to the advisor's conflictive roles and finds that advisors must constantly decide whether to take their role as student advocate or as institutional gatekeeper (Bresnahan 1992: 22). The gatekeeping style is more dynamic and intrusive, and gatekeeping can be manifested by:

> (a) invoking official rules and policies, (b) jumping-the-starting-gun tactics such as stating official positions before eliciting student premises, (c) 'stopping and frisking' (Erickson and Shultz 1982: 25), (d) advisor hyper explanation (a verbal overpowering move) which invokes positional authority, (e) using other detrimental conversational strategies which cause the student to lose face, (f) limited concession making from the outset of negotiation, (g) using positive and negative alter casting (statements suggesting a course of action that might have better been followed), and (h) distributive orientation.
>
> (Bresnahan 1992: 231)

Bresnahan's study concludes that the role of gatekeeper, fully embodying the supervisors' authority, power and higher status, is more frequently found when supervisors construct their identities in an academic counselling context. Similarly, Liu and Zhao (2007) claim that a teacher–student conference can be regarded as 'an unequal status encounter' in academic sessions, where the teacher with a higher status may serve as an authoritative figure in giving a suggestion. After exploring the process-oriented teaching practices of composition classes in America, they find that suggestions are regularly provided in an academic context, and the linguistic forms for suggestions are constrained by different relationships, power and distance between the interlocutors. This study offers a clear clue about the role of unequal power relationships in professional settings.

In contrast, He (1993, 1994, 1995, 1996a, 1996b) shows that academic supervisors are less authoritative than we assume because they avoid answering two kinds of questions: 'those concerning their personal opinions and judgements and those which may not warrant a definite answer' (He 1994: 313). Focusing on the conflicts between the expectations that students should be able to get the advice they need and the supervisors' official directives not to give personal opinions so that students can make up their own minds, her study shows that counsellors may not always establish their roles as experts as we presume; rather, they adapt their roles to different situations.

On the basis of the data collected from adult education centres and academic supervision, Vehviläinen (2001) explores the advice-giving in educational settings more comprehensively and identifies two types of counselling patterns. In Type 1, the counsellor asks questions to elicit the student's opinion, then the student responds by confirming or displaying the elicited opinion; in the end the counsellor gives advice that is grounded in the view established in the prior turns. In Type 2, the counsellor initiates the activity by eliciting the student's ideas or plans regarding a particular task, then the student responds by describing these plans, ideas and intentions; finally, the counsellor gives advice by commenting on and evaluating the student's response. The patterns reveal that the roles of supervisors are multiple, the most important ones of which are as experts and helpers. It is evident that identity construction seems more complex in Vehviläinen's model. In addition, based on the videotaped data of thesis supervision in a Finnish university, Vehviläinen (2009) examines teachers' strategic uses of questions in advice-giving sequences and concludes that the question-prefaced advice is linked to the teacher's expert role as the commentator, critic and quality-checker of the student's work.

To sum up, most studies on advice-giving in educational settings have investigated the sequential characteristics of the speech act of advising, its linguistic realisations and discourse patterns, as well as the authoritative roles established by the advisor. However, considering that advice-giving is a face-threatening act, face theory and politeness principles have not been adequately used to account for such acts; second, those studies have paid primary attention to detailed description of advising sequences and linguistic strategies, thus calling for alternative theoretical explanations.

Although the dynamism of advice-giving has been partly explored (Ren 2014), the interplay between identity construction and politeness in the situated context is yet to be highlighted. Hence, this study aims to explore the dynamic relationship between identity construction and politeness in the performance of the speech act of advice-giving in PhD oral defences from the perspective of rapport-management theory (Spencer-Oatey 2000, 2002, 2005, 2008).

Methodology

The data for the present study were collected from PhD oral defences in a university of foreign studies in southern China. As an academic practice, the PhD oral defence, which is always open in China and welcomes audiences as participants, is considered the important and final stage before the doctoral degree is conferred. Normally, the oral defence committee consists of five experts, among whom are three professors from the host university and two from other universities either in China or other countries, or from universities in Hong Kong or Macau, and the chairperson is invariably from an external university. In our data, the members were experts of linguistics, most of whom were supervisors of PhD students; thus, in this study, the term *supervisor* is used rather than *teacher* or *expert*. After about 30 minutes of presentation made by the PhD candidate, the committee members make comprehensive evaluation about the quality of the PhD dissertation by making comments and asking questions. Sometimes the questions from the committee members are quite challenging, and the candidates are required to make relevant responses. Besides the speech acts of commenting, questioning and challenging, the experts from the committee also give some advice or make suggestions on what needs to be revised, refined or adjusted for bettering the final version of the dissertation, or what should be further explored in the future. As a result, the speech act of advice-giving and relevant sequences for giving advice were found pervasive in the oral defences, justifying that giving advice is one of the most essential tasks of the committee in academic settings.

Besides the committee members of the oral defences, the candidate's supervisor is often present in the audience so as to learn about the professional comments and advice from the committee. It is also a ritual for the supervisor to be present as a way of showing respect towards the committee members. Since oral defence meetings are open, the participants also include some PhD students and postgraduates, even some teachers from the university as well. Therefore, effort at face-keeping or face-maintaining, that is, rapport management, is expected since advice-giving is face-threatening.

For this study, ten PhD oral defences in English were recorded with a digital recorder in their naturally occurring environment. PhD candidates who had given permission for the use of the data in this study had not been told beforehand that their speech would be recorded for research purposes. For the sake of anonymity, the speech made by the experts was numbered T1, T2 or T3, and the speech by the PhD candidate was also marked. The focus of analysis was put on the phase of interaction, in which questions were asked and advice was offered by the experts from the committee.

Supervisors' collective identity construction

Basic conceptions of identity

Literature shows that the interrelatedness between identity and interaction has been approached from the perspectives of sociolinguistics, sociology, linguistic anthropology, literature and other disciplines. Identity can be regarded as how one conceives and labels self. In contrast, some scholars argue that identity only arises in social settings where there is social communication from which we assume our roles. According to Wenger, for example, '(i)dentity could be understood both as individual sense of self and as a collective notion of belonging to a social category' (1998: 146). In this study the notion of collective identity, which is clsely related to professional identity, will be discussed with the support of some examples.

Some early studies hold that identity is rigidly fixed (Omoniyi 2006) and is an equivalent of *role* on many occasions, consisting of a set of fixed and predetermined characteristics that a social group or an individual has. Contrary to this position, Johnson (2006) and Holmes, Stubbe and Vine (1999) analyse identity construction from the perspective of discourse analysis, viewing identity construction as a process which takes place in concrete and specific interactional contexts with various identities built in the discursive negotiation (De Fina, Schiffrin and Bamberg 2006). The flexible and contingent attributes of the identity that an individual or a social group constructs in specific interactional contexts are highlighted. In research of the relationships between discourse, identity and social practices, identity as a discursive construct has been widely accepted, just as Chen (2014) states that multiple and dynamic identities rather than single and static ones can be constructed in the process of communication. It is therefore worthwhile, by adopting a discursive approach, to explore the professional identities which are constructed on site by supervisors.

Supervisors' collective identity

In this study, the supervisors are those experts participating in the oral defences since they are normally supervisors of PhD students. Collective identity represents a self-concept that is derived from a significant group membership. In fact, individual and collective identity are closely related. The former can be taken as 'collective self' because of the profound influence of the latter, and the blending between the two accounts for why we care about 'who we are' and 'how others view us' when we construct our collective identity in a group (Yu and Cable 2010: 105).

When supervisors construct their collective identity in the PhD oral defences, their primary roles are to impart knowledge, provide research methods and advise the candidates about how to revise or adjust their dissertations, etc., which are all clearly task-oriented (Drew and Heritage 1992). Hence, the supervisors' collective identity has some distinct institutional features. In particular, they present themselves as authoritative, professional, dominant but also easy-going. All the supervisors involved are authorities with professional knowledge in a particular field of linguistics, and thus have professional power in this sense. The comment or advice they give is considered professional and authoritative. Furthermore, since one of the main purposes of PhD oral defences is to help candidates further improve their dissertations, what the committee members say is generally task-oriented and audience-friendly in order to facilitate the candidates' revision of their dissertations. These are some features of the collective identity the supervisors from the committee members construct for themselves.

Strategies used in collective identity construction

A speaker's identity is not simply reflected through linguistic forms, but is constructed by strategies (Yuan and Chen 2013: 529). In academic contexts, supervisors are likely to construct their collective identities by way of delivering advice. Abolfathiasl's (2013) updated taxonomy of strategies is used here to illustrate how supervisors construct collective identities in PhD oral defences, as shown in Table 7.1.

Table 7.1. Supervisors' strategies of identity construction and linguistic realisations

Strategies	Linguistic realisations	Examples
Direct	Performatives: performative verbs and noun of suggestion	I suggest/recommend/propose My suggestion/advice is that …
	Imperatives and negative imperatives	Ask them about … Don't try to use …
	Let's …	Let's work together on the project.
Non-conventionally indirect	Pseudo-cleft structures (impersonal)	All…is… One thing you could do is… One important thing to keep in mind is…
	Extraposed to-clauses (impersonal)	It might(not) be … to … It is … to …
	Hints	I've read/heard that …
Conventionally indirect	Modals and semi-modals	You … have to/need to/should (shouldn't)/ought to/can/could/might/ had better …
	Conditionals	If you …; If I were you
	Wh-questions (interrogative)	Why don't you …? How about …? Why not …?
	Yes-no questions (interrogative)	Would you consider …? Have you thought of …?

A. Direct strategies

When using direct strategies, a speaker clearly states his or her opinions through the use of performative verbs, a notion of suggestion and imperatives (Abolfathiasl 2013). In the chosen Chinese PhD oral defences, their presupposed role as an authority impels supervisors to use more direct strategies in order to construct their authoritative identity, as shown in (1).

(1)

01	T1:	我也不太清楚说这个东西到底可行吗？好像……因为你第一稿里面还说可以替换，我当时就质疑了。我当时查了你后面一些东西，我觉得你这个概念非常模糊。我还是建议你把flexible这个词去掉。
02	S:	我也一直在想这个事情。能不能把它换成common?
03	T1:	对！
04	T2:	我也觉得不行，要换掉。
05	T3:	我也觉得。那换成regular？

01	T1:	I'm not certain whether this is applicable. If I remember correctly … because in your first edition you claimed that it was substitutable. I doubted about it at that time … After all, I recommend you to remove the word 'flexible'.
02	S:	I've also considered this issue. I was wondering whether it could be replaced by 'common'?
03	T1:	Exactly!
04	T2:	I agree that it's not suitable and needs to be substituted.
05	T3:	I agree, too. How about 'regular'?

Example (1) is taken from a discussion about the use of the term 'collocation'. At the very beginning, T1 gives his suggestion directly by using the performative verb 'recommend'; in 04, T2 employs the expression 'needs to be' so as to require the student to make changes about those inappropriate expressions. In 05, there is no direct strategy of advising, but the agreement shown by T3 indicates that he is trying to convey the same advice for revising the inappropriate collocation, which has been put forward by T2 and T3.

B. Non-conventionally indirect strategies

In some contexts, there is no indicator of illocutionary forces in what is said, thus the hearer has to infer what is intended by the speaker (Abolfathiasl 2013), or what is advised. This is a case of using an indirect strategy. The uses of impersonal forms and hints are two major ways of making indirect suggestions or advice, as is presented in (2) and (3).

(2)

01	T1:	你这个研究呀，主要是语境因素的确定，可能你也回应了我提的一些问题哦。就是你提的这几个特征，可能是文献中的，你要结合你研究的问题怎么样整合成你自己的。文献中是从多个角度解释，提出的特征可能不能完全和你的吻合，可能表述方面和术语可能要注意一下。我刚才提的modifier，还有speaker knowledge，可能不完全是语义方面的。所以你这个表述，这个术语呀……

01   T1:   For your research, the main target is to identify the contextual factors. You might have answered some of my questions. To be specific, the features you've proposed, which might be obtained from the existing literature, need to be integrated into your research question … The literature approaches the issue from multiple perspectives, so that the proposed features might not exactly match those in your study. You might need to pay attention to wording. And diction might also need to be noticed. Just now, I mentioned 'modifier' and 'speaker knowledge', which might not be an exact semantic issue. So, this term …

(3)

01   T1:   …你在文中claim说有或者没有(相关研究)。姚美她查了，她给我讲相关研究很多很多。不是说没有或者很少，是相当多的这个哦。所以你对这个问题没有回应。

         …

02   T1:   我问了姚美，我说没有把握不要乱写哦，她说是有很多哦，这个点我没有把握哦。

01   T1:   … In the dissertation you claimed that 'there is' or 'there is no' (related research). Yao Mei has checked it. And she told me there were a lot of related studies. In other words, the related literature is neither scant nor limited, but a lot. So, you haven't responded to this question.

?   ?   …

02   T1:   I asked Yao Mei. If you are not sure, please do not make such a claim. She said there were indeed a lot. But I am not sure about this point.

In (2), the utterance 'The literature approaches the issue from multiple perspectives, so that the proposed features might not exactly match that in your study' implies that the student needs to revise the part concerning the proposed features. Note that in the mitigated expression of criticism and advice 'you might need to pay attention to wording', the word 'might' is a conventionally indirect strategy that we are going to discuss in the following part. In (3), the supervisor mentions a third person's opinion so as to express his implied disagreement and simultaneously to express his suggestion or advice that the PhD candidate should make his claims in a cautious way in his research.

C. Conventionally indirect strategies

When a conventionally indirect strategy is used to give advice, the directness of what is expressed or advised decreases (Abolfathiasl 2013). In interactional communication, some linguistic expressions are often used in a conventional way, especially in contexts in which the participants' face is likely to be threatened or lost, for example interrogative questions, the verbs 'should' and 'need', and conditionals can be taken as conventionalised indirect strategies for expressing suggestions or giving advice. Consider (4) and (5):

(4)

01	S:	但我是我把小v看成是
02	T2:	你把小v看成以后就不用区分大V小v了吗？就一个大V解决了？
03	S:	为什么，但它这个大V是词根吧？如果是我把大V看成一个词根，它在
04	T2:	一个词根是你说的一个词根啦。别人说我不一定认为是个词根，对吧？然后你为什么把一个大V一个词根，你说它们俩都有意义。它们俩有什么意义呢？一个不就完了吗？

01   S: But I see small v as

02   T2:   You see small v … then you don't need to distinguish small v and big V? One big V solves everything?

03   S: Why, but this big V is a root, isn't it? If I see big V as a root, it is

04   T2:   A root is what you mean a root. Others say I may not think it as a root. Right? Then why do you put a big V for a root? You say both of them have meanings. What are their meanings? Isn't one enough?

(5)

01   T1:   对。还有一个，你可能要把握两个概念，一个是holistic   view，   一个是pro-cessing advantage。

        …

03   T1:   就是你认定这三个问题，把这三个问题讲清楚为什么，让别人来认可你这个问题。…第一个层面就是说，如果你把这个问题提得更深，你的论文会更好。

01   T1:   Right, there is one more thing. You need to distinguish between two concepts. One is holistic view and the other is processing advantage.

        …

03   T1:   In terms of the three questions you proposed, you need to explicate the rationales behind the questions, so that others will approve of your questions … On the first level, if you make the question more profound, your dissertation will be better.

The interrogative questions in (4) are mainly wh-questions and yes-no questions which have fixed answers, showing that the expert as a supervisor asks questions with the aim of not transmitting information or controlling the interaction, but of directing the students to think deeply and finally achieve correct understanding of the discussed issues by themselves. In (5), the utterance 'you need to distinguish between two concepts' serves to advise by highlighting the need to make some revisions on defining concepts, and the conditional utterance 'if you make the question more profound, your dissertation will be better' in the example also implies the supervisor's specific suggestion, which is not difficult for the PhD candidate to understand. In the data, there are plenty of such conventionally indirect ways of advising as the two excerpted conversations shown above. Supposedly, these strategies can not only help supervisors transmit their suggestions efficiently but politely as well. In the next part, we will see how supervisors construct specific collective identities by employing these strategies.

Specific identities constructed by supervisors

In PhD oral defences, supervisors may utilise the above strategies to construct some specific identities.

A. Role as director

In the oral defences, the experts from the committee often act as directors while making comments, in particular pointing out weak points in the dissertations. They are most likely to give some advice or suggestions about how to make revisions, or to carry out further studies in the future in the light of the present findings. In this case they are directors, who are helpful to the candidates and other students about dissertation writing. As mentioned before, the feature of dominance implies a position of control which the supervisors embrace when establishing their roles as directors. The following is an example of how the use of conventionally indirect strategies helps the supervisor fulfil the role as a director.

(6)

01　T1:　从你的研究问题来看，你好像关心学生的行为。我不知道这是不是跟你这个习得相关的，我想问一下，从第5到第6页这里，你的research　question啦，啦，这好像是从一个角度说，在什么情况下学生他会做什么，并作出一些预设。我想说，你这个跟习得有关吗？还是说在不同的语境条件的，在使用冠词的时候会对学生产生什么影响？你觉得你在研究习得问题吗？也就是说，你在判断学生做的close里面，你没有判断对错?⋯我是说你有没有做这样的区分？

02　S:　我前面没有做，在做第四个的时候，我有考虑accuracy。

03　T1:　我好像没有印象说你的跟accuracy是有关的。⋯你有没有做出一种价值判断？

04　S:　我没有价值判断。我关注的是行为。

05　T2:　哦，那你这个就跟习得没有太大关系。在不同的语境下，学生用冠词的行为规律是什么？至于这些行为本身，它是不是符合标准英语习惯的用法？　你没有太在意。

06　S:　嗯

01   T1:   Judging from your research questions, it seems that your concern is about students' behaviour. I don't know whether this is related to the acquisition you studied. I wonder, from the fifth page to this point on the sixth page, what your research question is and … is it related to acquisition? Or are you talking about and making some presumptions that, in different situations, contexts would have some influence on students' use of articles? Do you think you are studying an acquisition phenomenon? That is to say, when you analyse the close (test) made by students, have you made a right-or-wrong judgment?… My question is, have you made such a distinction?

02   S: I didn't make it at the beginning. But when I was doing the fourth one, I considered accuracy.

03   T2:   I have no impression that I said your study is concerned with accuracy … Have you made any judgments concerning value?

04   S: I haven't made value judgment. My concern is about behaviour.

05   T2:   OK. So you don't concern acquisition much. Then what's the behavioural pattern of using articles in different contexts? As for these behaviours per se, do they obey the conventional usages in English? You've not paid much attention to this.

06   S: OK.

Asking questions is one of the conventionally used indirect strategies in rendering advice. Example (6) shows that asking questions can be considered quite performative, such as requesting that the student explain their ideas more clearly or further consider what is being discussed, and so on. It is found that as strategies of giving advice, supervisors commonly employ wh-questions and yes-no questions. The supervisors are not intending to get immediate answers from the students, but are making suggestions in an indirect way. This is also a way of exercising control or showing power in Chinese doctoral dissertation defences. As Labov and Fanshel (1977) point out, by asking questions, the speaker can show the role he is playing. In 01 of the above example, the supervisor uses some yes-no questions, which are actually meant to advise the student to think more about his study. In this way, the speaker exercises his expert power as a supervisor. The question 'is it related to acquisition?' implies that the research question has nothing to do with acquisition, which suggests that the research question needs to be improved. Once the student treats it as a piece of advice, the identity of the supervisor as a director is successfully constructed. Similarly, T2 also adopts yes-no questions and wh-questions so as to give his authoritative comments. This shows that the speakers as supervisors have constructed their role as directors, which is better considered as a collective identity rather than as an individual one. Clearly, questions, especially wh-questions and yes-no questions, can be treated as transparent devices to construct speakers' collective identity as directors.

B. Role as expert

An expert is by definition someone who knows much about a particular subject. Some features, such as professionalism and authoritarianism, can be well observed when a supervisor plays the role of an expert in making comments or asking questions about dissertations. In general, a supervisor who acts as an expert possesses more professional knowledge and enjoys a higher social status in his profession than the student(s) he or she supervises. In the collected PhD oral defences it is found that the supervisors often adopt different strategies to fulfil such role as an expert, which is also a collective type of identity. Consider (7):

(7)

01	T1:	就三个问题，每个问题一句话。What are EAs? Why are there EAs?… 这真的不是一个博士论文应该研究的问题（（大笑））。这是一个小的journal paper可能用这几个可能还可以。
02	T2:	对对对。你展开也展开不了。
03	T1:	是。你把它写得复杂点，起码看上去也像个研究问题。
04	S:	那在这个研究问题里再设小的研究问题。
05	T1:	不是，不是，就用一个复杂的句式把它写得看起来像那么回事。你现在像个小学生的东西，你知道吧，这样写。（（大笑））What are EAs? 这就是一个研究问题?（（继续笑））
06	S:	我还是会考虑看看，感谢。

01　T1:　For each of the three questions, you just use one sentence. What are EAs? Why are there EAs?… This is not a question that should be studied in a doctoral thesis ((laugh)). It might be okay for a journal article.

02　T2:　Yes, yes, yes. You can't elaborate it much.

03　T1:　Yes. Please make it more profound, so that it will at least appear to be a research question.

04　S:　How about proposing subordinate research questions under the general research questions?

05　T4:　No, no (.) Rephrase it using complicated sentences. Make it look like a decent one. Your current version resembles the work of a primary school student. You know, if you do like this. ((Laugh)) What are EAs? Is this a research question? ((Keep laughing))

06　S:　I will think more about it, thank you.

In the above excerpted interaction, the supervisors in making suggestions or giving advice apply all the direct, indirect and conventionally indirect strategies. What they comment on or clarify indicates what is the correct understanding to the student. By so doing, they indeed construct their expert identity, and their institutional power is exercised. In 01, T1 makes use of the comment 'it might be okay for a journal article' to indirectly give his advice on improving the research question for the dissertation. This is professional advice from an expert. The response from T2 in 02 proves that the supervisors are constructing the same identity in expressing their ideas. Furthermore, a direct strategy realised as the imperatives in 03 and 05 is employed by the supervisors to strengthen their collective identities as experts. The requirement in 03 'please make it more profound' exerts the illocutionary force of urging the student to do something, successfully transmitting the expertise that should be followed; the utterance 'rephrase it using complicated sentences' in 05 functions in the same way. Meanwhile, the conventionally indirect strategy is also taken to construct the speaker's expert identity. In 05, the utterance 'is this a research question' implies that the supervisor does not agree with the student about the research question. It is an implicit negation of the dissertation. This shows the speaker's authority as an expert in the institutional context. Evidently, all the committee members have presented similar standpoints as experts, through which their collective position and identity instead of individual ones are shown and meant to influence the students.

C. Role as helper

In the PhD oral defences, supervisors can also construct their role as helper for the students. It is not true that emotional closeness is less commonly enacted in PhD oral defences. Rather, besides making critical and negative comments about the dissertations, the experts on the committee often offer helpful advice for revisions or improvements and make suggestions about possible research on relevant topics, which will in effect bring the two sides closer together. This is also a collective feature of the advising activity. As has been discussed earlier, we emphasise that the purpose of keeping close or speaking in a helpful way is for the successful delivery of advice in a less face-threatening way. As a result, the supervisors often resort to less face-threatening conventionally indirect strategies to present their advice in the process of constructing their identity as helper. Normally, patterns such as 'you have to', 'you need to' and 'you shouldn't' are used by the supervisors to help students solve their specific problems, or to avoid some weak points. It might be argued that the illocutionary force of such expressions is so strong that it may not create intimacy between the participants. Instead, they are meant to be helpful as they show the speakers' concern with the dissertations. It is such necessary advice that the students find them less imposing than they sound. Here is an example.

(8)

01   S: 就是说，我的这个，但是它也有个结构的

02   T1:   就是说，在行文的时候，把它明明白白说清楚，知道吧！你的想法是好的，
但你需要在文章里面把它说清楚，把它明确地点出来。

03   S: 就比如像，就说我要写一个hypothesis

04	T1:	这个不需要写hypothesis，就别人之前做了什么东西，哪些别人做的，哪些你跟别人不同。…知道吧？就是你们写作的过程当中，就是说怎么清清楚楚明明白白地把它表达出来。
05	S:	嗯。
06	T1:	不是你认为怎么样，我们都知道你知道，但应该写明白嘛，写清楚嘛！
01	S:	That is to say, my work … but it has its structure.
02	T1:	That is to say, when you are writing, you should make it explicit. Do you know?! Your idea is good, but you should state and point it out clearly.
03	S:	Just like this … should I say I am writing a hypothesis=
04	T1:	You needn't write a hypothesis. That (is to say), what has been done by others, what are the differences between your work and what has been done by others … Do you know? In short, when you are writing your dissertation, you need to make it explicit.
05	S:	OK.
06:	T1:	Your thought is not penetrable to us. But you need to write explicitly!

In the above excerpt, when rendering advice, the supervisors often employ such structures as 'you need to …' and 'you can …' to construct their collective identities as experts and helpers as well. In responding to a student's query, T1 makes the suggestion 'you should state and point it out clearly' to fully meet the student's need for help. It can effectively draw the two parties closer in that the advisee will be grateful for the advisor's help in solving the problem he or she faces. Likewise, T2 employs a similar strategy to construct an identical identity in giving advice. Meanwhile, the responses made by the student in 03 and 05 show that the supervisor's suggestion is accepted and welcomed, which supports the supposition that closeness is created when supervisors identify themselves as helpers. Our data testify to the tendency that supervisors almost invariably establish their identity as helpers. Due to limited space, other strategies will not be discussed here.

D. Role as encourager

When giving advice or making suggestions about improvements to dissertations, supervisors from the committee are more likely to present constructive details or show their positive attitudes so as to encourage the students to overcome difficulties. This is a collective feature in PhD oral defences where the supervisors construct their identity as encouragers by playing the above roles. By getting positive feedback, the students will be encouraged to make greater efforts with regard to what has been advised or suggested, as shown below.

(9)

| 01 | T1: | 对。这个认知跟英语标准语法之间是不是对应，他的好像没有太大的关系。所以我建议你还是要凸显这种。 |

02   T2:   所以你的习得概念是这个[用对了还是用错了]，他的习得概念是对于他做选择有没有影响。

03   T1:   嗯，对对对！嗯，有没有影响。你的关注点是描写行为的。

04   T2:   所以你要把在什么层面研究习得说清楚。

05   T1:   对，对！···那么这个时候你应该要填的你没有填，我看看你习得正确率的百分之几呀，accuracy啦。这个东西在你的论文里面体现的好像不是很明显

06   T3:   不明显

07   T1:   所以你这个是个巨大的差异，颠覆人们对习得一种根深蒂固的观念(笑)。所以我想你应该做清楚。当然我并不是反对你这么做，但是你应该把这个事情讲得更加清楚一点。

01   T1:   Yes. Do the cognition and Standard English grammar correspond? His study appears to have little relationship. So I suggest you highlight it.

02   T2:   So your acquisition concept is this [the right use or wrong use], his acquisition concept is whether it has influence on his choice or not.

03   T1:   OK, right right right! OK, having influence or not. Your focus is on describing the behaviour.

04   T2:   So you have to clarify on which level you study the acquisition.

05   T1:   Right, right!… Then at this moment what you should accomplish has not been accomplished, let me see the percentage of your acquisition accuracy, accuracy. This part in your dissertation does not appear to be obvious.

06   T3:   Not obvious

07   T1:   So your study makes a huge difference. The deeply rooted notion of acquisition has been overturned. (laugh). So I think you should make it clear. Of course, I am not against what you are doing, but you should make it clearer.

It is clear that the above academic interaction is totally controlled by the supervisors. In so doing, the collective identity of expert has been constructed and presented. In this excerpt the supervisors have all made effort to give advice through different linguistic realisations. For example, T1 uses the verb 'suggest' in 01 to advise the student to highlight the notion he holds. A similar suggestion or advice is realised by T2. In 04, T2 uses the semi-model of 'have to'. And the impersonal statement made by T2 in 05 and T3 in 06 like 'does not appear to be obvious' also proves that the supervisors are highly consistent in rendering similar advice so as to construct the same collective identity. T1 expresses his appreciation to the student for his contribution by the utterance 'the deeply-rooted notion has been overturned' in 07, which wins the recognition of the other committee members. As a whole, all of the supervisors expect the student to expound on the issue more clearly, and in this way encouragement is made by the supervisors to clarify the point and finally improve the dissertation. In summary, the supervisors may adopt more than one strategy to construct their collective identity as experts. It is hard to draw a clear distinction between different types of identities; supervisors may construct multiple identities simultaneously. It is hard to draw a clear demarcation between director, expert, helper and encourager. In the next section, the pragmatic motivations behind these strategies for establishing collective professional identities will be explored in the light of the rapport management theory.

Rapport management behind supervisors' identity construction

Some basic ideas about rapport management

Language is used not only to convey information, but also to attain interpersonal goals (Brown and Yule 1983). It is often the case that the primary aim of interactional speech lies in building interpersonal relationships or managing certain social relations, which then create agreeable conditions for successful communication. Thus, building rapport is one of the goals of communication in all cultures. For this reason, the framework of rapport management is proposed to explain how language is used to promote, maintain or threaten harmonious social relations (Spencer-Oatey 2000). Managing rapport, which is collectively referred to as facework (Scollon and Scollon 2001), can be reflected in face-saving and face-giving behaviour. From Spacer-Oatey's perspective, the task of increasing, maintaining and destroying rapport reflects the management of face. In Goffman (1967), face is defined as the social recognition of the other's positive self-image. According to Brown and Levinson (1987), face consists of two related aspects, namely negative face and positive face. In their model, positive face is a desire for each of us to be approved of and negative face is a person's desire to be unimpeded and to be free to act. Because such understanding ignores the collective nature of face, Spencer-Oatey puts forward 'identity face' and takes it as the desire to be recognised for one's positive social identity, as well as one's individual positive traits. By her understanding, face and identity are similar in cognitive terms because they both relate to the notion of 'self-image' and both comprise multiple self-aspects or attributes (Spencer-Oatey 2007: 644). As an attempt to overcome the weaknesses of Brown and Levinson's face model, Spencer-Oatey proposes a refined framework. Within the new framework, she argues that in order to achieve both transactional and interactional goals in communication, we need to consider not only face as interpersonal needs, but also sociality rights and obligations. Face management is explained by Spencer-Oatey as follows:

> Face management ... involves the management of face sensitivities and, following Goffman (1967: 5), I define face as 'the positive social value a person effectively claims for himself [*sic*] by the line others assume he has

taken during a particular contact' … The management of sociality rights and obligations, on the other hand, involves the management of social expectancies, which I define as 'fundamental social entitlements that a person effectively claims for him/herself in his/her interactions with others'. In other words, face is associated with personal/relational/social value, and is concerned with people's sense of worth, dignity, honor, reputation, competence and so on. Sociality rights and obligations, on the other hand, are concerned with social expectancies, and reflect people's concerns over fairness, consideration, and behavioural appropriateness. Interactional goals refer to the specific task and/or relational goals that people may have when they interact with each other.

(Spencer-Oatey 2008: 11)

In face management, two aspects of human desire that need to be considered are i) quality face: the desire to be thought of positively in terms of personal qualities, and ii) identity face: the desire that social identities or roles be acknowledged and upheld. Similarly, sociality rights also include equity rights and association rights, with the former referring to the right to receive personal consideration and be treated fairly, and the latter the entitlement to association with or dissociation from others. Here, face is basically an identity that is admitted both individually and socially. Thus, face management is related to identity construction.

In order to describe relational management in interaction, several interrelated domains need to be mentioned. First, the concept of politeness applies to the illocutionary domain of rapport management, being separated from other aspects of interactional communication; second, the concept of facework is considered to be any (verbal or non-verbal) behaviour that aims at accommodating or damaging face (Spencer-Oatey 2000); third, facework is a broader term than the notion of politeness in Brown and Levinson's model.

By considering the relationship between interlocutors and rapport bases, we can see that interaction could be negotiated by participants in the interaction and developed in different ways. Spencer-Oatey (2000, 2008) acknowledges the complexity of communication by considering many other influencing factors. In communication, some bases of rapport have to be considered, such as conventions on speech act realisations, sociopragmatic interactional principles underlying communication, and power, distance and social roles between participants (López 2008). Rapport orientation is the key factor that influences the use of interpersonal strategies in interaction. That is, different strategies for establishing interpersonal relationships result from different rapport orientations, as explained below.

Supervisors' rapport orientations

According to Schiffrin, 'the ways in which speakers and hearers are related to their utterances – to their propositions, acts and turns – influence the ways in which they relate to each other' (1987: 27). Generally, people in interaction engage in rapport enhancement, rapport maintenance, rapport neglect or rapport challenge orientation, which are different rapport orientations (Spencer-Oatey 2008). Rapport-neglect orientation indicates a lack of concern or interest in the quality of relations between the interlocutors, and rapport-challenge orientation refers to a desire to challenge or impair harmonious relations between the interlocutors. In the context of PhD oral defences, the consideration of facework can help to establish relationships among the participants and prevent conflict from occurring due to disagreements about what is being commented about the dissertations, since facework is about the linguistic manifestations of face-maintaining behaviour (Planken 2005: 382). The following excerpt shows that, when supervisors construct their collective identities, they often hold rapport maintenance orientation. Look at (10):

(10)

01   T1:   不能说是有影响吧，你知道，只能说是这个数据跟这个数据有相关性吧。

02   S: 是。

03   T2:   也许它没有直接影响，只是有相关性吧。

04   S: 哦哦，是的是的。整个实验设计是这样的。

01   T1:   We can't say that it has influence, you know, but only that it has correlation with this data.

02   S: Yes.

03   T2:   Perhaps, it has no direct influence, only correlation.

04   S: Oh oh, yes, yes. The whole research design is like this.

In this excerpt, T1 and T2 both construct the identity of expert. Yet, it is noteworthy that T1 uses the mitigation marker 'you know' and T2 adopts the hedge 'perhaps' to reduce face threat to the student while making some negative comments and then giving advice about the dissertation. In interactional conversations, mitigation devices are viewed by Caffi (2007) as strategic devices, which have much to do with politeness and face considerations because they can remove or sweeten those unwelcome or negative effects of speech acts expressing orders, criticism, bad news, negative comments, etc. Thus, the devices can be utilised to enhance harmonious relationships between interlocutors. Since giving advice can more or less threaten the hearer's face, the speaker may try to adopt some politeness strategies to mitigate or soften the speech act, or to minimise the chance of offending the addressee (Martínez-Flor 2005). According to Kasper (1997: 1), 'such resources include pragmatic strategies like directness and indirectness, routines, and a large range of linguistic forms which can intensify or soften communicative acts'. Here, when supervisors make some negative comments or criticism about the dissertations, they employ linguistic mitigation, thus contributing a lot to keeping rapport or managing positive relationships between the supervisors as experts and the students as advisees.

(11)

01   S: 是。我其实是想如果把Chomsky那些小v，把它看成…然后他的观点

02   T1: 他的观点很清楚，你不要自己看成，你不要乱弄它。就在他那一块下，或者把它弄出来后，你自己界定。就像刚才张孝龙讲那个(Cupperman)的。如果(Cupperman)句法里的跟汉语里传统的补语和补足语，就不一样的东西。实际上，不同的时间段，不同的人，不同的学派，用的就差别更大了。

03   S: 问题是只要他们归到一点，都是找出语言的本质。

04   T1: 有的东西，它不一样。应该说它有的是没有共同语言的，他谈不一起的。所以说，你自己弄这个东西，要非常清楚

05   S: 问题是如果我这样理解，我认为Chomsky的东西可以用在事件框架下来，然后我做一个类比。然后就觉得Chomsky的小v它相当于v-to，v-be，v-go，说不定他们从不同角度出发还能

07   T2: Chomsky的小v跟你的v-to，v-be，v-go不一样。

08   T1: 它是个纯句法的东西。

09   T2: 对！它没有语义的内容。

01   S: Yes. I actually think that if seeing Chomsky's small v as … then his opinions …

02   T1: His view is very clear. You should not interpret it yourself, you should not mix it up. In reference to his definition, or singling it out, then you define it yourself. Like just now what Zhang Xiaolong talks about (Cupperman). If (Cupperman) that in syntax is different from the complement and complementary clause, they are different. In fact, in different periods of time, for different people, in different schools, usages have more differences.

03   S: The question is that if they can summarise it to one point, they can find the essence of language.

04   T1: Some things are different. Or we should say some have no common places. You should be very clear about your own work.

05   S: The question is if I understand it like this, I think Chomsky's work can be used under event framework, and then I can do an analogy. Then I think Chomsky's small v is v-to, v-be, v-go, or if I approach them from different perspectives, they can be.

07   T2: Chomsky's small v is different from your v-to, v-be and v-go.

08   T1:   It is a pure syntax matter.

09   T2:   Right! It has no semantic content.

In 02, T1 constructs an identity as director, commanding the student not to misunderstand Chomsky's opinion. Meanwhile, he also presents himself as an expert by implying in the utterance 'his view is very clear' that he is familiar with Chomsky's theory and indirectly advises the student to secure a clear understanding. And what is presented by T2 in 07 and 09 shows that the supervisor knows about Chomsky as well. However, neither T1 nor T2 criticises the student directly so as to keep the latter's face by showing their concern for it. In this way, they manage to maintain rapport without severely damaging the student's face. According to Spencer-Oatey, 'when people hold rapport maintenance orientation, their aim is to minimize the negative impact of such acts on the hearer by selecting appropriate rapport-management strategies' (2000: 30). Evidently, it is likely that the supervisors present their professional knowledge as an indirect strategy of giving advice in order to maintain the student's face. This is what is collectively done by the supervisors in the PhD oral defences. According to Abolfathiasl (2013), making hints is an essential indirect strategy of making suggestions, and presenting professional knowledge can be considered as a hint in rendering advice, which is illustrated in the above example.

From the above analysis, we can see the rapport maintenance orientation taken by the supervisors. Earlier, we discussed the four types of roles that supervisors play in PhD oral defences. These roles can be re-categorised as authority-based identity, intimacy-based identity and equality-based identity according to those distinctive features of different roles. The following parts will elaborate on the connection between rapport maintenance orientation and the above collective identity construction.

A. Authority-based identity and rapport maintenance

Interpersonal relationships vary according to power, social status and professional knowledge between interlocutors. In PhD oral defences, supervisors enjoy more power than the students, and quite likely they will construct their authority-based identity so as to produce intended effects, such as to make the student revise the weak points of their dissertation, or delete the unnecessary parts. Thus, these contexts might involve rapport-challenge or neglect. Under such circumstances, supervisors tend to employ linguistic strategies to make rapport-oriented effort in interaction. Contrary to the idea that politeness and face-threatening acts are static or fixed, Spencer-Oatey (2005) points out that what constitutes politeness is largely a subjective judgment about the social appropriateness of verbal and non-verbal behaviour. The judgment is made in terms of sociality rights and obligations, which has much to do with the relative power, authority or social status between participants. The following example shows how power acts on the supervisors' authority-based identity within the framework of rapport maintenance.

(12)

01   T1:   你这个研究呀，主要是语境因素的确定，可能你也回应了我提的一些问题哦。就是你提的这几个特征，可能是文献中的，你要结合你研究的问题怎么样整合成你自己的。文献中是从多个角度解释，提出的特征可能不能完全和你的吻合，可能表述方面和术语可能要注意一下。我刚才提的modifier，还有speaker knowledge，可能不完全是语义方面的。所以你这个表述，这个术语呀

02   S: Speaker knowledge不一定是语义。

03   T1:   你可以用自己的术语，你引用别人的东西，他讲的东西也不完全哦。

04   T2:   他们的框架都每个框架包含两个feature。

05   T3:   是的，他的包含在很多不同的feature中，这样不好吧？

06   T1:   是是。这是论文很关键的部分。

07   T3:   走来走去就这几个理论。所以我还是有充分的意见，选个好帽子吧。

01   T1:   Your research is mainly concerned with locating context factors. Maybe you have answered some of my questions. The features you mentioned may come from other literature. You need to take your own research into consideration and see how you can integrate it into your own work. The literature explains it from different angles and it may not fit your research completely. You may have to pay attention to the expressions and terms. The modifier I mentioned just now and speaker knowledge may not be totally about semantics. So, your expression, your terms …

02   S: Speaker knowledge may not be a semantic issue.

03   T1:   You may use your own terms, or you may cite others' work, and his explanation is not complete.

04   T2:   Each of their frameworks includes two features.

05   T3:   Yes, his framework has many different features. This is not good, is it?

06   T1:   Right right. This is the key part of the dissertation.

07   T3:   You can only choose from these several theories. So, I have some doubts. Please choose a correct 'hat'!

In order to adapt to their roles, because of the power difference involved, the supervisors need to attend to the students' face, particularly their identity face and sociality rights. In this excerpt, the supervisors utilise some strategies to give advice so as to save the student's face, and to further help the student solve the problems about his research. In 01, T1 provides hedged suggestions through such expressions as 'may', 'maybe' and 'some of my questions', which can prevent the student from losing his face, otherwise he could have constructed his authoritative identity by speaking more directly and forcefully about the weak points of the dissertation and then directly giving his advice. Meanwhile, in 02, what T2 said may also be considered an indirect suggestion for reconsidering the issue mentioned by T1, through which his expert identity is constructed in effect. In addition, T3 poses a loaded question in 05 to give advice in a conventionally indirect way so as to save the student's face and preserves his identity face by displaying his authoritative opinion. From this excerpt, it can be found that the experts on the committee take the strategies in interaction for interpersonal purposes, although they possess higher social status than the students. Such strategies or linguistic means are rapport-oriented.

More importantly, in so doing, the supervisors construct their collective identity as a group. T1 makes the suggestion that the student needs to reconsider how to use academic terms, which also gains positive responses from both T2 and T3, indicating that the committee members intend to build the same identity in such a context. In (12), the three supervisors have exerted expert power, which means they have some special knowledge or expertise. The utterances in 04, 05, 06 and 07 indicate that the speakers as experts and directors enjoy the power to impel the student to correct inappropriate terms and revise the theoretical part of his study. Since a rapport-oriented view is held, the supervisors could make the best of the power they enjoy to create authority-based identities in communication and to construct a collective identity as a director, helper and/or encourager.

B. Intimacy-based identity and rapport maintenance

Intimacy-based identity construction is related to rapport-maintenance orientation. For a clearer understanding of social distance or other social factors in identity construction, we need to know something about the asymmetric relationships between the participants in academic exchanges. According to Hutchby (1995), the essential feature of advice-giving is asymmetry. Hutchby (1995: 221) calls advice-giving 'an activity which assumes or establishes an asymmetry between participants'. It is also an emergent property of social structure and macro patterns of inequality which produces social distance between groups (Bonnin 2014: 2). As for the constraints of settings, Vehviläinen (2001) suggests that participants in institutional settings, such as educational counselling, are involved in dilemmas. On one hand, advice-givers tend to maintain the authority of their perspective, and on the other hand advice-recipients' autonomy of their own perspective and experience should be self-directed and respected.

There is not always a symmetrical relationship between participants. Rather, distance is described as a kind of solidarity and closeness to each other (Brown and Gilman 1972). It has different labels, like 'social distance', 'closeness', 'familiarity', 'relational intimacy' (Spencer-Oatey 2000: 33). Social distance is independent, to some extent, of institutionally defined roles. The supervisors and the students may be socially familiar, or know each other, but there exist asymmetrical roles and an asymmetrical relation as well between them. Whereas the supervisors are motivated with rapport orientation, the asymmetry will be balanced or adjusted through some strategies for shortening the social distance with the student. Thus, a kind of intimacy-based identity is likely to be built. In this sense, the social distance is close to asymmetry, though different. The following example shows how social distance is fully used by the supervisors to construct identity in giving advice.

(13)

01   T1:   有的，要不然不会写这个。当时看的时候明明白白，我忘了，看了两个月了原来那个版本。你现在让我想也想不起来了。肯定是有的，好像当时我们预答辩的时候陈老师也提了这个问题。你前面刚批了的？（（看着陈老师））

02   T2:   好像是有。

03   T1:   是，确实有这一点。我们俩都看了

04   T2:   当时她写得⋯我们也批了的。

05   T1:   对，当时有写这么一点，两个月了我现在记不得细节了。但确实是有的这么一点。

06   T3:   [不一致的矛盾]的地方我们提到过，提到过。

07   S: 我想的是

08   T1:   是，提到过。

09   S: 好，老师都提到过。问题是我自己写着论文嘛，我批判的观点我并没有采用了，我采用的好像是另外一部分可能是同一个文献中另外一部分没有批判到的观点。应该是这样子的，因为我自己的行文中我既然批判=

10   T1:   =你既然这样用你就肯定认为你自己没有矛盾，但是让我们看起来是有矛盾的（（大笑））。你至少要让读者清楚，没有自相矛盾了。

01   T1:   I have. Otherwise I won't write this. But at that time I was clear about it. I forgot. I read the original version two months ago. Now I can't recall it even if you ask me to do that. Definitely it has. It seems that Mr Chen also came up with this question when we had pre-defence. You criticised it before? ((looking at Mr Chen))

02   T2:   It seems I did.

03   T1:   Yes, exactly. We both did.

04   T2:   Her last version then. We criticised it.

05   T1:   Yes, at that time this point was written, but I can't remember the details as two months have passed. But it really exists.

06   T3:   The contradiction we have mentioned, mentioned.

07   S: I think so.

08   T1:   Yes, we have mentioned.

09   S: OK, you teachers have all mentioned. The question is when I wrote the disser-
          tation, I did not use the opinions I criticise. Maybe I used another part, maybe
          another part in the same literature which I did not criticise. It seems to be like
          this, because in my own dissertation I criticised …

10   T1: If you used it, you must think that you have no contradictions, but it makes us
          think it has contradictions ((laugh)). You have to make it clear to your reader
          that there's no contradiction.

In the above interactional conversation, the supervisors, who are familiar with the student, employ direct patterns, such as 'we criticised it', 'we have mentioned' to express their disagreement in a collective way. However, they do not make the same critical comments about the dissertation, in which there still exist some contradictions, although they have power to do so. This is rapport-oriented, which helps to decrease the distance and increase the familiarity between two parties. In 01, the utterance 'it seems that Mr. Chen also came up with this question when we had pre-defence' shows that T1 is trying to shorten the distance with the student and manage their rapport in a socially familiar way, and the hedged expression 'it seems …' as an indirect strategy can mitigate the face-threatening effect. It can be seen that the speaker makes an effort to establish a close relationship instead of exerting his power. As a result, favourable rapport is created. Similarly, the following responses from T2 and T3 indicate that the supervisors are not trying to break the mutual rapport, and their supportive behaviours are beneficial for keeping their collective identity face and social rights, which is a flexible adaptation to the ongoing interactive environment. Such responses as 'I think so' in 07 and 'OK, you teachers have all mentioned' in 09 provide evidence that the intimacy-based positive efforts made by the supervisors have then been well received by the student, who does not react with any defensive speech. Thus, appropriate strategies can be employed in a collective way for giving advice or make suggestions and keeping rapport as well between the interlocutors. That is, the advice-giving or suggestion-making acts can be rapport-oriented. Besides, in the above excerpt from the PhD oral defence, the frequently used deictic expression 'we' is helpful in creating the collective identity of the supervisors as a whole rather than as individuals. By so doing in such an institutional context, both transactional and interactional goals can be reached.

C. Equality-based identity and rapport maintenance

With rapport-maintenance orientation, supervisors can fulfil their interactional roles by using some linguistic strategies. According to Spencer-Oatey (2000), interactional roles may have a major influence on the choice of rapport-management strategies, and affect the assessments of rights and obligations. She argues,

[W]hen people interact with each other, they often take up clearly defined social roles, such as teacher-student, employer-employee, chairperson-committee member. These role relationships not only partially determine the power and distance of the relationship, but also help specify the rights and obligations of each role member. People have the right to expect certain things of the other member and an obligation to carry out certain other things.

(Spencer-Oatey 2000: 37)

In PhD oral defences, the supervisors commit themselves to giving comments and evaluations about the students' academic performance in terms of the weak and strong points of their dissertations. More importantly, they have obligations and rights to direct students to making necessary improvements, or provide some guidance for their future study. In considering the responsibilities they take, the supervisors will attach importance to identity constructed by linguistic strategies. Therefore, some equality-based identities would be wisely selected by the supervisors to fulfil their obligations in company with the goal of interpersonal rapport management or maintenance, as shown in (14):

(14)

01	S:	这个我觉得不好看
02	T1:	不是。有些有，有些没有。
03	T2:	怎么就不好看了？（其他人笑）
04	T3:	对。你看，有些写了，像Chicago Press 是全的，Cambridge 就变成了 CUP，OUP, Oxford 也是 OUP
05	T1:	对
06	T3:	我觉得你最好把全称写上。
07	S:	这样节约了很多空间我想=
08	T3:	你怎么老是计较这个空间的问题呀？没人给你多要纸钱，（（大笑））嗨，你！

01	S:	I do not think it is good-looking
02	T1:	But some have, some not.
03	T2:	Why isn't it good-looking? (Others laugh)
04	T3:	Yes, you see, some are written (in full names), like Chicago Press is complete, Cambridge is CUP, OUP, Oxford is also OUP
05	T1:	Right.
06	T3:	I think you'd better write down all the full names.
07	S:	Then it saves much space I think
08	T3:	Why do you always haggle about the space? Nobody asks more money for paper from you, ((laugh)) Hi, you!

In the above excerpt, T2 and T3 try to be humorous so as to lessen their negative comments about the bibliography and then to establish solidarity and equality-oriented relationships in the context. In 03, the utterance 'Why isn't it good-looking?' not only causes laughter, but also contributes to building an equal relationship. This question and what is said by T3 in 08 are more like mild sarcasm that has the effect of humour. As a result, a relaxed atmosphere is created, which helps to increase intimacy and affective bonds between the two parties. The shift from a serious mode to a humorous one indicates that the supervisors give up their authoritative identity and are managing to create a more equality-based identity. In order to help the student overcome his difficulties, both T2 and T3 employ non-serious interrogative questions to construct an equality-based identity, so as to lessen the tense atmosphere of the oral defence. In theory, the pre-fixed interactional roles obligate the supervisors to build a more favourable identity for their communicative needs, for instance giving advice, making comments or evaluations. In this excerpt, however, it might be argued that the utterance in 06 is giving a personal opinion and thus should be taken as an expression of individual identity construction. The expert T3 uses the pattern 'I think you'd better ...' to convey the same suggestion made by the questions in 03 and 08. This conventionally indirect strategy has taken the student's face needs into account and can reduce the imposition of the suggestion or advice. Evidently, the suggestion made in 03 is the same one with that given by T1 and T3, proving that the supervisors are endeavoring to create equality-based identity to accomplish their obligations endowed by their interactional roles. This is also the requirement of the supervisors' identity face and social rights.

To sum up, the orientation of rapport maintenance or management held by the supervisors contributes to their collective identities constructed in the institutional context. Since there exist differences of power and social distance, some appropriate strategies can be chosen to construct a certain collective identity, such as a director, helper and encourager, in a flexible way in contexts where giving advice or making suggestions is necessary in PhD oral defences. This is what is required of the supervisors on the committee: that is, the goal of making comments, making suggestions or giving advice has to be well achieved; at the same time, harmonious relationships need to be managed and maintained between the supervisors and the students. Therefore, we can find rapport orientations in choosing linguistic strategies. This is also why the supervisors adapt themselves to collective identity construction in interaction. These are some collective features about how the supervisors behave in PhD oral defences. So, it is necessary to further explore how speakers manage to achieve both transactional and interpersonal goals in an institutional context, and it is important to attend to the influences that a specific identity constructed dynamically exerts on interpersonal relationships from a pragmatic perspective.

Conclusion

In PhD oral defences, supervisors can provide students with some help for the improvement of their dissertations by making suggestions, giving advice or other guidance, and they may even provide some guidance for the students' academic and personal development in the future. These are obligations and tasks for the supervisors on the committee, which are related to their communicative goals and collective identities of experts acting as directors or helpers in the oral interaction. However, this study demonstrates that the supervisors also take into account interactional goals, which are about the management of personal or interpersonal relationships with the students. As a consequence, the supervisors are found to adopt some strategies for constructing collective identities as well for managing rapport relations with the students. This explains why rapport orientation is frequently found in the data, although there exist differences in power and social distance between the supervisors and the students.

The present study is limited in several ways. First, recognition of the specific identities constructed by the supervisors is a bit subjective, without resorting to operable criteria of judgment. Secondly, only qualitative analysis has been carried out in this study. As a consequence, it is not clear then which of the identities constructed by the supervisors is the most salient. Besides, identity is not the only factor to influence the supervisors' linguistic choices for advice-giving or suggestion-making. In the future, more contextual constraints could be explored from the perspective of interpersonal pragmatics. Last but not least, some contrastive and comparative studies are needed to reveal how different supervisors from the same Chinese cultural background give advice in the same setting. Therefore, a wide range of topics about identity or identity construction in interaction await further investigation, and relevant issues about them can be addressed from different pragmatic perspectives.

Acknowledgment

This study was funded by the MOE project on interpersonal pragmatic competence, our gratitude should thus be expressed.

References

Abolfathiasl, H. (2013) Pragmatics strategies and linguistic structures in making 'suggestions': Towards comprehensive Taxonomies. *International Journal of Applied Linguistics and English Literature* 2(6): 236–241. https://doi.org/10.7575/aiac.ijalel.v.2n.6p.236

Banerjee, J. and Carrell, P. L. (1988) Tuck in your shirt, you squid: Suggestion in ESL. *Language Learning* 38: 313–364. https://doi.org/10.1111/j.1467-1770.1988.tb00416.x

Bonnin, J. E. (2014) To speak with the other's voice: Reducing asymmetry and social distance in professional–client communication. *Journal of Multicultural Discourses* 9(2): 149–171. https://doi.org/10.1080/17447143.2014.890207

Bresnahan, M. (1992) The effects of advisor style on overcoming client resistance in the advising interview. *Discourse Processes* 15(2): 229–247. https://doi.org/10.1080/01638539209544810

Brown, R. and Gilman, A. (1972) Pronouns of power and solidarity. In T. A. Sebeok (ed.) *Style in Language* 253–276. Cambridge, MA: MIT Press. Reprinted in P. Giglioli (ed) *Language and Social Context* 252–282. Harmondsworth: Penguin Books.

Brown, P. and Levinson, S. (1987) *Politeness: Some Universals in Language Usage.* Cambridge: Cambridge University Press.

Brown, G. and Yule, G. (1983) *Teaching the Spoken Language.* Cambridge: Cambridge University Press.

Caffi, C. (2007) *Mitigation.* New York: Elsevier.

Chen, X. (2014) Current research on identity from the pragmatic perspective: Key issues and main approaches. *Xiandai Waiyu (Modern Foreign Languages)* 5: 702–710.

Decapua, A. and Dunham, J. F. (1993) Strategies in the discourse of advice. *Journal of Pragmatics* 20(6): 519–531. https://doi.org/10.1016/0378-2166(93)90014-G

Decapua, A. and Huber, L. (1995) 'If I were you...': Advice in American English. *Multilingua* 14: 117–132. https://doi.org/10.1515/mult.1995.14.2.117

De Fina, A., Schiffrin, D. and Bamberg, M. (2006) Introduction. In A. De Fina, D. Schiffrin and M. Bamberg (eds) *Discourse and Identity* 1–23. Cambridge: Cambridge University Press.

Drew, P. and Heritage, J. (eds) (1992) *Talk at Work: Interaction in Institutional Settings.* Cambridge: Cambridge University Press.

Erickson, F. and Shultz, J. (1982) *The Counselor as Gatekeeper: Social Interaction in Interviews.* New York: Academic Press.

Goffman, E. (1967) *Interactional Ritual: Essays on Face-to-Face Behaviour.* New York: Pantheon Books.

He, A. W. (1993) Exploring modality in institutional interactions: Cases from academic counselling encounters. *Text* 13: 503–528.

He, A. W. (1994) Withholding academic advice: Institutional context and discourse practice. *Discourse Processes* 18(3): 297–316. https://doi.org/10.1080/01638539409544897

He, A. W. (1995) Co-constructing institutional identities: The case of student counselees. *Research on Language and Social Interaction* 28(3): 213–231. https://doi.org/10.1207/s15327973rlsi2803_3

He, A. W. (1996a) Narrative processes and institutional activities: Recipient guided storytelling in academic counseling encounters. *Pragmatics* 6: 205–216. https://doi.org/10.1075/prag.6.2.01he

He, A. W. (1996b) Stories as academic counseling resources. *Journal of Narrative and Life History* 6(2): 107–121. https://doi.org/10.1075/jnlh.6.2.01sto

He, A. W. and Keating, E. (1991) Counselor and student at talk: A case study. *Issues in Applied Linguistics* 2: 183–209.

Heritage, J. and Sefi, S. (1992) Dilemmas of advice: Aspects of the delivery and reception of advice in interactions between health visitors and first-time mothers. In P. Drew and J. Heritage (eds) *Talk at Work: Interaction in Institutional Settings* 359–417. Cambridge: Cambridge University Press.

Holmes, J., Stubbe, M. and Vine, B. (1999) Constructing professional identity: 'Doing power' in policy units. In S. Sarangi and C. Roberts (eds) *Talk, Work and Institutional Order: Discourse in Medical, Mediation and Management Settings* 351–385. Berlin and New York: Mouton de Gruyter.

Hudson, T. (1990) The discourse of advice giving in English: 'I wouldn't feed until spring no matter what you do'. *Language and Communication* 10(4): 285–297. https://doi.org/10.1016/0271-5309(90)90014-3

Hutchby, I. (1995) Aspects of recipient design in expert advice-giving on call-in radio. *Discourse Processes* 19(2): 219–238. https://doi.org/10.1080/01638539509544915

Johnson, C. G. (2006) The discursive construction of teacher identities in a research interview. In A. De Fina., D. Schiffrin and M. Bamberg (eds) *Discourse and Identity* 213–232. Cambridge: Cambridge University Press. https://doi.org/10.1017/CBO9780511584459.011

Kasper, G. (1997) Can pragmatic competence be taught? Retrieved 24 March 2015, from Second Language Teaching and Curriculum centre: http://www.nflrc.hawaii.edu/NetWorks/NW06/.

Kouper, I. (2010) The pragmatics of peer advice in a live journal community. *Language@ Internet* 7: 1–21.

Labov, W. and Fanshel, D. (1977) *Therapeutic Discourse.* New York: Academic Press.

Leppänen, V. (1998) The straightforwardness of advice: Advice-giving in interactions between Swedish district nurses and patients. *Research on Language and Social Interaction* 31(2): 209–239. https://doi.org/10.1207/s15327973rlsi3102_3

Liu, Y. and Zhao, J. (2007) Suggestions in teacher-student conferences. *SLA and Teaching* 14: 59–74.

Locher, M. A. (2006) *Advice Online: Advice-giving in an American Internet Health Column.* Amsterdam and Philadelphia: John Benjamins.

López, M. D. L. O. H. (2008) Rapport management under examination in the context of medical consultations in Spain and Britain. *Revista Alicantina de Estudios Ingleses* 21: 57–86. https://doi.org/10.14198/raei.2008.21.04

Martínez-Flor, A. (2005) A theoretical review of the speech act of suggesting: Towards a taxonomy for its use in FLT. *Revista Alicantina de Estudios Ingleses* 18: 87–103. https://doi.org/10.14198/raei.2005.18.08

Martínez-Flor, A. (2010) Suggestions: How social norms affect pragmatic behaviour. In A. Martínez-Flor and E. Us o-Juan (eds) *Speech Acts Performance: Theoretical, Empirical and Methodological* 246–267. Amsterdam and Philadelphia: John Benjamins.

Omoniyi, T. (2006) Hierarchy of identities. In T. Omoniyi and W. Goodith (eds) *The Sociolinguistics of Identity* 11–13. New York: Continuum.

Pilnick, A. (1999) 'Patient counseling' by pharmacists: Advice, information, or instruction? *Sociological Quarterly* 40(4): 613–622. https://doi.org/10.1111/j.1533-8525.1999.tb00570.x

Pilnick, A. (2001) The interactional organization of pharmacist consultations in a hospital setting: A putative structure. *Journal of Pragmatics* 33(12): 1927–1945. https://doi.org/10.1016/S0378-2166(00)00079-5

Planken, B. (2005) Managing rapport in lingua franca sales negotiations: A comparison of professional and aspiring negotiators. *English for Specific Purposes* 24(4): 381–400. https://doi.org/10.1016/j.esp.2005.02.002

Ren, Y. (2014) A review of studies on advising abroad. *Waiyu Jiaoxu Lilun yu Shijian (Foreign Language Learning Theory and Practice)* 4: 49–54.

Schiffrin, D. (1987) *Discourse Markers.* Cambridge: Cambridge University Press. https://doi.org/10.1017/CBO9780511611841

Scollon, R. and Scollon, S. W. (2001) *Intercultural Communication: A Discourse Approach.* Oxford: Blackwell.

Searle, J. R. (1969) *Speech Acts: An Essay in the Philosophy of Language.* Cambridge: Cambridge University Press. https://doi.org/10.1017/CBO9781139173438

Spencer-Oatey, H. (ed.) (2000) Rapport management: A framework for analysis. *Culturally Speaking: Managing Rapport through Talk across Cultures* 11–46. London: Continuum.

Spencer-Oatey, H. (2002) Managing rapport in talk: Using rapport sensitive incidents to explore the motivational concerns underlying the management of relations. *Journal of Pragmatics* 34(5): 529–545. https://doi.org/10.1016/S0378-2166(01)00039-X

Spencer-Oatey, H. (2005) (Im)politeness, face and perceptions of rapport: Unpacking their bases and interrelationships. *Journal of Politeness Research* 1(1): 95–119. https://doi.org/10.1515/jplr.2005.1.1.95

Spencer-Oatey, H. (2007) Theories of identity and the analysis of face. *Journal of Pragmatics* 39(4): 639–656. https://doi.org/10.1016/j.pragma.2006.12.004

Spencer-Oatey, H. (2008) *Culturally Speaking: Culture, Communication and Politeness Theory.* London: Continuum.

Sun, Y. (2013) A study on supervisor team's collective identity construction: A case study of the use of first-person plural pronouns 'we/us'. *Waiyu yu Waiyu Jiaoxue (Foreign Languages and their Teaching)* 6: 11–14.

Vehviläinen, S. (2001) Evaluative advice in educational counseling: The use of disagreement in the 'stepwise entry' to advice. *Research on Language and Social Interaction* 34(3): 371–398. https://doi.org/10.1207/S15327973RLSI34-3_4

Vehviläinen, S. (2009) Student-initiated advice in academic supervision. *Research on Language and Social Interaction* 42(2): 163–190. https://doi.org/10.1080/08351810902864560

Wenger, E. (1998) *Communities of Practice: Learning, Meaning, and Identity.* Cambridge: Cambridge University Press. https://doi.org/10.1017/CBO9780511803932

Yu, K. and Cable, D. (2010) Exploring the identity and reputation of department groups: Whose opinions matter most to their members? *Human Resource Management Journal* 2: 105–121.

Yuan, Z. and Chen, X. (2013) A study of pragmatic identity construction from the perspective of linguistic adaptation theory – A case study of medical consultations. *Waiyu Jiaoxue yu Yanjiu (Foreign Language Teaching and research)* 4: 518–529.

PART III

Politeness in various conflictive Chinese situations

Rapport orientations of women guests when making refusals and obligations of hosts on Chinese reality TV dating shows

Tzu-Wei Hsiang and Victoria Rau

Introduction

Refusal is a high-risk face-threatening act (FTA; Brown and Levinson 1987) because it contradicts the expectations of the speaker when the interlocutor directly or indirectly says 'no' to a request, invitation, suggestion or offer. Many previous studies (e.g., Fukushima 1996; Le Pair 1996; Yu 2003) have indicated that different cultural backgrounds will affect the cognition of face maintenance. Although refusals occur in all languages, not all languages or cultures refuse in the same way (Abdullah 2007). Allami and Naeimi (2011: 388) point out that, in general, the current literature on refusals indicates that one's cultural orientation, language proficiency, interlocutor status and residence in the target community seem to affect the type and frequency of strategies used in making a refusal.

Many studies on refusals made by Chinese speakers have dealt with this speech act from either a cross-linguistic or cross-cultural comparative perspective (Beebe, Takahashi and Robin 1990; Gao 2009; Guo 2012; Peng and Yuan 2006). However, no systematic investigation has used an interactive sociolinguistic approach to investigate naturally occurring data from TV programmes, like TV dating programmes. Originating in Western countries, such as the UK, the programmes are widely broadcast in Taiwan and Mainland China, and yet entirely different styles seem to have evolved. Therefore, it is worth exploring the interaction between facework and (sub)culture by investigating and comparing the differences in expressing refusals between Taiwan and Mainland China with special reference to politeness orientations.

A TV dating show incorporates a societal dating system and matchmaking practices in the form of a selection game. Dating is a publicly expressed practice undertaken by romantically interested partners for the purpose of getting to know one another better (Eaton and Rose 2011: 844) with the possibility of leading towards marriage. A TV dating show, like other TV game shows, is considered a modern form of the folk games that used to be popular at fairs and public gatherings before the advent of television (Williams 1975). As the dating show is construed as a performance for public entertainment, our interpretations of the differences between women in Taiwan and Mainland China in terms of their manners of giving refusals need to keep this setting in mind. Therefore, the speech act of refusal in a TV dating show should be re-contextualised as the speech event of negotiation between male and female guests in order to find a potential dating partner. Meanwhile, the hosts' roles in the TV dating shows are discussed, since the hosts play a crucial role in determining whether male guests can successfully get the date.

Theoretical background

This study adopts Scollon and Scollon's (1995) interactive sociolinguistic approach to examine (sub)culture as a discourse system. In the following parts, the four elements of their discourse system are discussed.

History

Scollon and Scollon's (2004) nexus analysis treats a social action as the intersection of historical body, the interaction order, and discourses in place. An action of refusal has to be interpreted in its nexus which, according to Wortham (2006), refers to 'a repeated site of engagement where some type of social action is facilitated by a relatively consistent set of social processes'. When engaging the nexus of practice, people have to find its historical background, crucial social actors, observe the interaction order and determine the most significant cycles of discourse (Scollon and Scollon 2004).

In this study, women's refusal acts in TV dating shows are social actions, which cannot be properly interpreted without considering the women's dating history in their own time and place, the interaction order between female and male guests, and the significant cycles of choosing potential partners in the dating programme. The women's dating history influences their own thoughts and views when they choose potential partners. For example, some of them would say that they did not like a male guest with a particular sign of the zodiac, as they had previously broken up with such a partner before. Other women would say that they did not like particular occupations and use this reason to refuse to date a male guest. Meanwhile, the differences in the roles of the hosts and whether the males and females participate equally in the show place constraints on the interaction order in the two TV dating shows. The differences in the significant cycle of choosing partners also influence their styles of communication.

Ideology

The gender roles in TV dating shows are constructed based on a heterosexual ideology (Eckert and McConnell-Ginet 2003). A male guest construed as a king or prince has the privilege of choosing an attractive woman from a large group of women. However, before the male guest chooses his princess, the women will express their first impressions of the male guest. If they refuse to proceed to the next round of the game, they will turn off their light. The host may then ask some of them to give reasons for their refusal to go out with the male guest. At this moment, it can be seen that women from Taiwan and Mainland China have their own values and agendas when choosing a potential boyfriend or spouse. A Taiwanese female may consider the male guest's personality, family background and occupation to be just as important as his appearance, as they may be serious in looking for a date. A female from Mainland China may consider the male guest's 'height, wealth, and handsome appearance' (高、富、帥 in Chinese) as the only criteria because their intention of attracting the TV audience's attention often supersedes their goals of finding a potential mate (Yin 2011). We will see how the women refuse a male guest and how the hosts collaborate in the process.

Face

Spencer-Oatey and Franklin's (2010) rapport management and Arundale's (2006) ideas on face are used to explain the different strategies of refusal that women use in the TV dating shows. According to Spencer-Oatey and Franklin (2010), rapport management involves two main components: i) the management of face, and ii) the management of sociality rights. Face is associated with personal/social value, and is concerned with people's sense of worth, reputation and honour (Spencer-Oatey 2002: 540). Sociality rights, on the other hand, are concerned with personal/social entitlements, and reflect people's concerns for consideration and social inclusion/exclusion (Spencer-Oatey 2002: 540). Spencer-Oatey and Franklin (2010: 103) propose six competencies in rapport management: contextual awareness, interpersonal attentiveness, social information gathering, social attuning, emotion regulation and stylistic flexibility. Applying the six competences, they explain why a British engineering company and a Chinese business delegation have different points of view towards seating arrangements, team introductions and business relationships (Spencer-Oatey 2003, 2005). As Spencer-Oatey and Franklin's model promises a deeper understanding of the factors that influence people's dynamic judgments of rapport, we will use their six competencies in rapport management to analyse how females in Taiwan and Mainland China differ in making refusals on TV dating shows.

Sometimes, face is also viewed as an emergent property of relationships rather than a matter of the individual actor's public self-image. Arundale (2006: 200) proposes two kinds of face, namely connection and separation faces, which are in a dialectic relationship. Connectedness indexes a complex set of meanings and actions that may be apparent, like unity, solidarity and congruence, but separateness indexes meanings and action that may be voiced as differentiation, independence and divergence (Arundale 2006: 204).

Forms of communication

Since refusal is a face-threatening act, it requires special skills. Scollon and Scollon (1995) distinguish involvement (inductive) from independence (deductive) as two linguistic strategies in their face (politeness) systems and identify three politeness systems based on power (P) and distance (D): deference (−P, +D), solidarity (−P, −D) and hierarchical (+P, +/−D).

In addition to linguistic strategies, we also examine how non-verbal signs are used in collaboration with verbal messages to express refusals in TV dating shows. This kind of non-verbal communication cannot be easily transcribed in words, but it is very crucial to our understanding of the intended meaning in the interactions (Scollon and Scollon 1995: 156). Therefore, we will explore and compare the non-verbal signs seen at the same time as the women verbally give their reasons for refusal.

Background of the shows

Before the research questions are introduced, it is important to explain how the show runs. When the male guest first appears on the stage, he is asked to introduce himself and hand the name of his initial choice of woman to the host, based on the profiles he has seen backstage. The women are given the chance to indicate their lack of interest in him by pushing a button. After that, a video introducing the background of the man is played, accompanied by words from a recommender (in Taiwan) or a question time (in Mainland China). At this point, both women and men are allowed to ask questions of the other before the women are given the chance again to indicate their lack of interest by pushing a button, after which the host will ask some to comment on why they have refused the man. At the end, the man can choose two women from those who still remain interested and raise a question for each of them to answer. Finally, he will choose his princess and go out with the woman for a date arranged by the show organiser.

In the following, Hymes's (1986) SPEAKING grid (Setting, Participant, End,

Act sequence, Key, Instrumentality, Norm and Genre) is used to introduce the background of the two TV dating shows, as summarised in Table 8.1.

Table 8.1. Comparison of the two TV dating shows based on Hymes's (1986) SPEAKING grid

	Take Me Out, Taiwan (王子的約會) **Taiwan**	*Take Me Out!* (我们约会吧!) **Mainland China**
S (Setting)	The stage is smaller and simpler.	The stage is larger in scale and higher in production value.
P (Participant)	26 female guests and a maximum of 50 audience members.	30 female guests and nearly 100 audience members.
E (End)	Making friends with the opposite sex possibly leading towards marriage.	Mostly striving to become a famous and popular contestant.
A (Act sequence)	Includes a segment called 'Recommender'.	Includes a segment called 'Question time'.
K (Key)	Friendly, relaxed and funny.	Competitive, serious and formal.
I (Instrumentality)	Handwrites a woman's name on a small paper card.	Uses a hi-tech device, an iPad, to show his choice of woman.
N (Norm)	Entertainment	Entertainment
G (Genre)	Drama	Performance

The setting of Taiwan's TV dating show is different from that in Mainland China. The stage in Taiwan is smaller and simpler than the one in Mainland China. This indicates that the TV dating show in Mainland China has a much larger scale and higher production value than the one in Taiwan. The participants can be divided into four types: female guests, male guests, hosts and audience members. Except for the number of male guests per show, all of the other participant components differ. There are around 5 to 6 male guests per show in both Taiwan and Mainland China, depending on the time taken by each person. There are 26 female guests on Taiwan's TV dating show, but in Mainland China's TV dating show, 30 women are chosen to participate. The Taiwan show is jointly run by a host and a hostess, while the Mainland show is run by only one host. Regarding audience members, there is a maximum of 50 people in Taiwan, but nearly 100 people in Mainland China. Finally, there is a stipulation in both Taiwan and Mainland China that the guests must be single.

'Ends' and 'Keys' in this context refer to the purpose and manner of the two TV dating programmes, which clearly differ. The goal of the Taiwanese dating programme appears to be to help the females make more friends, possibly leading towards marriage. Therefore, the manner on the dating show is more friendly, relaxed and funny. However, most, if not all, of the female guests on the Mainland Chinese dating show seem to be striving to become famous and popular. As pointed out by Yin (2011), TV dating shows have become very popular in Mainland China recently for the following reasons. First, people in Mainland China are willing to show themselves to the mass population, and TV dating shows give them the opportunity. Second, many people think that participating in TV shows provides a chance to become famous around the country overnight. Due to the Internet and the ubiquity of handheld electronic devices, the TV shows have become a short-cut to fame. Yin indicates that Liu Lei, the TV producer of *Take Me Out!* (我们约会吧!) in Mainland China once said that the content of TV dating shows is more important than the rate of success in getting a date. 'The females in "Take Me Out我们约会吧!" in Mainland China dare to speak very much', according to Liu Lei. This unique characteristic of daring to speak is important in allowing the TV dating show participants to become popular and famous so quickly. Therefore, they are much more competitive, making the tone of the entire show much more serious and formal.

There are both similarities and differences in the act sequence of the two shows. In Mainland China, the question time involves the male guest being asked many questions related to his personality, daily life and thoughts about love. Taiwan's dating show has a segment called 'Recommender'. In this segment, the male chooses a person to recommend him to the females.

The instrumentality that males use to reveal their choice of desired soul mate prior to meeting the women also differs between the two shows. In Taiwan, the man handwrites a woman's name on a small paper card. However, the instrumentality in Mainland China is more hi-tech, employing an iPad.

The norms of public dialogue on TV programmes are different from the norms in private conversations. On this point, the TV programmes in Mainland China and Taiwan have similar norms, that is, public entertainment. Although the TV programmes have a similar norm, each TV programme has its own purpose, which will affect the way that participants behave. The genres of the TV dating shows in Taiwan and Mainland China are different. The former is more like a drama, with the hosts playing the role of a match-maker, while the latter is like a performance, with the host serving as a master of ceremonies.

Methodology

Research questions

The research questions in this study are as follows.

1. What different strategies of refusal are used by women in Taiwan and Mainland China when they refuse to date the male guests?

2. How do the two hosts of the two TV dating shows negotiate their roles in this face-threatening act?

3. How are non-verbal signs related to the women's verbal behaviour in refusals?

Data collection

As this study attempts to investigate and compare the refusal behaviours of women on TV dating shows in Taiwan and Mainland China, the data of this study was collected from two TV dating shows: *Take Me Out, Taiwan* (王子的約會) from Taiwan and *Take Me Out!* (我们约会吧!) from Mainland China.

The first two research questions aim to explore the different methods used by women guests who give refusals, and how the hosts negotiate their roles in the face-threatening act in Taiwan and Mainland China, thus conversations between males and females and the hosts' responses were collected and presented. Since the host typically mediates the interaction between males and females, including the refusals, most of the data could be used to address either of these two research questions. The third research question explores non-verbal signs used by women to represent themselves as they reject the male guest, so screen shots were taken for illustration.

Take Me Out! (我们约会吧!) in Mainland China aired twice per week, whereas *Take Me Out, Taiwan* (王子的約會) aired only once a week. Therefore, the number of episodes in mainland China and Taiwan differed. In order to balance the number of episodes examined from the two areas, the data was collected for different lengths of time. This study analysed 56 episodes of *Take Me Out!* (我们约会吧!) from Mainland China which aired from February 2013 to August 2013, and 48 episodes of *Take Me Out, Taiwan* (王子的約會) which aired from August 2012 to August 2013.[1] For the non-verbal data, screenshots were selected from these 104 episodes.

Data analysis

After the episodes were collected, they were categorised by area (Taiwan vs Mainland), and the episodes of the two areas were compared. In order to give a detailed analysis and comparison of women's usage of refusal in Taiwan and Mainland China, it was necessary to transcribe every conversation in which the women refuse male guests. As noted in the background, the refusal took place when a woman turned off her light, and was subsequently called on by the host to explain why she had turned it off so as to refuse to date the man. One unit of conversation exchange was counted as the female gave her reasons for refusing the male guest, along with the response of the male guest. Thus, each conversation between a female and a male guest, mediated by the host, was counted as one unit of conversation exchange, providing 1,292 units of conversation exchange as examples in this study. Due to space limitations, we only focused on the qualitative discourse analysis in this study. Quantitative data from the same study can be found in Hsiang (2014).

Results and discussion

This section aims to explore in detail the refusal strategies. There are three parts which address the women's refusal acts, the hosts' negotiation roles and the non-verbal signs, respectively. First, the Taiwanese females show different contextual awareness and interpersonal attentiveness than the females in Mainland China. For example, the Taiwanese females are found to have a tendency to save the face of the male guests by using an indirect way of expressing personal opinions in the refusal. In contrast, the females in Mainland China prefer to use a more direct approach when refusing male guests. In addition, the females in Taiwan prefer to use an enhancement and maintenance orientation when they refuse the male guests, whereas the females in Mainland China tend to use a neglect and challenge orientation. Second, the host of the Taiwanese TV dating show adopts a connection face when the female guests refuse the male guests, but the host of the Mainland Chinese TV dating show adopts a separation face when handling the same face-threatening act. Furthermore, the host in Taiwan adopts an involvement strategy and solidarity politeness system (−P, −D) while the host in Mainland China adopts an independence strategy and hierarchical politeness system (+P, +D). Finally, the Taiwan and Mainland China females use different social attuning and styles when they refuse the male guests.

In the following sections, sets of examples contrasting the Taiwan and Mainland China shows are presented, followed by explanations. 'F' means a female guest; 'M' means a male guest; 'H' means the host ('FH' and 'MH' the female and male host, respectively, in Taiwan). The examples listed in this section are all transcribed and selected from our database of the TV dating shows.

Women's refusal behaviour

In this section, examples of the women's refusal behaviour actions are presented first, followed by explanations based on Spencer-Oatey and Franklin (2010), Scollon and Scollon (1995) and Arundale (2006).

A. Height is the most important thing in the world! (高就是王道!)

(1) Taiwan

F: 我很喜歡運動，所以我不介意他是運動員，可是對我來說他太高大，我怕我們手牽手出去很像在牽小猴子。

F: I like exercising; so I don't mind that he is an athlete. But for me, he is too tall. I am afraid that he will look like a man holding a monkey when we walk together.

(2) Mainland China

F: 我不能接受比我矮的男生，第二個是我覺得他長得不是很厚道。

F: The first reason is that I can't accept a man who is shorter than I. The second reason is that I feel that he doesn't look honest and kind.

In this set of examples, the women refuse the male guests because of their appearance. The one in Taiwan comments about the male guest's height, while the other about his height and facial appearance.

The Taiwanese female first compliments the male guest by saying that she likes athletes; she gives her reason for refusal in an indirect way by means of self-degradation. She even compares herself to a monkey in the simile of 'we will look like a man holding a monkey' in order to save the face of the male guest. Therefore, the Taiwanese female's compliment of the male's athletic training addresses the male guest's face sensitivity in interpersonal attentiveness. Moreover, the female's contextual awareness positions the participants' relationship as equality and closeness.

In contrast, the female in Mainland China acts very differently by directly stating that the male guest is short and commenting negatively on his appearance, using very direct words to expresses her thoughts. Her contextual awareness positions the participant's relationship as inequality and distance. The way she expresses herself indicates that she ranks herself higher than the male guest. She also shows distance from the male guest by using a very direct criticism to refuse the male guest. She does not concern herself with saving his face; in fact, her words might make him feel humiliated.

B. Baby face and oil field! (娃娃臉與油田!)

(3) Taiwan

F: 王子你好，我覺得你長得很高也很帥，可是你的臉有一點太小了。女主持

FH: 娃娃臉。

F: 我們以後如果要自拍的話，我就要跑得很遠。

F: Hi Prince, I think you are very handsome and tall, but your face is a little bit too small.

FH: He has a baby face.

F: If we wanted to take a selfie, I would have to stand farther away.

(4) Mainland China

F:　　反光。

H:　　反光? 什麼意思?

F:　　油田，他臉出油出的太厲害了，而且再加上他的服裝面料選擇的是絲絨的面料，就更會顯的反光，我不想以後如果我的另一半跟我說悄悄話的時候，蹭我一臉油。

F:　　Reflection.

H:　　What do you mean by 'reflection'?

F:　　An oil field. His face looks very oily. Also, he chooses clothes made of velvet, which make his face look even more oily. I don't want my face to become oily when my better half whispers to me.

In these two examples, the male guests are both refused because of facial problems. The Taiwanese female compliments the male guest and then gives her reason for refusal in an indirect way. She thinks that the size of his face is small, and she jokes that she would have to stand farther away if they wanted to take a selfie. Before she gives her reason, she says a few good words about the male guest in order to save his face. As in the previous example, the Taiwanese female's compliment of the male's appearance addresses the male guest's face sensitivity in interpersonal attentiveness and her contextual awareness positions the participants' relationship as equality and closeness. When the female complains that the male's face is a bit too small, the host applies connection face by re-interpreting the small face positively as 'a baby face'.

In contrast, the female in Mainland China acts very differently, directly stating that the male guest has a very oily face and then further criticising his clothing. Her contextual awareness again positions the participant's relationship as inequality and distance. The way she expresses herself indicates that she considers herself higher than the male guest. She also shows distance from the male guest by using a very direct criticism to refuse the male guest, even using the third person singular pronoun to criticise his facial features in response to the host's question. She shows no concern for his face; in fact, her words are likely to humiliate him. The host also fosters a negative reply by simply asking the female to clarify her complaint about his oily face without re-interpreting it in a positive way, which is an application of separation face.

C. Age is more important than excellence (再優秀也沒有用!)

(5) Taiwan

F:　　他真的很優秀，可是…

H:　　我知道。

F:　　沒錯，超級優秀，膚色也好好看喔，可是我真的沒有辦法，就是接受年紀比我小的。

F: He is very excellent. However, I …

H: I know what you want to say.

F: He is very excellent and also his skin colour looks nice. However, I really can't accept someone younger than me.

(6) Mainland China

F: 因為你太小了所以不符合我，所以我就把燈給滅了。

F: Because you are too young to be my type, I turn off my light.

In these two examples, the male guests are refused because of age. The Taiwanese female compliments the male guest and then gives her reason for refusal in an indirect way. She thinks that he is excellent and she feels very sorry for not choosing him. The Taiwanese female's compliment of the male addresses the male guest's face sensitivity. Moreover, the female's contextual awareness positions the participants' relationship as equality and closeness. When the female complains about the male, the host applies connection face, in this case with the female, by agreeing with what she says.

In contrast, the female in Mainland China directly states that he is not qualified because of his age. Her contextual awareness positions the participant's relationship as inequality and distance. The way she expresses herself indicates that she ranks herself higher than the male guest. She does not care if the male guest is excellent or good-looking. She refuses him simply because of his age.

D. I don't like pets or bookworms (不喜歡寵物與書呆子)

(7) Taiwan

F: 其實我有看到就是王子你很孝順，然後你又很有專業，你對家人也都很好，我都很喜歡，但是就是在寵物方面，我對寵物就是有一點恐懼，沒有辦法接受太常與寵物在一起。

F: I can see, Prince, you show respect to you parents, and you have professional abilities. I really like these points. However, I am a little bit afraid of pets. I can't handle a life of living together with pets.

(8) Mainland China

F: 那個我覺得你這體型也不像健過身的呀，有點太瘦，我要找一個結實一點的，然後呢，我比較喜歡有藝術氣息的男生，我不喜歡書呆子氣息的。

F: I don't think your figure looks like you have exercised enough. You are a bit too thin. I want to find a man who is a little stronger. And I prefer a man with an artistic spirit, rather than a bookworm.

In these examples, the two females use their personal interests to refuse the male guests. One does not like pets, the other does not like bookworms. The Taiwanese female compliments the male guest about his filial devotion towards his parents and his professional ability and then gives her reason for refusal in an indirect way. Though the male guest has many advantages, she still cannot accept him due to the pet issue. Before she gives her reason, she says good words about him. As in the other examples, the Taiwanese female's compliment of the male's personality and professional abilities addresses the male guest's face sensitivity, showing interpersonal attentiveness. Moreover, the female's contextual awareness positions the participants' relationship as equality and closeness.

In contrast, the female in Mainland China acts very differently, directly stating that he did not exercise enough and then further criticising him for being bookish. As with the other women from Mainland China, her contextual awareness positions the participant's relationship as inequality and distance, and the way she expresses herself indicates that she considers herself superior to the male guest. She also shows more distance from the male guest by positioning herself as hard to please. As in the other examples, her words could make him feel humiliated rather than saving his face.

As can be seen from the preceding examples, Taiwanese and Mainland females use diametrically opposed strategies when giving refusals. The Taiwanese females all use an involvement strategy by showing warmth to the male guest. Moreover, they also use a solidarity politeness system, presenting no power difference or distance (−P, −D) between the participants. However, the females from Mainland China use an independence strategy. They distance themselves from the male guest by using very harsh words and very strong statements. In other words, they adopt a hierarchical politeness system (+P, +D) in their interactions with the male guests by being distant towards them.

In short, based on the previous examples and explanations, it is clear that the females in both Taiwan and Mainland China use excuses like age, face, height and personal interest to refuse the male guests. However, the females in Taiwan tend

Table 8.2. Comparison between refusal strategies employed by females on dating shows in Taiwan and Mainland China

		Taiwan	Mainland China
Spencer-Oatey and Franklin (2010)	Contextual awareness:	Equality, Closeness	Inequality, Distance
	Interpersonal attentiveness:	Complimenting, Face saving	Criticising, Humiliating
Scollon and Scollon (1995)		Enhancement/maintenance, Solidarity politeness system	Neglect/challenge, Hierarchical politeness system
Arundale (2006)		Connection face	Separation face

to use enhancement strategy and a solidarity politeness system when they refuse the male guests. In contrast, the females in Mainland China use the opposite strategies, neglect and a hierarchical politeness system. Moreover, they also have different contextual awareness and interpersonal attentiveness. These results are summarised in Table 8.2.

The hosts' mediation roles

Matching the styles of the female guests, the hosts play the role of either matchmaker or 'matchbreaker' when mediating the interactions between the female and male guests. The following examples provide details of how the hosts negotiate their roles in the TV dating shows in Taiwan and Mainland China.

A. *Persuasion vs sarcasm* (說客 *vs* 冷嘲熱諷)

(9) Taiwan

F:　就是王子看起來忠厚老實，但是因爲年紀真的太小。

H:　年紀太小了，但是其實說真的，以他的年紀，他那個談吐，我的感覺是，是穩重的耶。

F:　The prince looks honest and sincere, but he is really too young.

H:　Is he too young? But I think he is quite mature considering his age and based on his way of speaking.

(10) Mainland China

F:　身高差距，然後語言溝通能力。

M:　爲什麼會這麼講呢？

H:　這都這麼明擺著的還要問嗎？

F:　Our height and communication ability are different.

M:　Why do you say that?

H:　Do you have to ask? It's so obvious.

The two examples show that the hosts of the TV shows also act differently when they negotiate face in the face-threatening act of refusal between the guests. In the Taiwanese example, after the female says the male guest is too young for her, the host says that he thinks the male guest acts in quite a mature manner for his age. He is defending the male guest, indicating his contextual awareness of role obligation as a matchmaker for the TV dating show. He acts as a mediator to pass the words between the female and the male guest and save the face of both. Meanwhile, the host in Taiwan demonstrates emotional regulation by showing resilience and high social involvement in handling criticism and embarrassment skilfully.

By contrast the host in Mainland China acts likes an emcee in a talk show. His response towards the male guest indicates that he agrees with the female and feels no need for the male guest to ask for clarification. Instead of defending or saving face, the host makes a pointed comment that demeans the guest. As the programme is a dating show, it seems that the host's job and responsibility should be to increase the chances of successfully getting a date instead of ruining those chances. However, the host seems to have used a separation face so that he could remain detached in the battle and maintain independence in the negotiation of face.

B. Explaining in detail vs coping without concern *(詳細解釋 vs 隨便應付)*

(11) Taiwan

F: 我沒有辦法接受男生化妝。

M: 我沒有化妝。

F: 但是他剛剛說他化妝。

MH: 我也化妝啦，來這邊的都要畫，妳知道來這邊一定要化妝妳知道嗎，因爲這個燈光打到臉上，如果你不化妝你的臉就像一顆蛋一樣。

F: I can't accept a male who wears make-up.

M: I don't wear make-up.

F: But he said that he wore make-up.

MH: I also wear make-up. Everyone has to wear make-up when he/she comes onstage because of the lighting. If you don't wear make-up, your face will look like an egg.

(12) Mainland China

F: 雖然說我兩米多了，但是就是平時喜歡坐著。

M: 兩米多??

F: 對，我現在是坐著的，平常老站起來太累了。

H: 你是不是覺得我們這舞台上人講話，你都有點丈二和尚，摸不著頭緒。

M: 是呀! 我覺得我思維夠跳躍的了，她的思維我實在搞不清。

F: 是嗎! 那就沒溝通慾望啦~ 再見。

F: Although I am 200 cm tall, I like to sit down.

M: Really 200 cm tall?

F: Yes, I am sitting now. It is very tiring if I always stand.

H: Do you think that the female on stage speaks without reason? She is like a 200 cm tall monk. You can't reach her head.[2]

M: Yes. I thought that I was quite illogical sometimes, but I can't really understand what she thinks since her thinking is so illogical.

F: Really? Then I don't need to continue communicating. Goodbye.

The examples give further instances of how the hosts of the TV shows act in mediating refusals. In the Taiwanese example, after the female says that she does not like the male guest wearing make-up, the host rationalises his decision by stating that it is necessary for the guest to wear make-up due to the stage lighting. In saying this, he is defending the male guest, indicating contextual awareness of his obligation as a matchmaker for the show and saving face for both of them. Meanwhile, the host demonstrates emotional regulation by showing resilience and high social involvement in handling criticism and embarrassment skilfully.

However, the host in Mainland China asks questions to help clarify the intent of the interlocutors instead of defending anybody. Even though the female's opinion does not seem to make sense, the host does not disgrace her. Furthermore, he uses a literary allusion in a question to prompt the male guest to express his evaluation of the female. The literary allusion to a 200 cm tall monk is complex (lit. 'She is too tall for you to reach her brain'). It does not imply that the female is actually logical, but that her thinking is so complex that you cannot understand it. Hence, the host employs a separation face so that he can stay outside of the battle and maintain independence in the negotiation of face (Arundale 2006).

C. Helping the male guest vs not helping (幫腔 **vs** 扯後腿)

(13) Taiwan

F:　就是因爲流浪狗這件事，我覺得應該是要拿回家養，而不是在外面餵牠，他應該馬上給它抱回來。

M:　那時候正在打工，所以那時候大夜班趕快衝出去買，買回來給牠吃。

MH:　算是很有愛心耶！而且妳那個說法其實不太實際

F:　Regarding the stray dog, I think that he should have brought it home instead of feeding it outside. He should carry it home immediately.

M:　The reason is that I had a part-time job at the time. I had to go out to buy something to feed it when I was on the night shift.

MH:　You are so benevolent! What you (the female) said sounds a bit unrealistic.

(14) Mainland China

F:　從上場看你到現在你一直在晃腿，從沒停過。

M:　因爲比較緊張。

F:　你緊張就晃腿，一抖窮，二抖富。不對，男越抖越窮。

H:　女的呢？

F:　女…越抖越壞！

H:　沒話說了吧！

F:　沒話說了。

F:　Your legs have been shaking ever since you came onstage.

M: Because I am nervous.

F: When you are nervous, your legs will shake. You will become poor if you shake your legs once, but rich if you shake your legs a second time.[3] That's not right! A man will become poorer the more he shakes his legs.

H: How about a female?

F: A female … the more she shakes her legs, the more promiscuous she will become.

H: There's not much more to say!

F: Nope!

In (13), after the female says that she has a different opinion from the male guest, the host comments on the male guest's benevolent action. Therefore, he is defending the male guest, indicating contextual awareness of his obligation in his role as a matchmaker for the show. Meanwhile, the host also demonstrates emotional regulation by showing resilience and high social involvement in handling embarrassment skilfully.

In contrast, the host in Mainland China asks questions that humiliate the female, highlighting her failure to quote the literary allusion properly, instead of helping build the relationship or helping the male guest get a date. By remaining disengaged in the battle, the host is in control of the situation, again giving him higher status, allowing him to use a neglect and challenge orientation.

In summary, the contextual awareness and interpersonal attentiveness of the hosts in Taiwan and Mainland China are very different. The former adopt a matchmaker's involvement strategy while the latter choose an emcee's independence strategy. Furthermore, the orientations of the hosts in Taiwan and Mainland China are different. The Taiwanese hosts use an enhancement and maintenance orientation, whereas the hosts in Mainland China use a neglect and challenge orientation. Interestingly, our data indicate that the hosts and the females in the two TV dating show are consistent in their stances towards rapport management and orientation. In addition, the hosts and females in both Taiwan and Mainland China also demonstrate a consistent interactive face and politeness system. While the former use a connection face and solidarity politeness system (−P, −D), the latter adopt a separation face and hierarchical politeness system (+P, +D).

Table 8.3. Comparison between the Taiwanese host and the host in Mainland China

	Taiwan	Mainland China
Spencer-Oatey and Franklin (2010)	Matchmaker	Emcee
Scollon and Scollon (1995)	Solidarity politeness system, Maintenance strategy	Hierarchical politeness system, Challenge strategy
Arundale (2006)	Connection face	Separation face

Although the females and host in each place use similar strategies, it is impossible to determine from our data who have influenced whom, or whether both have adopted a system imposed by others.

The comparison between the hosts in Taiwan and Mainland China is summarised in Table 8.3.

Non-verbal communication in refusals

In the following paragraph, we briefly describe how non-verbal communication in social attuning (Spencer-Oatey and Franklin 2010: 102) is related to the women's refusal behaviour. For the females' privacy, we do not include any pictures of real people here.

The Taiwanese females smile when giving their refusal, whereas the females from Mainland China pull a long face and cross their arms over their chests, consistent with the connection or separation face they adopt in their verbal interaction. Therefore, social attuning complements contextual awareness and interpersonal attentiveness to form a type of collage in expressing refusals, a finding consistent with Eckert's ethnographic study (1989). Table 8.4 summarises the comparison of the non-verbal signs used by females in Taiwan and Mainland China.

Table 8.4. Comparison of the females' non-verbal signs

	Taiwan	Mainland China
Non-verbal signs	Smile	Long face, Crosses her arms, Looks down her nose at male guests.

Conclusion

This study uses an interactive sociolinguistic approach to investigate different strategies used by Chinese women when giving refusals on TV dating shows in Taiwan and Mainland China. Informed by Spencer-Oatey and Franklin's (2010) rapport management, Arundale's (2006) face system and Scollon and Scollon's (1995) intercultural communication, we have analysed the different verbal strategies and non-verbal signs of refusal used by women in Taiwan and Mainland China and the interactive face adopted by the hosts of the two TV dating shows in negotiating their roles during the face-threatening act. We find that the females in Taiwan and Mainland China have different contextual awareness and interpersonal attentiveness (Spencer-Oatey and Franklin 2010) and face systems (Arundale 2006; Scollon and Scollon 1995), as do the hosts of the two shows. The Taiwanese hosts are more like matchmakers, while those from the Mainland Chinese act like emcees. The hosts from the two places apply different face systems in their interactions with the guests.

The differences in how they perform the face-threatening act of refusal might be explained by the ideology and socialisation of the two Chinese speech communities. The competitiveness to achieve social mobility in Mainland China, as shown in the nature of the programme, might foster independence and separation in public presentation, while the Chinese heritage of Confucianism in Taiwan, as embodied in the purpose of the programme, might encourage self-denigration and connection in self-expression. Influenced by the respective sociocultural backgrounds, the females in Mainland China act in a more direct and competitive way, using a neglect and challenge orientation in their relationship, while the women in Taiwan use a more indirect and humble manner to give refusals, trying to maintain and strengthen the relationship between the interlocutors.

As this study is only based on a specific TV dating show within a limited time period, the interpretations of the Chinese women's refusal strategies are not meant to generalise to a wider population. For future research, one could use the same method presented in this study to investigate how Chinese women refuse to date men from non-Chinese cultures. In addition, it would be interesting to explore how Chinese men and women construct desirable men and women in the heterosexual marketplace.

Notes

1. All the data transcriptions can be accessed via the following link: https://mega.co.nz/#F!QNMQVKoK!zCNr_Wk_uNmsuRwQlERMqg.
2. This is a Chinese idiom. As the monk is too tall for people to reach his head, so can one's thought be too high and difficult to understand.
3. This is a literary illusion to 男抖穷、女抖賤 'If a man shakes his legs, he is poor; if a woman shakes her legs, she is promiscuous', but the female guest did not remember how to cite it properly.

References

Abdullah, A. A. E. (2007) Refusal strategies by Yemeni EFL learners. *The Asian EFL Journal Quarterly* 9(2): 19–34.

Allami, H. and Naeimi, A. (2011) A cross-linguistic study of refusals: An analysis of pragmatic competence development in Iranian EFL learners. *Journal of Pragmatics* 43(1): 385–406. https://doi.org/10.1016/j.pragma.2010.07.010

Arundale, R. B. (2006) Face as relational and interactional: A communication framework for research on face, facework, and politeness. *Journal of Politeness Research* 2(2): 193–216. https://doi.org/10.1515/PR.2006.011

Beebe, L. T., Takahashi, T. and Robin, U. W. (1990) *Pragmatic Transfer in ESL Refusals*. Cambridge, MA: Newbury House.

Brown, P. and Levinson, S. C. (1987) *Politeness: Some Universals in Language Usage.* Cambridge: Cambridge University Press.

Eaton, A. A. and Rose, S. (2011) Has dating become more egalitarian? A 35 year review using *Sex Roles. Sex Roles* 64(11–12): 843–862. https://doi.org/10.1007/s11199-011-9957-9

Eckert, P. (1989) *Jocks and Burnouts: Social Categories and Identity in the High School.* New York: Teachers College Press.

Eckert, P. and McConnell-Ginet, S. (2003) *Language and Gender.* New York: Cambridge University Press. https://doi.org/10.1017/CBO9780511791147

Fukushima, S. (1996) Request strategies in British English and Japanese. *Language Science* 18(3–4): 671–688. https://doi.org/10.1016/S0388-0001(96)00041-1

Gao, W. Y. (2009) A comparative study on refusals between male and female: Using Tainan residents as an example. *Journal of Humanities College of Liberal Arts National Chung Hsing University* 42: 143–170.

Guo, Y. L. (2012) Chinese and American refusal strategy: A cross-cultural approach. *Theory and Practice in Language Studies* 2(2): 247–256. https://doi.org/10.4304/tpls.2.2.247-256

Hsiang, T. W. (2014) Women's refusal behaviours in Chinese TV dating shows. Unpublished Master's thesis, Chiayi: Institute of Linguistics, National Chung Cheng University.

Hymes, D. (1986) Models of the interaction of language and social life. In J. J. Gumperz and D. Hymes (eds) *Direction in Sociolinguistics: The Ethnography of Communication.* Oxford: Blackwell Publishing.

le Pair, R. (1996) Spanish request strategies: A cross cultural analysis from an intercultural perspective. *Language Science* 18(3–4): 651–670. https://doi.org/10.1016/S0388-0001(96)00040-X

Peng, Y. and Yuan, J. -T. (2006) <漢語拒絕言語行為的跨性別差異> (Gender differences in the performance of Chinese refusals) *Journal of Jiangxi University of Finance* 19: 129–131.

Scollon, R. and Scollon, S. W. (1995) *Intercultural Communication.* Oxford: Blackwell.

Scollon, R. and Scollon, S. W. (2004) *Nexus Analysis: Discourse and the Emerging Internet.* London: Routledge.

Spencer-Oatey, H. (2002) Managing rapport in talk: Using rapport sensitive incidents to explore the motivational concerns underlying the management of relations. *Journal of Pragmatics* 34(5): 529–545. https://doi.org/10.1016/S0378-2166(01)00039-X

Spencer-Oatey, H. (2003) Managing rapport in intercultural business interactions: A comparison of two Chinese-British welcome meetings. *Journal of Intercultural Studies* 24(1): 33–46. https://doi.org/10.1080/07256860305788

Spencer-Oatey, H. (2005) (Im)politeness, face and perceptions of rapport: Unpackaging their bases and interrelationships. *Journal of Politeness Research* 1(1): 113–137. https://doi.org/10.1515/jplr.2005.1.1.95

Spencer-Oatey, H. and Franklin, P. (2010) *Intercultural Interaction: A Multidisciplinary Approach to Intercultural Communication.* New York: Palgrave Macmillan.

Williams, R. (1975) *Television: Technology and Cultural Form.* New York: Schocken Books. https://doi.org/10.4324/9780203450277

Wortham, S. (2006) Review of Ron Scollon and Suzie Wong Scollon, *Nexus Analysis: Discourse and the Emerging Internet.* Retrieved from http://repository.upenn.edu/gse_pubs/55/.

Yin, C. C. (2011) 電視相親類真人秀節目研究 (A study of TV dating shows). http://media.people.com.cn/BIG5/22114/44110/189065/13650476.html.

Yu, M. C. (2003) On the universality of face: Evidence from Chinese compliment response behavior. *Journal of Pragmatics* 35(10–11): 1679–1710. https://doi.org/10.1016/S0378-2166(03)00074-2

Panellists' rapport management in expressing disagreement at conference discussions

Liyin Zhang and Xiaoyan Wang

Introduction

When we respond to others' opinions, we often agree or disagree. Whereas agreement is generally considered a preferred activity by conversation analysts, disagreement as a kind of face-threatening act (FTA; Brown and Levinson 1987) that runs counter to the Agreement Maxim (Leech 1983) is generally thought of as 'dispreferred' (in CA terms) in communication. Thus, people tend to avoid or at least mitigate disagreement (Pomerantz 1984; Sifianou 2012).

Recent research (e.g., Georgakopoulou 2001; Sifianou 2012), however, indicates that disagreement is not necessarily negative, or results in conflicts or impoliteness, such that people deliberately avoid it. Instead, in some particular settings, disagreement can be a sign of intimacy and a facilitator of positive social relationships (e.g., Locher 2004). A systematic approach to the understanding of disagreement has been proposed and four observations towards disagreement have been debated therein by Angouri and Locher (2012). First, disagreeing or expressing different views is quite common in daily life. Second, the expression of disagreement is likely to be expected and is an essential component of certain practices, such as 'decision making and problem solving talk in either everyday or professional contexts' (Angouri and Locher 2012: 1549). Third, this speech act cannot be labeled as 'a priori negative act', but is perceived and enacted pursuant to different norms developed over time by communities. Fourth, the ways in which disagreement is expressed and expectations about how it is valued in a particular practice will have an impact on the relational issues and participants' choices as well.

This so-called 'dispreferred' act of disagreement is increasingly seen as far more complex and multifunctional than straightforward labelling (e.g., Spencer-Oatey 2000). The previous assumption is conditionally restricted to some extent, and has its validity rooted in small talk, but becomes questionable in confrontational activities, such as discussions or participative meetings where disagreements frequently take very direct and less mitigated forms (Bond, Zegarac and Spencer-Oatey 2000). Güthner (2000), for example, observes that once an argumentative and confrontational frame is established, the German participants express their disagreement in a much more focused and maximised way.

Despite the extensive literature on disagreeing activities and rapport management in the domains of workplace and daily communication, very little attention has been directed to the phenomenon of disagreement in academic settings. Conferences are common occasions where academics exchange views, in either a mild or a heated way, on their research through discussions. At conferences, participants may raise their queries on the discussed topics to probe further into the research process, the methodology and the results, or supplement the research with new perspectives or insightful interpretation. Above all, disagreement that occurs in the exchange process is generally or inevitably a characteristic feature of such an activity. It is intriguing to examine how panellists at conferences express their disagreement with speakers, raise their own point of view on the topics in discussion, and manage rapport in the meantime. However, there has been scant literature on such practices related to disagreement in this specific context. We may wonder whether panellists choose to adopt some strategies to maintain harmony while raising their dissenting or conflicting opinions at the same time.

Based on an in-depth analysis of the utterances collected from academic conference discussions in the field of linguistics and drawing on the rapport management framework proposed by Spencer-Oatey (2000, 2002, 2008), this study will focus on panellists' expression of disagreement and will try to show the common patterns Chinese panellists use, the strategies they adopt to manage face and sociality rights and interactional goals in the activity, and finally to investigate the influencing factors concerned. Our hope is that evidence can be found and added to the socially and situationally based interpretation of disagreement in academic settings. We also expect that the study will promote the understanding of management of relations in Chinese conference settings and contribute to further comparative study.

Rapport management in disagreements

Theoretical framework of rapport management

Communication is not merely a way of transmitting information, but also a site of managing social relations (e.g., Ran 2012; Spencer-Oatey 2000; Watzlawick,

Beavin and Jackson 1967). That is, as stated in Watzlawick et al. (1967), all communication has a content component and a relation component. Similarly, Brown and Yule (1984) identify the dual functions of language: the transactional function and the interactional function. Whereas the goal of the former is to convey information coherently and accurately, that of the latter is to communicate hospitality and good will.

A myriad of scholars have proved the crucial importance of face and/or (im) politeness in our relational interaction with people. However, Spencer-Oatey (2008: 12) suggests that the term 'face', with its focus mainly on the concerns for self, hardly touches upon the balance between self and other. In addition, the term '(im)politeness', often equated with formal terms and expressions, is interpreted inadequately in previous literature. As Fraser and Nolan (1981: 96) point out, politeness is actually a contextual judgment: no sentence is inherently polite or impolite. Only the conditions under which certain expressions are used can determine the presence or absence of politeness. In other words, the judgment of politeness is not embedded in words themselves, but is socially and situationally based. In this sense, politeness is practically a question of appropriateness. Further, another limitation of the term 'politeness' is that it emphasises the harmonious aspect of social relations, but fails to, at least partly, incorporate people's disagreement and other inharmonious aspects, which also frequently occur in communication (Culpeper 1996).

To provide a term with wider coverage and to include both the individual and social perspectives in the management of interpersonal relations, Spencer-Oatey (2000: 3; 2002, 2008) proposes the term 'rapport management' to refer to the use of language to promote, maintain or threaten/damage harmonious social relations. In her model, the term 'rapport management' rather than 'face management' is used in the discussion of the management of social relations, because Spencer-Oatey presumes that the term 'face' seems to be more concerned with self, whereas rapport management provides 'more of a balance between self and other' (2000: 12). The scope of rapport management is hence considered as broader and covers the way that language is used to construct, maintain and/or threaten face, and also includes the management of sociality rights and interactional goals.

The analytical framework first proposed by Spencer-Oatey (2000) regarding rapport management consists of the following interrelated aspects: the management of *face needs* and *sociality rights*, which can be further divided into *quality face* and *identity face*, and *equity rights* and *association rights* respectively. The framework, which has developed from Brown and Levinson's (1987) model of politeness, maintains the personal or individual conceptualisation of face with the terms 'quality face' and 'equity rights' (roughly corresponding to 'positive face' and 'negative face'), and adds the social/interdependent perspective to social relations – 'identity face' (the fundamental desire for people to acknowledge and uphold our social identities or roles) and 'association rights' (the fundamental belief that we are entitled to association with others).

In her later work (Spencer-Oatey 2005: 95; 2008), Spencer-Oatey makes minor changes to her framework, and adds a third component – the management of interactional goals. The content of the first two components is interpreted as the management of face sensitivities for face management, and the management of social expectancies for the management of sociality rights and obligations. In her words,

> [F]ace is associated with personal/relational/social values, and is concerned with people's sense of worth, dignity, honour, reputation, competence and so on. Sociality rights and obligations, on the other hand, are concerned with social expectancies, and reflect people's concerns over fairness, consideration and behavioural appropriateness. Interactional goals refer to the specific task and/or relational goals that people may have when they interact with each other.

(Spencer-Oatey 2008: 13)

Some traditional face-threatening acts (FTAs), primarily in relation to speech acts such as requests, offers, compliments and so on, may be viewed differently from the rapport management perspective. Orders and requests, for example, may not necessarily be face-threatening. At times, we may feel pleased or even honoured with the sense of trust in our abilities if someone asks us for help (Spencer-Oatey 2000). In this sense, the request actually gives us face. Therefore, within the framework of rapport management, speech acts are not associated with fixed interpretation of face threat. That is to say, the judgment is subjective and depends not simply on the form or content of the language used, but also on people's interpretations, the circumstances and so on.

Rapport management in disagreeing activities

Disagreement occurs as a result of the different views expressed by interlocutors in communicative activities, and is mostly described as confrontational and thus should be mitigated or avoided (Sifianou 2012). According to Bond et al., '[d]isagreement can be said to occur if some participant or participants in a situation of communication communicate(s) some belief or beliefs, which are partly or fully inconsistent with some other belief or beliefs publicly held by another participant (or participants) in the same situation' (2000: 62). The coverage of the examined utterances includes both the explicitly and implicitly communicated cases.

Disagreement and politeness are closely related. The functions of disagreement and their implications for participants from both sides are related to the issue of politeness (e.g., Locher 2004). Politeness devices are not universal but carry individually, situationally and culturally specific tendencies (Sifianou 2012). Seeking agreement and avoiding disagreement are not definite politeness strategies and cannot be classified as positive politeness devices unquestionably (Sifianou 1992). They could be negative in that 'they avoid imposition by wasting the addressee's time' (Sifianou 2012: 1561). Scott (2002) indicates that disagreements are not a uniform phenomenon and may carry many distinctions. Raising safe topics (for example, talking about the weather) as a device for seeking agreement may be safe, but also indicates distance at the same time.

Within the framework of rapport management, positive rapport or harmony between people can be threatened in three ways in accordance with the three components of rapport management: through face-threatening behaviour, through rights-threatening/obligation-rejecting behaviour and through goal-threatening behaviour. Spencer-Oatey explains that, if two people disagree with each other, there will be a content aspect to their disagreement concerning, for example, the 'suitability of a course of action' or 'disagreement over the accuracy of a piece of information' (2000: 2). Meanwhile, a relational aspect to their agreement is also involved concerning, for example, 'whether the expression of disagreement conveys lack of respect for the other person, or whether it leads to feelings of resentment or dislike' (2000: 2). The simple Chinese scripts for disagreement in meetings proposed by Bond et al. go like this: 'Present the information that supports your view. Give the hearers a communicative clue that will enable them to figure out your view(s). A rhetorical question is a useful communicative device for achieving this end' (2000: 65). It explains the phenomenon of disagreement in meetings to some extent, but still leaves room to be explored, such as patterns of disagreement, strategies of disagreement and their underlying factors.

This study

Disagreeing practices are complex and can either be a sign of hostility or affiliation (Sifianou 2012). Early CA research and politeness theories have restricted studies on disagreement to single utterances or the effects on participants' positive face. In addition, relevant research has primarily concentrated on internal structures and held the one-sided view that disagreeing is dispreferred and thus frequently prefaced, softened and delayed in contrast to preferred action (Sacks 1987). Nevertheless, these early research findings have laid the foundation for the general understanding of disagreement.

It is commonly understood that the Chinese characteristically desire to maintain harmony in social interaction. Politeness and face issues are inherently embedded in Chinese culture (Gu 1990) and in Chinese patterns of communication. Some studies have investigated (in)direct complaints (e.g., Chen, Chen and

Chang 2011), refusal strategies (e.g., Liao and Bresnahan 1996) and other FTAs. However, very little empirical research has to date been published on panellists' rapport management in their expression of disagreement at conference discussions. Based on Spencer-Oatey's (2000, 2002, 2008) rapport management framework, this study attempts to identify patterns of Chinese panellists' disagreeing expressions at conference discussions, the strategies they employ to manage rapport in the discussion sessions, and related influencing factors in the process of enacting and modifying the managing process in this setting. Naturally occurring interactions rather than elicited data will be examined in the study.

Methodology

Research questions

To achieve the purpose of the current study, three research questions are to be addressed:

1. What patterns do Chinese panellists adopt while expressing disagreements at conference discussions?
2. What strategies do they use to manage rapport while expressing disagreements at conference discussions? How do they implement these strategies pragma-linguistically?
3. What factors might enhance, maintain or damage the rapport between Chinese interlocutors at the panels?

Data collection

To answer the research questions, 14 episodes of conference discussions conducted in Chinese were recorded and then transcribed (see Table 9.1). Panellists' discussions were selected from panels of two conferences held in China, one international and one domestic. Both conferences arranged several panel discussions in Chinese and the topics centred on linguistics and applied linguistics. One conference was a national forum on applied linguistics. This conference, abbreviated as *Gw*, contributed nine episodes out of the recorded fourteen audio files. For each episode, the recorded data covered one discussion session, of which the arranged time period for discussion was around five minutes, but the time span varied slightly due to the length of the prefaced presentation and possible absence of speaker(s) in the same group. These nine episodes clipped from three panels, namely, academic discourse, media discourse and contrastive discussions, were recorded, transcribed and analysed.

The other one was an international conference, abbreviated as *Nj*, focusing on English language teaching and attracted over 600 participants around the world. Five episodes, conducted in Chinese, from a panel with its topic on the dictionary and English teaching were selected. The lengths for the episodes were supposed to be ten minutes, but varied for the same reasons mentioned above. The demographic information of speakers and power relationships between/among speakers and panellists for both conferences were also collected to facilitate the interpretation of the process of enacting and modifying the management of rapport in specific settings. Interactional and discursive approaches were jointly used to interpret the politeness involved in panellists' expression of disagreement.

Table 9.1. Display of the 14 episodes collected

Episodes	Duration	Time of start and end
1	4'06"	Gw1(12'56"–17'02")
2	9'38"	Gw1(38'12"–47'50")
3	2'19"	Gw2(26'05"–28'24")
4	4'17"	Gw2(52'23"–56'40")
5	5'27"	Gw2(75'25"–80'52")
6	10'07"	Gw3(0'15"–10'22")
7	9'56"	Gw4(2'16"–12'12")
8	10'00"	Gw5(14'40"–24'40")
9	7'52"	Gw5(32'41"–40'33")
10	10'08"	Nj1(25'25"–35'33")
11	11'21"	Nj2(30'56"–42'17")
12	12'22"	Nj3(36'30"–48'52")
13	17'00"	Nj4(28'24"–45'24")
14	11'46"	Nj5(26'54"–38'40")

Data analysis

The identification of panellists' disagreement patterns and strategies was mainly based on three major types of the wording of speech acts, namely, the semantic components of the speech acts, the degree of (in)directness and the type and amount of upgraders/downgraders (Spencer-Oatey 2000). A list of the disagreement strategies reported by Bousfield (2008), Culpeper (1996), Locher (2004) and Shum and Lee (2013) was also prepared for reference. To form the list, one researcher first identified the types of disagreement patterns and strategies, and then the other researcher cross-checked the results.

Patterns of disagreement at conference discussions

Academic conferences are a genre of communicative activity with fairly fixed patterns. Hence, a set of assumptions, rules or maxims of behavioural conventions related to the situation, termed as 'scripts' by Bond et al. (2000: 62), are to be observed. The collected data show that Chinese panellists mostly conduct the following behaviour types at conference discussions: expressing disagreement (12/72), raising content-based questions (28/72), providing suggestions (9/72), offering affirmative comments or relevant personal experiences (12/72) and providing further explanation (11/72). The results also indicate that panellists express their disagreement in eight episodes out of the total fourteen. That is to say, disagreement appears in more than half of the data and constitutes the second most frequently conducted behaviour together with providing suggestions. To some extent, such a finding proves Yeung's (cited in Bond et al. 2000) research on the issue of indirectness in Chinese and English participative decision-making discourse. In that study, 7% of turns taken by the Chinese contain disagreements with the superior, while only 1% of turns involve disagreement in the Australian data.

Güthner (2000: 226) reports in her study on the forms of organising dissent among Chinese participants in a conversation with German students. The German participants show more diversified features: a) The utterance containing the disagreement repeats parts of the prior utterance and either negates it or substitutes central elements through contradictory devices. b) The correction of the problem item is highlighted by prosodic (contrastive stress), lexico-semantic (such as antonyms; opposing categories) and/or syntactic means of contrast (syntactic parallelism). c) The dissent is sequentially organised in a way that the speaker of the 'problem utterance' receives no possibility for self-correction. However, compared with their German counterparts, only one continuously used strategy by Chinese participants is spotted. They tend to signal formal consent and then indicate a different position in the following turn without formal disagreement marking.

The collected data for the current research are strongly against the aforementioned view of Chinese participants following a monotonous pattern; rather, we find diversified patterns of expressing disagreement among them. The following lists a few common patterns observed to enable better and easier understanding of relevant Chinese interactions in the setting (P = Panellist; S = Speaker):

A. The utterance containing the disagreement repeats parts of the prior utterance and either negates it or substitutes central elements through contradictory devices, and then invites explanation in the form of question.

(1)

P: 你刚说，我看上面有一句，说是，对编码没有帮助的搭配，我不太清楚，我觉得好像所有的搭配对编码都会有帮助，你说的具体是指什么？

P: As you've just mentioned, I noticed that there was a sentence mentioning the collocations which were of no use to encoding. I'm not clear (about this). It seems to me that all the collocations will be useful for encoding. What do you refer to specifically?

(Nj5-14-2)

In (1), the panellist holds different opinions from the speaker on the issue of usefulness of collocation. The panellist starts with the commonly used preparator – the repetition of parts of the speaker's utterance – then comes up with the contradictory point of view, and ends with a question, as imposition downgrader, to invite explanation from the speaker. This set of scripts typically occurs at the initial round of the discussion session, and the repeated part may be the key terms, the central topics and the like.

B. The utterance is prefaced with a question to confirm the understanding of the panellist, and then the panellist proposes the different view and possible suggestions.

(2)

P: 我有几个（???）很受启发（???）我的问题也是作为一个学习者的角度来提，就是搭配的一些用法。首先，我是不是和你探索一下，你刚说的那个"非搭配"，我感觉这个，好像把它，就是"非"这个字好像已经把它排除掉了，它不是一个搭配了，对吧？

S: 是的，我是这么想的，但是，不知道。

P: 一般是他们还是在那个，就是continuum里面

S: 我也得承认一下，我故意写了这个题目，让别人引起这个注意……

P: 然后我就感觉是不是可以稍微使用一下，比如说叫"内搭配"，是吧？

S: 好，好

P: 因为如果你都非搭配了，然后你又说这个搭配…

P: I have several (???) very insightful (???). My question will be raised from the perspective of a language learner regarding the usage of collocation. First, is it possible for me to probe into the question with you? You have just mentioned a term 'non-collocation'. I feel this, it seems that the prefix, 'non-' has excluded it from being a collocation. It is not a collocation any more, right?

S: Yes, I think so. But, I don't know.

P: Generally, they are still within that, within that continuum.

S: I have to admit, to some extent, I used this title deliberately to arouse people's attention …

P: Then I feel it is possible (we) can use a little bit, for example, name it 'internal collocation', right?

S: Good, good.

P: Because if you use 'non-collocation', and then you mention THIS collocation …

[Note: (???) = unintelligible speech]

(Nj4-13-1)

In the above sequence, the panellist intends to discuss an essential term involved in the previous presentation, i.e., 'non-collocation'. In order to mitigate the negative effects of raising such a harsh opinion, the panellist adopts the question form in a rather explicit way by directly employing 'my question' or 'the question'. The panellist prefaces his comment with a question to confirm his/her understanding of the term, and then raises his interpretation about the 'continuum'. When the speaker expresses his uncertainty about the issue, the panellist kindly offers an alternative solution to the problem.

C.   The panellists express their approval of or thanks to the speaker in general, usually in very brief sentences, and then propose a different point of view.

(3)

P: 您好！就是刚听了您的这个讲座，我觉得很受启发，就是我们现在在编词典的时候可以有很多软件(???)，就是您刚提到这个GDEX这个软件，就是比如说最后在经过这样的筛选权重，然后比如说他每个词可以选出前20个，但是对于get 来说，有可能比如说这前20个例子，这里面还不能够全部反映这个词它所，它所典型地，或者比如说，就是信息量更全面的一些例子，是不是，您觉得是不是也有这个问题？

P: Hello! I feel very enlightened after listening to your presentation. Now we have a lot of software to choose from while compiling a dictionary (???). For example, the software, GDEX, you have just mentioned. The first 20 items for a single word can be selected through filtering based on their weight. But as for the word *get*, the first 20 items may not fully represent the typical usage of the word, or in other words, may not represent more informative examples, right? Do you think this problem exists?

(Nj1-10-2)

Example (3) illustrates the typical pattern used by the Chinese participants in Güthner's (2000) study. The panellist expresses her approval of or thanks to the speaker or tends to signal formal consent, and then indicates a different position in the following turn with/without formal disagreement marking. In this case, the explicit marking 'but' is used to preface the different view. Politeness is embedded in the careful organisation of the turns. With sufficient preparation at the beginning and a question giving room to the speaker at the end, this potential face-threatening act is more accessible to the listener and helps to maintain positive rapport between the interlocutors.

D. The utterance directly negates the central elements of prior utterance.

(4)

S: 但它的这个软件上，软件上是没有的，就是我刚才为您呈现的

P: 我记得是有的，我记得是有的（（听众笑））

S: But as for the software, the software doesn't cover this as I have shown to you just now.

P: I remember the software does cover this. I remember the software does cover this. ((audience laughs))

(Nj2-11-2)

Direct negation, as shown in the above example, often occurs in the middle of a discussion when the speaker fails to offer a satisfactory answer to the prior question. In this example, the panellist, the editor in charge of the dictionary the speaker is focusing on, is pretty confident about the functions of software designed for the dictionary and therefore directly negates the speaker's view with a lowered voice.

E. The panellist interrupts the speaker and makes negative comments on the issue, rather than on any specific question raised previously.

(5)

S: 因为我们这里面本身没有研究到话题的影响，就是叙事这个物件的，就是叙事的开始和结尾这两个截面，这与话题本身

P: 好像，好像，就有一个感觉吧，就好像是，好像你选的这个语料就是要适应你做的这个结论的((观众笑))，我不知道我说的对不对，反正就是供你去参考吧

S: Because we don't investigate the influence of topics in the research itself, and only (focus on) the narration itself, namely the two intersections – the beginning and the ending. This and the topic itself …

P: It seems, it seems, (I) just have a feeling. It seems, seems that you choose the data aiming to fit your conclusion ((audience laughs)). I don't know whether I'm right (at this point). Anyway, it is for your reference.

(Gw5-8-4)

Similar to (4), this pattern also appears in the middle or towards the end of a discussion session, but involves overlapping of the utterances of the speaker and the panellist. The panellist interrupts the speaker directly and expresses, oftentimes, fairly harsh opinion on the macro part of the presented research, such as the theoretical framework, the methodology and so on, rather than on any specific question raised previously. As in this case, the panellist shifts the topic of the ongoing discussion and points out the inappropriateness of the data collection process, and ends with the highlighting of the referencing function of the suggestion as the mitigator.

Panellists' rapport management strategies

Disagreement can easily threaten rapport, because it can affect people's face and sociality rights/obligation and interactional goals as well. As stated above, disagreement involves different views expressed by interlocutors in communicative activities, and is generally described as confrontational and should be mitigated or avoided. Unlike in some types of ordinary communication, disagreement at conference discussion is often welcomed by participants and takes up a large percentage of the session. Panellists are expected to express their opposite or different opinions while maintaining good relations with other participants, including the speaker and other participants. Thus, disagreement, in conference settings, is not necessarily face threatening. It can be a sign to show panellists' interest and active participation in the discussion. That is why speakers sometimes express their gratitude to the panellists for their challenge. However, it should also be highlighted that expressing disagreement can be risky. If people's perceived sociality rights and obligations are not fulfilled, interpersonal rapport can still be affected. In addition, speakers usually have specific interactional goals, such as spreading their academic opinions, building/enhancing their academic status and so on. The fulfilment of their 'wants' can significantly affect their perceptions of rapport. Any failure caused by panellists' expression of disagreement to achieve these goals may cause frustration, annoyance or even anger. This explains why panellists take care to use downgraders from time to time when expressing disagreement.

Every language affords a wide range of linguistic options that can be used to manage harmony/disharmony among people, and every level of language can play a role in each of the rapport management domains (Spencer-Oatey 2008). According to Spencer-Oatey (2008: 17), people give different weight to the components of rapport management and hence form different conceptualisation of the components. Some interactions are more goal-driven than others, whereas some are more face-sensitive or rights-sensitive. Based on the analysis of the interactions between British and Chinese business people, Spencer-Oatey and Xing (1998) suggest that the following domains are all important in the management of rapport: illocutionary domain, discourse domain, participation domain, stylistic domain and non-verbal domain.

Illocutionary domain has traditionally been the focus of studies on politeness and rapport management, and considerable attention has been paid to the wording of speech acts. Thus, this study only focuses on this domain in the following discussions. Illocutionary force (Brown and Levinson 1987) and the appropriate management of such domain are both vital to harmonious relations to be created and/or maintained. As Spencer-Oatey (2008) suggests, three important types of features are commonly analysed in a number of studies: the selection of speech act components, the degree of directness/indirectness and the type and amount of upgraders/downgraders. Let us take (6) for discussion.

(6)

P: 你刚说，我看上面有一句，说是，对编码没有帮助的搭配，我不太清楚，我觉得好像所有的搭配对编码都会有帮助，你说的具体是指什么？

P: As you've just mentioned, I noticed that there was a sentence mentioning the collocations which were of no use to encoding. I'm not clear (about this). It seems to me that all the collocations will be useful for encoding. What do you refer to specifically?

  Repeating the speaker's point of view (preparator)

  Head act
  Inviting an answer to the disagreeing issue from the speaker in question form (imposition downgrader)

S: 哦，比如说像，我刚举得例子来说，是we perform, we work, we run，其实你就可以这样自由的，没有提供的必要

S: Oh, for example, just like the examples I have used just now are *we perform, we work, we run*. You can be free like this actually. There's no need to offer (such collocations).

P: 啊，就是这个呀。

P: Ah, that's what you mean.

  Acknowledging the speaker's explanation

(Nj5-14-2)

In (6), the panellist initiates his/her utterances by repeating the speaker's point of view, as a preparator, then states the opposite opinion directly, and lastly invites an answer to the disagreeing issue from the speaker in question form. It should be noted that downgraders used in the example, such as the repetition of the speaker's viewpoint, the adoption of a hedge '我觉得好像' ('it seems to me') and the employment of the question form at the end work together to mitigate the imposition of this disagreement.

As for illocutionary domain, additionally, scholars have carried out research on the semantic components of disagreement (based on Beebe and Takahashi, cited in Spencer-Oatey 2000: 24) given in the following list.

    a. Explicit disagreement, e.g., *I'm afraid I don't agree.*
    b. Criticism or negative evaluation, e.g., *That's not practical.*
    c. Question, e.g., *Do you think that would work smoothly?*
    d. Alternative suggestions, e.g., *How about trying…?*
    e. Gratitude, e.g., *Thanks very much for your suggestion,* …
    f. Positive remarks, e.g., *You've obviously put a lot work into this,* …
    g. Token agreement, e.g., *I agree with you, but*…

The data of the current study not only show similar findings regarding the components of disagreement, but also suggest some differences. The components used in Chinese panellists' expression of disagreement are as follows:

Table 9.2. The list of components in Chinese panellists' expression of disagreement

a.	Panellists' interpretation of the topic discussed in the presentation
b.	Mentioning the issue to be argued upon
c.	Restating the question raised by another panellist
d.	Providing an affirmative comment on the presentation in general
e.	Repeating the speaker's point of view
f.	Panellist's confirming his/her understanding of the issue presented by the speaker (in question form)
g.	Stating different views with/without 'Do you agree?/ Do you think so?'
h.	Interrupting the speaker and repeating the answer in question form
i.	Inviting an answer to the disagreeing issue from the speaker in question form
j.	Panellist's interpretation of the disagreeing issue in discussion
k.	Providing suggestions
l.	Agreeing with the speaker's explanation

The first six items in Table 9.2, from *a* to *f*, are often used at the beginning of the utterances by the panellists to preface the following negative, possibly harsh, comment. The head act of disagreeing in the study is, in most cases, initiated with 'but' and prefaced or ended with different types of mitigating expressions, especially in cases where the panellists start a new topic and express their different views for the first time. If the speaker fails to offer a satisfactory answer or explanation to the issue, a more direct form is likely to be adopted, that is, directly stating the opinion without employing any mitigating components.

Directness/indirectness is another important feature to be analysed. The linguistic features of indirectness proposed by Yeung's (cited in Bond et al. 2000) study and Bond's (1991) study are: 1) the use of questions instead of statements; 2) the use of degree adverbs and hedges; 3) the avoidance of the first person singular pronoun; 4) the tendency to acknowledge the other's previously stated position, by repeating it for example; 5) the use of rhetorical questions. Bond et al. (2000) define communicative (in)directness as a function of the evidence for particular interpretations. To compare the Chinese rhetorical question strategy for disagreement and the Australian '*yes, but …*' strategy, the Chinese one is more indirect than the Australian '*yes, but …*' strategy since, other things being equal, a rhetorical question allows for a wider range of answers. In contrast, a '*yes-but …*' utterance explicitly indicates a) that the speaker acknowledges the hearer's point of view and b) that the speaker disagrees with some assumptions which follow from that view. In Spencer-Oatey's (2000: 24) study, however, direct strategies are reported to be used more frequently in Chinese than in English, and are often used in situations where a conventionally indirect form would be likely in English. Such direct utterances, however, are not considered as rude in Chinese, because they are usually softened with particles, affixes or tone of voice.

Findings of the current study partly diverge from the two statements above. Direct strategies (e.g., explicit statements of different views), conventionally indirect strategies (e.g., utterances which contain a query for explanation or a suggestion to do something) and non-conventionally indirect strategies (e.g., strong or mild hints) are all frequently observed in the collected data, and, more importantly, direct strategy is seldom used alone. The norm followed goes typically like this. Expressions of disagreement are often prefaced with semantic components with mitigating effects as shown in the above list (items *a* to *f*) with/without a question for confirmation or consent. The mitigating preface is mostly an integral part of the whole utterances to avoid direct threat to the speaker. The data also show that statements conveying negative comments or different views can be used independently only in the process of discussion, but not at the beginning. It should be admitted that Chinese panellists, who are of the same nationality as those subjects in Spencer-Oatey's (2000) study, prefer to use the devices of particles, affixes or tone of voice to soften their tone apart from their selection and combination of semantic components. Some typical examples found in the data are '吧' (*ba*), '啊'(*a*), '是啊' (*shi'a*) and '呢' (*ne*).

Now, let us turn to panellists' use of downgraders (or termed as hedges or downtoners), which is the third feature frequently analysed by researchers. Like speech acts such as apologies, expressions of gratitude and compliments, downgraders also have a mitigating effect for disagreements (Spencer-Oatey 2008). In other words, they function to reduce any negative impact associated with the disagreement. In our data, downgraders, such as '一下' ('a little'; often used together with a verb), '好像' ('it seems'), '那么' ('well') and so on, are used frequently in disagreeing utterances.

Factors influencing the choice of rapport management strategies

Disagreement is one type of face threatening act which, by its nature, runs counter to the face wants of the addressee and/or of the speaker (Brown and Levinson 1987: 65). The first key factor that influences people's strategy use is their rapport orientation (Spencer-Oatey 2008). There are four types of rapport orientation: rapport-enhancement orientation, rapport-maintenance orientation, rapport-neglect orientation and rapport-challenge orientation.

In our data, panellists' expressions of disagreement are mainly associated with two types of orientations, namely rapport-maintenance and rapport-neglect orientation. Panellists' primary purpose in the activity is to exchange ideas and handle this face threatening act appropriately so as to maintain the current quality of relationship and minimise possible threats involved. However, at times, panellists may have limited or little control of the quality of the relationship between interlocutors, especially when they fully focus on the target matter, and tend to express their opinions in order to perfect the current research and provide possible new perspectives for it. The data show that panellists tend to be more direct and show less concern for the speaker's face when they are of superior status. That is especially true when they are more professionally privileged than the speaker, as when the panellists are the speakers' academic supervisors or the acknowledged experts in the field. Their disagreeing activities are conducted not much for change as for maintenance of relations.

The second set of factors influencing Chinese panellists' choice of rapport management strategies are contextual variables (Spencer-Oatey 2008), which include a wide range of items, such as participants' relations, social/interactional roles and activity type. The relationship between the speaker and the panellists in this study shows a diversified distribution. Panellists may be academic supervisors and instructed students at PhD level or Master's level, dictionary editor and dictionary researcher, scholar and his/her fellows, and so on. These different patterns of relationship are reflected in the representation of participants' utterances in such an academic setting. Panellists in more intimate relations with the speaker or with more power, such as 'expert power' in Spencer-Oatey (2000: 33), tend to select more casual or direct patterns (e.g., Example (4)), whereas people with less intimacy or with comparable status tend to express their disagreement in a more indirect way, often by using sentences or expressions with mitigating effects (e.g., Example (3)). In (4), the panellist, the editor of the dictionary under discussion, enjoys authority over the speaker, a researcher on lexicography. He interrupts the speaker directly and only mitigates the directness with lowered pitch to avoid threatening the speaker's face. In (3), on the contrary, the panellist and the speaker are peer research fellows. They have almost equal status. The utterance, therefore, is prefaced with panellists' approval of and thanks to the speaker, and the disagreement is expressed in a rather mild way.

Thirdly, the contents of disagreeing raised by the panellists also seem to have a closing bearing on the panellists' choice of strategies and the sequence of sentences. Regarding the cost-benefit considerations, if the issue or the problem pointed out can be easily solved, and the incurred costs are not too much to the speaker, the degree of indirectness is usually small. On the other hand, if the correction of the problem takes great efforts, more indirect strategies are to be favoured. For example, criticism of the methodology or theoretical framework (see Example (5)) could possibly mean the negation of the whole study and the efforts exerted by the speaker. Such disagreeing activity can be potentially threatening to the relationship between the panellist and the speaker, and should be treated with great care. In contrast, disagreeing on some relatively minor issues, such as the typology of data or the naming of certain concepts (see Example (2)), has less threatening effects, and could possibly take more direct form or be followed by the panellist's personal suggestion.

Admittedly, the list of contextual variables is open and inexhaustible. New items can be added according to different contexts. For example, the timing of the utterances also influences the patterns of the activity. If the different view is newly expressed, or raised for the first time, panellists tend to adopt a more indirect approach, whereas in the middle or towards the end of the discussion, direct expressions are frequently observed.

It should be noted that the factors mentioned above cannot be analysed separately. The inclusion of the dynamicity of these factors would be very useful for the overall assessment of context. It involves the process of accommodating people's conventionalised experiences to the course of a practical interaction. All the factors need to be re-evaluated dynamically together. The same disagreeing utterance may be viewed as enhancing, maintaining, neglecting or challenging the interlocutors' relationship in different contexts. The amount, degree and weight of the factors contribute to the communication as a whole. For example, utterances initiated with 'but' can be decoded into various interpretations when factors such as the relationship between interlocutors, the position of 'but' in the sentence, the adoption of hedges or even the tone of voice are considered. When 'but' occurs in a disagreeing sequence, it can either indicate the panellist's lack of concern for the quality of relations with no mitigating sentences adopted in the beginning or at the end of the sequence, or show the panellist's desire to maintain a harmonious relationship with the speaker by using politeness strategies, such as mitigating expressions, downgraders or questions in contexts such as conference discussions, where different opinions are invited rather than avoided. Were the same 'but' sequence to occur in daily communication, however, it would possibly be interpreted with some threatening effects to the relations of the interlocutors. Disagreement, a typical type of potentially face-threatening act, can be invited, expressed frequently, and deeply appreciated at conference discussions, although certain conventions are to be observed by participants at the same time.

Conclusion

The current empirical study indicates that disagreement, though a risky communicative act, is not necessarily meant to be face threatening, but subject to comprehensive and sufficient interpretation on the basis of social and contextual factors. The expressions of disagreement by Chinese panellists at conference discussions tend to show the multiple purposes of language, not only for the transmission of information, but also for the management of rapport between or among interlocutors. These expressions follow certain norms and conventions driven by face concerns and contextual variables, among others. Panellists craftily choose the components of disagreement together with other strategies to fulfil the purpose of relationship management. Also, the strategies are not employed at random; rather, their use is dynamically influenced by a myriad of factors. The findings of the current study, to some extent, reveal the conventions and patterns of Chinese panellists expressing disagreement while trying to fulfil the multiple functions of language at the same time. Hopefully, this study can promote the understanding of the management of relations in Chinese conference settings and contribute to further comparative study on related topics.

A lot of issues remain to be explored in the future. To begin with, further research may focus on the micro perspective of disagreeing activities and explore some influencing factors uncovered in the current study, such as the number of participants and pragmatic principles and conventions, preferably analysed with the help of interlocutor interviews. In addition, the management of rapport in domains other than the illocutionary domain, such as the discourse domain, participation domain, stylistic domain, and non-verbal domain (Spencer-Oatey

2008), in the conference setting calls for careful observation and discussion. Last, but not least, research across cultures, contexts and participants is also expected to reveal similarities and differences concerning the strategies of disagreement for rapport management in similar contexts.

References

Angouri, J. and Locher, M. A. (2012) Theorising disagreement. *Journal of Pragmatics* 44(12): 1549–1553. https://doi.org/10.1016/j.pragma.2012.06.011

Bond, M. H. (1991) *Beyond the Chinese Face*. Hong Kong: Oxford University Press.

Bond, M. H., Zegarac, V. and Spencer-Oatey, H. (2000) Culture as an explanatory variable: Problems and possibilities. In H. Spencer-Oatey (ed.) *Culturally Speaking: Managing Rapport through Talk across Cultures* 47–71. London: Continuum.

Bousfield, D. (2008) *Impoliteness in Interaction*. Amsterdam and Philadelphia: John Benjamins. https://doi.org/10.1075/pbns.167

Brown, G. and Yule, G. (1984) *Teaching the Spoken Language*. Cambridge: Cambridge University Press.

Brown, P. and Levinson, S. C. (1987) *Politeness: Some Universals in Language Usage*. Cambridge: Cambridge University Press.

Culpeper, J. (1996) Towards an anatomy of impoliteness. *Journal of Pragmatics* 25(3): 349–367. https://doi.org/10.1016/0378-2166(95)00014-3

Chen, Y. S., Chen, C. Y. D. and Chang, M. S. (2011) American and Chinese complaints: Strategy use from a cross-cultural perspective. *Intercultural Pragmatics* 8(2): 253–275. https://doi.org/10.1515/iprg.2011.012

Fraser, B. and Nolan, W. (1981) The association of deference with linguistic form. In J. Walters (ed.) *The Sociolinguistics of Deference and Politeness* 93–111. The Hague: Mouton.

Georgakopoulou, A. (2001) Arguing about the future: On indirect disagreements in conversations. *Journal of Pragmatics* 33(12): 1881–1900. https://doi.org/10.1016/S0378-2166(00)00034-5

Gu, Y. (1990) Politeness phenomena in modern Chinese. *Journal of Pragmatics* 14(2): 237–257. https://doi.org/10.1016/0378-2166(90)90082-O

Güthner, S. (2000) Argumentation and resulting problems in the negotiation of rapport in a German–Chinese conversation. In H. Spencer-Oatey (ed.) *Culturally Speaking: Managing Rapport through Talk across Cultures* 217–239. London: Continuum.

Leech, G. N. (1983) *Principles of Pragmatics*. London: Simon and Shuster.

Liao, C. and Bresnahan, M. I. (1996) A contrastive pragmatic study on American English and Mandarin refusal strategies. *Language Sciences* 18(3–4): 703–727. https://doi.org/10.1016/S0388-0001(96)00043-5

Locher, M. (2004) *Power and Politeness in Action: Disagreements in Oral Communication*. Berlin: Mouton de Gruyter. https://doi.org/10.1515/9783110926552

Pomerantz, A. (1984) Agreeing and disagreeing with assessments: Some features of preferred/dispreferred turn shapes. In J. M. Atkinson and J. Heritage (eds) *Structures of Social Action: Studies in Conversation Analysis* 57–101. Cambridge: Cambridge University Press.

Ran, Y. (2012) Rapport orientation of mitigators and their interpersonal pragmatic functions. *Contemporary Foreign Languages Studies* 11: 4–10.

Sacks, H. (1987) On the preference for agreement and contiguity in sequences in conversation. In G. B. Button and J. R. E. Lee (eds) *Talk and Social Organisation* 54–69. Clevedon: Multilingual Matters.

Scott, S. (2002) Linguistic feature variation within disagreements: An empirical investigation. *Text & Talk* 22(2): 301–328. https://doi.org/10.1515/text.2002.011

Sifianou, M. (1992) *Politeness Phenomena in England and Greece: A Cross-Cultural Perspective*. Oxford: Clarendon Press.

Sifianou, M. (2012) Disagreements, face and politeness. *Journal of Pragmatics* 44(12): 1554–1564. https://doi.org/10.1016/j.pragma.2012.03.009

Shum, W. and Lee, C. (2013) (Im)politeness and disagreement in two Hong Kong Internet discussion forums. *Journal of Pragmatics* 50(1): 52–83. https://doi.org/10.1016/j.pragma.2013.01.010

Spencer-Oatey, H. (2000) Rapport management: A framework for analysis. In H. Spencer-Oatey (ed.) *Culturally Speaking: Managing Rapport through Talk across Cultures* 11–46. London: Continuum.

Spencer-Oatey, H. (2002) Managing rapport in talk: Using rapport sensitive incidents to explore the motivational concerns underlying the management of relations. *Journal of Pragmatics* 34(5): 529–545. https://doi.org/10.1016/S0378-2166(01)00039-X

Spencer-Oatey, H. (2005) (Im)politeness, face and perceptions of rapport: Unpacking their bases and interrelationships. *Journal of Politeness Research* 1(1): 95–119. https://doi.org/10.1515/jplr.2005.1.1.95

Spencer-Oatey, H. (2008) Face, (im)politeness and rapport. In H. Spencer-Oatey (ed.) *Culturally Speaking: Culture, Communication and Politeness Theory* 11–47. London: Continuum.

Spencer-Oatey, H. and Xing, J. (1998) Relational management in Chinese–British business meetings. In S. Hunston (ed.) *Language at Work* 31–46. Clevedon: British Association for Applied Linguistics in association with Multilingual Matters.

Watzlawick, P., Beavin, J. B. and Jackson, D. (1967) *Pragmatics of Human Communication: A Study of Interactional Patterns, Pathologies, and Paradoxes*. London: Norton.

CHAPTER 10

Politeness and disagreement in Hong Kong Internet discussion forums

Cynthia Lee and Winnie Shum

Introduction

It has been in vogue to freely express one's opinion or discuss an issue in public discussion forums on the Internet in the contemporary world. These online discussion forums, like some computer-mediated communication (CMC) devices such as chatrooms and blogs, allow interactions in real time. CMC, which is characterised by 'anonymity and freedoms of time and space, and absence of audio-visual context in cyberspace' (Benwell and Stokoe 2006: 245), allows interlocutors to interact and express opinions towards a certain issue on an equal status. The co-occurrence of 'interactive modes' and 'self-presentation modes' (Haugh, Chang and Kádár 2015: 73) in real time on an equal basis may result in opposite views, and disagreement seems to be an avoidable social behaviour in online Internet forums.

Recent studies have investigated the linguistic politeness strategies of direct and indirect disagreement in intercultural and intracultural conversations (e.g., Cheng and Tsui 2009; Edstorm 2004; Mullany 2010; Pan 2000), experimental settings (e.g., Liang and Han 2005) and CMC (e.g., Nishimura 2008, 2010; Hongladarom and Hongladarom 2005; Shum and Lee 2013). Among them, some studies have reported a variety of disagreement strategies that are interpreted with reference to the interlocutors' cultural norms or beliefs, including Venezuelans (Edstorm 2004), English (Mullany 2010), Chinese (Cheng and Tsui 2009; Kádár 2012), Japanese (Nishimura 2008, 2010), Greek (Kakava 2002) and Thai (Hongladarom and Hongladarom 2005).

In this study, we wish to make a modest contribution to the burgeoning body of work on disagreement by showing the ways in which Chinese classical works are directly referred to when interlocutors disagree in Internet discussion forums using verbatim quotes, words and phrases in the speech act performance in context. Based on the data collected from two Internet discussion forums in Hong Kong, ten instances of verbatim quotes, words and phrases from Confucius and neo-Confucius ethics and works were identified, manifesting how the Cantonese interlocutors presented opposite views when they disagreed. The identified instances indicated the interlocutors' adherence to their traditional values to do justice and make moral judgment, and showed how the interlocutors employed these as tactics for implicit disagreement and empowerment. Such implicit disagreement was particularly enacted with the aim of preserving others' face and avoiding hurting their positive face directly (Brown and Levinson 1987), a speaking practice that is largely in line with the Chinese conception of politeness in interpersonal communication practice (Gao 1998; Gao and Ting-Toomey 1998; Pan 2000; Kádár and Pan 2011).

Disagreement and politeness

Disagreement is a common speech act that exists in daily interactions (Angouri and Locher 2012). When a speaker disagrees with the hearer, s/he will present a viewpoint or an opinion opposite to the latter's stance and support it with evidence or facts (e.g., Takahashi and Beebe 1993; Rees-Miller 2000 cited in Zhu 2014a). When the speaker performs the act, it can threaten the hearer's positive face want (Brown and Levinson 1987). Positive face refers to the 'positive consistent self-image or personality (crucially including the desire that this self-image be appreciated and approved of) claimed by interactants' (Brown and Levinson 1987: 61). As the speech act of disagreement runs counter to the Agreement Maxim (Leech 1983), it has the potential of being impolite. Therefore, according to Brown and Levinson (1987), the force of the act should be minimised or mitigated so as to minimise the threat to the hearer's positive face. Unlike this classical view on politeness, the postmodern view is no longer limited to face work and covers all kinds of relational work (Locher and Watts 2005), emphasising the discursive co-construction of politeness according to agreed social norms during conversations.

Both classical and postmodern approaches have invigorated numerous research studies on politeness and disagreement in face-to-face interactions in different settings and across cultures (e.g., Bargiela-Chiappini and Kádár 2010). Some studies (e.g., Zhu 2014a, 2014b) have revealed the ways in which disagreement (strong disagreement) can serve rapport in conversations. Some have identified a range of direct and indirect linguistic disagreement strategies to address (im)politeness (e.g., Bousfield 2008; Culpeper 2005; Locher 2004), and factors underlying the use of disagreement strategies such as the interlocutors' traditional cultural norms (Edstrom 2004; Hongladarom and Hongladarom 2005; Grainger 2010), cultural attitudes (Cheng and Tsui 2009), conversational styles, speech situations, age and status (Locher 2004), gender and workplace culture (Mullany 2010), discussion topics (Kakava 1993, cited in Locher 2004: 98), and semantic content and identity (Angouri and Tseliga 2010). Yet, so far, only very limited studies have explored how netizens attend to politeness when performing disagreement in the CMC context (but see Shum and Lee 2013).

Disagreement, politeness and communication in Chinese culture

Politeness, face work or *mianzi/lian* (面子/臉) is one of the unique and core values in Chinese culture, encompassing 孝 'filial piety', 關係 'social networking/interrelationships', 人情 'interpersonal sentiment', 仁 'benevolence', 禮 'propriety' and 道德 'morality', as researched in Chinese psychology (Kulich and Zhang 2010). Drawing on Brown and Levinson's politeness model (1987) and Leech's politeness maxims (1983), Gu (1990: 230), in his pioneer work on Chinese politeness, admits that, while politeness is a universal phenomenon, it is also culture-specific and language-specific. He examines the Chinese politeness phenomenon and proposes four categories of related maxims, namely, the Self-denigration Maxim to denigrate self and elevate others in ten personal, interpersonal, professional and familial spheres; the Address Maxim to recognise an interlocutor's social status and mutual relationship such as 同志 'comrade'; the Generosity Maxim and the Tact Maxim to demonstrate attitudinal warmth and refinement during invitation and food plying. Although the extent of politeness varies over time and setting in modern China (Kádár and Pan 2011), the maxims still prevail, and their representation is bound to change in accordance with discourse situations or settings (Gu 2010). In Gu's recent paper on Chinese politeness (2010), he revisits the concept of Chinese politeness in the modern world by adopting a postmodern discursive approach (Watts 2003). He further argues for politeness as 'an experiential phenomenon coexistent with a society or culture' (Gu 2010: 137) and discusses how politeness varies with the four-borne discourse: written-word-borne discourse (WWBD), air-borne situated discourse (ABSD), land-based situated discourse (LBSD) and web-based situated discourse (WBSD), each of which characterises different spatial-temporal engagement and personal involvement. He also explicates how anonymity and absence of social hierarchy between interlocutors in web-based situated discourse, in particular, challenge the traditional view of politeness, promote equality and weaken the deference embedded in the Chinese social hierarchy (Gu 2010: 141–143).

Alternatively, Pan and Kádár (2011) trace the development of Chinese linguistic politeness ideologies and norms. Historically speaking, Chinese social hierarchy is inherited from Confucianism (儒家) and neo-Confucianism (理學), both of which consist of key principles and proper social behaviour with the purpose of maintaining harmonious relationships in family and state and among people. The key concepts of Confucianism include benevolence (仁), righteousness (義), propriety (禮) and filial devotion (孝), all of which provide a set of unambiguous moral guidelines and principles for related social behaviour (Ji, Lee and Guo 2010). For instance, the rites of propriety (*li*) describe the proper social behaviour to be performed in front of people of various roles and status (Kádár 2007 as cited in Pan and Kádár 2011: 1528). These rites of propriety, as argued by Pan and Kádár, are not exactly identical to the notion of politeness, but polite behaviour quintessentially demonstrates the appropriate forms at linguistic and discourse levels.

Without the appropriate use of *li* or social behaviour, a person may take the risk of making himself or others lose face or *mianzi* (面子) in front of people. The concept and importance of face or *mianzi* in interpersonal and intercultural communication between Chinese speakers and between Chinese and other cultural groups in various domains have been widely discussed (e.g., Bond and Hwang 1986; Pan 2000). Knowing how to enhance and save one's and others' face helps maintain harmony and relationships (Bond and Hwang 1986). In addition to such face-directed communication strategies, Gao (1998) points out the importance of *hanxu* (含蓄 'implicit communication') and *zijiren* (自己人 'a focus on insiders'). Hwang (1999: 166–168) explains how the Chinese interact with one another based on the indigenous Chinese concept of *guanxi* (關係), a social networking which consist of many types of interpersonal relationships. These interpersonal relationships are role-directed based on whether the interlocutors are considered as insiders or outsiders. He argues that people in Chinese society adopt different rules of exchange when interacting with others of various relations. The rules for social exchange are formed based on the person's judgment of his or her *guanxi* with others. There are three kinds of interpersonal relationship including relationships between people who interact for a particular purpose known as instrumental ties, relationships with acquaintances outside the family known as mixed ties, and relationships among family members known as expressive ties (Hwang 1999: 167). People's interactions and reactions vary with the three types of ties. Given all these discussions above, it remains to be explored how Chinese people interact politely in CMC situations.

Disagreement, politeness and Chinese culture

The values, beliefs and conceptions of implicit communication, social networking, insiders or in-group membership and harmonious relationship in Chinese culture are realised in linguistic behaviour and are referred to when researchers interpret disagreement made by Chinese learners or speakers of English. For instance, Shen (2006) argues that power and social relations (e.g., *guanxi*) are the major factors affecting Chinese preference and management of disagreement strategies in business negotiation in addition to business interest. Shen finds that direct and explicit disagreement is preferred for in-group negotiations, whereas indirect disagreement is chosen for out-group negotiations. Similarly, in a discourse-completion test, Liang and Han (2005) ascertain that the level of politeness of disagreement displayed by Mandarin Chinese college students varies with the interlocutor's social distance. When there is a great social and power distance, the Chinese students tend to be politer in disagreement. When there is little or no social and power distance, their disagreement will be less polite. Cheng and Tsui (2009) find from their recorded intercultural face-to-face communication between Hong Kong Chinese and native English speakers that Hong Kong Chinese frequently disagree and express disagreement indirectly with mitigation and redressive language such as prefacing opinions with hedges (e.g., 'I think'), using token agreements (e.g., 'yeah') and providing justifications for and elaborations on disagreements. As done in the research by other researchers who refer to interlocutors' cultural practices (e.g., Edstorm 2004; Hongladarom and Hongladarom 2005), indirect disagreement behaviour is interpreted with reference to Chinese values that stress harmony, face work and consideration. Nevertheless, such generalisation may not hold true when communication takes place in another discourse situation. Shum and Lee (2013) find that Hong Kong Cantonese Internet discussion forum interlocutors are prone to violating traditional speaking practices, role-directed relationship and face-directed communication strategies. Such behaviour is in consonance with Gu's view on the challenge of WBSD on politeness. Anonymity and absence of social and power distance may have encouraged the emergence of direct and impolite behaviour such as profane language, cursing and reprimanding.

The foregoing review shows that the key Chinese values and communication processes can indirectly influence disagreement behaviour in face-to-face conversations, though it may not necessarily be so in online communication due to its unique feature. This study attempts to contribute to the growing body of research on disagreement and its relations with culture, with particular reference to the issue of politeness and Chinese values in Internet discussion forums. It is this we turn to next.

Data description

The data for this study were ten posts written by native Cantonese speakers of Chinese in Hong Kong in two Internet discussion forums (see Shum and Lee 2013). The interlocutors of both Internet forums communicated in written Cantonese, a vernacular form of Chinese in some Hong Kong magazines and newspapers (Snow 2004). Their traditional values, like those of many Chinese in the world, are largely inherited from the classical works of Confucianism and neo-Confucianism. For the sake of completeness, the selection of the posts, forums and instances is summarised below.

The two Internet discussion forums are popular public and open forums in Hong Kong as revealed by their high monthly ranking calculated by a web information company known as Alexa. The two Internet forums, Internet forum A and Internet forum B, ranked 7 and 19 respectively during the research period. The selected post topics were about studying overseas (G1, D1) and a newspaper commentary on a girl who had died after saving her little sister from a fire in Hong Kong (G2, D2). The former topic (G1, D1) was classified as a more general and less-controversial type of topic, whereas the latter one (G2, D2) was classified as a relatively controversial type because moral value or judgment was addressed during discussion. Despite the difference in the nature of the two types of posts, both of them successfully attracted over a hundred responses. Based on the interactional approach, a total of ten disagreement episodes were identified from each topic and type of post at the discourse level. Six posts of the less-controversial topic and four posts of the controversial topic were selected from the two Internet forums. A detailed profile is provided in Table 10.1.

Table 10.1. Selected post types, topics and number of episodes

Forum	Post types	Post topic	Number of episodes identified
Forum A	Less-controversial	Studying overseas (G1)	3
	Controversial	A girl died after saving her little sister in a fire accident (G2)	2
Forum B	Less-controversial	Studying overseas (D1)	3
	Controversial	A girl died after saving her little sister in a fire accident (D2)	2

The authors identified 99 disagreement instances in total. Among them, ten instances that were categorised as disagreement genres involved elements of Chinese values such as verbatim quotes, words and phrases related to Confucianism or neo-Confucianism. These were extracted, analysed and interpreted in the context of Confucian and/or neo-Confucian ethics and beliefs to fulfil the aim of the study.

Demonstrating disagreement in a polite and indirect manner by making reference to Confucian and neo-Confucian ethics and beliefs

Each identified instance consists of two parts: 1) Cantonese discourse and 2) a translated and edited English version. The identified Chinese value- or ethics-related expressions are underlined. To focus attention on the relevant parts, the irrelevant part is replaced by the symbol '…'.

Among the six posts on both the less controversial and controversial topics, one instance was found in which ethics was referred to by the interlocutors.

(1)

J:	去國家B嘅留學生話: (建議)如果要去外國讀書，首選國家B, 因爲國家B …所以, 樓主去國家A體驗留學樂趣嘅原因, 放諸四海皆準。 [in response to the post-opener-interlocutor A]
K:	好! 完全表達到我想說的,這就是天真與成熟層次的區別。
For A, post-opener:	夏虫不可以語于冰,非無冰也,而是未見冰也.

J: An overseas student of country B said: (suggestion) If you are going to study overseas, country B will be the first option, because country B … So, post-opener (interlocutor A), the reasons for you to experience the pleasure of overseas study in country A apply accurately to every place in the world.

K: Great. It entirely expressed what I wanted to say. This is the difference between naivety and maturity.

For A, post-opener: The reason why summer insects cannot understand a talk about ice is that they have not seen ice before. It is not because there is no ice.

The verbatim quote '夏虫不可以語于冰' originates from 《秋水篇》 (*Qiushuipian*, a piece of literary work written by Zhuang Zi, a Chinese Taoist philosopher around 369–286 BC). The sentence explains that summer insects fail to talk about ice because of their ignorance rather than because of the non-existence of ice. Summer insects are analogous to people who are short-sighted and make allegiances without factual support. In (1), Interlocutor K explicitly agrees with Interlocutor J's view. However, the verbatim quote is written for Interlocutor A, the post-opener, who expresses some biased views about studying abroad in one country but not others. The quote indicates Interlocutor's K disagreement with Interlocutor A's view and implicitly ridicules the limited knowledge of Interlocutor A; that is, Interlocutor A's ignorance is analogous to that of summer insects.

Among the four posts of the controversial topic, eight instances are identified and listed as follows.

(2–4)

> F:　甘都叫靚…? 香港冇靚女…
>
> K:　你有仁義禮智嗎? (2) <u>人皆有不忍人之心</u> (3)。
> <u>先王有不忍人之心，斯有不忍人之政矣。以不忍人之心，行不忍人之政，治天下可運之掌上。所以謂人皆有不忍人之心者，今人乍見孺子將入於井，皆有怵惕惻隱之心，非所以內交於孺子之父母也，非所以要譽於鄉黨朋友也，非惡其聲而然也。由是觀之，無惻隱之心，非人也；無羞惡之心，非人也；無辭讓之心，非人也；無是非之心，非人也。惻隱之心，仁之端也；羞惡之心，義之端也；辭讓之心，禮之端也；是非之心，智之端也。</u> (4)
>
> F:　You call that pretty …? Hong Kong really doesn't have pretty girls then …
>
> K:　Do you possess benevolence, righteousness, propriety and wisdom? All men have a mind which cannot bear to see the sufferings of others.
> … <u>the feeling of commiseration is essential to man</u> (originally stressed by the participant), that the feeling of shame and dislike is essential to man, that the feeling of modesty and complaisance is essential to man, and that the feeling of approving and disapproving is essential to man. The feeling of commiseration is the principle of benevolence. The feeling of shame and dislike is the principle of righteousness. The feeling of modesty and complaisance is the principle of propriety. The feeling of approving and disapproving is the principle of knowledge.[1]

As the post is to mourn for the girl who has died after saving her sister from the fire, Interlocutor K does not admit the view of F, who criticises another interlocutor's comments on the girl's appearance. His disagreement is expressed indirectly by means of the four virtues of Confucian ethics, namely, benevolence, righteousness, propriety and wisdom, supplemented by a piece of classical writing related to commiseration written by Mencius, a prominent philosopher in Confucianism from 372 to 289 BC. According to the text, commiseration is essential behaviour for all people. Without it, people will not have any feelings of shame, modesty or approval. The verbatim quote implies not only K's indirect disagreement, but also K's moral judgment of F.

(5)

> B:　又少個人爭飯食 good [in response to interlocutor A]
>
> D:　你@@有@[2]無惻隱之心, 惻隱之心人之皆有…
>
> B:　It's good to have fewer people to compete with.
>
> D:　Do you xxx have heart of commiseration? All men have a heart of commiseration …

Likewise, another instance comes from Interlocutor D, who holds different views from interlocutor B. This time Interlocutor D disagrees more explicitly and strongly by questioning the heart of Interlocutor B's commiseration. Both phrases '惻隱之心' ('heart of commiseration'; in (5)) and '不忍人之心' ('a mind which cannot bear to see the sufferings of others'; in (3)) originate from the work of Mencius regarding people's heart of commiseration. In the same way as Interlocutor K (in (4)), Interlocutor D also questions the moral standard of Interlocutor B, and the quote represents Interlocutor D's evaluation of Interlocutor B.

(6)

    B: 又少個人爭飯食good.

    C: 估唔到有人話少個對手, 我相信你媽咪有大把對手。

    B: 你媽咪…先係。

    C: 狗口長不出象牙。

    B: It's good to have fewer persons to compete with.

    C: (I) could not imagine that someone would talk in this way. I believe your mum will have many competitors.

    B: Perhaps your mum ... is.

    C: A dog's mouth can't grow an elephant's tusks.

In response to the same message posted by Interlocutor B, Interlocutor C rebuts and draws attention to other family members. Interlocutor B fights back and Interlocutor C's fury and disagreement end in a reprimand by means of a Chinese proverb '狗口長不出象牙' ('A dog's mouth can't grow an elephant's tusks'). In Chinese culture, ivory is perceived as expensive and elegant, while a dog is seen as a representation of things that are of a lower status and ignominious. The proverb signifies that wicked people will not be able to say anything nice and civilised. Interlocutor C's implied meaning could be interpreted correctly only if Interlocutor B understands the proverb.

(7)

    M: 個社會講外表講手段架…

    M: Society is about appearance, wheeling and dealing ...

(8)

    U: 如果你覺得上網講野大晒, 可以唔理後果, 亂咁講野…我唔係好人, 都唔 係君子, 但我知道有咩可以講, 有咩心諗都唔好講來做人係咁, 上網都係咁, 因爲亂咁講野唔係對唔住D KEYBOARD FIGHTER,…都對唔住老豆養育之恩…

    U: If you feel that you have the absolute right to speak whatever you like over the Internet and ignore the results, I feel bad for you because you are not able to distinguish right and wrong. I am not a good man, and I am not a noble man either. But I know what can and can't be said as a person and on the Internet. You should feel sorry for what you have said and to other KEYBOARD FIGHTERS ... and your dad who rears you.

Interlocutor U does not agree with Interlocutor M's view about the practice in society. Interlocutor U feels that Interlocutor M should speak appropriately and claims that he is not good enough to be named as '君子' ('a noble gentleman'). He asks the interlocutor to reflect on their parents' grace – '養育之恩' ('the grace of bringing up a child'). The concept and deeds of '君子' ('a noble gentleman') can be traced from the Analects, a collection of sayings and ideas attributed to Confucius and written from 475 to 221 BC.

人不知，而不愠，不亦君子乎？

(論語I)

Even though I am not understood, I will not be furious. Isn't that a behaviour of a noble gentleman?

(Analects I)

According to Confucianism, a noble gentleman should behave well by not expressing fury when his deed is misunderstood, and not showing off in front of people. These decent modes of social behaviour are implicitly relayed from the interlocutor to others by means of the two words. In addition, filial devotion, which is an important value in Confucianism, should not be overlooked. Parents' and children's filial duties are stressed in Confucianism (Hwang and Han 2010: 490). Parents have the responsibility to rear their children. In return, children are obliged to take care of their parents when they are old. Interlocutor U enhances the force of the message by associating it with Chinese values.

Functions of verbatim quotes, words and phrases

The use of verbatim quotes, words and phrases by native Cantonese speakers of Chinese in Hong Kong in two Internet discussion forums, which mainly make reference to Confucianism and neo-Confucianism, is functional in two ways: empowering the disagreement and mitigating face threat, the latter being an important means of politeness.

A. Empowering disagreement by indicating moral judgment

The first function of using verbatim quotes, words and phrases from classical texts is to accuse others of indecent social behaviour which is against the traditional norms, ethics and expectations inherited from Confucianism and neo-Confucianism. They indicate the interlocutors' value judgment on what is said by others, whereby the interlocutors can claim the moral high ground. For example, in (2), Interlocutor K condemns Interlocutor F for ridiculing the appearance of the girl who has died, and reprimands Interlocutor F for not knowing anything about the four virtues – benevolence, righteousness, propriety and wisdom – and questions her absence of a heart of commiseration. All these virtues are key concepts and deeds in Confucian ethics. It is Interlocutor K's negative assessment of F's moral judgment that drives him/her to disagree and decide on the type of tactics appropriate to the context. Moral judgment and the feeling of being morally better are indicated prior to the performance of the face-threatening act in particular.

B. Mitigating face threat due to disagreement

The second function of using quotes, words and phrases from classical texts is to employ traditional Chinese values as tactics for implicit disagreement and thereby mitigate its face threat. As shown in the eight instances, the interlocutors draw on the dominant ideologies of Confucianism and neo-Confucianism to express disagreement either implicitly or explicitly. Table 10.2 gives an overview of the implied meaning of each disagreement, the related cultural ideology to which the interlocutors are referring, and the original source.

Table 10.2 An overview of the eight instances

Instance	Implied meaning and related cultural ideology	Original source
1	Ignorance/limited knowledge	Neo-confucianism – Zhuang Zi (Taoist)
2	Lacks the four virtues	Confucianism – Confucius
3	Not having a heart of commiseration	Confucianism – Menicus
4	Not having a heart of commiseration	Confucianism – Menicus
5	Not having a heart of commiseration	Confucianism – Menicus
6	Not being able to speak in a nice and civilised manner	Proverb
7	Not being a noble gentleman	Confucianism – Confucius
8	Filial duties of children	Confucianism – Confucius

The eight instances reveal two tactics intentionally adopted by the interlocutors in disagreement. The first tactic is to disagree implicitly and indirectly. The interlocutors of instances (1) to (6) cite classical texts and a proverb verbatim without mentioning any disagreement with others' views openly. This tactic is implicit and indirect in the sense that the interlocutor involved is expecting others to infer the implied meaning from the classical texts. By doing so, the interlocutor who disagrees can avoid attacking or hurting others' face or positive face (Brown and Levinson 1987) in public. The quotes are an alternative to the use of mitigated language reported in the literature, such as in the studies of Cheng and Tsui (2009) and Edstrom (2004), and this act is consistent with the Chinese belief about talk in daily communication – 含蓄 'implicit communication', emphasising meaning that lies beyond words (言外之意) (Gao 1998: 170). In other words, the tactic has taken into consideration the positive face want or the face of others, and can be glossed as an indirect way of expression in daily communication among Chinese.

The second tactic is to incorporate expressions or words extracted from classical works or ideologies into disagreement discourse for further support and intensification. This tactic is more explicit than the first one because the interlocutor points out the inappropriate behaviour or wrong deed directly in the written discourse. The interlocutors of instances (7) and (8) demonstrate the use of the second tactic. The word君子 'noble gentleman' and the phrase 養育之恩 'grace of bringing up a child' describe obligatory Confucian social behaviour and responsibility in the theoretical model of Confucian ethics that regulate people's interpersonal and familial relationships (Hwang 1999: 167). As proposed by Hwang, 'the theoretical model of Confucian ethics for ordinary people is a template for ethical arrangements in interpersonal relationship' (1999: 167). Ethics for ordinary people includes filial devotion to parents, respect for others and loyalty to superiors, and benevolence to inferiors (even father to son). All these modes of social behaviour and responsibilities are emphasised in familial and ordinary societal relationships. In Hwang and Han's view, filial devotion is an unconditional positive duty for ordinary people and is the 'core value of benevolence' (Hwang 2001, cited in Hwang and Han 2010: 490). Filial duty stresses the idea of 'benevolent father, filial son': two out of the ten things which are considered to be right in *Li Chi* (禮記). People are obliged to carry out their duty.

> What are the things which humans consider righteous (*yi*)? Kindness on the part of the father, and filial duty on that of the son … These are the ten things which humans consider to be right.
>
> (*Li Chi*, Chapter 9, as cited in Hwang 1999: 169)

The traditional values and quotes intensify the impact of the interlocutor's message.

Conclusion

To conclude, this study has provided some instances to illustrate how interlocutors incorporate Chinese traditional values into disagreement when verbatim quotes, words and phrases are referred to. In addition, it has identified two disagreement tactics in relation to the use of Confucian ethics and has explained the use with reference to Confucianism, Chinese politeness and communication practice. It is argued that the verbatim quotes, words and phrases represent and indicate an interlocutor's moral judgment of others. The moral judgment drives the interlocutor to search for appropriate Chinese values and norms from Confucianism and neo-Confucianism to support his/her stance. The traditional values and norms empower the interlocutor's disagreement and intensify the force of the speech act. The cited texts, words and phrases express disagreement implicitly and empower the force of the act, leaving room for the interlocutors to infer the implications in context. No matter how the verbatim quotes, words and phrases are used, they expound the role that Chinese values and ethics play in Chinese disagreement discourse, even in the cyber world, and complement the rudeness of disagreement discourse in the same two Internet discussion forums reported in Shum and Lee's paper (2013). Although studies on disagreement by Chinese in face-to-face communication have identified some mitigated expressions to avoid directness (e.g., Cheng and Tsui 2009) and have argued for Chinese politeness from a historical perspective (Pan and Kádár 2011), none of them are able to show any instances similar to those in the present study.

Since there are only eight Chinese belief- and norm-related disagreement instances of verbatim quotes in this study, more samples from daily conversations or other forms of computer-mediated communication are yet to be collected to ascertain their functions and the identified tactics reported in this study.

Notes

1. Chinese text project (n.d.). *Gong Sun Chou I*. Retrieved 24 April 2012 from http://ctext.org/mengzi/gong-sun-chou-i
2. The discourse has been edited and profane language is replaced by the symbol @.

References

Angouri, J. and Locher, M. A. (2012) Theorising disagreement. *Journal of Pragmatics* 44: 1549–1553. https://doi.org/10.1016/j.pragma.2012.06.011

Angouri, J. and Tseliga, T. (2010) 'You have no idea what you are talking about!' From *e-disagreement* to *e-impoliteness* in two online fora. *Journal of Politeness Research* 6: 57–82. https://doi.org/10.1515/jplr.2010.004

Bargiela-Chiappini, F. and Kádár, D. Z. (2010) *Politeness across Cultures*. London: Palgrave Macmillan.

Benwell, B. and Stokoe, E. (2006) *Discourse and Identity*. Edinburgh: Edinburgh University Press.

Bond, M. H. and Hwang, K. K. (1986) The social psychology of Chinese people. In M. H. Bond (ed.) *The Psychology of the Chinese People* 213–266. Hong Kong, Oxford, New York: Oxford University Press.

Bousfield, D. (2008) *Impoliteness in Interaction*. Amsterdam and Philadelphia: John Benjamins. https://doi.org/10.1075/pbns.167

Brown, P. and Levinson, S. C. (1987) *Politeness: Some Universals in Language Usage*. Cambridge: Cambridge University Press.

Cheng, W. and Tsui, A. B.M. (2009) 'Ahh ((laugh)) well there is no comparison between the two I think': How do Hong Kong Chinese and native speakers of English disagree with each other? *Journal of Pragmatics* 41: 2365–2380. https://doi.org/10.1016/j.pragma.2009.04.003

Culpeper, J. (2005) Impoliteness and entertainment in the television quiz show: *The Weakest Link*. *Journal of Politeness Research* 1: 35–72. https://doi.org/10.1515/jplr.2005.1.1.35

Edstorm, A (2004) Expressions of disagreement by Venezuelans in conversations: Reconsidering the influence of culture. *Journal of Pragmatics* 36: 1499–1518. https://doi.org/10.1016/j.pragma.2004.02.002

Gao, G. (1998) 'Don't take my word for it." – Understanding Chinese speaking practices. *International Journal of Intercultural Relations* 22: 163–186. https://doi.org/10.1016/S0147-1767(98)00003-0

Gao, G. and Ting-Toomey, S. (1998) *Communicating Effectively with the Chinese*. Thousand Oaks, CA: Sage.

Grainger, K. (2010) Indirectness in Zimbabawean English: A study of intercultural communication in the UK. In F. Bargiela-Chiappini and D. Z. Kádár (eds) *Politeness across Cultures* 171–193. London: Palgrave Macmillan.

Gu, Y. G. (1990) Politeness phenomena in modern Chinese. *Journal of Pragmatics* 14: 237–257. https://doi.org/10.1016/0378-2166(90)90082-O

Gu, Y. G. (2010) Modern Chinese politeness revisited. In F. Bargiela-Chiappini and D. Z. Kádár (eds) *Politeness across Cultures* 128–148. London: Palgrave Macmillan.

Haugh, M., Chang, W. L. M. and Kádár, D. Z. (2015) 'Doing deference': Identities and relational practices in Chinese online discussion boards. *Pragmatics* 25: 73–98. https://doi.org/10.1075/prag.25.1.04hau

Hongladarom, K. and Hongladarom, S. (2005). Politeness in Thai computer-mediated communication. In R. T. Lakoff and S. Ide (eds) *Broadening the Horizon of Linguistic Politeness* 145–162. Amsterdam and Philadelphia: John Benjamins. https://doi.org/10.1075/pbns.139.14hon

Hwang, K. K. (1999) Filial piety and loyalty: Two types of social identification in Confucianism. *Asian Journal of Social Psychology* 2: 163–183. https://doi.org/10.1111/1467-839X.00031

Hwang, K. K. and Han, K. H. (2010) Face and morality in Confucian society. In M. H. Bond (ed.) *The Oxford Handbook of Chinese Psychology* 479–498. Oxford: Oxford University Press. https://doi.org/10.1093/oxfordhb/9780199541850.013.0029

Ji, L. J., Lee, A. and Guo, T. Y. (2010) Chinese thinking. In M. H. Bond (ed.) *The Oxford Handbook of Chinese Psychology* 155–167. Oxford: Oxford University Press.

Kádár, D. Z. (2012) Historical Chinese politeness and rhetoric: A case study of epistolary refusals. *Journal of Politeness Research* 8: 93–110. https://doi.org/10.1515/pr-2012-0006

Kádár, D. Z. and Pan, Y. (2011) Politeness in China. In D. Z. Kádár and S. Mills (eds) *Politeness in East Asia* 125–146. Cambridge: Cambridge University Press. https://doi.org/10.1017/CBO9780511977886.008

Kakava, C. (2002) Opposition in modern Greek discourse: Cultural and contextual constraints. *Journal of Pragmatics* 34: 1447–1471. https://doi.org/10.1016/S0378-2166(02)00075-9

Kulich, S. and Zhang, R. (2010) The multiple frames of Chinese's values: From tradition to modernity and beyond. In M. H. Bond (ed.) *The Oxford Handbook of Chinese Psychology* 241–278. Oxford: Oxford University Press.

Leech, G. (1983) *Principle of Pragmatics.* New York: Longman.

Liang, G. D. and Han J. (2005) A contrastive study on disagreement strategies for politeness between American English and Mandarin Chinese. *Asia EFL Journal* 7: article 9. Retrieved on 6 November 2014 from http:asian-efl-journal.com/quarterly-journal/2005/03/29/a-contrastive-study-on-disagreement- strategies-for-politeness-between-american-english-mandarin-chinese/

Locher, M. A. (2004) *Power and Politeness in Action: Disagreement in Oral Communication.* Berlin and New York: Mouton de Gruyter. https://doi.org/10.1515/9783110926552

Locher, M. A. and Watts, R. J. (2005) Politeness theory and relational work. *Journal of Politeness Research* 1: 9–33. https://doi.org/10.1515/jplr.2005.1.1.9

Mullany, L. (2010) Im/politeness, rapport management and workplace culture: Truckers performing masculinities on Canadian ice-roads. In F. Bargiela-Chiappini and D. Z. Kádár (eds) *Politeness across Cultures* 61–84. London: Palgrave Macmillan.

Nishimura, Y. (2008) Japanese BBS websites as online communities: (Im)politeness perspectives. *Language@Internet* 5: article 3. Retrieved on 26 April 2012 from http://www.languageatinternet.org/articles/2008/1520

Nishimura, Y. (2010) Impoliteness in Japanese BBS interactions: Observations from message exchanges in two online communities. *Journal of Politeness Research* 6: 33–35. https://doi.org/10.1515/jplr.2010.003

Pan, Y. L. (2000) *Politeness in Chinese Face-to-Face Interactions.* Stamford, CT: Ablex Publishing Corporation.

Pan, Y. L. and Kádár, D. Z. (2011) Historical vs. contemporary Chinese linguistic politeness. *Journal of Pragmatics* 43: 1525–1539. https://doi.org/10.1016/j.pragma.2010.10.018

Shen, L. (2006) A discourse analysis of Chinese disagreement management strategies in business negotiation. Unpublished PhD thesis, The University of Arizona. Retrieved on 1 November 2014 from http://arizona.openrepository.com/arizona/bitstream/10150/194733/1/azu.etd_1469_sip1_m.pdf

Shum, W. and Lee, C. (2013) (Im)politeness and disagreement in two Hong Kong Internet discussion forums. *Journal of Pragmatics* 50: 52–83. https://doi.org/10.1016/j.pragma.2013.01.010

Snow, D. (2004) *Cantonese as Written Language: The Growth of a Written Chinese Vernacular.* Hong Kong: Hong Kong University Press.

Takahashi, T. and Beebe, L. M. (1993) Cross-linguistic influence in the speech act of correction. In G. Kasper and S. Blum-Kulka (eds) *Interlanguage Pragmatics* 138–157. Oxford: Oxford University Press.

Watts, R. J. (2003) *Politeness.* Cambridge: Cambridge University Press. https://doi.org/10.1017/CBO9780511615184

Zhu, W. H. (2014a) Managing relationships in everyday practice: The case of strong disagreement in Mandarin. *Journal of Pragmatics* 64: 85–101. https://doi.org/10.1016/j.pragma.2014.01.010

Zhu, W. H. (2014b) Rapport management in strong disagreement: An investigation of a community of Chinese speakers of English. *Text and Talk* 34: 641–664. https://doi.org/10.1515/text-2014-0021

PART IV

Backchannelling and politeness in various Chinese interactions

CHAPTER 11

Backchannelling for positive politeness in Chinese TV interviews

Chunmei Hu and Rong Chen

Introduction

Backchannelling refers to listener response in primarily one-way communication. In such communication, there are two channels of communication operating simultaneously. The predominant channel is that of the speaker who directs the primary speech flow. The secondary channel of communication (i.e., backchannel) is that of the listener who provides signals for her participation (Atkinson and Heritage 1985; Drew 2013; Schegloff 2007, among others).

Since its introduction by Yngve (1970: 568), backchannelling has been one of the most recognised topics in conversation analysis. Among the huge literature on backchannelling, its function has been investigated in a wide range of speech situations. For instance, Blum-Kulka and Olshtain (1984) include backchannelling as an important feature in their cross-linguistic study of requests and apologies (see also Anna 2011; Felix-Brasderfer 2005; Lee 2009; Lindstrom 2005, all about backchannelling in requests), Edwards and Stokoe (2007) examine how backchannelling functions in calls for help with problem neighbours in a British context, Drew and Heritage (1992) and Zimmerman (1992) place backchannelling in the context of professional and institutional settings, and Kent (2012) demonstrates that backchannelling assists the speaker in her effort to respond to directives. From the conversation analysis tradition, these studies have identified backchannelling as a means of sequencing conversations (Drew 2013; Edwards 1994; Sidnell and Stivers 2013; Schegloff 2007; Zimmerman 1992), expressing various attitudes and stances towards what the dominant-channel interlocutor has to say (Goodwin and Cekaite 2013; Stivers and Hayashi 2010) and helping the speaker to turn the conversation to a particular direction (Drew 2013; Schegloff 2007).

This study continues the conversation analysis tradition with a decidedly different focus. Instead of looking at the specific organisational functions of backchannelling, we explore the interconnection between backchannelling and politeness in TV interviews aired in Mainland China, Hong Kong and Taiwan. We will demonstrate that, while backchannelling varies a great deal in this particular genre, it is motivated by the speakers' consideration for the dominant speakers' positive face. Simply put, positive politeness undergirds almost all instances of backchannelling in Chinese TV interviews. In the sense that politeness has emerged in the area of pragmatics and has continued to figure prominently in the pragmatics literature, our study can be seen as an attempt to help the two fields inform each other.

We will omit what would seem to be a must-have section for a chapter like this: a literature review on backchannelling in TV interviews. As a matter of fact, studies on this topic are scarce. The only one we have found is Yu (2003), who views backchannelling as being primarily supportive in function, falling into two types: general and intensified. The former includes tokens such as 嗯, 啊, 噢 'umm', and the latter includes 对对对 'yes', 没错 'right', 是这样的 'that's true', 多温馨啊 'how sweet' and 谢谢 'thanks'.

Politeness

The notion of politeness, originating in Lakoff (1973, 1977), has led to a number of important theories, the most notable of which are Leech's (1983) Politeness Principle, Brown and Levinson's (1987) universal theory of politeness, Locher's (2006) relational theory of politeness and Spencer-Oatey's (2005) theory of politeness as rapport management.

Of the four theories, the first two, by Leech and by Brown and Levinson, are similar in that they are based on classical theories of conversational implicature and speech act, respectively. The second two, by Locher (and colleagues) and by Spencer-Oatey, can be seen as reactions to Leech and Brown and Levinson based on more recent research findings that communication is more dynamic, various, interactional and context-specific than seems to have been assumed by the former group of theories.

As can be gleaned from the literature on politeness, Leech and Brown and Levinson's respective theories, particularly the latter, have been criticised widely for what is supposed to be a 'Eurocentric' bias, its theoretical assumption of rationality, and the underlying view that communication is static (see Chen 2010 for a summary of these criticisms). Despite this, however, we will use Brown and Levinson's theory in this study. Our decision to do so is manifold. First, the criticisms of Brown and Levinson do not seem to have discredited the theory, as it has continued to be the framework for many studies. Second, we do not necessarily agree with the assessment of some of these criticisms. Take, for instance, the allegation that the theory is 'Eurocentric'. It is Eurocentric, it seems, because it is based on rationality, a notion that has come from the European philosophical tradition. However, in these critical works, the notion of rationality is never carefully defined, and the assumption that non-Europeans are not 'rational' is not sufficiently substantiated. Third, contrary to what seems to be believed, we view Brown and Levinson's model of politeness as capable of handling the dynamism and interactionality of a real-life conversation (cf. Chen, He and Hu 2013). We will come back to this point in the conclusion after we have demonstrated how it can do so.

Brown and Levinson hold that members of a society have face, defined as wants and needs to maintain their public image approved of by other members of society. The notion of face is further divided into negative and positive types. Negative face refers to 'the want of every "competent adult member" that his actions be unimpeded by others'; positive face refers to 'the want of every member that his wants be desirable to at least some others' (1987: 62). When it comes to the performance of speech acts, it is claimed that these acts very often threaten the face of the speaker or the hearer or both; hence Brown and Levinson call them face-threatening acts (FTAs). Therefore, speakers use politeness strategies, as presented below, to mitigate the damaging effects of FTAs:

(1)

1. Without redressive action, baldly
2. Positive politeness
3. Negative politeness
4. Off record
5. Withhold the FTA

The choice of a particular strategy is determined by the weightiness of an FTA: the weightier the FTA, the higher the number of strategies – as seen in (1) – a speaker will choose. An FTA's weightiness is computed using the following formula:

(2)

$$Wx = D(S,H) + P(H,S) + Rx$$

According to the authors, 'Wx is the numerical value that measures the weightiness of the FTA x, D(S,H) is the value that measures the social distance between S and H, P(H,S) is a measure of the power that H has over S, and Rx is a value that measures the degree to which the FTA x is rated an imposition in that culture' (Brown and Levinson 1987: 76).

Since a higher numerical value of any of the three factors will result in a higher value for the weightiness of the FTA, which will in turn lead to a higher-numbered strategy, the formula in (2) predicts that the greater distance there is between the speaker and hearer or the more power the hearer has over the speaker or the more imposing the FTA is, the more effort she will make to mitigate the face-threatening force of the intended speech act.

In our discussion part, we will make use of Brown and Levinson's theory to analyse the findings of our study. As we have indicated, positive politeness dominates our discussions, as negative politeness seems to be largely absent in our data. The reasons for this will be explored in our concluding remarks.

Methodology

The data used in our study were from recent Chinese TV talk shows. Since we were interested in backchannelling, which requires a 'dominant channel speaker', we decided on the kind of talk shows that featured guests who were viewed as 'experts' in their respective areas of expertise. The typical format of these shows was that the host introduced the guest, opened the topic, and invited the guest to express their views. Therefore, the guest was often the dominant channel speaker, quite often talking at great length, and the host was the backchannel speaker, providing minimum responses to the guest.

In order to have as wide a representation as possible for our data, we collected material from a pool of major TV shows from Mainland China, Hong Kong and Taiwan. These shows varied in topic, covering issues in politics, diplomacy, national defence, the economy, the environment, technology and religion. These shows enjoyed high ratings in their respective regions and were all 'serious' programmes, aiming at providing in-depth analysis as opposed to those that were for entertainment purposes. A careful screening resulted in ten shows for our data: three from Mainland China, three from Hong Kong and four from Taiwan. Information about them is presented in Table 11.1.

All these shows were transcribed, with detailed notations marking out features such as tones, speech errors, facial expressions and kinetics, especially those parts where interaction between the host and the guest occurred. Instances of backchannelling were then identified and categorised according to form and function. In terms of form, backchannelling was first classified as either verbal or non-verbal, with the uttering of linguistic sounds as the criterion. Verbal backchannelling therefore referred to those instances in which the speaker uttered something while non-verbal meant that the speaker did not utter anything but signalled her intention through facial expressions or kinetic movements such as nodding the head. The category *verbal* was further divided into *lexical* and *non-lexical*.

Table 11.1. Source of data

Region	Show	Number of episodes	Running time
Mainland China	Yang Lan One on One	10	311'18"
	Global Watch	1	24'44"
	A-Views	4	73'35"
Hong Kong	News Line	2	45'10"
	News Today	5	131'34"
	From Phoenix to the World	3	61'43"
	Global News	3	145'33"
Taiwan	Critical Moment	2	215'56"
	News Tornado	2	99'46"
	New Taiwan Starry Avenue	1	73'11"
Total		33	1122'30"

Lexical backchannelling consisted of recognisable linguistic expressions, ranging from sentences to fragments to words. Non-lexical, on the other hand, referred to those linguistic sounds used for phatic purposes, sometimes even barely audible. It should be noted that those instances under 'verbal' were often accompanied by non-verbal elements, which we will refer to in our discussions in the next section. The frequencies of occurrences of these forms are presented in Table 11.2, in the next section.

Lastly, we categorised all the instances of backchannelling in our data by function: what they seemed to be doing. Nine such functions were identified: *Following, Agreeing, Responding, Rephrasing, Adding, Interrupting, Repeating, Commenting* and *Repairing*. The result of this tabulation is presented in Table 11.3 and the definitions of these functions are provided afterwards.

We were aware that some of the functions might have corresponding notions in the conversation analysis literature. *Responding* seemed to be what conversation analysts call 'reactive expressions' and *Rephrasing* was close to what conversation analysts called '(re)formulation'. However, not every one of these functions had a conversation analysis counterpart, but all of them could be named following the speech act tradition: using a performative verb to label the speech act in question. We therefore opted to follow the framework of speech act theory.

In identifying these functions of backchannelling, we relied on 1) the semantics of backchannelling tokens and 2) semantics plus non-linguistic features as indicated above. Functions such as *Rephrasing* were easily identified using the first criterion, as the meaning of the token was often enough to tell us that the backchannel speaker was saying what the dominant channel speaker had said in a different way. Other functions needed to be identified with the help of non-linguistic features. To tease apart *Following* from *Agreeing*, for example, semantics was often not enough, as the tokens were nodding and short utterances such as 是*shi* 'yes' or 对*dui* 'yes; right', which could indicate both *Following* and *Agreeing*. Non-linguistic features we had noted during the transcription came in handy: In *Agreeing*, what the dominant speaker had said was usually an opinion, often one that was controversial, and the backchannel token was delivered with phonetic emphasis and eye contact. In *Following*, on the other hand, what the dominant speaker had said tended not to be a position or opinion that could be agreed to, and the backchannel tokens were delivered with less phonetic emphasis and with or without eye contact.

Interrupting also belonged to this hard-to-identify group of functions. It was identified by a combination of these criteria: 1) the frequency of backchannel tokens: sometimes, the backchannel speaker, often the host, delivered several umms in succession, indicating that s/he wanted to cut in; 2) facial expressions: the backchannel speaker – again often the host – showed anxiousness on her face to keep the time, sometimes even impatience; and 3) subsequent conversation: once an interrupting token was delivered, the backchannel speaker would try to obtain the floor.

Just as an instance of backchannelling could be realised through multi-forms, it could serve multi-functions as well. For multi-functional backchannelling, we counted all functions but categorised them under the most important function. Therefore, the total numbers of instances in Table 11.3 are greater than those in Table 11.2.

Results and discussion

As is seen in Table 11.2 below, of the three categories, *Non-lexical* is the most frequent form of backchannelling, *non-verbal* is the middle, while *lexical* is the least frequently adopted form. Compare the three regions in terms of frequency as measured in numbers per minute (the rightmost column): Mainland China TV interviews display the most frequent backchannelling, followed by Hong Kong, with Taiwan the least. Due to space considerations and the focus of our study, we do not dwell on these statistics but move to the discussion of the functions of backchannelling.[1]

Although we have listed the functions of backchannelling by region in Table 11.3, we do not dwell on regional differences, as the types of shows and the personal styles of the anchor reviewers could be factors for such differences as well as region.

In our discussions below, we will use DCS to stand for *dominant-channel speaker* and BCS to stand for *backchannel speaker*. DCS is often the guest speaker and BCS, the host. However, that is not always the case, as the host is found to be

Table 11.2. Forms of backchannelling in three regions

	Mainland China	Hong Kong	Taiwan	Total
Length (m)	409	241	472	1122
Non-verbal	365	193	178	736
Lexical	322	115	125	562
Non-lexical	1406	731	531	2668
Total	2093	1039	834	3966
No/m	5.12	4.31	1.76	3.13

Table 11.3. Functions of backchannelling in three regions

	Mainland China	Hong Kong	Taiwan	Total
Following	1634	791	414	2839
Agreeing	227	134	222	583
Responding	73	25	117	215
Rephrasing	143	27	42	212
Adding	49	31	19	99
Interrupting	34	19	6	59
Repeating	20	15	13	48
Commenting	9	8	11	28
Repairing	6	6	0	12
Total	2195	1056	844	4095

the DCS sometimes, particularly at the beginning when she lays out the topic and at the end when she summarises the interview. We ignore the identities of DCSs and BCSs most of the time and make reference to them only when necessary.

A. Following

Following refers to signals that the speaker is following the guest. Tokens of it are mostly non-verbal (nodding of the head) and non-lexical responses such as 嗯 'umm'. As is seen in Table 11.3, *Following* is the most frequent function of back-channelling in the context. An example is provided below.

(3)

DCS:　近些年可能最牵动公众神经的就是有关舌尖上的安全的问题哈

BCS:　[点头]

DCS:　啊一会是这个父母们都跑到香港去办奶粉哈，一会是黄浦江上又飘来了死猪哈，就是这样的一个，呃…过程当中，让公众对自己餐桌上的安全产生了一个很大的一种忧虑啊

BCS:　嗯

DCS: 但是我们也知道，在食品安全的控制链上，有多头的管理，有工蔺的，有什么质量技术监督的

BCS: [点头]

DCS: The hottest topic in the public discourse in recent years has been food safety.

BCS: [nodding]

DCS: People hear parents going to Hong Kong to buy baby formulas, dead pigs floating on the Huangpu River. These things have caused great anxiety in the public about what they eat.

BCS: *Umm.*

DCS: But as we know, the control of food safety belongs to multiple government agencies such as the Bureau of Commerce and offices for quality control and production oversight.

BCS: [nodding]

In (3), the BCS provides frequent nodding of the head and non-lexical responses *umm*. These tokens help make the interview appear to be a two-way conversation rather than a monologue. In the traditional conversation analysis approach, this function is seen as a means for sequencing and expressing interest.

The politeness approach would emphasise the 'expressing interest' aspect. When a guest is invited to appear on TV, much of her image is at stake. These guests are called '嘉宾' ('distinguished guests') or '专家' ('experts'). As such, they want their audience to like and respect what they have to say. In a TV interview context, the audience is not present in the studio, nor is it decided beforehand when the show is aired. The interviewer, being the only audience, provides those signals of interest, showing respect to the guest, a positive politeness strategy.

B. Agreeing

Agreeing refers to those backchannelling tokens that signal the sharing of a particular view by the guest. According to Brown and Levinson, agreeing is yet another positive politeness strategy. In our study, agreeing is found to be the second most frequently occurring function of backchannelling. We cite two examples below.

(4)

DCS: 我就给你讲，如果是这样的话呢，第一个我们可能搜寻的区域不对，就你的概率搜寻就已经错了

BCS: 当然

DCS: This is what I can say. If this is true, we were searching in the wrong region. Therefore, an error has been made about the probability of where the incident might have taken place …

BCS: *Of course.*

(5)

DCS: 当然，在创了这个历史纪录的同时，大家心里想，第一，为什么大立光表现这么
强，其实它有几个重点，第一个的话呢，它够专业

BCS: 对

DCS: 在之前它做光学镜头，那么很多人，可能从数位相机着手啦，可能从投影机着
手，它专注在手机，结果手机发展得最快，再下来的话呢，它也不交际，也不应
酬，它不做什么第二摊的这种交际，对它来讲的话，怎么样把事情做好，聚焦
是最重要的。

BCS: 没错

DCS: Of course … when *Daliguang* broke the record, people were wondering how they managed to have done that. There are several reasons. The first is their expertise …

BCS: *Yes.*

DCS: Previously, *Daliguang* was making optical lenses. At that time, others were focusing on mobile phones, digital cameras or projectors. Second, they did not pay much attention to promotion or making business connections. To them, the most important thing was to do things right. Their objective was to solve the focus problem [of cameras].

BCS: *Right.*

Example (4) is about an aeroplane accident.[2] The DCS (the guest in this case) is analysing the reasons for the failure in locating the plane days and months after the accident. In (5), the DCS is offering his opinions on how *Daliguang*, a company specialising in optical products, has succeeded where its competitors have failed. Both topics are technical, requiring specialised knowledge on the part of the guests. As such, the DCS's views may or may not be readily acceptable to the audience. It is in this context that the politeness function of backchannelling by the BCS is seen: by agreeing with the guest DCS with tokens such as 'of course' (4) and 'yes' and 'right' (5), the host BCS lends validity to the guest's analysis, which enhances the DCS's positive face.

C. Responding

The two functions of backchannelling discussed above are at the mega-discourse level: *Following* indicates interest in what the DCS has to say and makes the interview seem to be interactive while *Agreeing* conveys the BCS's support of the DCS's opinions and views. *Responding*, on the other hand, signals politeness at the level of the specific propositional content of the interview. In (6), two guests are present (hence multiple BCSs).

(6)

DCS: 所以所以你就像一个吸尘机一样每天早上非常负责地在北京的公园　里啊负责把
这些脏空气吸进去

BCSs: [笑]

BCS1:   哈哈吸了一点点

DCS: So, you would be like a vacuum cleaner, sucking up the dirty air in Beijing parks dutifully every morning

BCSs: [laughing]

BCS1:   *Haha … Yes. I sucked in a little*

The DCS's simile comparing a human being to a vacuum cleaner sucking in dirty air involuntarily in Beijing is meant to be a clever joke. The success of a joke is seen in the audience's response: not to generate laughter is a sure sign of failure. Both of the two listeners – BCSs – provide precisely what is expected: laughter.

In the conversation analysis literature, joking and laughing may be seen as an adjacent pair: once a joke is delivered, laughing (on the part of the listener) becomes immediately expected as its 'Preferred Second'. In terms of politeness, laughing is 'preferred' because it satisfies the politeness needs of the joking speaker by expressing understanding and appreciation of the joke. This is yet another strategy geared towards the positive face of the joking speaker.

The BCSs in (6) do not stop here. One of them, BCS1 (last line), goes further, adding support to what the DCS says by admitting that he 'sucked in a little [dirty air]', implying that he is indeed a vacuum cleaner for the city of Beijing. Note that a speaker of a joke is often not serious about the propositional content of the joke. When saying that Beijing citizens are like vacuum cleaners, the DCS does not mean that they *are* vacuum cleaners. BCS1, however, 'goes out of his way', as it were, to imply that he *is* a vacuum cleaner, hence further enhancing the DCS's positive face by showing 'apparent' agreement.

D. Rephrasing

Rephrasing refers to utterances that express a statement in a different way.

(7)

DCS: 第一是农民工工作几十年要他回农村养老是不公平的，那么他在城里边呆着，就应该跟城里人同工同酬同待遇，享受同等市民待遇，这是个公平问题．

BCS: 社会公益角度

DCS: First … Migrant workers have worked in the city for decades. Now you want them to retire in the countryside they originally come from. This is not fair. They have been living in cities. They deserve the same benefit as those living in cities. This is an issue of fairness.

BCS: *The perspective of social welfare*

Summarising his discussion about the retirement system for migrant workers – those who leave their hometowns in the countryside to work in urban areas – the

DCS says that it is not fair to send these people back to the countryside while they have lived in cities and contributed to the development of cities. The BCS rephrases the view into 'The perspective of social welfare'. By so doing, the magnitude of the issue is clarified and increased: the issue of fairness is an issue of 'social welfare', a serious issue for a government (or even any government) to cope with.

The rephrasing function of backchannelling therefore serves to strengthen the DCS's point, in an interview environment in which the image of the DCS, the guest in this case, depends in part on the importance and validity of his arguments and points. By supporting and strengthening the DCS's points, rephrasing offers the BCS an opportunity to enhance the DCS's public image, which is the very goal of Brown and Levinson's positive politeness strategies.

(8)

DCS: 我们可以看到就是说在1997年韩国发生金融风暴的时候，韩国是多么　的努力，把自己往上去推上去，但是从这一次的事件我们可以看到就是说有两个问题，我们必须要去思考说为什么韩国的官员变成了这个样子，第一个就是说其实我们可以看到，就是说韩国从2000年之后，它就把自己的重点放在签FTA和经济发展。

BCS: <u>全部都要拼经济</u>。

DCS: As we have seen, Koreans worked very hard after the financial crisis in 1997. They wanted to improve, to get better. This leads to two points. We must think about why the Korean government was so determined. In other words, after 2000, they have been focusing on signing FTAs and economic development.

BCS: *All out for economy.*

In this example, the DCS states that the Korean government 'has been focusing on signing FTAs and economic development'. His 'focusing on' is turned into 'all out' and the two things he has emulated – signing FTAs and developing economy – are subsumed under one notion, 'economy', by the BCS in her paraphrasing. So, what the BCS does in (8) is similar to what the BCS does in (7): strengthening the point made by the DCS, which adds to the positive face of the interlocutor.

E. Adding

Adding refers to a BCS's providing of what the DCS is going to say. It typically takes place when the DCS is searching for the right word at the time.

(9)

DCS: 可是这一星期呢我确实受不了因为我本身有点感冒感冒刚刚好啊所以这个嗓子呢就对PM2.5 比这个王教授的…（停顿1.3秒）

BCS: <u>仪器哈哈</u>

DCS: 仪器还准确 稍微一高我就受不了呼吸就有点困难

DCS: But this week, I really could not stand it. I had a cold. So, my throat was reacting to the PM2.5 value more accurately than Professor Wang's [1.3 seconds delay]

BCS: *Instrument, haha*

DCS: More accurately than his instrument. A slight increase would cause difficulty in breathing.

The DCS is searching for the right word, as is indicated by the delay. The BCS comes to his rescue, as it were, by providing that word, which is readily taken by the DCS: he repeats the word 'instrument' in his subsequent turn. The next example is similar:

(10)

DCS: 竟然西方的两个重要人物，第一个就是，这个美国的这个共和党的啊

BCS: 议员

DCS: 呃老总，他是主席。啊他呢，跑到乌克兰去，去挑动那。这也是很典型的美国

BCS: *John McCain* 麦凯恩

DCS: 麦凯恩

BCS: 参议员

DCS: 参议员，他就是去挑动这个

BCS: 情绪

DCS: 情绪. 一下之后呢就说，我支持你这个，这个西乌克兰人是不是，去反政府。

DCS: Two of the most important politicians in the West … one of them is a Republican … umm …

BCS: *Senator*

DCS: Umm. Yes. He is the chairman. He went to Ukraine to provoke. This is typical of him …

BCS: *John McCain. McCain.*

DCS: McCain.

BCS: *Senator.*

DCS: Senator. He went to provoke the … this …

BCS: *Sentiment*

DCS: Sentiment. He went there and said, 'I support you'. This means the Ukrainians should go against their government.

In (10), the DCS seems to face some difficulty in finding the right word. He stumbles four ftimes: over the word *senator*, *John McCain* (the name of the senior US Senator from Arizona, Chairman of the Senate Arms Services Committee), the word *senator* again and, finally, the word *sentiment*. Each time, the BCS supplies the right word and each time he accepts it, either by responding with 'yes' or by repeating the word given him in the next turn.

Therefore, the 'coming to the rescue' analogy of the adding function of back-channelling seems to be quite apt. The guest DCS, appearing on national TV, has much at stake. He is supposedly the expert on the issue surrounding Ukraine and expert on international affairs in general. Not being able to readily produce relevant information – and the relevant information in this case seems to be common knowledge to an average viewer – threatens his positive face. The BCS's providing of the much-needed information helps him save his face, helping the interview to go along.

F. Interrupting

To interrupt can hardly be said to be polite. However, we will show that, in a TV interview context, *Interrupting* may serve politeness purposes, or at least it is not impolite. Consider the following example.

(11)

DCS: 其实不光是股市和房地产，股市和房地产这个数字看得大家就心里有点寒心，而且近期我们从一季度的各项数据，公布的各项指标来看，其实大家也都是这个，几乎是达到了十年来的一个最低值了…

BCS: 呃 [打断]

DCS: 各项数据。可以说下行下行，

BCS: 对 [打断]

DCS: 下行这个词大家都已经板上钉钉都确认的事情了

BCS: <u>对，事实上因为这几年我一直在谈，我说给大家在普及一个常识，就是中国经济不可能像过去三十多年一样增长速度。</u>

DCS: Not only the stock market and housing market. The stock market and housing market are a bit depressed. Other numbers, statistics that have been made public. All suggest … the numbers are the lowest in ten years.

BCS: *Yeah …* [interrupting]

DCS: All numbers are going down.

BCS: *Right* [interrupting]

DCS: Negative growth is widely recognised. It is a sure thing.

BCS: *Yes. In fact, I have been saying this all along. It has to be common knowledge that the Chinese economy cannot grow at the same rate as it has in the past thirty years.*

During his speech, the DCS is interrupted twice. Since possession of the conversation floor translates into power and to interrupt is an indication of taking away that power, would the BCS's two interruptions, which clearly threaten the DCS's positive face, be seen as strategies for impoliteness per Culpeper (1996)?

The answer is in the negative once we look at the interview more carefully. The reason for the two interruptions, as it turns out, is that the BCS wants to offer support for the DCS. In the last turn of (11), when the BCS finally gains the floor, he makes the point that the DCS has been making all along, that the (Chinese) economy cannot sustain the rate of growth as it has been in the past three decades. Since the DCS has been pointing out the decrease in the growth rate, the BCS's point offers direct support for him, hence enhancing his positive face.

There seems to be another possibility. In (11), both the DCS and the BCS are guests. As such, they both have the right to the floor. The interruptions that occur are also seen as signals for the BCS to negotiate the floor. In the sense that the right to speak helps one's own positive image, particularly when one is a member of a panel of 'experts', the interruptions by the BCS can be seen as a strategy for his self-politeness, per Chen (2001). However, we will not dwell further on this, as self-politeness does not appear to figure prominently in our data.

The following example is similar.

(12)

DCS:　赵主任呢?

BCS:　我也…[打断]

DCS:　您出行我想也会坐一些公交车啊?

BCS:　是的。

DCS:　坐一些地铁是吧。您体会这个高峰期的地铁的这个拥挤程度吗？

DCS:　How about you, Director Zhao?

BCS:　*Me too* … [interrupting]

DCS:　I think you take buses sometimes, right?

BCS:　*Yes.*

DCS:　And also the subway. What is your experience of the peak time in the subway?

The interruption in this example seems to be the result of improper signalling by the DCS. The DCS asked the BCS a question ('How about you, Director Zhao?'), which prompts the answer 'Me, too' from the DCS. 'Me, too' is an interruption because it is uttered before the DCS finishes her question. However, as it turns out, the DCS – the host – has no intention of getting answers from the BCS. The questions about the BCS using the subway had been assumed all along. All she seems to want to do is to lead to the BCS's experience with the crowdedness of the Beijing public transportation system.

G. Repeating

Repeating refers to the exact verbal reproduction of the previous utterance in an interview. In (13), below, the BCS repeats the DCS's '26 times', which gets further repeated by the DCS himself.

(13)

DCS: 这是一个原因 但是呢 第二个原因我们分析发现呢这里边的硫酸盐增高了26倍

BCS: <u>26倍</u>

DCS: 26倍

DCS: This is the first reason. The second reason we have found after analysis is sulphate went up 26 times.

BCS: *26 times*

DCS: 26 times

Repetition serves the function of emphasising and reinforcing the point. This excerpt comes from an interview about air pollution in China. The increase of sulphate – known as a greenhouse effect-causing agent – in the environment by 26 times is an alarming statistic. By repeating it, the BCS assists the DCS in strengthening and consolidating the latter's point. The DCS obviously appreciates this positive politeness strategy: He repeats '26 times' one more time before going on with his discussion.

(14)

DCS: 铁达尼号，这个跟铁达尼号是完全不同的两个事实，铁达尼号是在那里沉，已经没有办法，束手无策的一个状况，他们掏出了那么多的人，是你根本眼睛看不见的。这个是眼睛睁着看在那里耶。

BCS: <u>眼睁睁地看它沉进去</u>。

DCS: (The Sewol Ferry[3] is) different from the Titanic case. Very different. In the Titanic case, the ship was sinking. There was nothing to do about it. Nothing. Many people were taken out of cabins later but you didn't see them while in this case you see the ship going down right in front of your eyes.

BCS: *The ship going down right in front of your eyes.*

Likewise, the repetition in this example, 'The ship going down right in front of your eyes', enhances the DCS's positive face by reinforcing the horrifying scene of the Sewol Ferry's sad fate.

H. Commenting

Commenting refers to utterances that express the BCS's views about what the DCS has said. Consider (15).

(15)

DCS: 现在中国的穆斯林呐，我们统计，就是两千三百万。两千三百万呢，是我们中国五十六个民族当中的十个少数民族，对，十个少数民族集中在一起是两千三百万。

BCS: <u>非常庞大的一个数字</u>。嗯。

DCS: The population of Muslims in China, according to our census, is about 23 million. Twenty-three million is the total of ten average-sized minority ethnic groups. Yes. Ten other ethnic groups put together.

BCS: *A huge number. Umm.*

The DCS's entire turn is aimed at demonstrating the size of the Muslim population in China. After providing the census number – 23 million – he states that 23 million is ten other ethnic groups combined. As if that is not enough, he reiterates that idea one more time. The BCS apparently accepts his point: she comments on it by saying, 'A huge number'.

The support for the DCS is more obvious in the following.

(16)

DCS: 关键是如何有序地进入，老百姓的爱心应该得到保护；但关键是你如何分流。如何用一些地图或地标或者用一个协调机制，把这些爱心最大限度地激发起来。

BCS: <u>说得太好了</u>。<u>这是重要的</u>。

DCS: The key is how to enter the disaster areas in an orderly and organised manner. Sure, you have to care for the people. But you have to find the best ways to distribute the rescue crews. You must use all available navigation systems and landmarks. You should have a coordinating mechanism. Only this can show your care for the victims.

BCS: *Very well put. This is important.*

The backchannelling provided by the BCS is an explicitly positive assessment of the points that the DCS has made, clearly a positive politeness strategy that enhances his public image in front of the TV audience.

I. (Other-)Repairing

In the conversation analysis literature, two types of repair – correction of a mistake – are recognised: self-repair and other-repair. A repair often goes through two steps: initiation and repair. Putting the two together, one ends up with the following possible organisational possibilities:

(17)

Types of repair

1.   Self-initiation, self-repair

2.   Self-initiation, other-repair

3.   Other-initiation, self-repair

4.   Other-initiation, other-repair

Type 1, self-initiation and self-repair, can be illustrated by utterances such as 'I've had a tough time this year … I mean this quarter'. Type 2 can be seen in the following:

(18)

    A: He had dis … uh Mistuh W- whatever k- I can't think of his first name, Watts on, the one thet wrote l/ that piece,

    B: Dan Watts.

(Adopted from Schegloff, Jefferson and Sacks 1977: 364, Ex. 13)

The third type, other-initiation, self-repair, is exemplified by the following, all adopted from Schegloff, Jefferson and Sacks (1977: 377–378):

(19)

    A: The first time they stopped me from sellin' cigarettes was this morning

           (1.0)

    B: From selling cigarettes?

    A: From buying cigarettes.

(20)

    A: 'E likes that waiter over there,

    B: Wait-er?

    A: Waitress, sorry,

    B: 'ats better.

(21)

    A: But y'know single beds'r awfully thin to sleep on.

    B: What?

    A: Single beds. //They're-

    B: Y'mean narrow?

    A: They're awfully narrow yeah.

The last type of repair, both initiated and done by other, is illustrated in (22):

(22)

    A: Stay home and pine about work.

    B: Not about work. About money.

(Adopted from Schegloff, Jefferson and Sacks 1977: 378, Ex. 67)

According to Schegloff, Jefferson and Sacks (1977), the order in which the four types of repair are listed in (17) coincides with the order in which these types are preferred by conversationalists: Type 1 is the most preferred and Type 4, the least. If we apply Brown and Levinson's politeness theory to repair, we see why that is the case: The order in (17) is also the order in which the threat to the positive

face of the speaker who has made the error increases. In other words, it is more 'face-saving' for one to realise and correct her own mistake than have it realised and corrected by others.

In our data, however, all backchannelling repairs are other-initiated and other-performed:

(23)

DCS: 潘总说了说他第一次关注到PM2.5是我记得是2001年10月份对吧

BCS1:   [点头]

BCS2:   <u>2010年</u>

DCS: According to Mr Pan, he began to pay attention to PM2.5, I remember, in the October of 2001, right?

BCS1:   [nodding]

BCS2:   *In 2010*

(24)

DCS: 但是我们也知道，在食品安全的控制链上，有多头的管理，有工商的，有什么 质量技术监督的…呃…有这个卫生的，然后也有农业部的

BCS: <u>嗯。农业的</u>

DCS: As we know, the chain of control for food safety includes many sectors: commercial, quality oversight, umm, sanitary, and Ministry of Agriculture.

BCS: *Umm. Agricultural.*

(25)

DCS: 就是怎么样呢，他们现在不是美国忽然之间，他们已经发现他们这个天然气

BCS: <u>液燃气</u>

DCS: 他们把这变为液体，把这液体以后，将来，以后运着卖给这个…

DCS: So, the US, all of a sudden, they discovered that natural gas …

BCS: *Liquefied gas.*

DCS: They liquefied natural gas and, in the future, sell it to …

In all these instances, the BCSs deliver the repair straightforwardly. They do not give the DCS the opportunity to realise the errors (so that he could initiate the repair). Neither do they initiate (e.g., 'You mean X?') the repair for the DCS (so he can perform the repair himself). Such 'blunt' repair work indicates to the DCS that 'You are mistaken and haven't realised it. I will correct your mistake for you', something that would no doubt threaten positive face of the DCS. However, the DCSs do not take offense. Neither do we as viewers feel that the BCSs are 'impolite' in those cases. How would a politeness approach account for this difficulty?

We believe that the answer to this question lies in Brown and Levinson's formula for computing the weightiness of an FTA as presented in (2) above, particularly the factor Rx, defined as 'a value that measures the degree to which the FTAx is rated an imposition in that culture'.

Other-repair is supposed to have a very high Rx value ordinarily. But TV interviews are not 'ordinary' conversations. For one thing, TV shows of any kind are subject to stringent time constraints. However, self-initiation and self-repair takes time and can fail. In one example in Schegloff, Jefferson and Sacks (1977: 364, Ex. 9), a conversationalist waits a total of 5.7 seconds in four turns for the other to self-initiate and self-repair before they both admit failure, which we do not cite due to space limitations. Their Example 12 (1977: 364), however, is short enough for us to cite below:

(26)

Ken:	Is Al here today?
Dan:	Yeah.
	(2.0)
Roger:	-> He is? hh eh heh
Dan:	-+ Well he was.

Note that Roger waits two seconds for Ken to self-initiate a repair before he does it himself. Then the conversation takes two more turns to repair the misuse of the *be* verb. Two seconds would seem quite long on TV. We believe therefore that the TV interview context would reduce the Rx value of other-repair drastically.

Second, a mistake in a TV interview may be more consequential than it is in a different context. In daily conversations, speakers are frequently found to misspeak, and many of the resulting errors are accepted and then forgotten. But TV interview guests have more at stake. They are 'experts', held to be intelligent and knowledgable, and are hence less tolerated by their audience for errors. In this sense, repairing their errors is doing them a favour.

Third, the 'source' of the error may also play a role in making it possible for DCSs to deliver other-repair. In (23), the error has to do with memory – the DCS is pulling the year out of his mind off hand – and he is not fully committed to what he manages to recall, as is seen in the tag question 'right?' at the end of his turn. In (24), the error seems to be a slip of the tongue: the DCS may have intended to say '农业的' ('agricultural') but ends up saying '农业部的' ('Ministry of Agriculture'), whereby the difference is the additional morpheme '部' ('Ministry'). These are common occurrences, and therefore to correct them may not be very threatening to the DCS's face.

We argue that, due to all these reasons, the Rx – degree of imposition – of other-repair in a TV interview would be very low. The low value of Rx would lead to a low value of Wx, which, in turn, would lead to a more direct politeness strategy, as is seen in (1). The strategy that is seen as the most direct is Strategy 1, 'Without redressive action, baldly'.

In sum, the instances of other-repair found in our data turn out to also be politeness strategies. They are delivered without mitigation because the TV interview context calls for it. Besides, Brown and Levinson's FTA weightiness formula allows for this possibility. In our understanding of Brown and Levinson, whether an utterance is polite or not does not depend on how direct it is but on how it is motivated by the speech situation as reflected by their formula in (2).

Conclusion

In this study, we have investigated how backchannelling seems to work for the purpose of politeness in Chinese TV interviews. Specifically, we have identified nine functions of backchannelling and argued that positive politeness underlies all of them. In this concluding section, we discuss three issues that have arisen from our findings: reasons for the connection between positive politeness and our data, the implications of our findings for politeness research, and the interception between conversation analysis and pragmatics.

First, our finding that all the nine functions in our data are accounted for very elegantly by Brown and Levinson's notion of positive politeness is hardly surprising. The interviews we have studied seem to be homogeneous in important ways. As regular programmes on the air, they are all subject to stringent time constraints and are conducted in similar and consistent formats. This means that the interviews follow a well-defined structure, with the roles of the hosts and guests clearly spelled out. This results in the fact that very few, if at all, directives such as requests or orders are found, for the reason that these speech acts potentially threaten negative face.

The identity of the invited participants also matters. All guests in the interviews in our study are experts on their respective topics. In our opinion, while similar interviews in societies such as the US exist, the status of expert seems to be more highlighted in the Chinese context. For instance, guests in these interviews are explicitly referred to as 专家 'experts' or 嘉宾 'distinguished guests', which does not seem to be the case in channels like CNN or other national TV programmes in the US.[4] Therefore, the image of these guests on the air is very important. The same holds for hosts. Most of the hosts in our data are regular anchors. The popularity – and the existence – of their shows depends a great deal on their image. It is hence vital for both the guests and the hosts to maintain and, better still, to enhance their respective images. Positive politeness strategies thus become a handy tool, as they are 'designed' to reduce the threat to their positive face.

The cooperative relationship between the host and the guest is relevant, too. In the shows in our data, the hosts and their respective guests seem to have shared goals and shared views on their topics. This sharing makes it possible to help each other in the maintaining and enhancing of their public image. In a different kind of show, however, things would be different. The host Bill O'Reilly of 'The O'Reilly Factor', on *Fox News*, for example, often invites guests known to have opposite views to his own, and the interviews can be very confrontational. His interview with Barney Frank, Democratic Congressman, is one of the many in which the two openly attack each other's face.[5] One would expect to find a different set of things, more likely to be 'strategies' for impoliteness per Culpeper (1996) or for self-politeness per Chen (2001), in programmes of this sort.

Second, our findings are relevant to discussions about politeness theories. As indicated in the introduction, Brown and Levinson's (and, to a lesser degree, Leech's) politeness theory has been criticised for not being able to take care of factors that are context specific. Our analysis of other-repair seems to suggest the opposite. To reiterate, while other-initiation, other-repair is the least preferred type of repair work in conversation analysis, hence the least 'polite', it appears as a positive politeness strategy, functioning to maintain the positive face of the DCS in the same way as do other types of backchannelling. Brown and Levinson's theory, as we have demonstrated, can explain this seeming contradiction nicely. This may be suggestive of greater explanatory power and therefore greater validity of Brown and Levinson's theory than has been believed by many (cf. Chen 2010).

Third and lastly, we see our work as an attempt to combine insights from conversation analysis and pragmatics. Coming into being in more or less the same time (late 1960s to early 1970s), conversation analysis and pragmatics have made landmark contributions to the study of language. However, the two 'sisters' have not been talking to each other as much as they should have. For instance, reading the vast literature on conversation analysis, one finds only passing reference to works in pragmatics, and vice versa. In this study, we hope we have succeeded in demonstrating how the two can inform each other and wish more effort will ensue in the near future.

Notes

1. An anonymous reviewer suggests that we delete Table 11.2 and our discussions of forms of backchannelling. While we agree that Table 11.2 is not entirely relevant to the rest of the study, we felt that the potential value of what is presented in it for interested readers outweighs the cost of the little space it takes up.
2. Malaysia Airlines Flight 370 (MH370/MAS370), a scheduled international passenger flight, disappeared on 8 March 2014 while flying from Kuala Lum-

pur International Airport near Kuala Lumpur, Malaysia, to Beijing Capital International Airport in Beijing, China.

3. The sinking of the MV Sewol occurred on the morning of 16 April 2014 en route from Incheon to Jeju. The Japanese-built South Korean ferry capsized while carrying 476 people, mostly secondary school students from Danwon High School (Ansan City). In all, 304 passengers died in the disaster.

4. In those programmes, the guest is often introduced by name, followed by a brief bio to show that she is knowledgable about the topic at hand. However, the word *expert* is seldom used. Besides, the Chinese words专家 'experts' and 嘉宾 'distinguished guests' have been made into proper names. At a formal banquet, for instance, there are often 嘉宾席 'seats reserved for distinguished guests'. The codification of these statuses in language, we believe, indicates their importance.

5. https://www.youtube.com/watch?v=Unj-kcGOe5I, accessed on 19 May 2015.

References

Anna, V. (2011) Cross-cultural and situational variation in request behaviour: Request strategies in American English and Hungarian. *Argument* 7: 95–106.

Atkinson, J. M. and Heritage, J. (1985) *Structures of Social Action: Studies in Conversation Analysis*. Cambridge: Cambridge University Press. https://doi.org/10.1017/CBO9780511665868

Blum-Kulka, S. and Olshtain, E. (1984) Requests and apologies: A cross-cultural study of speech act realization patterns. *Applied Linguistics* 3: 196–213. https://doi.org/10.1093/applin/5.3.196

Brown, P. and Levinson, S. (1987) *Politeness*. Cambridge: Cambridge University Press.

Chen, R. (2001) Self-politeness: A proposal. *Journal of Pragmatics* 33: 87–106. https://doi.org/10.1016/S0378-2166(99)00124-1

Chen, R. (2010) Pragmatics East and West: Similar or different? In Anna Trosborg (ed.) *Pragmatics across Languages and Cultures* 167–186. Berlin: Mouton de Gruyter.

Chen, R., He, L. and Hu, C. (2013) Chinese requests: In comparison to American and Japanese requests and with reference to the 'East–West divide'. *Journal of Pragmatics* 55: 140–161. https://doi.org/10.1016/j.pragma.2013.05.012

Culpeper, J. (1996) Towards an anatomy of impoliteness. *Journal of Pragmatics* 25(3): 349–367. https://doi.org/10.1016/0378-2166(95)00014-3

Drew, P. (2013) Conversation analysis and social action. *Journal of Foreign Languages* 3: 2–19.

Drew, P. and Heritage J. (1992) *Talk at Work: Interaction in Institutional Settings*. Cambridge: Cambridge University Press.

Edwards, D. (1994) Script formulation: An analysis of event descriptions in conversation. *Journal of Language and Social Psychology* 13(3): 211–247. https://doi.org/10.1177/0261927X94133001

Edwards, D. and Stokoe, E. (2007) Self-help in calls for help with problem neighbors. *Research on Language and Social Interaction* 40(1): 9–32. https://doi.org/10.1080/08351810701331208

Felix-Brasderfer, J. C. (2005) Indirectness and politeness in Mexican requests. In D. Eddinton (ed.) *Selected Proceedings of the 7th Hispanic Linguistics Symposium* 66–78. Somerville, MA: Cascadilla Proceedings Project.

Goodwin, M. H. and Cekaite, A. (2013) Calibration in direct/response sequences in family interaction. *Journal of Pragmatics* 46: 122–138. https://doi.org/10.1016/j.pragma.2012.07.008

Kent, A. (2012) Compliance, resistance and incipient compliance when responding to directives. *Discourse Studies* 14(6): 711–730. https://doi.org/10.1177/1461445612457485

Lakoff, R. (1973) The logic of politeness, or minding your p's and q's. *Papers from the Ninth Regional Meetings of the Chicago Linguistics Society* 292–305. Chicago, IL: Chicago Linguistics Society.

Lakoff, R. (1977) What can you do with words: Politeness, pragmatics, and performatives. In A. Rogers, B. Wall and J. P. Murphy (eds) *Proceedings of the Texas Conference on Performatives, Presuppositions, and Implicatures* 79–106. Arlington, VA: Centre for Applied Linguistics.

Lee, S. (2009) Extended requesting: Interaction and collaboration in the production and specification of requests. *Journal of Pragmatics* 41: 1248–1271. https://doi.org/10.1016/j.pragma.2008.09.013

Leech, G. (1983) *Principles of Pragmatics*. London: Longman.

Lindstrom, A. (2005) Language as social action: A study of how senior citizens request assistance with practical tasks in the Swedish home help service. In A. Hakulinen and M. Selting (eds) *Syntax and Lexis in Conversation* 209–233. Amsterdam: John Benjamins. https://doi.org/10.1075/sidag.17.11lin

Locher, M. (2006) Politeness behaviour and relational work: The discursive approach to politeness. *Multilingua* 25: 249–267. https://doi.org/10.1515/MULTI.2006.015

Schegloff, E. A. (2007) *Sequence Organization in Interaction: A Primer in Conversation Analysis,* I. Cambridge: Cambridge University Press. https://doi.org/10.1017/CBO9780511791208

Schegloff, E. A., Jefferson, G. and Sacks, H. (1977) The preference for self-correction in the organisation of repair in conversation. *Language* 53: 361–382. https://doi.org/10.1353/lan.1977.0041

Sidnell, J. and Stivers, T. (eds) (2013) *Handbook of Conversation Analysis*. Chichester: Blackwell Publishing.

Spencer-Oatey, H. (2005) (Im)politeness, face and perceptions of rapport: Unpackaging their bases and interrelationships. *Journal of Politeness Research* 1(1): 95–119. https://doi.org/10.1515/jplr.2005.1.1.95

Stivers, T. and Hayahi, M. (2010) Transformative answers: One way to resist a question's constraints. *Language in Society* 39:1–25. https://doi.org/10.1017/S0047404509990637

Yngve, V. (1970) On getting a word in edgewise. In R. I. Binnick (ed.) *Papers from the Sixth Regional Meeting of the Chicago Linguistic Society* 567–577. Chicago: University of Chicago Linguistics Department.

Yu, M.-C. (2003) On the universality of face: Evidence from Chinese compliment response behaviour. *Journal of Pragmatics* 35: 1679–1710. https://doi.org/10.1016/S0378-2166(03)00074-2

Zimmerman, D. H. (1992) The interactional organisation of calls for emergency assistance. In P. Drew and J. Heritage (eds) *Talk at Work: Interaction in Institutional Settings* 418–469. Cambridge: Cambridge University Press.

CHAPTER 12

Backchannelling and politeness in the interaction of medical consultations

Yansheng Mao and Kun Yang

Introduction

The use of the term 'backchannel' dates back to Yngve (1970: 568), who defines backchannels as short message signals that the speaker receives from the listener while holding the floor. According to Yule (1996), backchannels refer to those vocalisations in a conversation, short words and phrases such as 'yeah', 'no', 'right' and 'sure' (Yule 1996). However, though backchannelling is considered a necessary part of conversation and meaningful in linguistic research, it has not received adequate notice or attention (Shelley and Gonzalez 2013). What is more, while backchannelling behaviour seems to be a universal feature of human communication, how the behaviour varies from language to language and from culture to culture is also underexplored (Sharifi and Azadmanesh 2011). Although a backchannel token may sometimes serve more than one function within a speech community, it may have different interpretations from community to community. As stressed by Berry (1992), Mizutani (1988) and Wieland (1990), each language has a different system of contextualising cues, including backchannels, and the difference inbetween often leads to misinterpretation of each other in intercultural communication. For this reason, some studies (e.g., Berry 1992; Ishida 2006) have been carried out in the fields of interlanguage and crosscultural pragmatics in order to identify related differences in the sociolinguistic or sociocultural rules between individual speech communities, and to explore learners' competences with regard to the backchannelling rules of the target language.

Many researchers, working from diverse perspectives, have considered backchannel feedback, along with other turn-taking phenomena, to be a phenomenon of special interest, as being prototypical of social interaction in general (Fiske and

Duncan 1985; Sacks, Schlegoff and Jefferson 1974; Ward 1997; Yngve 1970) or a signal marker (Yngve 1970). All these studies, conducted in relation to speech acts or conversation analysis, have tended to focus on the investigation of production strategies with regard to the categories of backchannels. As yet, however, the potential of backchannelling as a politeness strategy (dealing with how rapport or coordination is managed between language users by means of backchannels) has received relatively little attention. As we shall demonstrate, the knowledge of the categories and strategic functions of backchannels may serve to prevent potential failures or misunderstanding in the process of interpersonal communication.

Specifically, this study focuses on the use of backchannels as a strategy of politeness in call-in consultation. This genre of communication has recently assumed prominence as a means of promoting appropriate use of health care services and ensuring that callers are matched with the most appropriate and least costly services (Lynda, Nauright, Moneyham and Williamson 1999). It also has the potential to provide effective medical treatment whilst simultaneously maximising efficiency and improving access to care (Warren, Mackie and Leary 2012). Taking all these into account, this study reports on a qualitative study on the relationship between backchannels and politeness management with regard to the perception and interpretation of backchannelling as it occurs in spontaneous conversation between Chinese consultants and callers (with questions) on the radio.

Literature review

In the existing studies, backchannels as feedback have been variously delimited and discussed in regard to their definitions, sub-types and related phenomena (e.g., Clancy, Thompson, Suzuki and Tao 1996; Drummond and Hopper 1993; Horiguchi 1997; Maynard 1989; Mizuno 1988; Schegloff 1982). By and large, the term 'backchannel' refers to listener responses, both verbal and non-verbal in nature (Ishida 2006), in a primarily one-way communication, which are frequently considered to be phatic expressions (Ward and Wataru 2000). In essence, backchannels serve social or meta-conversational purposes, rather than involving substantial two-way communication. Characteristically, backchannels have three features: a) they are used to respond directly to the content of an utterance of the other, b) they are optional, c) they do not require acknowledgment by the other, as commented below by Faerch and Kasper:

> In real life communication, there is a constant need for speakers to both self-monitor their own speech production and to monitor the reaction of their interlocutors. There is a need for listeners to ensure that their interpretation of the speaker's communicative intention in fact matches what

he wanted to say. And occasionally, there is a need for both speakers and listeners to solve problems as they crop up

(Faerch and Kasper 1982: 72).

Since the idea of backchannelling was first put forward by Yngve in 1970, many researchers have considered backchannels to be a phenomenon of special interest (Ohira 1994). Among the various studies, the most notable is the functional categorisation of backchannels. It has been found that the functions of backchannels could be classified into four kinds: a) backchannel as a continuer, with the function to maintain the flow of conversation and the desire of the current speaker to continue his turn (White 1997); b) backchannel as captured interest token, indicating that the listener pays attention to what is said, as well as the continuer, the difference being in the relation to the uttered information (Pipek 2007); c) backchannel as consonance token, which informs the speaker that the listener agrees with the standpoint of the speaker or that the listener is in convergence with the conveyed idea (Pipek 2007); d) backchannel as information confirmation token, which means the stated information has been received (Pipek 2007).

Beside the numerous studies on the functional categorisation of backchannels, several other kinds of studies are also worthy of mention. Among others, Ward and Wataru (2000) conducted research into the prosodic differences in backchannel responses between English and Japanese. In Ishida's (2006) study, the receptive strategies used by learners of Japanese are investigated, focusing on their perception of a backchannel cue that occurs in spontaneous conversation between native speakers of Japanese. It reports on qualitative differences between native speakers and learners of Japanese with regard to the interpretation of the backchannel cue and the social context in which it is used. Wanis-St. John (2006), focusing on the backchannelling negotiation in international bargaining, indicates that backchannelling negotiation can not only facilitate the attainment of breakthrough agreements, but can also damage a peace process by reinforcing some uncertainties. Some dimensions of register like field and tenor may show direct relation on the use of backchannel, and backchannelling itself would change the outcome of the interaction (e.g., politeness). Thus, the study on backchannels should consider the effects of social context (gender, power, distance) on the use of backchannelling, the function and distribution of backchannels in conversation, and the relation between backchannelling and politeness.

So far, little research has been carried out with regard to Chinese people's use of backchannelling and politeness (but see Hu and Chen, this volume) and in Chinese institutional contexts (for example, the context of medical consultation, which has attracted a lot of attention in both linguistics and sociology research). Thus, the present study might not only contribute to our further understanding of backchannelling, including its functions and effects on politeness, but also improve the understanding of the current tense relationship between medical penalties and patients.

Methodology

Research questions

In view of the research gaps pointed out above, this study is intended to reveal how the use of backchannels signals politeness in consultant-callers' conversations on the radio. The following specific questions will be addressed:

1. What types of backchannels do consultants use in their conversations with callers on the radio?
2. How do they use them to signal politeness?

Data collection

All the data in this study were collected from caller telephone counselling radio programmes with a digital voice recorder. This method had several advantages: a) owing to the general accessibility of radio broadcasting, the researcher could collect data without having to consider the restriction of research ethics; b) the researcher could collect data wherever possible instead of going to the fixed venue; c) with the re-play function of a digital voice recorder, the researcher was able to listen to the collected data time and again. Moreover, during the data-collecting process, the researcher could avoid collecting interaction data that would seem to be apparently fake. (The 'fake interaction' would happen in front of the hospital gate, where the *yaotuo* (drug agent) would boast or lie to the patients of the effects of certain medicines.) With the supervision of governments or media agents, the consultants could barely boast or lie to the audience through online consultation.

Specifically, the data were collected from two caller radio programmes in China, *Medical Health Consulting* and *Voice of Health*, both broadcast in July 2015. As shown in Table 12.1, four records of medical health consultants were taken from the *Medical Health Consulting* programme, and another six records were taken from the *Voice of Health* programme. All the contents of the records were transcribed into words by the researchers who were familiar with the transcribing rules so as to ensure the reliability of the data (according to ANOVA and Turkey test, R= 0.960, which meant that the data were of high reliability).

In China, perhaps also in many other countries of the world, social factors like ill-balanced doctor–patient relationships and expensive medical costs have forced the public to turn to non-governmental medical institutions and medical

Table 12.1. Sources of data

Radio programme	Frequency	Gender (consultant–caller)	Duration
Medical Health Consulting	FM196.6	Male–Male	18′15″
Medical Health Consulting	FM196.6	Male–Female	13′13″
Voice of Health	FM105.9	Female–Male	15′59″
Voice of Health	FM105.9	Female–Female	13′29″

consulting service institutions. According to a report in *China Daily* in December 2014, China's healthcare system is faced with corruption, often endangering the relations between doctors and patients. In a report by *TMT Post* (an Internet news journal in China, see details in http://www.tmt.com) in July 2015, the reporter believes that a real-time telehealth service could ensure sufficient communication between patients and doctors and improve the accuracy of diagnoses. In response to these factors, some radio stations have set up telephone counselling radio programmes, aiming to establish a platform between medicine factories (medicine recommending) and patients (disease consulting). According to Drew and Heritage (1992), such telephone consulting interaction between consultant and caller is institutional by nature.

After setting up the telephone consulting model, the authors categorised the backchannels in terms of form and function. While analysing the politeness of backchannelling in the consultation context, the authors adopted the Grand Strategy of Politeness by Leech (2005, 2014) as the main framework of reference: In order to be polite, S expresses or implies meanings which place a high value on what pertains to O (O = other person[s], [mainly the addressee]) or place a low value on what pertains to S (S = self, speaker).

In pursuing GSP, the S will express meanings as presented in Table 12.2:

Table 12.2. Communicative constraints in GSP (adapted from Leech 2014: 92)

Constraints	Label for this constraint	Typical speech act type(s)
(1) Place a high value on O's wants	Generosity	Commissives
(2) Place a low value on S's wants	Tact	Directives
(3) Place a high value on O's qualities	Approbation	Compliments
(4) Place a low value on S's qualities	Modesty	Self-evaluation
(5) Place a high value on S's obligations to O	Obligation of S to O	Apology, thanks
(6) Place a low value on O's obligation to S	Obligation of O to S	Responses to thanks and apologies
(7) Place a high value on O's opinion	Agreement	Agreeing/disagreeing
(8) Place a low value on O's opinion	Opinion-reticence	Giving opinions
(9) Place a high value on O's feeling	Sympathy	Expressing feeling
(10) Place a low value on O's feeling	Feeling-reticence	Suppressing feeling

Here in this study, Leech's Grand Strategy of Politeness (GSP) is applied as the main framework of reference for the following major reason. Specifically, back-channelling is not the primary act that its user intends to perform. As Hu and Chen (this volume) suggest, it is directed towards the positive face of the addressee. The adoption of Leech's (2005) GSP can serve to complement their study.

Results and discussion

This section presents the quantitative distribution of the various functions of the backchannels and discusses their implications of politeness.

Quantitative display of the forms and functions of backchannels

To address our first question of what types of backchannels consultants used in their conversation with the callers on the radio, we analyse our data from two perspectives: forms and functions.

In terms of forms, backchannels are first classified as lexical and non-lexical, with the former consisting of lexical forms and the latter, mimetic units (for details see Table 12.3). According to Pipek (2007), lexical backchannelling includes 'yeah', 'right', 'sure', etc., whereas non-lexical backchannelling includes sounds like 'mm', 'en', 'mhm', etc

Table 12.3. Forms of backchannels in our data

	Verbal		Total	No/m
	Lexical	Non-lexical		
M–M	55	82	137	7.48
M–F	33	66	99	10.99
F–M	17	40	57	3.57
F–F	21	19	40	2.96
Total	126 (37.8%)	207 (62.2%)	333 (100%)	5.47

No/m represents the use of backchannels per minute.

From Table 12.3, it is clear that the interactants use significantly more non-lexical backchannelling than lexical backchannelling (62.2% vs 37.8%). For the former, sounds in radio recordings like 哎 ('yes'), 嗯 ('en') are frequently used non-lexical backchannels. According to Ward (2006), non-lexical backchannels serve to agree to the opposite partner's utterances and ideas. According to the fact that non-lexical backchannels are the most frequent forms in the data, and the interpretation of non-lexical backchannels by Ward, it is supposed that consultants intend to express agreement or following during the conversation, which is a manifestation of positive politeness. For the latter, the Chinese characters in the radio recordings like 当然 ('Of course'), 对 ('Yeah'], 确实('true') are frequently used lexical backchannels. These also signal agreement. In addition, according to Rieger (2001), lexical backchannels fulfil social, interactional and symbolic functions, such as engaging the addressee and making the conversation sound friendlier. Thus, both the lexical and non-lexical backchannels are tightly related with politeness, as stated in Post's comments on conversation, and elaborated later:

> In conversation, as in most things, the 'middle road' is best. Be neither too silent nor too glib. Know when to listen to others, but know also when it is your turn to carry the conversation ... Remember that the sympathetic listener is the delight of delights. The person who is eager for your news or enthralled with your conversation, who gives you spontaneous and undivided attention, is the one to whom you would rather talk than any others.

> (Post 1969: 1943)

With regard to the functions, eight types of functions (following, responding, repeating, agreeing, commenting, interrupting and rephrasing) are identified according to their roles in the data with reference to Ohira (1994), Limbertz (2011) and Chen and Hu (this volume), which emphasise the importance of listenership and their role in conversation. Our findings are shown in Table 12.4, where *following* ranks the highest (257) in terms of frequency, followed by *Responding (33), Repeating (21), Agreeing (9), Commenting (8), and Interrupting (4),* with *Rephrasing (1)* being the least.

Table 12.4. Functions of backchannels in our data

	M–M	M–F	F–M	F–F	Total
Following	108	86	42	21	257
Responding	3	5	9	8	25
Repeating	15	2	1	3	21
Agreeing	2	1	0	6	9
Commenting	6	2	0	0	8
Interrupting	1	1	1	1	4
Rephrasing	1	0	0	0	1
Total	136	97	53	39	325

Backchannel functions and their politeness interpretations

It is demonstrated that both lexical and non-lexical backchannels are found in the consultation interaction between consultant and caller. As discussed in previous studies, the use of backchannels is related to politeness. This section tries to demonstrate in detail how the backchannels used by the consultants signals politeness with examples from our records.

A. Following

The term 'consultation' is definable as a collaborative problem-solving process between a consultant and a caller. The purposes of consultation are to reduce the patients' uncertainty, ease anxiety and stress, and help them to make informed decisions about medical treatments. So, how to manage the consultation in a polite and efficient way is of great importance in the medical interaction. Without competence in consultation skills, all the other skills of a clinician become almost irrelevant (Hugo and Couper 2005). In acknowledgment of this, consultants are generally expected to show, above all, that they are following the caller at the time.

Following backchannels refer to signals that suggest that the listener is being attentive to the speaker's words. It is found that tokens of this type are mostly non-lexical responses such as 嗯 'emm'. It is quite understandable why following backchannels occur most frequently. Above all, the consultants could not see the callers on the radio. Using following backchannels, they can indicate their presence and attention during the conversation. Also, the consultants need to follow the callers or show signals of following to reduce the latter's uncertainty about whether the consultant is giving heed to their need, which is believed to place a high value on S's qualities and feeling according to GSP. As is seen in Table 12.3, following is the most frequent function of backchannelling when the participants are in the process of consultation. When backchannels are functioning as following, they sound like turns, thus involving speaker-shift, though not very obviously in terms of contribution to the proposition content; they are often uttered simultaneously with part of the ongoing talk, but mostly uttered in a fairly low voice, often with characteristic intonation. Here is an example.

(1)

1	Caller(M):	我就想问一下马老师啊
2	Consultant(M):	嗯
3	Caller(M):	您看我中午加上一次行不行啊？
1	Caller(M):	Mr Ma, I have a question
2	Consultant(M):	Emm
3	Caller(M):	Is that ok if I drink one more time at noon?

In (1), the consultant utters 'Emm' as a non-lexical response to the caller. The use of the token helps to make the caller feel the presence of the consultant at the other end of the line. More relevantly in this context, the consultant's attention to the caller's question expresses his interest in and care for the caller. Thus, in (1), the consultant's use of attention-indexing backchannel 'Emm' is a polite move as it indicates he is interacting with the caller and thus encouraging the speaker to continue with the description of physical conditions in progress. In terms of politeness, the consultant's use of 'Emm' suggests his consideration of the caller's physical state; that is, he is implicitly placing a high value on the latter's feelings, which is consistent with the Maxim of Sympathy according to Leech's (2005) Grand Strategy of Politeness.

B. Responding

Charon, Greene and Adelman (1994) examine the structure of clinical consultation as an activity type which involves collaboration and complexity, and the consultant is often thrust into complex ethical and psychosocial situations (Jimenez, Esplin and Hernandez 2015). Naturally, how to initiate and keep smooth rapport with the caller is quite meaningful for the sake of a successful consultation with the help of backchannelling cues. Quite different from following backchannels, which are often neutral or less opinionated (Gardner 1997), responding backchannels usually convey an explicit opinion about the interlocutor's utterance, aiming to place a high/low value on the O's opinion, consistent with the Maxim of Agreement in GSP. In other words, while following backchannels are usually used during the continuous speaking of the caller, responding ones occur when there is pause or question from the caller in the conversation. It is found in our data that backchannelling functions as a responding act. Take (2) for example:

(2)

1	Consultant(M):	提前使用三七粉，不用多，早上一次，晚上一次，没什么问题，完全可以…
2	Caller(F):	那我就给她用上？
3	Consultant(M):	<u>哎，对，</u>你爱人不是有血压高么？
4	Caller(F):	<u>嗯，血压高</u>
5	Consultant(M):	我们现在正在搞一个活动…
1	Consultant(M):	(Let her) use notoginseng powder twice a day, once in the morning and once in the evening. Don't worry. It's fine for her
2	Caller(F):	So, I would tell her to use the notoginseng powder?
3	Consultant(M):	*Yes, right.* And your husband is suffering from high blood pressure?
4	Caller(F):	*Yeah, high blood pressure*
5	Consultant(M):	The medicine is on promotion now …

In the third line of the conversation, the consultant responds to the question 'I would tell her to use the notoginseng powder?' with a responding 'Yes, right', indicating that he understands the question of the caller, and the responding backchannel has the same function as 'bingo, you got the point'. Here the consultant's responding backchannels are not to make any new contribution to the content of conversation since no new information is provided. Rather, the consultant is showing his agreement with what the speaker has proposed. As has been seen, with the use of 'responding' backchannels, the consultant successfully manages the conversation smoothly while helping himself to elicit the information of the caller as expected. Therefore, the consultant signals to the caller his full understanding that the caller is asking him for confirmation. In short, the consultant's use of 'responding' backchannels comprises two functions: indicating comprehension of the prior turn and signalling agreement to the caller's proposal. In the latter case, the consultant is observing the Maxim of Agreement according to the Grand Strategy of Politeness (Leech 2005, 2014); that is, she is 'placing a high value on O's opinion' (a proposal for a course of action in this case).

C. Repeating

It is acknowledged that emotions, especially negative ones like frustration, shame and helplessness, play an important role in the complexity of consultation (Stone 2014). Understandably, it is crucial to politely and skilfully identify and manage these troubling emotions to ensure effective consultations. Thus, it is often necessary to repeat the old information provided by the caller, with the purpose of maintaining the quality of conversation (in a more polite way, see GSP). In our data, backchannelling is used for this purpose. Repeating refers to the fact that the exact verbal reproduction of the previous utterance is employed repeatedly for a certain purpose. Consider (3):

(3)

1	Caller (M):	我用这个三七啊
2	Consultant (M):	啊
3	Caller (M):	一个月零三天了
4	Consultant (M):	<u>一个月零三天哈</u>
1	Caller (M):	I have used the notoginseng …
2	Consultant (M):	Ah
3	Caller (M):	A month and three days
4	Consultant (M):	*A month and three days*

In (3), the consultant repeats the caller's line 'A month and three days' so as to echo him in a follow-up manner, therefore driving himself into a collaborative brainstorming. Unlike the backchannelling of following made possible by the use of non-lexical backchannel cues, repeating involves the use of lexical words or phrases. Through repeating or merely echoing, the consultant engages himself in joint development of the conversation, thus avoiding distancing himself from the caller. In this way, he is complying with the Maxim of Generosity, that is, by placing a high value on the caller's want (of attention).

D. Agreeing

Consultation is characterised by mutual ownership of the identified problem, and the recognition of individual differences in developmental progress (Wanis-St. John 2006). Accordingly, how to signal agreement between the consultant and the caller means a lot for a rewarding consultation on the radio. Our data reveal that, apart from giving agreement at a turn level, backchannelling can also function as a marker of agreement. In our study, agreeing is found to be the third most frequently occurring function of backchannelling, where backchannelling tokens are used to signal agreement to the opinions of the caller by the consultant. As stated by Leech (2005), 'in responding to others' opinions or judgement, agreement is the preferred response and disagreement is dis-preferred'. Therefore, the consultant's use of agreeing backchannels is helpful for the construction of politeness in the conversation. Here is an example from the data:

(4)

1	Caller(F):	我只是认为你这产品，我实实在在说，你这产品在我身上，起到了很好的效果。
2	Consultant(F):	没错，啊，其实呢，很多的老爸爸老妈妈都是这样的实话实说。啊，大家呢，啊，都是有病的人，身体当中有了疾病以后，都渴望健康。
3	Caller(F):	对
1	Caller(F):	To tell the truth, I think your product is pretty helpful for me.
2	Consultant(F):	*Right.* Actually, many elders, both male and female have said the same kind of words as you, especially those who have a sickness who would always desire health.
3	Caller(F):	*Yeah.*

In (4), the caller and the female consultant are talking about the effects of a certain medical product. At first, the caller tells the consultant that the product is effective in the control of his disease, and the female consultant agrees with the caller with the backchannel word 'right' (it is not a unit of turn because it is not used to answer a yes-no question). In other words, the consultant is showing agreement with the caller. We can observe that the consultant uses 'right' to signal that he shares the caller's idea. After using the backchannel, the consultant takes the turn of the conversation and emphasises that to be healthy is the good wish of many people, suggesting that the consultant is actively listening and contributing to the conversation. Interestingly, she is also fed back with a backchannel of agreement, i.e., 'Yeah' from the caller. According to the Grand Strategy of Politeness (Leech 2005, 2014), it is polite to 'place high value on others' opinion'; therefore, it is polite for the consultant, as well as the caller, to observe the Maxim of Agreement by responding to each other with the backchannel of agreement.

E. Commenting

Brown (2015) conducts a study on politeness as strategic attention to 'face', believing that politeness relies on cooperation between or among the conversationalists. It is hypothesised that politeness strategies are tightly related with functions of backchannels when people are doing face-threatening acts like commenting on the others. Here, commenting refers to the use of backchannels, instead of occupying a separate turn, which conveys the speaker's views about what has been said. That is to say, the consultant chooses to use backchannels in a more hedged way in order to earn the trust of the caller, and the conversation also contributes to the O's feeling of trust. Thus, it is believed that a hedged commenting backchannel could save the O's face and maintain politeness. For instance:

(5)

1	Caller(M):	你说说一咳嗽啊就咳的我满头大汗
2	Consultant(M):	哦，(那)挺厉害的
3	Caller(M):	你说这出的这气儿啊也不出来
4	Consultant(M):	这就感觉不对劲了
1	Caller(M):	You know I would always be covered with sweat when I cough.
2	Consultant(M):	*Oh, (that is) terrible.*
3	Caller(M):	Also, I can't breathe very well.
4	Consultant(M):	That is worse.

Here in (5), the consultant is commenting on the severity of the illness of the caller. By expressing his concern and worry, he is showing his sympathy with the caller. It is polite of him to do so, because, according to Leech (2005: 19), it is polite when we put a high value on other people's feelings.

G. Interrupting

According to Chang and Haugh (2011), background knowledge about the participants' ongoing relationship helps them interpret the interactional practices in a contextually grounded and 'accurate' way. However, sometimes the consultant has to interrupt the caller to gain a better sense of the background information. In this situation, politeness is required to free the caller from unhappiness. We found in our study that backchannels are employed as a politeness marker when used for interrupting. According to Zimmerman and West (1975), interruption is 'a device for exercising power and control in conversation' or 'a violation of speaker's turns at talk'. In other words, interruption is 'essentially a spoken interjection into another person's "turn", an attempt to gain the conversation floor' (Edelsky 1981). However, within the 'face'-based strategy model (Brown and Levinson 1987), affiliative interruption is instantiated as an addressee-oriented, face-saving strategy, preferred second pair parts of adjacency pairs used for the initiation/ development of affiliative topics and affiliative topic change/shift, etc. Disaffiliative interruption, on the other hand, consists in the antagonistic performance of all the above.

(6)

1	Caller(F):	啊，我.我.我.因为吧…，我和我爱人，也都有血压高的情况嘛。
2	Consultant(M):	嗯嗯嗯。
3	Caller(F):	嗯.再加上，他还有点心肌供血不足
4	Consultant(M):	对
5	Caller(F):	睡眠也不行…
6	Consultant(M):	对
7	Caller(F):	所以我们用了也就无妨。
1	Caller(F):	My husband and I both have hypertension.
2	Consultant(M):	Emm.
3	Caller(F):	And, he is a little myocardial ischemic …
4	Consultant(M):	*Yeah*
5	Caller(F):	Also, he doesn't sleep well …
6	Consultant(M):	*Yeah*
7	Caller(F):	So, we might as well use it …

Here in (6), the consultant interrupts the caller twice with the backchannel cue 'Yeah' in the fourth line and the sixth line of the conversation. Unlike that in the case of commenting, the consultant's use of the backchannel here is not meant to respond to an opinion or an act. Nor does it occur at an explicit pause position. Whereas interruption can hardly be said to be polite in general, the interruption by the consultant in this case is not to be taken as a violation of the caller's floor right or conversation dominance, for the reason that the consultant's interruption here functions to inform the caller of the current state of their communication. At this stage of the conversation in progress, what the caller needs most is the attention of the consultant, otherwise, it is like talking to a dead phone. Therefore, unlike what happens in normal conversation, the consultant's attention is given more priority than formal courtesy. According to the Maxim of Generosity, that is, 'placing a high value on O's want', of the Grand Strategy of Politeness (Leech 2005), showing one's active attention is arguably polite. Therefore, the consultant's interruption here is not disaffiliative but affiliative in essence.

H. Rephrasing

Hugo and Couper (2005) put forward a new classification of consultation models in terms of process and interaction, which consists of facilitation, clinical reasoning and collaboration. In general, consultation is impossible without recasting or rephrasing the contents of communication so as to realise facilitation, reasoning and collaboration in the process of consultation. Rephrasing is a process used in oral discourse organisation, and it is therefore considered to be a metalinguistic phenomenon. It can be performed by the speaker (self-rephrasing) or by the interlocutor (other-rephrasing). It guarantees textual cohesion and facilitates discursive progression as it helps to reduce any existing communicative defects of a text. In our study, the rephrasing backchannels are generally conducted by the consultants to show that they are responsible for/in charge of the whole medical consultation. In other words, the consultants are loading high values on the wants of the caller in this information-giving context. This is supported by our study, where backchannelling cues are used for rephrasing acts. For instance:

(7)

1	Caller(M):	那时候我买药都得偷偷地买。
2	Consultant(M):	嗯。
3	Caller(M):	孩子们不让，老是怕我买些没效果的药。
4	Consultant(M):	<u>上当受骗</u>
5	Caller(M):	对，怕我上当受骗。
1	Caller(M):	I have to buy medicine secretly.
2	Consultant(M):	Emm.
3	Caller(M):	To buy medicine is not allowed by my children. They are always afraid that I would buy some fake medicine.
4	Consultant(M):	*Deceived.*
5	Caller(M):	Yes, they are afraid that I would be deceived.

Here in (7), by rephrasing, the consultant makes a retrogressive interpretation of the previous utterance 'They are always afraid that I would buy some fake medicine' so as to explain, reconsider and summarise it. Since rephrasing is metalinguistic by nature, it does not make a contribution to the propositional content of the current conversation. In the context of consultation, rephrasing is politeness-driven from the side of the consultant in the following sense: it is necessary for the consultant to manage a coherent conversation. Now that it is polite to 'place high value on others' opinion' (here the caller's opinion that some medicine has no effect at all) according to the GSP (Leech 2005), it is polite of the consultant to observe the Maxim of Agreement by indicating his agreement to what the caller is saying.

From the discussion above, we can see that the consultants use different forms of backchannels to perform a variety of conversational functions. These functions are by and large polite, evidencing the argument that a successful consultation is largely dependent on the use of politeness in interaction, as interpersonal equilibrium is difficult to maintain without this (Spencer-Oatey 2011).

Conclusion

So far, a number of studies have been conducted to examine the backchannelling acts of various linguistic or cultural groups in different contexts, yet more work still remains to be done in Chinese conversation with the help of naturally occurring data. In this connection, the present study has filled a gap by exploring the use of backchannels in consultant–caller conversations on the radio. In particular, we have explored what forms and functions of backchannels are used and their politeness implications. It has been found that both lexical and non-lexical backchannelling are used in the consultation between consultant and caller, and the function of backchannelling could be classified as responding, repeating, agreeing, commenting, interrupting and rephrasing.

With regard to the relationship between backchannelling and politeness, it is found that all of the functions of the consultants' backchannels may have the implication of politeness in the context of consultant–caller communications. More specifically, it is revealed that consultants use a lot of backchannels in the conversation with the callers for the sake of politeness, which means that they place a high value on what pertains to the callers. Their politeness orientations are mainly set towards the callers' need for attention, agreement and sympathy. Thus, by and large, the consultants' use of backchannelling is not only riveted on the act of consultation alone, but also motivated towards interpersonal interaction, which might contribute to medical service and product promotion in the long run.

This study suffers some obvious limitations, which may more or less reduce the validity of the research findings. First, the size of the corpus is not accommodating enough and the sources of consultation episodes are not adequately diversified. Second, the procedure of data identification and analysis is not free from slips, which might be bettered if non-verbal or multi-modal backchannelling signals had been included in the analysis of the data. Third, the possible variation in the consultant's use of backchannelling is not dealt with due to the limited size of the data for each consultant. Last, but not least, due to the limit of time and effort, the effect of identity or gender of the consultant as well as the callers has not been addressed. Future effort might follow in these directions.

References

Berry, A. G. (1992) Spanish and American turn-taking styles and the misinterpretation of each in cross-cultural conversations. Unpublished Master's thesis, University of Illinois at Urbana- Champaign.

Brown, P. and Levinson, S. C. (1987) *Politeness: Some Universals in Language Use.* Cambridge: Cambridge University Press.

Brown, S. (2015) Should a syllabus ever tell students what not to say? *The Chronicle of Higher Education* 30 September.

Chang, M. and Haugh, M. (2011) Strategic embarrassment and face threatening in business interactions. *Journal of Pragmatics* 43(12): 2948–2963. https://doi.org/10.1016/j.pragma.2011.05.009

Charon, R. M., Greene, G. and Adelman, R. D. (1994) Multi-dimensional interaction analysis: A collaborative approach to the study of medical discourse. *Social Science and Medicine* 39(7): 955–965. https://doi.org/10.1016/0277-9536(94)90207-0

China Daily (December 2014) Investor 'pill' for China's healthcare reform. http:// www. usa. chinadaily. com. cn.

Clancy, P. M., Thompson, S. A., Suzuki, R. and Tao, H. (1996) The conversational use of reactive tokens in English, Japanese and Mandarin. *Journal of Pragmatics* 26: 355–387. https://doi.org/10.1016/0378-2166(95)00036-4

Drummond, K. and Hopper, R. (1993) Back channels revisited: Acknowledgment tokens and speakership incipiency. *Research on Language and Social Interaction* 26: 157–177. https://doi.org/10.1207/s15327973rlsi2602_3

Drew, P. and Heritage, J. (1992) *Talk at Work: Interaction in Institutional Settings.* Cambridge: Cambridge University Press.

Edelsky, C. (1981) Who's got the floor? *Language in Society* 10: 383–421. https://doi.org/10.1017/S004740450000885X

Faerch, C. and Kasper, G. (1982) *Phatic, Metalingual and Metacommunicative Functions in Discourse: Gambits and Repairs.* Abo: Abo Akademi.

Fiske, D. W. and Duncan, S. (1985) *Interaction Structure and Strategy.* Cambridge: Cambridge University Press.

Gardner, R. (1997) The conversation object mm: A weak and variable acknowledging token. *Research on Language and Social Interaction* 30: 131–156. https://doi.org/10.1207/s15327973rlsi3002_2

Horiguchi, S. (1997) *Nihongo Kyoiku to Kaiwa Bunseki* (Japanese Conversation by Learners and Native Speakers). Tokyo: Kuroshio.

Hugo, J. and Couper, I. (2005) The consultation: A juggler's art. *Teaching Exchange* 597–604.

Ishida, H. (2006) Learners' perception and interpretation of contextualization cues in spontaneous Japanese conversation: Back-channel cue *Uun Journal of Pragmatics* 38: 1943–1981. https://doi.org/10.1016/j.pragma.2005.08.004

Jimenez, X. F., Esplin, B. S. and Hernandez, J. O. (2015) Capacity consultation and contextual complexities: Depression, decisions, and deliberation. *Psychosomatics* 6: 1–17. https://doi.org/10.1016/j.psym.2015.06.002

Leech, G. (2005) Politeness: Is there an East–West Divide? *Journal of Foreign Languages* 160(6): 3–31.

Leech, G. (2014) *The Pragmatics of Politeness.* Oxford: Oxford University Press. https:// doi.org/10.1093/acprof:oso/9780195341386.001.0001

Limbertz, K. (2011) Back-channelling: The use of 'yeah' and 'mm' to portray engaged listenership. Retrieved 9 December 2015 from http://www.griffith.edu.au/_data/assets/ pdf _file/0005/ 384017/Lambertz-backchannelling.pdf.

Maynard, S. K. (1989) *Japanese Conversation.* Norwood, NJ: Ablex.

Mizuno, Y. (1988) Chugokugo no aizuchi (Back-channel feedback in Chinese). *Gengo* 7(12): 18–23.

Mizutani, N. (1988) Aizuchi-ron (On 'Got it'). *Nihongogaku* 7(12): 4–11.

Nauright, L. P., Moneyham, L. and Williamson, J. (1999) Telephone triage and consultation: An emerging role for nurses. *Nursing Outlook* 5: 219–226. https://doi. org/10.1016/S0029-6554(99)90054-4

Ohira, K. (1994) Have you changed? Pragmatic transfer of back-channel behaviour by Japanese English Learners. Unpublished PhD dissertation, University of Illinois at Urbana-Champaign.

Pipek, V. (2007). On backchannels in English conversation. PhD thesis, Masaryk University, Brno, USA.

Post, E. (1969) *Emily Post's Etiquette.* New York: Funk and Magnalls.

Rieger, C. L. (2001) Idiosyncratic fillers in the speech of bilinguals. ISCA Archive. Retrieved from http://www.isca-speech.org/archive

Sacks, H., Schegloff, E. A. and Jefferson, G. (1974) A simplest systematics for the organization of turn taking for conversation. *Language* 50: 696–735. https://doi.org/10.1353/ lan.1974.0010

Schegloff, E. A. (1982) Discourse as an interactional achievement: Some uses of 'uh huh' and other things that come between sentences. In D. Tannen (ed.) *Analyzing Discourse: Text and Talk* 71–93. Washington, DC: Georgetown University Press.

Sharifi, S. and Azadmanesh, M. (November 2011). Speaker's cues inviting back channel responses in spontaneous Persian conversations. Retrieved 9 December 2012 from http://profdoc.um.ac.ir/articles/a/1025339.pdf

Shelley, L. and Gonzalez, F. (2013) Back channeling: Function of back channeling and L1 effects on back channeling in L2. *Linguistic Portfolios* 2: 98.

Spencer-Oatey, H. (2011) Conceptualising 'the relational' in pragmatics: Insights from metapragmatic emotion and (im)politeness comments. *Journal of Pragmatics* 43: 3565–3578. https://doi.org/10.1016/j.pragma.2011.08.009

Stone, L. (2014) Managing the consultation with patients with medically unexplained symptoms: A grounded theory study of supervisors and registrars in general practice. *BioMed Central Journal* 15: 1–29. https://doi.org/10.1186/s12875-014-0192-7

TMTpost (July 2015) Why video telehealth service can't make its leap in China? http:// www. tmtpost. com.cn.

Wanis-St. John, A. (2006) Back-channel negotiation: International bargaining in the shadows. *Negotiation Journal* 22(2): 119–144. https://doi.org/10.1111/j.1571-9979.2006.00091.x

Ward, N. (1997) Responsiveness in dialog and priorities for language research. *Cybernetics and Systems* 28: 521–533. https://doi.org/10.1080/019697297126038

Ward, N. (2006) Non-lexical conversational sounds in American English. *Pragmatics and Cognition* 14(1): 129–182. https://doi.org/10.1075/pc.14.1.08war

Ward, N.and Wataru, T. (2000) Prosodic features which cue back-channel responses in English and Japanese. *Journal of Pragmatics* 32: 1177–1207. https://doi.org/10.1016/S0378-2166(99)00109-5

Warren, M., Mackie, D., & Leary, A. (2012) The complexity of non face-to-face work with patients affected by metastatic breast cancer and their carers. The 'hidden consultations' of the clinical nurse specialist. *European Journal of Oncology Nursing* 16: 460–464. https://doi.org/10.1016/j.ejon.2011.10.009

White, R. (1997) Backchannelling, repair, pausing, and private speech. *Applied Linguistics* 18(3): 314–344. https://doi.org/10.1093/applin/18.3.314

Wieland, M. (1990) Politeness-based misunderstandings in conversations between native speakers of French and American advanced learners of French. Unpublished doctoral dissertation, Indiana University, Bloomington.

Yngve, V. (1970) On getting a word in edgewise. In R. I. Binnick (ed.) *Papers from the Sixth Regional Meeting of the Chicago Linguistic Society* 567–557. Chicago: University of Chicago, Department of Linguistics.

Yule, G. (1996) *Pragmatics*. New York: Oxford University Press.

Zimmerman, D. and West, C. (1975) Sex roles, interruptions and silences in conversation. In B. Thorne and N. Henley (eds) *Language and Sex: Difference and Dominance* 105–129. Rowley, MA: Newbury House.

CHAPTER 13

Backchannelling in Internet interactions: Implications for netiquette

Xiyun Zhong

Introduction

In conversation, when one speaker holds the floor, the other gives vocal feedback such as 'uh huh' or nonverbal messages like head nods (Heinz 2003). Yngve (1970) was the first to call these types of reaction 'backchannels'. It is a general consensus that backchannel behaviour is a universal conversational feature which indicates that one is listening and indirectly granting the speaker the right to continue talking (Miyata and Nisisawa 2007).

The bulk of the related literature has been devoted to identifying the functions of backchannels in a wide range of genres, such as face-to-face conversations (Goodwin 1986), TV interviews (Yu 2003), business negotiations (Bjørge 2010) and narrations (Tolins and Tree 2014). It has been discovered that backchannels can signal attention to, understanding of, support for, empathy with and evaluation of the current speaker, encouraging him/her to continue talking (Goodwin 1986; Maynard 1997; Oreström 1983; Schegloff 1982; Yngve 1970). These studies are conducted within the field of conversation analysis, focusing on the organisational role of backchannels.

From a different line of research on backchannels, a few studies have suggested the possibility of considering backchannels from the perspective of politeness (Bjørge 2010; Clancy, Thompson, Suzuki and Tao 1996; Heinz 2003). For instance, Heinz views backchannel behaviour as 'a required contribution when the Cooperative Principle is enacted, when one interlocutor … holds the floor and the other wants this alignment to continue for the time being' (2003: 1114). Bjørge (2010) discovers that the frequency of backchannels is much higher in a less conflictive situation, indicating that backchannels might help to manage rapport in negotiations. The (im)politeness role of backchannels is more prominent when researchers try to explain different patterns and values of backchannelling across cultures. According to Clancy et al. (1996), whereas Japanese people regard the use of backchannels as a kind of considerateness to one another's face, Americans and Chinese consider the use of too many backchannels as an interruption of the ongoing narration and an intrusion into the speaker's freedom to continue talking. All of these studies seem to imply that the use of backchannels is linked to politeness.

However, none of the previous studies have elaborated on how the use of backchannels gives rise to politeness, nor have they investigated the practice of backchannels in genres other than face-to-face communication, in which the identities of the interactants are known to one another. Gu (2011), a vanguard on Chinese politeness, claims that the anonymity on web-borne situated discourse has challenged the traditional conception of politeness in China and urges researchers to pay attention to this recent phenomenon. The present study, therefore, aims to examine how and why Chinese participants backchannel on Internet forums from the perspective of politeness. It is presumed that the practice of backchannelling on the Internet is a strategy of showing politeness or netiquette, which is different from that in daily conversations.

Literature review

Identifying backchannel expressions

The interest in listener's feedback in conversational interaction may date back to Fries's observation of 'those single free utterances … that have as responses continued attention' (1952: 49). Among the many terms that have been used to describe those utterances of non-primary speakers, such as 'accompaniment signal' (Kendon 1967), 'listener response' (Dittmann and Llewellyn 1968), 'acknowledgement token' (Jefferson 1983), 'backchannel' is by far the most influential one. The term was first coined by Yngve as a response 'over which the person who has the turn receives short messages such as *yes* and *uh-huh* without relinquishing the turn' (1970: 568). Following him, Oreström describes backchannel as 'a brief, spontaneous reaction to the content of the speaker's turn supplying him with direct feedback' (1983: 104). While his definition of backchannel is restricted to such minimal verbal expressions as 'yeah', 'God' and 'really', others have expanded the notion to include sentence completions, brief restatements and requests for clarification (Duncan 1974; Duncan and Fiske 1977), assessments (Goodwin 1986), head nods (Dittmann and Llewellyn 1968), head shakes (Duncan 1974) and laughter (Clancy et al. 1996).

Difficulties and divergences remain when scholars try to differentiate a backchannel turn from a separate turn. Oreström (1983) discards requests for clarification as backchannels in that they are very similar to ordinary question/answer paired turns, and therefore may interrupt the ongoing conversation and lead the talk in another direction. Duncan and Niederehe (1974) find that the line between speaking turns and backchannels is uncertain if the backchannel behaviour is manifested as brief restatements. Fortunately, Cutrone (2005, 2014) and Maynard (1986, 1997) have proved Markel's conception of turn to be quite effective in identifying backchannels. According to Markel (1975), a speaking turn begins when one interlocutor starts solo talking; for every speaking turn, there is a concurrent listening turn, which is the behaviour of one or more non-talking interlocutors present. That is to say, a question like 'Is that so?' is regarded as a backchannel when it serves only to react to what the primary speaker is saying and not to add any new information to the conversation. In this study, the broader definition is used and Markel's criterion is adopted to identify backchannels.

Functions of backchannels

Researchers have attributed many functions to backchannel behaviour from the perspective of conversation analysis. Oreström (1983) and Yngve (1970) believe that backchannels have a supportive function, signalling the listener's understanding of and agreement with the speaker. Schegloff (1982) claims that backchannels serve as continuers, thus yielding a regulative function. This idea is then developed by Goodwin (1986), who divides backchannels into continuers (or generic backchannels) and assessments (or specific backchannels). According to him, continuers such as 'huh' and 'mmm' are listeners' responses to let speakers continue talking, whereas assessments like 'Wow' and 'Great' are context-sensitive, signalling listeners' evaluation of speakers' narration. Maynard (1997) identifies six categories of possible functions of backchannels: continuer, understanding, support and empathy, agreement, emoting and minor additions. Tolins and Tree (2014) conclude through experiment that generic backchannels trigger discourse-new information from the speaker, while specific backchannels elude elaborative narration on previous events.

A few other investigations have implied that the functions of backchannelling can be explained in terms of politeness. Bjørge (2010) examines the use of backchannelling in ELF (English as Lingua Franca) negotiations. He divides the negotiations into three phases, namely, relationship-building, information exchange and conclusion. He finds that the frequency of backchannels is considerably higher in the first and third phase, where a less-conflict situation is enacted. In this case, backchannels seem to help manage rapport in negotiations. Hu and Xu (2007) argue that backchannels can be divided into positive, neutral and negative ones. Positive and neutral backchannels are means of showing attitudinal warmth, mainly functioning as understanding, support and continuer, while negative ones are intended to yield a turn. They further claim that negative back-channels are rare in daily conversations, as people tend to show politeness to one another. According to Grice (1975), people have the desire to cooperate in interactions. Providing backchannels can therefore be thought of as 'a required contribution when the Cooperative Principle is enacted, when one interlocutor … holds the floor and the other wants this alignment to continue for the time being' (Heinz 2003: 1114). Despite no explicit discussion, these studies seem to imply that backchannelling may act as a strategy to show politeness.

Chinese backchannelling practices

So far, research on Chinese backchannelling practice is rather rare. Some scholars mention it only in passing when comparing it to other cultures. Some studies seem to suggest that backchannelling is not perceived as a predominant feature of Chinese daily use. Both Liu (1987) and Mizuno (1988) claim that Chinese speakers use backchannels less frequently than Japanese. Also, Tao and Thompson (1991) note that Chinese speakers use backchannels less frequently than English speakers. Following them, Clancy et al. (1996) draw on data collected from these three languages and discover that a) the use of backchannels in Chinese is strikingly infrequent, b) Chinese backchannels tend to occur in places other than the middle of the primary speaker's clause and c) Chinese backchannels are lexically more contentful. Based on these findings, they further speculate that the Chinese avoidance of backchannelling is a reflection of not infringing on the speaker, being consistent with Lakoff's (1970) rules of politeness and Brown and Levinson's (1987) conception of negative and positive face. However, it is note-worthy that all of their data are collected from face-to-face, non-argumentative daily conversations among friends, making no reference to the possible effect of social status on the use of backchannelling.

Yu (2003) might be the only one who has conducted a thorough investigation of Chinese supportive backchannels in TV interviews. He divides supportive backchannels into general and intensified ones. The former are manifested as 'En', 'Ah' and 'Oh', whereas the latter contain acknowledgment tokens 'Yes' or laugh, agreement tokens 'Right' or 'True', evaluation expressions, gratitude token 'Thank you' and help-offering utterances. He concludes that the host employs more general backchannels than the interviewee because the former is institutionally more powerful than the latter. His study has shown how backchannels are used in a particular genre: TV interviews. More importantly, he has touched upon how power, as one of the factors of politeness, affects the choice of backchannels, apart from linking the functions of backchannels to politeness.

Previous literature has been very enlightening in several aspects. First, different functions of backchannels in different genres have been identified. Second, the possibility of regarding the practice of backchannels as a means of showing politeness has been suggested. However, quite a few questions remain to be answered: how are backchannels performed in genres other than daily conversations or TV interviews? In what ways is the use of backchannels polite in those genres of communication? The present research intends to address these questions within the framework of politeness. As Gu (2011) points out, in addition to land-borne, written-borne and air-borne situated discourse, the web-borne situated discourse in China is a very recent phenomenon and presents a challenge to politeness on the Internet or, in Yus' (2010) terms, 'netiquette', as anonymity on the Internet has made everyone equal, which further undermines the pressure to exhibit deference. Accordingly, this study chooses Internet communication as a particular genre, arguing that backchannelling is a strategy to convey netiquette and that the netiquette has some unique features, as shown in the practice of backchannelling.

Netiquette

Netiquette, a portmanteau word ('net' + 'etiquette'), refers to 'a set of rules governing acceptable behaviour for participants in chatrooms and other online forums', according to A Dictionary of Media and Communication (2011). Within the field of linguistics, netiquette specifically means 'politeness on the Net'. Researchers such as Yus (2010) and Landone (2012) have all tried to apply various politeness models to the study of this new type of communication.

Among the current politeness theories, Leech's (1983) 'Principle of Politeness' is one of the most pioneering and influential efforts, although some criticisms have been brought against him. Luckily, in his latest work, *Pragmatics of Politeness* (2014), Leech responds to these criticisms and provides a revised framework. In this study, we will use this revised version for the following reasons.

First of all, Leech's proposal of a Grand Strategy of Politeness (GSP) and his maxims coincide with our general observation of Chinese backchannelling on Internet forums. Leech (1983, 2014) believes that the Principle of Politeness (PP) is a constraint observed in human communicative behaviour, leading us to avoid communicative discord or offence and to maintain or enhance communicative concord or comity. To conform to PP, the speaker will employ the GSP that 'associates a favourable value with what pertains to O or associates an unfavourable value with what pertains to S (S = self, speaker; O = Other)' (Leech 2014: 90). He further lists ten maxims as specific manifestations of GSP in interactions. As we will show later, the practice of backchannelling on the Internet forums is such a strategy of showing politeness, and the functions of backchannelling correspond to some specific maxims.

Secondly, Leech's notion of pos-politeness and neg-politeness is more appropriately defined than Brown and Levinson's (1987)'s conception of positive politeness and negative politeness. For one thing, Brown and Levinson's positive and negative politeness have poor correspondence to their own distinction between positive and negative face. For another, Brown and Levinson's conception of politeness as a way of protecting face against face-threatening acts only sees one side of face (face mitigation) and neglects the other side (face enhancement). For them, positive politeness is simply an additional set of strategies for avoiding face threat.[1] In view of this, Leech (2014) redefines pos-politeness as a means of assigning positive value to the addressee and neg-politeness as a way of assigning negative value to self. As is indicated in the literature review and will be proved in the section of Results and Discussion, backchannelling is primarily intended to enhance face value rather than to mitigate face threat. Accordingly, Leech's definition of pos- and neg-politeness is adopted in this study because it fits better.

Methodology

Research questions

The present study attempts to answer the following two questions.

    a.   How do the Chinese use backchannels on Internet forums?
    b.   In what ways does their use of backchannels mean politeness?

Data collection

The data for this study were collected from Internet forums mainly due to their anonymity and assumed equality. Unlike other computer mediation such as Twitter or Facebook, participants on Internet forums are total strangers. Without the effects of social status, the data could well reflect the differences between the Internet and face-to-face conversations. In this sense, it is also an echo of Gu's concern that 'the anonymity on the Internet has made everyone equal and further undermines the pressure to exhibit deference' (2011: 130).

Specifically, two Internet forums, *Tianya* and *Baidu*, were searched, with the former being the most influential Chinese forum in the world and the latter the biggest. Hence, in a way, these two forums could be assumed to represent Chinese interactions on Internet forums.

A total number of 40 posts were studied, with topics varying from society, to entertainment, to emotion, to travel. These posts were picked out for three reasons. First, topics on these four themes were found on both forums, so that a generalisation could be drawn from the comparison of the results. Second, posts concerning society and entertainment comment on events happening in the societal and entertaining circle respectively, and thus were considered argumentative and other-oriented, whereas posts on emotion and travel, which narrate personal emotion and travel experience, were therefore regarded as non-argumentative and self-oriented. Since backchannels are related to politeness and face, it was assumed that the use of backchannels might vary across posts. Third, the number of replies to these posts was constrained to a manageable size, around 100 per post. The detailed information is provided in Table 13.1.

Table 13.1. Information of the data collected from *Tianya* and *Baidu* forums

	Number of posts on *Tianya*	Number of replies on *Tianya*	Number of posts on *Baidu*	Number of replies on *Baidu*	Total number of posts	Total number of replies
Society	5	415	5	325	10	740
Entertainment	5	365	5	451	10	816
Emotion	5	620	5	572	10	1192
Travel	5	391	5	446	10	837
Total	20	1791	20	1794	40	3585

To probe into the reasons for using backchannels, interviews were conducted as empirical evidence for our observations and speculations. We showed eight posts (each post about a different topic) to five students and asked them to answer the following questions: i) will you give a reply to the post? ii) If yes, what will you write? and why? iii) If no, why not?

Data analysis

On an Internet forum, the primary speaker is the one who posts a new topic and the non-primary speaker is the one who replies. The number of non-primary speakers is more than one in normal cases as the replies to a single post may be up to thousands. In this study, we call the primary speaker the sender and the non-primary speaker the recipient, so as to distinguish them from daily interactions. To be sure, conversations not only happen between the sender and the recipient, but between recipients or among the sender and multiple recipients as well. This study, however, only examined interactions between the sender and the recipients. Each reply was considered as a recognisable unit, either a turn or a backchannel. A turn could be the sender's or the recipient's. The sender's turn was identified other than his/her first post, including both his/her later solo-talking and responses to the recipients; the recipient's turn was in contrast to the backchannel, which is not a separate turn by itself. Following previous literature (Cutrone 2005, 2014; Markel 1975), we define a backchannel response on the Internet forum as a direct reaction to the post sender without providing new information or interrupting the sender's solo-talking. Look at the following replies.

(1)

(Context: The post sender pointed out the graft phenomenon in *Tianma Village* and appealed for action on anti-corruption.)

Reply A: 顶…正义永存

Up … Justice lasts forever

Reply B: 将反贪斗争进行到底！坚持就是胜利！

Carry through the anti-corruption fight to the end! Who perseveres will succeed!

Reply C: 那个岳麓区政法委副书记叫什么名字，发个照片咯，他说这话有录音没有？！

What's the name of that deputy secretary of law and committee in Yuelu District? Post a picture of him. Do you have an audio record of what he was accused of?

Reply D: 美女主持人纪英男…"反腐英雄"的美名…

The beautiful host J. I. Yingnan … has the reputation of 'Anti-corruption Heroine' …

In (1), Replies A and B were identified as backchannel turns since the recipients did not add new information. For Reply A, the recipient explicitly stated his attitude; for Reply B, the recipient provided a summary and paraphrase of the post. Reply C, however, posed a question that required an answer from the sender, thus interrupting the ongoing solo talk. In a similar vein, Reply D had added much new information and even led the conversation in a new direction.

After identifying the backchannels, the study was ready to answer the research questions. To answer the first question, the frequency of backchannels was first calculated across forums and topics; the frequency was the number of backchannel turns divided by the number of replies. Then the functions of backchannels were identified and calculated as well. To answer the second question, the researchers examined the results of the first question and drew some conclusions based on the interviews as well. Both results were interpreted within Leech's framework (2014).

Results and discussion

Frequency of using backchannels

In general, participants do employ a certain number of backchannels in Internet interactions, probably more than those in daily conversations. Table 13.2 shows that the general frequency of using backchannels on Internet forums reaches as high as 30.71%, with 26.74% on *Tianya* and 36.67% on *Baidu*. The result seems to be in contrast with that found in Clancy et al.'s (1996) study, in which the use of backchannels in Chinese daily conversations is strikingly low.

Table 13.2. Frequency of using backchannels on the Internet forums

	Tianya	Baidu	Total
Number of backchannel turns	479	622	1101
Frequency	26.74%	34.67%	30.71%

A further calculation of the statistics shows that the frequency of backchannels varies from one topic to another. Figure 13.1 indicates that on both forums, the recipients provide the highest percentage of backchannels on topics of travel, a relatively high percentage on topics of society and entertainment, but a quite low percentage on the topic of emotion. A tentative explanation of these frequencies will be given later.

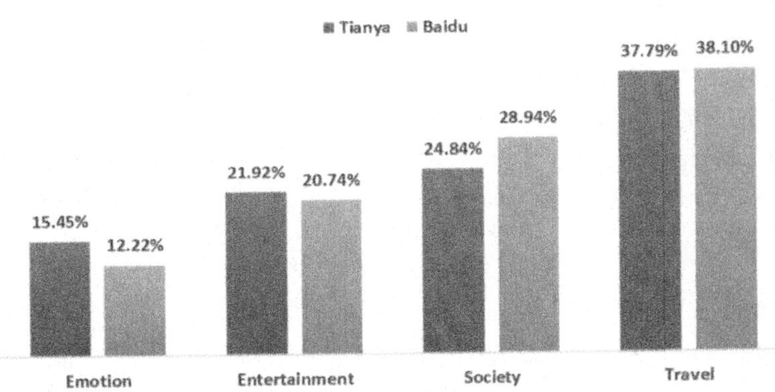

Figure 13.1. Frequency of backchannel turns across topics

Functions of using backchannels

Through analysis, we have identified seven functions of backchannels on Internet forums, namely, emoting, endorsement, evaluation, acknowledgment, attention, gratitude and disapproval, each conforming to a sub-maxim of Leech's (2014) GSP, as presented in Table 13.3.

Table 13.3. Functions and politeness orientations of backchannels on the Internet forums

Function	Number	Maxim	Politeness orientations
Emoting	294	Sympathy	Pos-politeness
Endorsement	242	Approbation	Pos-politeness
Evaluation	210	Agreement	Pos-politeness
Acknowledgment	193	Agreement	Pos-politeness
Attention	115	Generosity	Pos-politeness
Gratitude	28	Obligation of S to O	Pos-politeness
Disapproval	19	Opinion reticence	Neg-politeness

A. Emoting

In this study, emoting refers to the expression of shared feelings of the recipients with the post sender. It is the most frequent function used on Internet forums. The function of emoting corresponds to Leech's Maxim of Sympathy, for the reason that recipients use emotive backchannels to give a high value to other's feelings.

In our study, there are two scenarios in which emotive backchannels may occur: one is when the post expresses a positive feeling; the other is when the post conveys a negative feeling. For instance:

(2)

啊啊啊啊啊啊

Ahhhhhhhh

(3)

好逍遥自在啊！

What a carefree day!

(4)

摸摸

pat pat

(5)

哎，感同身受

(sigh) I feel the same.

In a post that describes an enjoyable trip to Hong Kong, two recipients respond like (2) and (3). They use interjections such as 'Ah' and an exclamatory sentence to convey the admiration of the sender. On the other hand, in a post that narrates a bad break-up, the recipients provide responses like '摸摸' ('pat pat') in (4) or '感同身受' ('I feel the same') in (5) to commiserate with the sender. In both scenarios, the recipients use backchannels to sympathise with the sender.

The way to present emotive backchannels on the Internet exhibits some unique features as well. Some of the recipients tend to appeal to emoticons. For example:

(6)

学霸 😳😳

curve wrecker

(7)

😬

In (6), the recipient wants to show intense love for her idol Zhang Guorong; instead of using words 'kiss, kiss', she chooses the corresponding emoticon to convey her love, which is vivid and direct. Similarly, the recipient in (7) also employs an emoticon to manifest his uncontrollable anger towards the official corruption found in the rural areas of China.

B. Endorsement

By endorsement, we suggest that the recipient thinks highly of the post. This function is a manifestation of Leech's Maxim of Approbation, i.e. give a high value to other's qualities. In this study, the qualities cover various aspects: the general gist of the post, such as (8), (9) and (12), or the spirit of the sender, like (10), or a specific point of view, like (11), or a combination of the above aspects, like (13).

(8)

顶。

Up.

(9)

赞！

Thumbs up!

(10)

加油！

Fighting!

(11)

将反贪斗争进行到底！坚持就是胜利！

Carry through the anti-corruption fight to the end! Who persevere will succeed!

(12)

顶顶顶顶顶顶！

Up up up up up!

(13)

Internet Anti-corruption
Fighting, Netizens!

It is noticed that the linguistic expressions used, particularly '顶' ('Up') and '赞' ('Thumbs up'), are typical Internet terms, and the way to convey endorsement can be quite exaggerated as well. For instance, (11) uses a slogan-style sentence; (12) employs multiple 'Up's to strengthen the tone; (13) even exploits multi-modality to strengthen his/her strong attitude. By exaggeration, the recipients further enhance the sender's positive face.

C. Evaluation

By evaluation, we mean the recipient implicitly agrees with the post sender by giving short comments. This function abides by Leech's Maxim of Agreement, that is, giving a high value to other's opinion. At times, the way to present the agreement is quite implicit. For example:

(14)

这才是天涯正常的画风，隔壁黑子太能蹦跶了。

This is the normal style of posting on Tianya. Other post senders are too active in deprecation.

(15)

楼主去香港住这么大的屋，必须是壕啊！

You stayed in such a big room when travelling to Hong Kong. You must be very rich!

In a gossip post, recipient (14) agrees with the post sender by comparing it with another one and evaluates it as an objective model on the forum; on a travel topic in which the post sender introduces his hotel room to others, the recipient (15) agrees with his choice of room by evaluating him as a rich person. In both examples, the recipients resort to Internet terms such as '楼主' ('you', referring to the post sender), '画风' ('style'), '黑子' (people who enjoy themselves by deprecating others) and '壕' (a combination of '土' and '豪', referring to the newly rich).

D. Acknowledgment

Acknowledgment means the listener accepts or understands the speaker's content by using explicit backchannel tokens. The function of acknowledgment also reflects Leech's Maxim of Agreement, but in an explicit way. For instance, in an anti-rural-corruption post, the recipients use such lexical words as 'Right' and 'Yes' to explicitly convey their agreement with the post sender, like (16). Yet, unlike daily conversations or TV interviews, in which backchannels tend to be short (Goodwin 1986; Yu 2003), the Internet forum is loose on synchronicity; the listener has more time to produce longer backchannels. For example:

(16)

对，没错。

Yes. That's right.

(17)

对啊，要从根抓起。

Right. We have to start from the root.

(18)

是的，杀鸡儆猴不管用。

Yes. Warning does not work.

(19)

太对了，现在的村干部都特别特别黑，而且不讲理。

Can't agree more. The current village cadres are deeply corrupt and unreasonable.

In addition to using 'Yes' and 'Right', unlike (16), Examples (17) and (18) express to what specific extent they accept the post sender's view, while (19) gives a minor elaboration relevant to the post.

E. Attention

By attention we mean that the recipient uses backchannels to indicate his/her attention to the post sender. According to Leech, in order to be polite, the speaker gives a low value to his/her own want and gives a high value to the other's want. The attentive backchannels, by contrast, do not exhibit a high value to the other's want as in (20), and even place a high value to the speaker's want as in (21) and (22):

(20)

马克，楼主快八。

Mark. Continue gossiping.

(21)

坐等！

Go on!

(22)

楼主怎么不八了，还等着看呢！

Why not continue gossiping? We are waiting for more!

However, the purpose of posting on the Internet is to attract people's attention and interest (Cao 2011). In this light, giving a response in (20)–(22) has already met the sender's want, as it is not so compulsory as in face-to-face interaction. When recipients demand more information, they not only satisfy their own needs, but also satisfy the sender's needs. Therefore, the function of attention mirrors Leech's Maxim of Generosity.

F. Gratitude

The recipient may convey gratitude by backchannelling, conforming to Leech's Maxim of Obligation of the speaker to the other, such as in (23):

(23)

谢谢楼主！

Thank you!

A closer look at data like (23) suggests that though Internet participants are equal, the recipient may promote the sender's status or lower his/her status to show deference when thanking the post sender. Here are similar examples:

(24)

感谢楼主的指导！

Thank you for your guidance!

(25)

谢啦！好好研究一下下啊

Thanks! I will thoroughly study your post.

In (24), the recipient uses '指导' ('guidance') to portray an expert image of the sender, further abiding by the Maxim of Approbation; by comparison, in (25), through '研究' ('study') and the intensifier 'thoroughly', the recipient downgrades herself by acting as a layman.

G. Disapproval

A few backchannels show the recipient's disapproval of the post sender. Yet, these backchannels aim to minimise their disapproval, conforming to Leech's Maxim of Opinion reticence. For example:

(26)

额

Er

(27)

呵呵

Hehe

On the Internet, '额' ('Er') in (26) and '呵呵' ('Hehe', meaning sneer, implying that the speaker has nothing else to say) in (27) are normally associated with a negative attitude. Instead of using explicitly impolite phrases, the recipients use these short phrases to show their disagreement with the post sender, but in order to protect his face, they choose to say nothing more.

Reasons for using backchannels: Implications for netiquette

The following reasons might well account for the use of backchannels on the Internet, as we have observed.

A. Backchannelling as a strategy of pos-politeness on the Internet

The results above, together with the interviews, have confirmed that, similar to daily conversations, the reason for using backchannels on Internet forums is to show politeness, in particular, to enhance the positive face of the post sender. In other words, backchannelling is a strategy of pos-politeness on Internet forums. This conclusion can be drawn from several observations.

In general, the practice of backchannels on Internet forums is a way to enhance communicative concord. Results in the earlier part have shown that the functions of backchannels conform to Leech's Grand Strategy of Politeness. Specifically, a majority of the functions of backchannels reflect the observance of the Maxims of Agreement, Approbation, Sympathy, Generosity and Obligation of S to O, all of which are pos-politeness maxims. The only instance exhibiting the maxim of neg-politeness also seems to reduce the impoliteness to a minimum degree. In addition, as all the interviewees have admitted, they provide backchannel responses as a means of expressing politeness. For instance,

(28)

| Interviewee C | 觉得有用就简单回个谢谢，比较礼貌。 |
| Interviewee C | The post is quite informative. I will reply with a 'thanks'. It is polite to do so. |

(29)

| Interviewee D | 可能发个表情什么的。别人辛辛苦苦写了这么多，不表示一下总是不好意思的。 |
| Interviewee D | I may give an emoticon or so. Since the post sender has written so much, it seems impolite not to reply anything at all. |

Obviously, Interviewee C directly relates the backchannel to politeness, while Interviewee D claims that the lack of a backchannel suggests impoliteness. Both have acknowledged the function of backchannelling as being polite.

Secondly, the practice of backchannels as a pos-politeness strategy varies. While the majority of the functions are pos-politeness maxims, they show varying frequencies across topics. As is presented in Figure 13.1, the recipients provide a relatively high percentage of backchannels on topics concerning society, entertainment and travel, but a quite low percentage on emotion. It might be speculated that the Internet participants are not likely to provide backchannels on emotion topics that are all about break-up themes because they are too face-threatening to the post sender. Backchannels are considered an expression of attitudinal warmth on the listener's part. It is how you show yourself to be more polite than normal. Nevertheless, when one encounters a speech act that is essentially face-threatening, i.e. impolite in nature, using backchannels is useless in mitigating the threat. The interviews back up such a speculation. On the emotion posts, Interviewees A to D gave the following responses.

(30)

Interviewee A	这个帖子我可能看过就算了。分手是比较伤感和私人的事情，不知道说什么好。
Interviewee A	I may just flip through this post. Break-up is actually a pretty sad thing and too personal. I don't know what to say.

(31)

Interviewee B	分手这么悲催的事情，别人说啥都不对。安慰吧，她也难受。批评吧，她更难过！
Interviewee B	Break-up is too sad to say anything right. Any remark, be it consolation or criticism, only causes more pain.

(32)

Interviewee C	当然要回了！我会告诉她自己的故事，并且鼓励她。谁都经历过分手，我太了解这时候有人安慰有多重要！
Interviewee C	Of course I will respond to it! I will share my own story to encourage her. Everyone has the same experience. I know how comforting it is to have someone consoling you at the moment.

(33)

Interviewee D	会回的。她既然写出来，就是希望得到别人的安慰啊！大概会写一下我自己分手后的感受吧，让她知道以后会好的。
Interviewee D	I will respond to the post. she wrote the post in the hope of getting consolation from us. So I will share my experience and let her know that we will get better eventually.

In these statements, Interviewees A and B are afraid of giving any feedback since the emotion posts are too face-threatening. On the other hand, Interviewees C and D will yield a full turn rather than a backchannel turn since the latter is not enough to express their consolations. Although their opinions diverge to some extent, all of them agree that they will not resort to a backchannelling turn to mitigate a face-threatening speech act.

This finding is also supported by the results from other topics. The percentages using backchannels concerning society and entertainment lie in between. These two topics are argumentative in nature, thus more face-threatening than information-sharing travel topics but less face-threatening than sad personal emotion topics. This is consistent with Bjørge's (2010) findings that, in negotiations, the frequency of backchannels is considerably higher in a less-conflict situation. While Bjørge provides no explanation for why it is so, we choose to argue that this is because backchannelling is essentially a pos-politeness strategy that can enhance other's face rather than to mitigate face threats.

B. Backchannelling as a result of fewer constraints on netiquette

That backchannelling on the Internet presents some unique features might be attributed to the characteristics of the computer-mediated communication (CMC). Among others, the Internet has fewer constraints on netiquette than daily conversations. But this is not the whole story.

Apparently, Internet forums provide recipients with the freedom not to respond out of politeness, and thus not to backchannel. If we compare the total amount of responses with the number of readers, the percentage would be extremely low. That is to say, on the Internet, when audiences are often strangers to one another, most of them choose not to provide any feedback at all. According to Gu (2011), the equality resulting from anonymity on the Internet undermines the pressure to exhibit deference. Here, the virtuality of the Internet forum has undermined the pressure to conform to Leech's GSP. Interviewee A's and B's statements have supported this observation as well.

(34)

Interviewee A	一般我都是潜水的，他应该也无所谓一个陌生人留不留言吧，而且他也不知道我是谁。
Interviewee A	Usually I would not bother to respond. I think the sender won't care whether a stranger leaves messages or not; even if he cares, he does not know who I am.

(35)

Interviewee B	不回。上网的好处不就是可以不说话又能得到信息嘛。
Interviewee B	I won't respond. One good thing about the Internet is that you can get whatever you want to know, but you don't have to engage in any real conversations.

Interviewee A believes neither side on the Internet needs backchannels. In his opinion, the post sender does not 'care' to receive a backchannel while the post responder does not 'bother' to give one, and this is due to the anonymity of both sides. Interviewee B further argues that such an attribute is a benefit of the Internet. Apparently, the Internet has undermined the pressure on those who are unwilling to 'talk' on the Internet, like Interviewees A and B.

However, for those who are willing to participate, the Internet forum has provided a friendly environment for the recipient to give backchannels. For one thing, the post sender actually cues the responses from the recipients when he/she publishes the first post, even though he/she does not finish describing the event. In other words, the sender explicitly demands some reaction from the audience. Clancy et al. (1996) find that Chinese backchannels tend not to occur in the middle of the speaker's clause, as they do not intend to infringe on others. On the Internet, however, backchannels can only appear between sender's turns. In this sense, backchannels are not considered as an infringement, but a fulfilment of the sender's expectation. For another thing, the Internet forum has allowed more time for the recipient to produce backchannels. In daily conversations, the speaker may also pause and wait for the hearer to give some feedback. The difference is that the post sender has enough time to get a response while the speaker is obliged to continue even if the hearer does not exhibit any reaction as expected. Clancy et al. (1996) claim that Chinese backchannels are lexically more contentful. If this is really the case, Chinese people may not have time to speak them even if they want to. Yet, the Internet can resolve this problem well, due to the lack of synchronicity. In short, this is probably why the current study finds more backchannels on the Internet than those in Clancy et al.'s findings.

C. Backchannelling as alignment in netiquette

Presenting backchannels in the above-mentioned way might well be motivated by the desire for alignment. This, in turn, suggests that pursuing alignment might be a norm for netiquette in Chinese.

Alignment is exhibited on two levels: one on language, and the other on content. On the linguistic level, participants resort to Internet terms when providing backchannels. The analysis in the earlier part exhibited that people tend to employ emoticons and Internet-style language. It seems that all functions of backchannels have more or less exploited Internet terms such as '楼主' ('the post sender'), '顶' ('up'), '赞' ('mark'), etc. On the content level, the Maxims of Agreement, Sympathy and Approbation are the most used ones when providing backchannels. Gu (1990) argues that modesty is a feature of Chinese politeness. This study finds, however, that giving a high value to other's opinions, feelings and qualities is more important than giving a low value to self's qualities. This is probably due to the fact that Internet forums are places where people with the same interest gather together to discuss a topic (Cao 2011). Alignment on these two levels can therefore quickly help participants build common ground and establish an in-group identity. As Interviewee E concedes, she uses backchannels to gain trust from the post-sender so that the post-sender will in turn follow up on her posts.

(36)

Interviewee E	一般我都会简单回一下 '路过' 、 '顶' 之类的，这样既不麻烦，也可以让楼主关注到我。互动是双方的嘛，我回他，他也会回我。
Interviewee E	Normally I will respond with terms like 'pass by' or 'up'. They are quite simple but can attract his attention to me. Interaction is a two-way street. If I respond to him, he will respond to me in return.

Conclusion

This study examined backchannel practice on Chinese Internet forums, by combining quantitative and qualitative analyses, and integrating interviews with observations. It was discovered that i) the number of backchannels on Chinese Internet forums is higher than that in daily conversations and the frequency varies across topics; ii) the functions of backchannels conform to Leech's Grand Strategy of Politeness, and each function corresponds to a certain sub-maxim; iii) most backchannel tokens are represented in an Internet style. The reasons for using backchannels in this way can be well interpreted in terms of Leech's Principle of Politeness and the characteristics of Internet-mediated communication.

This study thus has three implications for Internet netiquette: a) the practice of backchannelling is a pos-politeness strategy on Internet forums; b) the Internet forum has fewer spatial and temporal constraints on politeness; i.e. it provides more time for recipients to generate longer backchannels; c) searching for alignment might be the norm for netiquette. Though Gu (2011) worries that anonymity on the Internet may have challenged the practice of politeness in China, this study, by examining backchannels, has discovered that it is the means and norms that have changed in showing politeness on the Internet.

Acknowledgments

This study has been funded by the MOE project on interpersonal pragmatic competence, our gratitude should thus be expressed.

The author wishes to express her heart-felt thanks to Cynthia Allen for her generous support and guidance in the research for and writing of this chapter.

Note

1. For Leech's criticisms of Brown and Levinson's positive and negative politeness, refer to his *Pragmatics of Politeness* (2014: Sections 1.2.6.2 and 4.4.2).

References

Bjørge, A. K. (2010) Conflict or cooperation: The use of backchanneling in ELF negotiations. *English for Specific Purposes* 29: 191–203. https://doi.org/10.1016/j.esp.2009.04.002

Brown, P. and Levinson, S. (1987) *Politeness*. Cambridge: Cambridge University Press.

Cao, J. (2011) Network communication and persuasion of public opinion forum. *Nanjing Journal of Social Sciences* 10: 110–116.

Clancy, P. M., Thompson, S. A., Suzuki, R. and Tao, H. (1996) The conversational use of reactive tokens in English, Japanese and Mandarin. *Journal of Pragmatics* 26(1): 355–387. https://doi.org/10.1016/0378-2166(95)00036-4

Cutrone, P. (2005) A case study examining backchannels in conversations between Japanese-British dyads. *Multilingua* 24: 237–274. https://doi.org/10.1515/mult.2005.24.3.237

Cutrone, P. (2014) A cross-cultural examination of the backchannel behavior of Japanese and Americans: Considerations for Japanese EFL learners. *Intercultural Pragmatics* 11(1): 83–120. https://doi.org/10.1515/ip-2014-0004

Dittmann, A. T. and Llewellyn, L. G. (1968) Relationship between vocalizations and head nods as listener responses. *Journal of Personality and Social Psychology* 9(1): 79–84. https://doi.org/10.1037/h0025722

Duncan, S. (1974) On the structure of speaker–auditor interaction during speaking turns. *Language in Society* 2(1): 161–180. https://doi.org/10.1017/S0047404500004322

Duncan, S. and Fiske, D. (1977) *Face-to-face Interaction: Research, Methods, and Theory*. Hillsdale NJ: Erlbaum.

Duncan, S. and Niederehe, G. (1974) On signalling that it's your turn to speak. *Journal of Experimental Social Psychology* 10: 234–247. https://doi.org/10.1016/0022-1031(74)90070-5

Fries, C. (1952) *The Structure of English*. New York: Harcourt Brace.

Goodwin, C. (1986) Between and within: Alternative sequential treatment of continuers and assessments. *Human Studies* 9(1): 205–217. https://doi.org/10.1007/BF00148127

Grice, H. P. (1975) Logic and conversation. In P. Cole and J. Morgan (eds) *Speech Acts* 41–58. New York: Academic Press.

Gu, Y. (1990) Politeness phenomena in modern Chinese. *Journal of Pragmatics* 3: 237–257. https://doi.org/10.1016/0378-2166(90)90082-O

Gu, Y. (2011) Modern Chinese politeness revisited. In F. Bargiela-Chiappini and D. Z. Kádár (eds) *Politeness across Cultures* 128–148. London: Palgrave. https://doi.org/10.1057/9780230305939_7

Heinz, B. (2003) Backchannel responses as strategic responses in bilingual speakers' conversations. *Journal of Pragmatics* 35: 1113–1142. https://doi.org/10.1016/S0378-2166(02)00190-X

Hu, J. and Xu, H. (2007) Backchannels in Conversations. *Journal of Anhui University* 2: 58–62.

Jefferson, G. (1983) Notes on systematic deployment of the acknowledgment tokens 'Yeah' and 'Mmhm'. *Tilburg Papers in Language and Literature* 30: 1–18.

Kendon, A. (1967) Some functions of gaze-direction in social interaction. *Acta Psychologica* 26(1): 22–63. https://doi.org/10.1016/0001-6918(67)90005-4

Landone, E. (2012) Discourse markers and politeness in a digital forum in Spanish. *Journal of Pragmatics* 44: 1799–1820. https://doi.org/10.1016/j.pragma.2012.09.001

Lakoff, R. (1970) The logic of politeness: Or, minding your p's and q's. In *Papers from the Ninth Regional Meeting, Chicago Linguistic Society* 292–305. Chicago: Chicago Linguistic Society.

Leech, G. (1983) *Principles of Pragmatics*. London: Longman.

Leech, G. (2014) *The Pragmatics of Politeness*. Oxford: Oxford University Press. https://doi.org/10.1093/acprof:oso/9780195341386.001.0001

Liu, J. (1987) Chinese–Japanese comparison of the frequency of backchannels over the phone. *Language* 16(12): 88–92.

Markel, N. (1975) Nonverbal behaviour associated with conversation turns. In A. Kendon, R. M. Harris and M. R. Key (eds) *Organisation of Behaviour in Face-to-Face Interaction* 189–197. The Hague: Mouton.

Maynard, S. (1986) On backchannel behaviour in Japanese and English casual conversation. *Linguistics* 24(6): 73–105. https://doi.org/10.1515/ling.1986.24.6.1079

Maynard, S. (1997) Analyzing interactional management in native/non-native English conversation. *International Review of Applied Linguistics in Language Teaching* 35(1): 37–60.

Miyata, S. and Nisisawa, H. Y. (2007) The acquisition of Japanese backchanneling behaviour: Observing the emergence of *aizuchi* in a Japanese boy. *Journal of Pragmatics* 39: 1255–1274. https://doi.org/10.1016/j.pragma.2007.02.012

Mizuno, Y. (1988) Chinese backchannels. *Japanese Language Studies* 7(12): 18–23.

Oreström, B. (1983) *Turn-Taking in English Conversation*. Lund: Lund University Press.

Schegloff, E. (1982) Discourse as an interactional achievement: Some uses of 'UHHUH' and other things that come between sentences. In D. Tannen (ed.) *Georgetown University Roundtable on Language and Linguistics, Analyzing Discourse: Text and Talk* 71–93. Washington, DC: Georgetown University Press.

Tao, H. and Thompson, S. (1991) English backchannels in Mandarin conversation: A case study of superstratum pragmatic 'interference'. *Journal of Pragmatics* 16(3): 209–223. https://doi.org/10.1016/0378-2166(91)90093-D

Tolins, J. and Tree, J. E. F. (2014) Addressee backchannels steer narrative development. *Journal of Pragmatics* 70: 152–164. https://doi.org/10.1016/j.pragma.2014.06.006

Yngve, V. (1970) On getting a word in edgewise. *Chicago Linguistic Society* 6(1): 567–578.

Yu, G. (2003) A conversational analysis of supportive verbal feedback. *Journal of Foreign Languages* 5: 23–29.

Yus, F. (2010) *Cyberpragmatics: Internet-mediated Communication in Context*. Amsterdam: John Benjamins.

Index

CPSIA information can be obtained
at www.ICGtesting.com
Printed in the USA
BVOW06*0929031117

498909BV00005B/5/P